CAVALRY FROM HOOF TO TRACK

CAVALRY FROM HOOF TO TRACK

Roman Jarymowycz

Foreword by General Donn A. Starry

War, Technology, and History
Robert Citino, Series Editor

Praeger Security International
Westport, Connecticut · London

Library of Congress Cataloging-in-Publication Data

Jarymowycz, Roman Johann, 1945–
Cavalry from hoof to track / Roman Jarymowycz ; foreword by General
    Donn A. Starry.
      p. cm. — (War, technology, and history, ISSN 1556–4924)
    Includes bibliographical references and index.
    ISBN-13: 978–0–275–98726–8 (alk. paper)
    1. Cavalry—History.   2. Cavalry horses—History.   3. War horses—History.
I. Title.
UE145.J37   2008
357.09—dc22   2007034941

British Library Cataloguing in Publication Data is available.

Library of Congress Catalog Card Number: 2007034941
ISBN-13: 978–0–275–98726–8
ISSN: 1556–4924

First published in 2008

Praeger Security International, 88 Post Road West, Westport, CT 06881
An imprint of Greenwood Publishing Group, Inc.
www.praeger.com

Printed in the United States of America

The paper used in this book complies with the
Permanent Paper Standard issued by the National
Information Standards Organization (Z39.48–1984).

10 9 8 7 6 5 4 3 2 1

Illustrations, Maps and Cartoons by Roman Jarymowycz

Contents

A photo essay follows page 152

Series Foreword

Military historians can be a contentious, feisty lot. There is little upon which they agree. The importance of attrition vs. maneuver, the relative qualities of "deep battle" and "Blitzkrieg," the command abilities of Patton and Montgomery: put two military historians in a room and you'll likely get three opinions on any of these questions. And yet, there is one thing that unites military historians across the spectrum. Virtually everyone within the field recognizes the crucial role that technology has played in the development of the military art. Indeed, this is almost axiomatic: the very first man who picked up a club against his neighbor was wielding "technology" of a sort. The outcome of wars has been profoundly affected by the technological context in which they were fought. From spoke-wheeled chariots to the M1A1 tank, from blades of Toledo steel to the AK-47, from primitive "bombards" to the MOAB ("mother of all bombs"), the problem of technology has stood at the forefront of military history.

Beyond that unifying proposition, however, problems can still arise in analyzing the precise role of technology. Consider for a moment the impact of the Industrial Revolution. Just as it transformed society, economy, and culture, it changed the appearance of war beyond all recognition. It was the age of the mass army, "railroads and rifles," and the telegraph. The growth of industry allowed military forces to grow to unheard-of size. In 1757, Frederick the Great triumphed over the French at Rossbach with an army that totaled 22,000 men; at Königgrätz in 1866, well over 400,000 men would be contesting the issue, and Austrian casualties alone, some 44,000 men, would be precisely twice as large as Frederick's victorious host at Rossbach. The railroad allowed these hordes to move, quite literally, twenty-four hours per day, and the problem of the slow-moving supply column that had bedeviled military operations from time out of mind seemed to have been solved. Moreover, the introduction of the telegraph meant that armies could be kept on a tight leash, even by commanders hundreds of miles away.

For each advantage of the new technology, however, there was a corresponding difficulty. It was soon clear that commanding and controlling the mass army was a huge, even insurmountable, problem. It is generally agreed that Napoleon I had serious problems in this area in 1812, and that he was at his best with armies that totaled 85,000 men or less. It was foolish to expect an army of several hundred thousand men to maneuver nimbly across the countryside, wheel like a company, and whack the opponent a surprise blow in the flank. In fact, getting them to maneuver at all was a stretch. The telegraph was a modern marvel, true, but the vision it offered of total control of far-flung operations turned out to be a mirage. Tied to a static system of poles and wires, it was far more useful to the defender than to the attacker, and it was nearly useless in any kind of mobile campaign. The mass army, then, was a huge body with a small brain, and had a very difficult time doing much more than marching straight ahead and crashing into whatever happened to be in front of it.

At that point, a mutual slaughter began. The other great technological advance of the era was introduction of new firearms—the rifled musket, or simply "rifle." It dramatically improved the range and firepower of infantry and the 1860's would see another breakthrough, the breech-loader, which greatly increased rate of fire. With long-range rifles now in the hands of the defenders, assault columns could theoretically be shot to pieces long before they struck home. In place of the old-style assault, there now arose the firefight, with extended skirmish lines on both sides replacing the formations of line and column. It was an "open order revolution," the logical culmination of tactical developments since the French Revolution. Open order tactics, however, rarely allowed enough concentration of fighting power for a successful assault. Both sides lined up and fired. There were casualties, enormous casualties, often for little gain. It was the great conundrum of the era. Clearly, technology was not so much a solution to a problem on the 19th century battlefield; it was more like the problem itself.

These are the issues that will form the heart of Praeger's new *War, Technology, and History* series. Books in the series will focus on the crucial relationship between warmaking and technological advance in the past 200 years. During that period, new machines like the rifle, the railroad, and the telegraph (in the 19th century) and the machine gun, the airplane, and the tank (in the 20th) have transformed the face of war. In the young 21st century, the U.S. Army has been emphasizing the ways in which information technology can have an even more radical transformative impact. Historically, armies that have managed to integrate these new technologies have found corresponding success on the battlefield, and their victories have as often as not come at the expense of those who have failed to ground their warmaking doctrine squarely in the available technology. The question is, therefore, much wider than a simple list of technical "specs" for various weapons. Books in the series will link technology and doctrine—that is, the weapons and the manner in which they were employed on actual battlefields of the day. The series is intended for a wide readership, from buffs and wargamers to scholars and "operators"—military officers and policymakers.

It is hard to argue with the notion that technological change has held the key to understanding military history, and in our contemporary era of information management and smart weaponry, technology continues to change the face of battle. Questions remain, however. Is technology our master or our servant? Are there limits to its usefulness? Does it alter the nature of war, or is war based on timeless, unchanging principles? These are a few of the themes to be explored by the authors—recognized experts all—in this new series. It presents no party line or previously agreed-upon point of view. Nor does it offer any simple answers to any of these questions. Welcome to *War, Technology, and History.*

Robert M. Citino, Series Editor

Foreword

Fifty years ago the distinguished U.S. historian Edward Katzenbach published an essay titled *The Horse Cavalry in the Twentieth Century: A Study in Policy Response*. In that essay was cited the need for change in operational concepts for fighting battles, and making war in general, which would largely reflect dramatic effects of the Industrial Revolution on battle and warfare demonstrated in or suggested by battles and operations in the First World War. Machine guns and indirect fire artillery, most evident on the western front, were the best evidence of the Industrial Revolution. But there were suggestions of more changes, yet probable, which would eventually result in development and deployment of armored vehicles (read tanks) and aircraft (primitive though they may have been in 1914–1918).

Then, reviewing postwar attempts of all the First World War's principal contenders to recognize the full dimensions of the need for change and accomplish something (anything) meaningful as a result, the latter reflecting what he called bureaucratic inertia, Katzenbach concluded that the most technically advanced nation on earth (he thought it to be the United States) entered what would become the Second World War with large parts of its army deeply wedded to notions of land warfare equally deeply rooted in the eighteenth and nineteenth centuries, singling out horse cavalry as the most remarkable example.

Exception should be taken to the assertion that the United States was, at the onset of the Second World War, the most industrially advanced nation on earth. There is no question that the industrial potential was indeed enormous, but of all the First World War's principals, the United States was by no means either the most industrially advanced or the most guilty of bureaucratic inertia. Further, contrary to Katzenbach's, in the United States there was no "policy" pronouncement set forth as to which response was required. The size and shape of any nation's armed forces are, as ever, determined by national strategy and derivative national military strategy. Nor was there such a policy statement in any other country where mechanization of armed forces was debated, and sometimes experimented with, in the years 1919–1939, resulting in the forces fielded at the onset of the Second World War. Nonetheless, it is likely fair to assert that in all armies in those two interwar decades, the challenge to mechanize fell heavily on horse cavalry.

Perhaps the foremost reason for that is reflected in observations by the baron Antoine de Jomini, who, with Clausewitz, was one of the most frequent observers of Napoleon's campaigns. It was Jomini who declared that "the principal value of cavalry is derived from its rapidity and mobility."[1] Interestingly enough, he added to that observation the caveat that "to these characteristics may be added its impetuosity, but we must be careful lest a false application be made of this last."[2] Napoleon himself is quoted in John Ellis' book *Cavalry: The History of Mounted Warfare* to the effect that "without cavalry, battles are without result."[3]

The motto of the U.S. Army's cavalry arm—We Thrive by Mobility—was the conceptual key to mobile warfare, and cavalry in any army had long been king of mobile warfare. For historically, horse cavalry's principal role in battle had been to move rapidly through breaches in enemy forces created by what was frequently called "open warfare" (that being the combined action of infantry and artillery), or to go quickly around—seek flanks and the rear of enemy force formations. In either case, the objective was to go deep into the enemy deployed force in order to disrupt and/or destroy follow-on forces, logistics, command-control, and other support structure, thus collapsing whatever the enemy tactical and operational level scheme may have been, followed by pursuit and destruction of enemy forces in the field. The latter was considered the key to victory as perceived by Jomini, perhaps the most perceptive observer of Napoleon's method of war.

For it was in the shadow of this traditional tactical and operational level conceptual framework that contending powers in the run-up to the First World War fielded, by one count, on the western front alone 1,254 squadrons of horse cavalry, mounting in all more than half a million horse cavalrymen. On the eastern front, of course, there was quite a different war. Famous battles—Gumbinnen, Tannenberg, Masurian Lakes, and others—featured large horse cavalry forces, German on the one side, regular Red Army as well as Cossack horse cavalry units ranging in size up to Cavalry Corps on the other. However, since the war in the East virtually ended in 1917 with collapse of the Czar's armies and government, and the onset of revolution in Russia, there was no common experience in the East reflecting either the military or national trauma of attrition warfare so dramatically demonstrated on the western front. For when all was done, in the West in the First World War, no horse cavalry fought a significant engagement, traditional style. Horse cavalry had been preempted from the battlefield, largely by machine guns and maneuverable indirect fire artillery. And soon many of its principal capabilities would become vested in organizations comprised primarily of all-arms units built around tanks, aided and abetted by air forces whose rapidly growing technical prowess made for air–land forces whose capabilities far extended those of horse cavalry.

So it was that mechanization of all military branches became the principal focus of armed forces of all nations in the interregnum between 1919 and 1939—as everyone prepared for the next war. Mechanization of cavalry was a particularly difficult factor in the equation of change. For commencing perhaps late in the nineteenth century, horse cavalry would be found riding hard to get to the scene of battle, but once engaged, dismounting to fight on foot— more as dragoons than as cavalry.

Responding to this reality, emphasis began to shift to employment of horse cavalry on three related missions. First, as a gatherer of information—reconnaissance in order to locate, identify, and report on enemy forces and their activity. Second, as a security force providing early warning of enemy forces and activity ahead, on the flanks, or in the rear of friendly forces. Finally, as an economy force, holding off or disrupting enemy forces in order to protect the principal mass of friendly force from enemy interference with its mission.

That being so, then, in the race to modernize (mechanize) in the 1919–1939 years, what role (if indeed any role) cavalry? Conceptually there were several related questions. Should (could) cavalry be light enough, and therefore agile enough, to deploy with alacrity, but heavy enough to fight effectively once engaged with enemy forces armed with "modern" weapons? For adding modern weapons to cavalry to satisfy the "heavy enough" requirement defied the need to be light enough to move about with traditional alacrity.

Related questions followed. On reconnaissance missions, should cavalry be organized and equipped to fight for, as well as just look for, information of enemy forces, forces which would likely be equipped with heavier modern weapons? Simply put: should cavalry be employed as a "sneak and peek" force, or as a heavier fighting force in seeking information? On reconnaissance, how should cavalry be equipped, trained, and organized to rapidly convey its reconnaissance findings to whatever central information collecting facility (yet to be defined) would be provided? As a security force (covering force, advance or rear guard, flank protection), should cavalry be organized and equipped heavily enough to be effective against modern artillery, modern anti-armor cannon or rocket systems, all capabilities that would render cavalry far less mobile than historically traditional cavalry?

So it was that the cavalry subset of modernization questions focused attention on the fundamental question: just what would be the function (if any) of cavalry in battles between mechanized forces? Whatever might be the answer to that question, would the force still be called "cavalry"? What would be its operational modus? And what might provide the rapidity and ease of motion, perhaps even the impetuosity so highly touted by Jomini observing Napoleon's horse cavalry?

From the 1919–1939 experiments with mechanization came different answers in each country—France, Germany, the UK, the USSR, and the United States—not only to the question of what function cavalry, but also to related mechanization questions with regard to other branches of military arms of the respective nations. All have been resolved in one fashion or another. Those solutions reflect systemic uncertainties in extant or developing national political strategies and their supporting national military strategies, in (frequently uncertain) opportunities offered by "modern technology," and in (and not least) the defining cultures of the military establishments of the several nations.

Included in the latter category—defining military cultures—is the ever important (perhaps all important) consideration of doctrine for deployment and employment of the military power of the nation in pursuit of national goals and aims (read: national strategy). Doctrine for strategic, operational, and tactical level operations consistent with national goals. Modern doctrine must reflect the reality that in a world that now includes threats to national security ranging from nuclear Armageddon to improvised explosive devices in insurgency operations, there is a sure certainty that military force may be able to handle only a part of modern conflict, and that it will require concerted, well-devised political, economic, social, as well as military programs to secure national goals, especially in the insurgent environment.

It is not difficult, therefore, to conclude that relevant doctrine, in the context just framed, is the "first and great commandment." Relevant doctrine is not however a new requirement. In the early decades of the Christian era, the Apostle Paul wrote about the matter to his friend Timothy:

> I solemnly urge you: proclaim the message; be persistent whether the time is favorable or unfavorable; convince, rebuke and encourage, with the utmost patience in teaching. For the time is coming when people will not put up with sound doctrine, but having itching ears, they will accumulate for themselves teachers to suit their own desires, and will turn away from the truth and wander away to myths.[4]

In the story so brilliantly characterized by Roman Jarymowycz in *Cavalry from Hoof to Track,* there is "something about the cavalry." It was and remains something of substance. For the teachings of cavalry have historically focused on sound doctrine, formulae for remarkable military operations in support of national goals and aims, superbly thought-out tactical and operational concepts, well-trained soldiers, and extremely competent leaders all joined in highly effective units—units trained to fight together with all the panache that once elicited observations by Jomini, and by Napoleon himself.

Gen. Donn A. Starry, U.S. Army, Retired

Preface

You don't break these animals; you come to an understanding with them.
—Cowboy maxim

My best memory of teaching at the Army Staff College was the riding. Fort Frontenac is a walled bastion on the shores of Lake Ontario just across the bay from the Royal Military College. It boasted the last great officers' mess in the traditional meaning of the term and attracted a cohort of associated members—retired *grognards*—now settled in the Thousand Islands area. That is where I met Maj. Norman "Moe" Shackleton. He had joined the cavalry as a boy soldier in the 1930s. Forever a member of the Royal Canadian Dragoons, he eventually served during the Second World War and in every cold-war or peacekeeping garrison available to the United Nations or the Canadian Army from 1945 to 1975. He was a loquacious, opinionated staff officer, had written a still-quoted analysis of the combat in Normandy, and was a regular contributor to the *Whig Standard,* that renowned Loyalist newspaper from Lower Canada. We shared a common interest in military history and passionate criticism of how the modern army was "going all to hell."

Moe had a horse farm outside of Kingston with a barn full of nags in various states of operational readiness—from show horses to sickly retirees awaiting the knacker's truck—Baldur, Old Joe, and Sneaky Pete, to name but a few. My teaching partner was a Marines Corps lawyer from Cleveland who generously took the early classes so that I might drive to Shackleton's farm across the Cataraqui River. We were in the saddle by 0630, and I particularly recall the sun cutting through the low-lying fog. Afterward, my morning was spent in cleaning tack, being industrial with the hoof pick and curry comb, and finally, using a clean sponge to wipe the ears, eyes, nostrils, and, of course, the dock. Some mornings I would help Moe shoe horses—mostly by handing him stuff. You could always tell when the horses were happy, as the barn resonated with contented chuckles. The stable was well set to the prevailing wind, a sunny corridor that was a waft of fresh breezes. The cleaned stalls were sprinkled with a carpet of wood shavings Moe bought from a local mill. "This is what a proper stable smells like; don't believe that crap about horse stench and stable stink—that's just an excuse for not taking good care of the stalls." I can recall several afternoons reclining on a bale of hay, reading tactical catechisms, completely at peace surrounded by that rustic horsy aroma. Mucking out instilled a dash of humility. After a morning of service to my four-footed friends, I was far more decent to my two-legged students, or at least more patient. I was at peace, fitter, and probably far more pleasant. Once, on a particularly perfect morning, going through a lazy draw, the sun breaking through the maples and the horses quietly chortling, the major turned to me and said matter of factly: "The best thing for the inside of a man is the outside of a horse."

My summers with horses also reminded me of their all too human qualities—they were gullible, easily rattled, stubborn, and sometimes foolish. They are both fearless yet easily intimidated. Major Shackleton's horse, Baldur, was a black stallion measuring 19.5 hands high. I had ridden him a couple of times, but I knew well, as Baldur did, that he was only being polite. Should I have displeased him, I would quickly have become a crumpled pile of chaps and gabardine in a handy ditch. Peter Gray observed philosophically: "We have almost forgotten how strange a thing it is that so huge and powerful and intelligent an animal as a horse should allow another, and far more feeble animal, to ride upon its back."[1] Baldur had eyes like embers of coal—likely descended from one of the stallions Beelzebub's lieutenants rode in Hades' horsy levels. Only Moe could handle him. I watched Moe rule Baldur with a stalk of dried straw. If the horse was moody or uncooperative, the major pulled a piece of straw from a nearby bale and stared at Baldur. His voice was low and cautionary: "Do you want me to use this?" Baldur's eyes grew alert, fearful—he backed into his stall. A low concerned snort—it sounded like "nooowaay." "Will you be a good horse?" Compliance. The major confided, "Of course it's all because I've never touched him with the straw—if he ever finds out it's just straw, it's all over."

The history of the warhorse in style, temperament, and equipment has been well chronicled. This book is a selective review of the doctrinal application of cavalry and its use in the operational art: reassessment but not necessarily revisionist. I have made much use of secondary sources, and I am indebted to a host of folks who kindly and patiently assisted me in preparing this manuscript.

I extend my thanks to colleagues Maj. Michael Boire and Maj. John R. Grodzinski, historians at the Royal Military College, Kingston. Michael's expertise with the French army minutiae and invaluable support in digging up documents and providing books from Kingston's libraries rescued me at a time when I was particularly swamped. I am also indebted to Maj. Dan Acre who translated the nuances of the Israeli army and kindly reviewed interpretations and offered advice on many chapters; Dave Keough, archivist, U.S. Army War College, and an admirable source of American military history who guided my American cavalry-armor studies; Lt. Col. Ian McCulloch, authority on eighteenth-century militaria; Dr. Chuck Briscoe, U.S. Army Special Operations Command; Brig. Gen. Huba Wass de Czege, Lt. Col. Will Townend, Secretary Royal Artillery Historical Society, and Maj. W. G. Clarke, Royal Horse Artillery; and Captain Tony Schnurr, historical collector and authority on military costume. I was guided by medieval historian and jousts trainer, Richard Alvarez; master arrowsmith Hector Cole explained toxophilite mysteries; equestrians and medievalist historians Roy William Cox and Ken Turner were instrumental; and David Kuijt and Dianne Karp, who conducted trials on the mounted attack, were patient and helpful. Historians Per Inge Oestmoen, Nino Oktorino, Ned Eddins, and George Vogler generously shared their research. I am in debt to linguists Valerie Mollard, who corrected French phrases, and Grazyna Murawski, who reviewed my attempts at Polish translation; Sgt. Maj. William J. Stewart, riding master, RCMP Musical Ride Branch, who reviewed the realities of lance drills; Australian military vehicle collector Douglas Greville, who provided information on the nuance of armored-car design; Capt. Douglas Baum and particularly his wife, Ulle, who corrected my Russian; and Col. Robert ffrench Blake, Queens Light Dragoons, who knows everything worth knowing about polo. Valued military sources included Gen. William R. Richardson, Col. Richard Sinnreich, Col. David Pittfield Maj. Gen. Tim Grant, and Lt. Gen. Rupert Smith. Lt. Col. Paul Young of the Parachute Regiment, a cavalier at heart, assisted me in key research; Lt. Col. Charles Branchaud accompanied and often directed my investigation in England and France; and Maj. David Redpath, Robert Mason, and the ecclesiastic Dr. Cajetan Menke patiently and exactingly reviewed chapters. Military historians Robert Citino, George F. Hofmann and McGill Professor Emeritus, Desmond Morton, offered valued assistance and encouraging support.

Special thanks are extended to Lt. Gen. Don Holder, U.S. Cavalry, for his encouragement. He genially contributed comments and reviewed the chapters dealing with modern doctrine. His invaluable expertise gave me courage to drift into analysis.

I am delighted that Gen. Donn A. Starry graciously consented to write a foreword. His association with the history of the warhorse in literature and battle is unique among armored cavalry commanders. Finally, my editor, mentor, and patient wife, Sandra, who endured the terrible ordeals of my birthing a horse. She is emblematic that the hardest arithmetic to master is that which enables us to count our blessings.

Roman Johann Jarymowycz

Beaconsfield, 2007

In dealing with a girl or a horse, one lets nature take its course.

—Fred Astaire, *Top-Hat* (1935)

The Charger: "Warhorse? My dear fellow, you are a Beast of Burden..."

Chapter 1

Cavalry and the Operational Art

Cavalry is a state of mind.

—Maj. Gen. Robert W. Grow

The history of cavalry begins well before classical times and ends, it may be argued, at the turn of the twenty-first century. The saga of the warhorse is a roller coaster through millennia as cavalry gained, lost, then regained ascendancy via technical and doctrinal metamorphosis. Mechanization imposed an epiphanic moment that resurrected cavalry, yet finally abandoned the warhorse to its temporal restrictions—though not its temperament and style. By the mid-twentieth century, cavalry had embraced tanks and had resurrected so-called armored cavalry. Converts to mechanization argued that this restored prowess and that massed tanks, like Mongol armies, were well nigh to a strategic arm. The Second World War, the apex of armored warfare, was also the last great theater for mounted cavalry operations. The warhorse, dragooned into service beside the tank, endured a few years of dramatic activity and then was pronounced obsolete. It persevered via technical transmutation as armored cavalry—a modern cathedral to medieval tactics. At the acme of its operational triumph (1991), cavalry was a multifaceted, all-arms juggernaut. Following the Gulf War, the cataphract host was declared an anachronism as the U.S. Army embraced the cybernetic revolution. Robotic reconnaissance devices and collections of digitized formations appeared with enthusiastic fanfare. Anxious cavalrymen, veterans of the last great cavalier host that fought in the Arabian Desert, sounded the alarm as military progressives dictated the future of air-mobile, mix-and-match armies:

The current organizational design and intellectual underpinning of our Future Force do nothing less than signal the demise of Cavalry within the conventional forces of the United States Army, assuring its placement on the ash heap of history along with coastal artillery.[1]

In the spring of 2006, the Pentagon announced plans to close Fort Knox (the revered "Home of Armor and Cavalry") and move its chattel to the Infantry School. The future of armored cavalry may rest in philosophical definition, specifically the thesis presented by Maj. General Robert W. Grow. The cavalier general, a decorated commander of the 6th Armored Division and veteran of spectacular romps through Normandy and spirited panzer battles in Lorraine, concluded that "Cavalry is a state of mind." General Grow's thesis offered hope to modern cavaliers. There exists the predictable caveat: any defense of cavalry threatens to become a polemic for the warhorse. Guilty.

Warhorse is a quixotic term and has many references—from musical (Beethoven's Fifth Symphony, Vivaldi's *The Four Seasons,* "Hail to the Chief") to personalities (Gen. Robert E. Lee referred to General Longstreet as his Old War Horse). The term suggests a solid, trustworthy persona. The warhorse and its tribal collective, the cavalry, evolved from a tactical arm to an operational, even strategic, instrument of war. The horse, despite the triumph of technology, continues to occupy a beloved and special place in modern society. Man loves the horse.

During the 2006 running of the Preakness Stakes, a thoroughbred named Barbaro pulled short after the start with a badly broken leg—victim of an accidental contact with another horse. Barbaro was spared and initially rescued via costly surgery and rehabilitation. The drama made the evening news and front pages for months. When Barbaro was subsequently diagnosed with systemic laminitis (a disease of the hoof) in his other hind leg, that too made front-page news and shared copy with wars, typhoons, and terrorist attacks.[2] Barbaro, though a pampered prima donna, could not have been more appreciated had he carried the secretary of war into a Taliban stronghold. Conversely, had a rocket or road mine destroyed an Abrams tank lovingly stenciled *Barbaro* across its 120 mm gun, its reduction to junkyard status would not have merited any more notice than a fender-bender in New York City.[3] Therein lies the difference between cavalry and tanks.

Man's affection for the horse embraces visions of a noble loyal steed. It is, of course, true. But the horse is also a nasty bit of work—moody, skittish, and vindictive. It requires expert care, patient training, and expensive accoutrements. It enjoys a snotty class system—the best-looking chargers are not necessarily the best warriors but certainly the most popular. The classic Arab is far more appreciated than the shaggy little Afghan. Both went to war. Some breeds emerged by accident, and others after careful husbandry to produce either mobility or the stamina to carry armored warriors. Cataphract cavalry (from the Greek for "armored cavalry") appeared regularly throughout history; it reached a zenith during the Middle Ages, particularly after gunpowder appeared. Europeans encased themselves in metallic suits and strapped themselves onto gargantuan steeds.

The characteristics of the warhorse are essentially maneuver mixed with shock. As the last vestige of chivalry, the armored warhorse was a plodding furniture van—the same nickname given to Tiger tanks by their crews during the Second World War. When Gen. Jean Baptiste Chedeville noted, in 1918, that "Le Char est très délicat" (The tank is delicate), he was referring to its operational limitations. The tank's initial similarities to the warhorse were a fragile constitution, a constant need for attention, and vulnerability to both rough ground and high-velocity weapons. It also mirrored the warhorse's best martial quality—the capability to deliver shock. However, the tank carried none of the horse's symbiotic associations or charming tendencies.

A WARHORSE LEXICON

The military terminology associated with the cavalry and the operational art, a vocabulary that includes *Auftragstaktik* and *deep battle,* begs some clarification—if only by means of a selected lexicon. *Strategy* and *tactics* are familiar yet misleading terms. The military lexicon includes a cornucopia of terms inspired by technology, and though dated, many survive, ubiquitous enough to remain useful. *Auftragstaktik* (German: *auf,* "from"; *trag,* "task") refers to mission-directed tactics that are inspired actions by subordinates, which, while not specifically ordered, serve to secure the higher goals and visions of a great commander in chief.

These lend themselves well to cavalry operations but require inspired leadership from a captain blessed with *Fingerspitzengefühl* [finger spitz en ghe full], which is a sixth sense, intuitive comprehension: "thinking in the saddle." *Auftragstaktik* includes the expectation that junior leaders will use their initiative "even if it entails deviating from the mission and/or *disobeying orders* [emphasis added]."[4] A modern German interpretation of *Auftragstaktik* contends its origins were Prussian introspection after the defeat. Helmut von Moltke, the creator of operational command and control, defined it as how "the subordinate is to act within the guidelines of his superior's intent."[5]

Other Cavalry Terms

Reconnaissance or Recce [Rhe kee] (Cavalry Slang)

This refers to getting information about the enemy. In addition to being a strike or pursuit force, the cavalry provides commanders with early warning and intelligence via reconnaissance patrols or operations. Modern reconnaissance is increasingly electronic, but traditional reconnaissance operations were conducted by cavalry for about four millennia. The last formal military reconnaissance using both the horse and tank was conducted by the French and Russian armies, although the new century has recently witnessed surreal incidents in the mountains of the Hindu Kush.

Cavalry Screens

Cavalry patrols are thrown out in front of an advancing army or in the path of an invader to act as a trip wire. The so-called screen sniffs out the enemy and often resorts to sneaky-peeky tactics, but offensive screens must be robust and capable of fighting for information. The defensive screen is more than a cordon sanitaire; it also provides vital information. Its aim is to offer enough resistance to force the enemy to push harder and reveal his intent—the direction of his attack. Effective reconnaissance requires aggressive horsemen and inspired leadership. Great generals cannot practice the operational art without precise reports.

Vanguards

Represent the leading edge of an attacking force. This first formation is partly reconnaissance in that it seeks information and develops the situation. It is usually a combination of all arms (infantry, cavalry, armor, artillery, engineers, and immediate logistics). The vanguard moves quickly and secures key terrain or frustrates countermaneuver. It is strong enough that if it cannot defeat the enemy to its front, the commander of the main body is made aware he faces a mass of the enemy or has found a spot the enemy intends to defend resolutely.

Blitzkrieg

The term *blitzkrieg* [bliz kreeg] means, literally, "lightning war"—a grand tactical cocktail that used air attack and mechanized armies to disrupt the enemy via speed and shock. Blitzkrieg has many fathers and many variations, but the original tank with airplane version is German, circa 1930s, inspired by the British military philosophe General John Frederick Charles Fuller, and developed by a succession of Prussian generals from von Seeckt to Guderian. Blitzkrieg begins with a formal attack to achieve breakthrough. The central effort (*Schwerpunkt*[6]) creates a rupture large enough to introduce armored divisions. These units, combining tanks and armored infantry, race deep into the enemy territory creating terror and collapse. It is intimately supported by ground attack from its air force. Blitzkrieg, as so-called grand tactics, is a major part of the mechanized operational art and causes enough chaos to create military and political collapse—good examples are Attila the Hun in the fifth century, the German invasion of France in 1940, and both American invasions of Iraq.

Deep Battle

The term *deep battle* refers to big-league tactics—the ultimate operational statement. The technique thrusts a large mobile or mechanized force deep into enemy terrain. The extent of the penetration is gargantuan and capable of surrounding capitals or entire groups of armies. Deep battle can dispatch a nation or series of nations. It requires great sophistication and a complex organization. It can also be practiced by a force culturally disposed to do so—Attila the Hun's or Genghis Khan's armies. Deep battle was made modern by the Russians. Marshal Mikhail Tukhachevskii called it *Glubokii Boi* (*Hlib* as in "glib," *boi* as in "boy"). It continues to be practiced by modern armies as a dynamic solution—a step beyond blitzkrieg. Recent examples are Operation Cobra in Normandy (1944), the Destruction of Army Group Center, eastern front (1944), and Operation Cobra II, the 2003 tsunami against Iraq.

Basic Military Organizations

The Troop versus the Platoon

Both are essentially the same thing—the smallest tactical unit led by an officer, usually a lieutenant. Each is approximately 30 soldiers. Troops are cavalry organizations but are used by artillery and engineers in many armies. A troop is the horsy equivalent of the platoon.

Squadrons versus Companies

Squadron is again a cavalry term but is often used by other arms and services. It is a larger grouping of troops. The American cavalry squadron is equivalent to a battalion or regiment.

Regiment

A regiment is a grouping of at least two squadrons—more than four is rare. It is often confused with the term *battalion*. Regiments may be tactical organizations or ad hoc groupings. A regiment is also a tribal term or a parent company. Regiments carry the traditions and historical battle honors of their particular clique. They may spawn siblings, each a carbon copy of the parent organization. For example, the Black Watch, Royal Highland Regiment raised several battalions for war—identified as 1st or 2nd Black Watch. American examples include the United States Marine Corps—the First Marine Regiment comprises four battalions (its 4th Marine battalion is sometimes referred to as "the Fourth of the First"). While British Commonwealth regiments are parental administrative organizations, many countries (the United States and Russia, for example) also use the term *regiment* as a tactical unit. The largest cavalry outfit is the American Armored Cavalry Regiment (ACR), a robust formation festooned with tanks, scouts, artillery, and helicopters—the final word in cavalry clout.

Brigades

These are a collection of battalions. The brigade is often the first organization to offer formal groupings of so-called arms. The combat arms comprise three types of fighting troops: infantry, cavalry, and artillery (combat engineers were formally included after the technological contests of the Second World War). Two or more brigades make up a division. Two or more divisions make a corps—these are the largest organizations to actively deal in maneuver and combat. Two or more corps form an army—although the term *army* is regularly used to describe any larger fighting corporation.

Modern brigades, divisions, and particularly corps are large corporate toolboxes. They feature complex headquarters, various attached specialized units, and cadres that include everything from medicine to public relations. A corps, often augmented by specialist brigades, is capable of operational maneuver. It is much like a holding company—it sends out its divisions to conduct tactical battles while it controls a campaign (a series of battles).

Corps are capable of strategic results; for example, a couple of panzer corps reached the English Channel in 1940, cutting apart the French army, which soon led to the surrender of Paris and an armistice.

The Three Classic Tactical Maneuvers

There are three great tactical maneuvers in military history: the frontal attack and single envelopment (the battle of Gaugamela, Alexander the Great); the double envelopment (the battle of annihilation at Cannae, Hannibal); and the feint and flank attack (Leuthen, Frederick the Great). In the 1960s, the American army added a fourth classic maneuver via the helicopter—the vertical envelopment.

The Operational Art

This is a relatively modern term that describes the mechanics of warfighting. Initially a Russian (Soviet) idea introduced by Alexsandr Svechin, it was carefully ignored during most of the cold war—as were all Red Army achievements. The West, particularly the U.S. Army, embraced the concept of operation art during its military renaissance and the writing of its own deep battle doctrine, *AirLand Battle*, during the 1980s. Operational art deals with the business of war and incorporates the three strata: tactical, operational, and strategic.

Doctrine

Doctrine refers to a body of teachings or prescribed methods. In the military, it simply means "how we do things." This carries social baggage because doctrines invariably reflect the culture and beliefs of the practicing army. Doctrine is influenced by the weapons available, such as the horse, and technology; it also reflects the cultural philosophy of the originating nation. The concept is best explained by the grand master of the operational art, Eric von Manstein: "It has always been the particular forte of German leadership to grant wide scope to the self-dependence of subordinate commanders. . . The German method is really rooted in the German character . . . [which] finds a certain pleasure in taking risks."[7]

However, in an age where the movements of even individual tanks can be followed via satellite and laptops, freedom to take risks or deviate from prescribed plans is virtually impossible. Doctrine is like haute couture. Changing and dynamic, exciting doctrines are slavishly emulated by all armies.

Tactics

The word *tactics* comes from the Greek *Taktikē,* the art of managing military forces. It is concerned with the techniques of combat, sometimes cobbled with a new term, *warfighting.* Tactics reflect doctrine. For example, a submarine can fire a tactical missile at a target—this constitutes a tactical strike. However, if the weapon is nuclear and takes out Beijing or Tel Aviv, it is at once a strategic strike. One of the favored definitions is one that despite apparent simplicity, is both accurate and functional: Tactics is kicking over the pail of milk. Strategy is killing the cow. The Russian military philosopher, A. A. Svechin, notes that "tactics makes the steps from which operational leaps are assembled; strategy points out the path. . . Battle is the means of the operation. . . Tactics are the material of operational art."[8]

Strategy

Strategy suggests decisions with large-scale, long-term consequences (from the Greek *strategos,* or "general's art"). Modern strategists include politicians as well as military philosophes: from foreign policy to titanic visions of the conduct of mass war, from J.F.C. Fuller to Tukhachevskii, from Alexander to Napoleon, from Sun Tzu to Carl von Clausewitz. The difference between tactics and strategy is simply size.

This manuscript is a selected review of the operational history of cavalry with special emphasis on the horse as it morphed from symbiotic weapon to partner with the rude mechanical and, finally, a manifestation of its former medieval self as armored cavalry.

Charger: "I simply won't do it – it's grotesque and it smells."

Chapter 2

The Classical Horse

Why did this animal that had prospered so in the Colorado Desert leave his amiable homeland for Siberia? . . . He wandered into France and became the mighty Percheron, and into Arabia, where he developed into a lovely poem of a horse, and into Africa where he became the brilliant zebra, and into Scotland, where he bred selectively to form the massive Clydesdale. He would also journey into Spain, where his very name would become the designation for gentleman, a caballero, a man of the horse. There he would flourish mightily and serve the armies that would conquer much of the known world.

—James Michener

The association of the horse with warfare is buttressed with romance and routinely gives away to wistfulness. The horse became the preferred battle partner because of its attendant attributes: handsomer and easier to maneuver than the war elephant, smarter than the rhino and more effective than a war dog. Its complicated affiliation with the military is less influenced by bellicose bravado than veterinary knowledge and breeding techniques. The evolution of the horse as weapon of war, from harbinger of galloping conquest to doctrinal nuance, is based on *mass*. Cavalry was most effective when there was lots of it.

The raising of cavalry forces was best achieved in lush valleys and open steppes—from Macedonia to the American prairie. The appearance of the horse on the North American plains, via Spanish trading and clever rustling, created an aboriginal horse culture that evoked a particular type of chivalry that dominated the buffalo and European immigrants. The North American warhorse was a renaissance marking the return to its place of origin of *Eohippus,* a 10 inch, four-toed mammal, which had appeared one million years ago. Its eastern migration through Alaska and into Asia resulted in the Asian and European *equus*. The Bering Sea washed closed the land bridge to the Americas; predators, climate change, and disease eliminated the last of the American ponies. The horse, much like the Polish ancestors of the American buffalo, flourished in Asia and Europe where vast Mongolian prairies, steppes, and *pushta* generated great herds.

Until man learned to domesticate it, the horse initially was hunted as another source of food. Thousands of years passed before the horse was ridden. Catching horses was difficult; trapping risked death and injury. Eventually the tribes of the Euphrates domesticated the horse; excavations in Syria produced the earliest evidence of horsemanship. The Mesopotamian kingdom of Nineveh, associated with the king Sennacherib and the epic of Gilgamesh, boasted light cavalry, but they were defeated by the Babylonians who had developed the war chariot. The chariot was less cavalry and more personnel carrier.

In the close assault the warhorse was the symbiotic cohort to its warrior master. Bucephalus carried Alexander into the midst of enemy armies, ignoring the disruptive exotic smells of camels and elephants as well as their riders. The warhorse responded to control by knee or thigh, not reins. A good fighting horse demonstrated steadiness in confused situations and cooperated usefully with the method of attack or melee. Warhorses differed from working or sports horses in that they were specifically bred and trained for combat and required a subtle blend of individual bravado and group dynamics. They had to respond to commands that were often mere pressure by the rider's thigh, and they were taught to ignore the sounds of war—consisting of cries of the wounded as well as the blare of accompanying martial music and drums.

Considerable time was spent to overcome the horse's aversion to the smell of blood and its natural disinclination to trample a human. Horses were trained to cripple and kill by slamming, bodychecking, and butting with their chest or flanks. They were deadly with kick, stomp, or bite. Napoleon's cavalier, Capt. Marcellin, the Baron de Marbot, described his mare, Lisette, at the battle of Eylau: "She sprang at the Russian and at one mouthful tore off his nose, lips, eyebrows and all of his face, making him a living death's head, dripping with blood."[1]

Classical and medieval cavalry was built around the champion warrior—the armored knight. The challenge was to breed a warhorse with speed and litheness yet capable of bearing heavy metal. Battle chargers remained the private accessories of the rich and socially prestiged. The expense of training and equipping a mass of armored cavalry meant that only organized kingdoms with sizeable treasuries meddled in the operational art's most glamorous tool—massed cavalry. The tactical result was rather standard. The cavalry charge at Crécy was much like the ones at Cannae or Waterloo: measured approach breaking into either controlled canter or fanatical gallop, followed by a confused, determined melee. The charge was but the last act in a complex procedure of training and drill that could easily go wrong in an instant. Mounted attack was an intricate combination of courage, bravado, skill, and occasion. It was as much a triumph of the will, both human and animal, as it was a shrewd bit of timing or maneuver.

THE HORSE AS BATTLE TAXI

> A chariot of lapis lazuli, brass, ivory and golden wheels shall you have. On it pulled by horses created from thunderheads.
> —*The Epic of Gilgamesh,* Tablet VI: The Hero Returns

While chariots are on the periphery of cavalry attack, they represent an important stage in the evolution of the warhorse. *Juggernaut* is a term derived from Sanskrit (*Jagannatha,* "Lord of the universe") and cited to describe unstoppable, all-crushing armies. It also suggests a gargantuan war wagon but is only loosely applicable to an offensive by mass chariots. Nevertheless, during its brief domination of mobile warfare, the chariot was a fearsome weapon. Horse driven and combining the attributes of infantry assault with mobility, it preceded the tank. Like armor, it was beset with technical breakdown and thwarted by terrain and steady, disciplined infantry. The first chariots (from Latin, *carrus*), were four-wheeled carts pulled by oxen, tamed asses, or onagers. There were various types, and eventually the two-wheeled horse-drawn chariot proved most popular and efficient. Used for transport as well as warfare, they were common to the Bronze and Iron Ages; their use was limited to open terrain, and their weakness was the power train and suspension. The horses were relatively small—no more than ponies—while axles and wheels quickly deteriorated under the stress of weight and uneven ground, much like modern tanks. The spoked wheel improved mobility and control. Still they were no more than "battle taxis" for heroes—permitting great warriors to quickly close and duel with enemy champions.

Massed chariots were more a type of self-propelled artillery delivering direct and indirect fire: a barrage of arrows and javelins or lunges with spear and sword to clear off skirmishers and archers and then disrupt steady formations. The vulnerability of chariots was that the engine was at the front and easily wounded by missiles or direct assault. Chariots with scythe blades rotating from the axles were awesome and deadly if driven through troops in open order. Direct attack depended entirely on the horse's willingness to throw itself onto a wall of armed infantry. A phalanx's unwavering wall of spears reduced attack to harassment at a distance. The ability to shock was mostly psychological—horses could not be made to break into formed steady masses covered by sharp objects, whether spears or bayonets. This was as true at Waterloo as it was at Arbela.

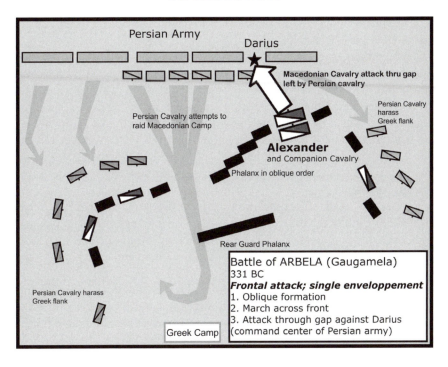

Persian Army

Darius

Macedonian Cavalry attack thru gap left by Persian cavalry

Persian Cavalry harass Greek flank

Persian Cavalry attempts to raid Macedonian Camp

Alexander
and Companion Cavalry

Phalanx in oblique order

Rear Guard Phalanx

Persian Cavalry harass Greek flank

Greek Camp

Battle of ARBELA (Gaugamela)
331 BC
Frontal attack; single enveloppement
1. Oblique formation
2. March across front
3. Attack through gap against Darius
(command center of Persian army)

The costs associated with the chariot limited its use. The principal warrior depended on a chauffeur and an armed subordinate like the squire of medieval knights. The subsequent battle was pretty much a raid by the rich and famous. Expensive chariots suddenly appeared and disgorged gold-chained, Armani-clad fellows swaggering into battle accompanied by pipes and Arcadian rap. Chariots delivered attackers but, perhaps more important, permitted quick escape. A noble facing capture or the onslaught of more dangerous opponents counted on his driver, parked with the chariot conveniently facing the rear, to be at the ready to deliver him to safety.

The chariot's tactical popularity appears to have peaked with the pharaoh Ramses and an action sometimes dubbed "the mother of all battles" fought in what is today Syria: the battle of Kadesh (1274 B.C.). Ramses' invading army consisted of Egyptian infantry and a strike force of war chariots, comprised mostly of nobles, who were well matched by Hittite charioteers. Hittite vehicles, drawn by two horses, were made of wood and were tougher than the rattan vehicles used by Ramses. Lighter wheels and a better axle gave them good cross-country performance; the crew did not dismount but fought from the vehicle via long spears and javelins. The Hittites supplemented their mounted attack with attendant infantry runners who killed off wounded enemy charioteers or crippled horses left behind by an initial charge. The attending infantry were delivered into battle by chariot but dropped off before a maneuvering attack; the dismounted cadre could also be employed as skirmishers, slingers, or archers.

The Egyptian army (about 20,000) was surprised by the Hittite king, Muwatallish, who outmaneuvered them with a force of about 2,000 chariots and 35,000 foot, of which over 2,500 were runners in support of the chariots. The Hittites surrounded the Egyptian camp and then assaulted from several directions and began to loot, which proved to be their undoing. Muwatallish's aim should have been to destroy Egyptian high command (Ramses and his nobles); this was a tactic Alexander used dramatically at Gaugamela, 900 years later. It was to become the essence of blitzkrieg doctrine—cripple the decision-making leadership.

Ramses was saved by the timely arrival of reinforcements and Hittite avarice. In the confusion of the pillage, Ramses organized a desperate breakout which soon became a counterattack. Leading a small force of chariots, the Egyptians attacked Hittite groups in sequence, gobbling them up and snatching victory from defeat.

In North Europe, Celtic Britons confronted Julius Caesar with bravado and light chariots: "They drive about in all directions and throw their weapons and generally break the ranks of the enemy with the very dread of their horses and the noise of their wheels; and when they have worked themselves in between the troops of horse, leap from their chariots and engage on foot."[2] The Celtic chariot carried a driver and a warrior; tactics included a rapid approach, close quarter battle, and timely withdrawal. Once dismounted, the Celts fought with a berserker ferocity that unnerved garrison troops. Forced to melee against veterans, the Britons were soon disorganized and eventually dispatched by armored and better drilled opponents. Celtic chariots had iron wheel rims and wicker work for upper armor; this combination made for a lighter battle taxi with good all-terrain capability. The Roman occupation of Britannia was challenged in A.D. 60 by Boudicca, queen of the Inceni, who lived in what is now Norfolk. "Boudicca, with her daughters before her in a chariot, went up to tribe after tribe, protesting that it was indeed usual for Britons to fight under the leadership of women."[3] Her ferocious attacks badly mauled the IX Hispania Legion and drove the Romans out of several towns, including London. The legions fled to the continent which made the emperor Nero consider abandoning Britannia all together. Regrouping in Gaul, the Romans returned with two battle-hardened formations (XIV Gemina and the XX Valeria Victrix) and gave battle in a skillfully chosen defile. Desperate charges by Inceni chariots and foot were easily defeated by an experienced heavy infantry and disciplined horse: "The cavalry, at the same time, bore down upon the enemy, and, with their pikes, overpowered all who dared to make a stand."[4]

The continental chariot was considered obsolete by 400 B.C., particularly when confronted by armor and firepower. Longer ranged bows and cataphract cavalry relegated the war chariot to the *circus maximus*. Its most famous version was the four-horsed *quadriga* and is perpetuated via magnificent equestrian sculptures atop the Wellington Arch in London, Berlin's Brandenburg Gate, Venice's Triumphal Quadriga, and the Arc de Triomphe in Paris.

CLASSICAL CAVALRY—THE GREEKS AND ALEXANDER

> In 480 B.C. Persian cavalry under a general Masestivs had an authentic shock action and melee.
>
> —George Patton Jr.[5]

Cavalry armed with javelin, short swords, and mail shirts appeared circa 705 B.C. The Assyrians used cavalry organized in pairs; one warrior was armed with a bow, while the other, who was unarmed, directed the horse of his companion. This soon evolved into one rider, an archer with reins around his neck, giving fire while at the gallop. In 595 B.C., the Persian monarch, Cyrus the Great, armored his cavalry and organized it into groups of one hundred, armed with lances for throwing or charging. The narrow valleys and rocky ground of the Peloponnesus did not lend itself to the raising of cavalry forces. The arm of tactical decision, the axis of Greek military strength, was the *phalanx*. Sparta raised infantry, Athens developed a formidable fleet, but Philip of Macedon fielded a formidable cavalry comprised of well-equipped horses including a squadron of royal horse guards. This required considerable economic and political clout.[6]

Mycenaean Greeks made some use of chariots, but it was Alexander's use of cavalry as a shock weapon that gave the Greeks military dominance via a tactical balance of the heavy infantry phalanx and supporting arms. In battle, Greek cavalry hovered near the phalanx—an anvil upon which lesser arms broke. But properly led, cavalry could hammer out victory. When Alexander invaded the great empire in 334 B.C., the Persians still preferred the chariot for the attack. They are credited with having developed the original four-horsed chariots augmented with a devilish infantry-slicing sickle blade on each wheel hub. This scattered skirmishers and infantry in unsteady formations but did not worry disciplined hoplites (armored infantry). The phalanx, a veritable hedgehog of spears, stood as a rock in a sea of chariots.

Alexander instructed his army to create open lanes when threatened by chariot attack. The advancing horses simply followed the path of least resistance and galloped through, falling victim to flank assaults from missiles, javelins, or spears. The wheeled fighting vehicle would not make a dynamic reappearance until the combustion engine made armored cars and tanks practical cross-country weapons.

BUCEPHALUS—ARCHETYPAL WARHORSE

The warhorse of the Heroic Age was not large, averaging 13–14 hands. A "hand" is 4 inches—this unit of measure for equines is based on the width of a palm. The average Peloponnesian warhorse stood about four and a half feet from hoof to withers (the prominent ridge where the muscles of the neck and the back join, considered the horse's highest constant point). The best Greek horses came out of Thessaly and regularly bred with Persian, Scythian, and much prized Ferghana horses from Turkistan. The small-bodied Greek horses were subsequently improved by masses of horses imported from the East.[7] After defeating Darius, Alexander demanded a war tribute of 50,000 horses, which dramatically enhanced Mediterranean cavalry.

Alexander's warhorse, Bucephalus, rivaled the mythic status of his master. His legend was enhanced by the Delphic oracle, which foretold that the destined master of the known world would be a warrior whose horse carried the symbol of an ox head. Bucephalus may have carried this mark, but it is more likely Alexander named him *Boukephalos* (Greek for "ox-head") because he had a full-bodied head, like that of a bull. Alexander bet with his father he would ride Bucephalus—a feat none of the royal handlers had managed. "'And if you do not,' said Philip, 'What will you forfeit for your rashness?' 'I will pay,' answered Alexander, 'the whole price of the horse.' At this the whole company fell a-laughing."[8] This was only partly bravado, for Alexander had studied the horse and noted that Bucephalus bolted at the sight of his own shadow. He led him to face the sun and then lightly stroked his neck. The "horse whisperer" technique was known in Greece where good riders sought to control a horse via calm presence, smell, and finally, touch. Force or words of command were considered unnecessary, particularly with intelligent, spirited horses: "Stroking him gently when he found him begin to grow eager and fiery, he let fall his upper garment softly, and with one nimble leap securely mounted him, and when he was seated, by little and little drew in the bridle, and curbed him without either striking or spurring him."[9] The act moved Phillip: "shedding tears . . . kissed him as he came down from his horse, and said, O my son, look thee out a kingdom equal to and worthy of thyself, for Macedonia is too little for thee."[10]

As a cavalry general, Alexander had more than one war horse. Bucephalus was but one of his chargers; however, it was his favorite and brought him good fortune. "So long as [Alexander] was engaged in drawing up his men, or riding about to give orders or review them, he spared Bucephalus, who was now growing old . . . but when he was actually to fight, he sent for him again."[11] The horse inspired the army. From the phalanx to the cavalry, it was easily recognized on the battlefield: "There is something about this horse that strikes a responsive chord in even the most jaded viewer."[12] The spirited black charger (although an ancient fresco portrayed him as a bay) proved itself in a score of battles and was wounded in several. His larger than life status evoked spectacular myth.

Bucephalus was depicted as anthropophagous—a man-eater, a combatant that ripped foes and tore into their flesh. After carrying Alexander through his victories at Issus, Granicus, and the greatest of them all, Gaugamela, Bucephalus' luck ran out at Battle of the River Hydaspes, 326 B.C., where he succumbed to his battle wounds. Plutarch says Bucephalus was "thirty years old"[13] when he died—rather old for a warhorse. Alexander mourned him as he would his bravest captain, ordering a state funeral and personally leading the procession. A new city, Bucephala, was founded in his warhorse's honor. It survives as the Pakistani river city of Jhelum, where the Military College Jhelum is based.

ALEXANDER'S CAVALRY BATTLES—GAUGAMELA, THE CLASSIC FRONTAL

> Read over and over again the campaigns of Alexander, Hannibal, Caesar, Gustavus, Turenne, Eugene and Frederic. … This is the only way to become a great general and master the secrets of the art of war.
>
> —Napoleon Bonaparte, *Military Maxims*

Gaugamela (also known as Arbela, 331 B.C.) is taught by staff colleges as the first of the three great maneuvers in warfare—the frontal attack. It featured a decisive assault at a central point, followed by penetration and the envelopment of one wing. Its most effective result was the direct paralysis and elimination of the Persian army command. Although Alexander's army was outnumbered, his heavy infantry was superior to Darius' infantry, despite the presence of Greek mercenaries and Persian royal bodyguards known as the Immortals.

Darius enjoyed a distinct advantage with masses of cavalry, chariots, elephants, and foot consisting of at least 250,000, perhaps as many as 600,000, against 50,000 Greeks who arrived with only 7,000 horse and 40,000 infantry. The Macedonian heavy cavalry, Alexander's bodyguard Companions (the Hetairoi), numbered about 1,700 men in eight cavalry regiments called *hipparchies*. During the Persian campaign, the entire Greek cavalry was organized into five regiments, each *hipparchy* with an attached squadron of Companions. Alexander's immediate consort was a squadron of 300 selected Companions. Horse furniture comprised a bridle and *shabraque* (horse blanket); combat was given without saddles and, more importantly, without stirrups. Heavy cavalry was armed with long heavy spears, round shields, cuirasses of metal and leather, and helmets. The Greeks' longer spears gave them considerable advantage over the Persian cavalry who were equipped with short stabbing javelins.[14]

The emperor Darius could not manage his army and dabbed at the Greeks with uncoordinated piecemeal attacks. Alexander responded with maneuver.

He marched his army obliquely across the Persian front and unnerved Darius who began to lose tactical control. Maneuver should not have troubled the Persians as they fielded enough men to swamp the Greek force, but they seemed mesmerized by Alexander, the essence of dynamic leadership. He was called *Eskandar* in Persian—a synonym for "expert." Alexander cast himself as the avenging angel, resplendent in shimmering armor. One painting has him wearing a golden helmet made to look like the leering face of a god—he was an overwhelming spectacle. Catching sight of Darius' chariot just beyond a slight gap in the front line, he charged. As the Companions cut toward the Persian emperor, command was lost. Darius became petrified, fixated with the approaching storm as Alexander clearly had one goal, to kill him: "The lances of Alexander's cavalry and the pikes of the phalanx now pressed nearer and nearer to him. His charioteer was struck down by a javelin at his side; and at last Darius' nerved failed him."[15] Darius fled. His abandoned army, leaderless and broken in spirit, collapsed.

It would be unfair to characterize Gaugamela as a cavalry victory. The steadiness of the phalanx offered Alexander a base of attack as well as a safe haven; however, this action emphasized the effectiveness of the dynamic offensive. Shock action was limited; without stirrups, the classical warhorse did not produce the jolt of medieval cavalry, but Alexander smartly made up the difference with flamboyant leadership and a sudden thrust at the point of greatest decision. The mounted attack created enough psychological shock to develop exploitable momentum. Equally important was Alexander's good fortune. His victories were hard fought, he constantly risked death and often emerged with heavy wounds—the penultimate captain of cavalry.

It may be argued that cavalry victories began with Alexander, even though Greek warfighting centered on the heavy infantry. Alexander's mounted successes took classical warfare beyond the hoplite, elevating cavalry to an arm of decision. His personal élan secured victory, with a brief nod to the other half of the symbiotic partnership, his warhorse.

HORSES, INFANTRY, AND THE ODD ELEPHANT: HANNIBAL VERSUS ROME

Despite Alexander's use of elite cavalry, heavy infantry continued to dominate ancient wars. The Roman legion treated its cavalry as auxiliaries and was content with hiring conquered tribes to fill in. The advent of Hannibal briefly changed this attitude. Phoenician cavalry (a mix of African and Spanish levies) was superior to the Roman horse in quality, though not in breeding or size. The Latin warhorse was sturdy: "His neck is carried erect; his head is small; his belly short; his back broad. Brawny muscles swell upon his noble chest. A bright bay or a good grey is the best colour; the worst is white or dun."[16]

Roman mounts were trained for close combat and, like all spirited chargers, sensed battle and were drawn toward it: "If afar the clash of arms be heard, he knows not how to stand still; his ears prick up, his limbs quiver; and snorting, he rolls the collected fire under his nostrils."[17]

The introduction of war elephants created a temporary tactical advantage centered on shock and momentum. The exotic smell also terrified European horses. Hannibal's elephants were few and, like tanks in the early twentieth century, relatively delicate. The journey from Africa to Spain, through Southern France, across to snow covered passes of the Alps and finally the northern valleys of Italy eroded their numbers. It is a tribute to the veterinary skills of the Carthaginian army that any elephants arrived at all. The first major action fought between the Roman Republic and the Carthaginian invader was the Battle of Trebia in December of 218 B.C. It was the tactical precursor to Cannae and a good example of lessons learned turning against the student. It introduced the war elephant to the Romans and demonstrated the superiority of the Carthaginian cavalry.

Carthaginian elephants and cavalry drove into the Roman front and blitzed the Roman horse away from the flanks of the attacking army. The Gauls, terrified by the war elephants, broke first. The trapped Romans kept their cool and fought with determination, actually breaking through the Carthaginian center. This brief success was soon savaged from three sides as Hannibal's disciplined cavalry returned and the remaining elephants trampled through the cohorts. Trebia alarmed the Senate, which promptly raised four new legions and commanded the army to drive Hannibal out of Italy. This did not occur. The better led and faster marching Carthaginians completely out maneuvered the Romans and looted the rich countryside. Finally, Hannibal lured the Romans to Lake Trasimine (217 B.C.) where he sprang a devastating ambush. When the Romans restored the army, their generals would lead it into the worst defeat in the empire's history.

CANNAE—THE CLASSIC MODEL

> Every ground commander seeks the battle of annihilation; so far as conditions permit, he tries to duplicate the classic example of Cannae.
> —Gen. Dwight D. Eisenhower

The battle of Cannae (216 B.C.), the second great maneuver of military studies, remains the magnum opus for modern general staffs. Although cybernetic technology has just about taken surprise out of operational maneuver, Cannae continues to be studied at staff colleges as the *pas de cheval* of tactical ballet. The lesson the Romans chose to learn from Trebia was that disciplined Roman heavy infantry, using its ripping assault, could tear the heart out of any formation. The Senate's new commander, Gaius Terentius Varro, was determined to repeat the frontal attack. The maneuver problem, which featured superior Carthaginian cavalry and the threat of turned flanks, was given secondary concern. The Romans fielded 70,000 infantry and 2,500 cavalry; Hannibal managed less than 50,000 infantry, 40,000 of which were armored, but all his elephants were dead. However, he could deploy 8,000 cavalry, and they were to be the dramatic key to the battle of annihilation. Varro, recalling Hannibal at Trebia and Trasimine, selected open ground where everything was in the shop window. The plain favored cavalry operations but initial betting favored Varro. Roman legionnaires were a homogeneous lot, whereas Carthaginian forces varied. Hannibal placed his best infantry on the wings while his cavalry covered the flanks. As Varro began his advance to contact, the Carthaginian cavalry attacked the Roman cavalry and drove it off the field. The Carthaginians followed in hot pursuit. Herein lay the key to cavalry operations: discipline and control. According to Denison, "[Carthaginian] cavalry must have attained a very high degree of discipline, or they could never after a victorious charge have been kept so well in hand and recalled so readily."[18]

Hannibal deployed by *offering his front*—his army deployed as a bulge, inviting, daring a Roman attack. The cohorts promptly and systematically hacked through the center formations until the concave bulge had developed into a convex protrusion like a balloon stretched, about to burst. Hannibal permitted his infantry to fall back, thus drawing Varro's cohorts into a center mass, anticipating an imminent collapse. As the Romans crowded into the salient, Hannibal sprang loose the heavy infantry on his right and left; like two swinging doors they drove into Varro's flanks. This was the classic double envelopment, the vaunted *pincer movement*. The Romans began to appreciate the looming disaster when Carthaginian cavalry returned and delivered a demoralizing attack against the Roman army's rear, cutting them down mercilessly. The army became a panicking mass. Roman historians recorded as many as 60,000 dead, including consuls, tribunes, and senators. The status of Cannae as the perfect battle has been lauded by modern strategists:

> A battle of annihilation can be carried out today according to the same plan devised by Hannibal in long forgotten times. The enemy front is not the goal of the principal attack . . . The annihilation is completed through an attack against the enemy's rear . . . To bring about a decisive and annihilating victory requires an attack against the front and against one or both flanks.[19]

Cannae's fame rests on its result—total annihilation. According to Will Durant, "it was a supreme example of generalship, never bettered in history . . . and [it] set the lines of military tactics for 2,000 years."[20] This invites debate and discussion regarding ancient command and control as well as battlefield

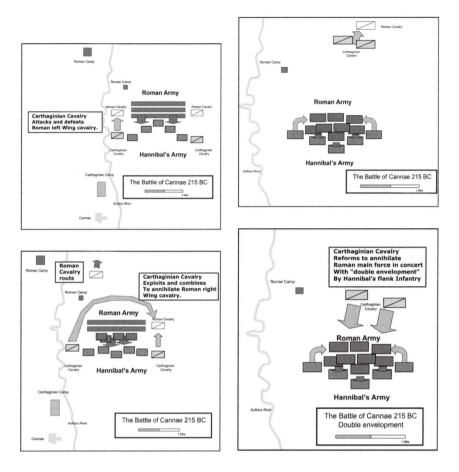

maneuver. Cannae was a fortunate result, made possible via shrewd deployment by a general who knew his army and owned an effective cavalry that arrived at the right moment to instigate chaos.

Hannibal met his end in North Africa. The battle of Zama (October, 202 B.C.) concluded the Punic Wars and destroyed Carthage. The contest featured the Roman army at its best and the Carthaginian at its worst. Few veterans of Trebia or Cannae remained, and the hastily assembled force did not boast the superb cavalry that had so effectively contributed to Roman disasters. Like Alexander facing Darius' chariots, Scipio ordered open lanes, in effect, killing zones, to tempt the 80 war elephants. Hannibal's "tanks" cooperated and ignored the Roman formations; rather than trampling through the maniples, they ambled past them, taking savage attack to their exposed flanks and rear from thrown *pilums* (javelins). Scipio's defeated Carthaginian horses then regrouped to deliver a coup de grace attack upon Hannibal's rear. The Carthaginian army and the once great empire collapsed.

The Roman legions went on to conquer the Mediterranean world. The civil war that followed Julius Caesar's assassination (44 B.C.) ended with a division of the empire amongst the members of the Triumvirate. One of its more greedy members, Marcus Licinius Crassus, was drawn into a campaign that shocked the empire into an appreciation of light cavalry: the eastern horse archer.

THE PARTING SHOT AND THE GOLDEN COCKTAIL

The Battle of Carrhae (53 B.C.) is the first recorded example of a defeat of heavy infantry by horse archers. The Parthians (remnants of the Persian Empire, modern Iraq) decisively vanquished Rome's legions, pitting an all-cavalry field force of 9,000 mounted archers supported by 100 cataphract cavalry against that most ubiquitous military tool box, the legion. The Roman army was impressively larger and comprised about five legions (28,000 foot) but failed to match the Parthian mounted arm deploying only 400 cavalry, mostly mercenary. Crassus confronted the Parthian general Surena on the arid plain just north of the Syrian border near present day Harran, Turkey. An ambitious military amateur, Crassus refused professional advice, maneuvered away from the Euphrates River, and allowed himself to be drawn into the desert in pursuit of Parthian plunder.

The outnumbered Parthians played their one trump card of mobility. Their horse-based army permitted strategic gambit. Parthian King Orodes II divided his force into two parts; he sent his infantry into Armenia to punish Crassus' only effective ally, while his cavalry force was dispatched to torment, then destroy, the invading Romans. The Parthian cavalry comprised two elements: cataphract horse (armored warriors, capable of blunting any attack by Roman cavalry) and horse artillery (missile-launching regiments of horse archers armed with the composite bow, which was allegedly able to pierce through two men at once). The horse archers practiced every form of maneuver warfare, but their most effective tactic was the feigned retreat.

Forces drawn into the pursuit were subjected to the so-called Parthian shot—archers turning and delivering well-aimed volleys of arrows into the chasing force. Stirrups were not used, but an early form of loop stirrups (cord or rings for the big toe) appeared in the Middle East circa A.D. 1. The Parthians depended on strong thighs and splendid balance to deliver fire. The archers tormented the enemy with a rain of arrows, and then, if attacked by heavy cavalry, pretended to rout, encouraging reckless pursuit. The tactic survives in the English lexicon to this day, as the "parting shot" or last jibe in spirited debate. The horse archers required considerable arrows, which were provided via the camel trains. After a battle, the Parthians generally were left holding the open ground, and spent arrows were retrieved.

The attack by fire was accomplished by a Parthian circle. Tactical groups, the *drafshi* (about 1,000 horse archers) or the *washt* (a squadron equivalent to about 300 horse archers), approached to give stand-off fire and then trotted in a lazy ring. As the archers reached the arc closest to the enemy, they let loose with a deadly barrage and then fitted new arrows at leisure as they moved with the circle. Both the arrow circle and Parthian shot were an "attack by fire." The only defense was lots of cavalry, archers, or a seeding of caltrops ("star nail" or *makibishi:* four or more iron spikes forged together) to impede cavalry advance. Scattered before an advancing force, the caltrops pierced the soft hooves of horses and camels or elephants and barefooted infantry.

The greatest advantage of the horse archer was eliminating the need to close with the target and expose the horse to either weapon fire or ambushing ground spikes. It had worked in previous battles: "The Legion strewed the field of battle with caltrops, and the horses that drew the chariots, running full speed on them, were infallibly destroyed."[21] Not this time. The battle was a gradual slaughter in the blazing sun. The legionnaires suffered the storm and attempted a missile defense via the testudo, or "tortoise," wherein legionnaires hoisted shields over their heads to form an overlapping armored roof against arrows or slingers' shots. The Parthians gave direct fire against the exposed torsos; the testudo also invited probing charges from spear-equipped cataphract cavalry. Plutarch recorded "When [Crassus' son] exhorted them to charge the armoured horsemen, [the Legionnaires] showed him that their hands were riveted to their shields and their feet nailed through to the ground, that they were helpless to either flee or fight in self-defence."[22] The combination of thirst, heat, and constant attack eventually made the Roman infantry incapable of effective defense, and the Parthians turned the battle into dusty target practice. Crassus' army broke. The greater part was hunted down or captured in one of the most complete defeats in Roman history, second only to Cannae.

Crassus was captured and brought before Surena. He was a multimillionaire better suited to politics and the grain market than war command. Surena contemptuously reminded his prisoner that it was his greed for pillage that led him to invade and pronounced a sentence he considered apt for an avaricious affluent foe: molten gold was poured down Crassus' throat.

One legacy of the battle was the introduction of silk into the Roman Empire. Campaign survivors described seeing luminous, iridescent standards; this allegedly led to the Silk Road and initial trade with China. The greater military effect was the realization that heavy infantry could not defeat a balanced cavalry army in open terrain.

Chapter 3

The outside Pony: **"This *Parthian Shot* stuff – it's so last millennium."**

The West in Decline: Mongol Cavalry

> The nation of Huns surpasses all other Barbarians in wildness of life. And though the Huns do just bear the likeness of men (of a very ugly pattern), they are so little advanced in civilization that they make no use of fire, nor any kind of relish, in the preparation of their food, but feed upon the roots which they find in the fields, and the half raw flesh of any sort of animal.
>
> —Ammianus Marcellinus, *History of Rome*[1]

The Roman Empire's decline was hastened by barbarian invasions; the cavalry army of the Hun Empire was particularly devastating. The Huns swept through the Roman Empire isolating Constantinople and penetrating as far west as France before being defeated at the Battle of Châlons. They were a nomadic confederation of Eurasian tribes seemingly devoted only to war. They had no system of writing, no capital; their world was the horse, and their *patria* the saddle. Initially the Huns had no monarchs, but by the middle of the fourth century, they were led by an emperor. The western borders of their empire were formed by the Rhine and Danube rivers, including present-day Germany, Hungary, Russia, Romania, Poland, and Ukraine. The Huns' ability to conduct hit-and-run raids was coupled with their skill in establishing a feudal stranglehold over conquered lands, ensuring compliance through terror and vengeance.

The Huns are synonymous with what may be described in modern terms as *strategic operational maneuver*. Their equestrian army was in a constant state of operational readiness and capable of both maneuver and shock. Hunnish horses were particularly suited to the rigors of a campaign, exhibiting extraordinary endurance for work and resistance to cold and hunger. The Huns likely used the toe-ring stirrup, but early versions of the traditional model may have been introduced. Their bow was a devastating technological advancement made from horn, sinew, and wood. The reflex composite bow was particularly suited to cavalry in that it was smaller than the longbow, was powerful, had a better range, and was easy to use on horseback. The Huns engaged their foes directly in a reasonably accurate barrage, often before their opposite numbers had loosed their first volley. The reputation of Hun archers prompted false bravado: "We fear neither the Huns nor their hornbows."[2]

Hun cavalry, like the Mongols 800 years later, did not use horseshoes. Protection for horses' feet was known to the early Romans but not in general use: "Mules and beasts of burden were sometimes provided with a metal or wooden shoe (called a *solea*), which was held in its place by thongs of leather crossed over the hoof. This however seems to have been the exception rather than the rule."[3] Roman cavalry may have been shod, but terrain was the deciding feature. Traditional nailed-on shoes were used during Celtic occupation, but the strapped-on *hippo sandal,* or detachable horseshoe, was common. Detachable shoes made attack at the gallop extremely difficult, if not impossible. Nailed shoes were common by the sixth century but required forges and smiths. Large cavalries trusted to the sturdiness of their horses' feet and good veterinary care.

It appeared as if the Huns fought in no fixed order or set doctrine; in fact, the simple sophistication of an all-cavalry force required both discipline as well as central command. The sudden appearance of cavalry on flanks or the reappearance of a force believed to have been broken and dispersed belied the experienced technique of a professional cavalry force. Barbarians by definition only, Attila's horde conducted deep battle and maneuver warfare with the grace and agility of a drilled corps de ballet.

The ability of their *vanguard* to spread terror, yet deny information, permitted sudden unexpected attacks. Speed added to their terror. Their startling arrival and merciless slaughter swept Europe like a mass of hungry locusts. The sighting of even small reconnaissance bands created panic—the Huns seemed to be everywhere, at once. A cavalry army is impossible to entrap unless it is confronted with an equally skilled force of light horse. It was clear that the Huns' army depended on silage, but short of laying waste to every meadow in Western Europe, it was impossible to deny them rations or cut their supply lines as there were no lines of supply.

A cavalry army must travel reasonably dispersed to permit forage and efficient pillage; it must also be able to concentrate quickly for selected attack. Operational maneuver in an age where only the crudest maps existed and information was passed verbally, was practically impossible without a highly developed system of reconnaissance and command and control. While tactical maneuver demands esprit and almost reckless bravado, in-the-saddle decisions demand a good eye and dynamic leadership. The Huns employed aggressive screens to fix the main body and then smack them in the flank or rear. Their approach marches were difficult to determine, particularly since, in juxtaposition to the forces they faced, the Hun hordes could turn on a dime. Their assault featured fire and maneuver before melee:

> The oriental never has used the cohesive shock of lines of horsemen. He gallops at his foe in loose unaligned masses and from his first appearance in history, is spoken of as circling. He uses a horizontal cut to increase the drawing effect of his weapon and takes his time to kill his man, continually circling him until he sees an opening and trusting to the agility of his horse for his parries.[4]

The apparent rustic simplicity of Hun cavalry masked the complex dexterous machine that made war with terrible efficiency.

ATTILA VERSUS ROME

Rome initially managed to check Asiatic probes by hiring Goths to reinforce the legions. The Huns' recurring peripheral raiding became serious with the appearance of a new leader in the western confederacy—the great cavalry captain, Attila. Attila's effect on the greater European psyche was second only to that of Adolf Hitler; his horrifying successes and demonic aura created continental anxiety and a psychological necessity for his elimination. To the rural peasant or town burgher, he was the devil incarnate. However, for a barbarian, he was reasonably sophisticated. Indeed, he could have passed for a patrician.

Attila the Hun was more of a returning tourist. He had been educated in Rome where he was held as a political hostage since the age of 12 and raised in the court of Emperor Honorius. The Roman diplomat Priscus, who met Attila, described him as "a short, squat man with a large head, deep-set eyes, flat nose, and a thin beard."[5] He was comfortable in the customs and peccadilloes of Roman society and had grown accustomed to the opulence and decadence of the eternal city. Attila had been made to attend ambassadorial conferences and been schooled in protocol and bureaucratic procedure; had he not become a captain of apocalyptic cavalry, he could have easily succeeded as a high placed official in the Roman or Byzantine courts. Although inheriting a taste for the empire's luxuries, he left with contempt for its culture. After 14 years of Roman finishing school, Attila returned to the East.

In A.D. 432 King Ruga, who had united the Hun tribes, died in his capital in present-day Hungary. Royal succession was bestowed to his nephews Bleda and Attila. The ceremony was conducted in a manner befitting an empire based on the warhorse. Attila and Bleda met with the representatives of the Hun imperial diet, all of whom were seated on horseback. They were given sectors of the empire and immediately set about securing and expanding their personal domains. Attila reappeared on the Roman borders in A.D. 440 and, after harassing commerce, crossed the Danube in a formal test of the empire's defenses. It was not a daunting task. When he assumed control, he inherited the perfect force with which to challenge an empire groaning under bureaucratic corruption and an unchanged conservative operational art. Attila's field force flooded past the crumbling levees of Danube forts. Every Balkan city fell before the army, which behaved with particular cruelty to any opposition, slaughtering entire tribes but ensuring that a few survivors were set free to spread news of the coming terror. Before long, Attila was called "the Scourge of God."

His offensive stopped at Constantinople because the Huns did not have the engineers to conduct a grand siege and because they were offered tribute by the emperor. The arranged peace and bribe simply whetted Attila's appetite. In A.D. 445, after Bleda mysteriously died (rumored to have been killed by Attila himself), Attila took the throne as undisputed lord of the Huns. He again turned his attention toward the empire, returning to his western seat on the Danube and hovering menacingly over the peripheries of Roman control. In A.D. 447 Attila invaded; his cavalry overwhelmed Roman and Gothic coalitions and again threatened Constantinople. During the negotiated armistice, the Roman emissary observed Attila during a banquet in his tented cavalry encampment:

> A luxurious meal, served on silver plate, had been made ready for us and the barbarian guests, but Attila ate nothing but meat on a wooden trencher. In everything else, too, he showed himself temperate; his cup was of wood... The sword he carried at his side, the latchets of his Scythian shoes, the bridle of his horse were not adorned, like those of the other Scythians, with gold or gems or anything costly.[6]

A neurotic cavalier, Attila once remained seated on his horse during an entire fête. The Huns did not take well to peaceful coexistence. One of the drawbacks of having a dynamic force of cavalry is that the horses, warriors, and their captains are high strung, easily grow restless, and function best when they are on campaign. Attila could not simply administer a fighting horde in grassy retirement. He soon received a serendipitous rationale for going to war again.

CHÂLONS: A CAVALRY BATTLE

> Quadrupedumque putrem cursu quatit ungula campum. [And the hoof of the horses shakes the crumbling field as they run.]
>
> —Virgil, *The Aeneid (XI, 875)*

The Battle of Châlons featured a Roman coalition led by General Flavius Aëtius, the empire's designated supreme allied commander. Aëtius commanded a European force that included the Visigoth king, Theodoric. Their alliance confronted the operational might of Attila's equestrian horde, ostensibly bent on restoring honor, but mostly after plunder. The battle was sort of a Helen of Troy affair kindled by Princess Honoria, the disgraced sister of the Western Roman Emperor Valentinian. She had conducted a scandalous affair with her chamberlain and had been implicated in a plot to overthrow her brother. Her lover was executed, and Honoria, allegedly pregnant, was exiled to a secluded convent. She smuggled out a letter to Attila, seeking to make him her champion; the letter included a ring, as a sign of trust. Attila chose to interpret this as a proposal of marriage and immediately demanded from Valentinian a fitting dowry of half the empire. When the emperor refused, the cunning Attila professed immeasurable anguish from the imperial insult and invaded Western Europe. Was Honoria the face that launched 30,000 warhorses? Unfortunately, no pictorial record remains.

The Hun horse archers crossed the Rhine early in A.D. 451 and penetrated into Gaul, capturing a dozen important centers including Paris. But as Orléans was besieged, Attila was confronted by the grand alliance. Patricius (supreme military commander) Aëtius led a coalition of Visigoths, Alans, and Burgundians: "The Visigoths, who at that time were in the mature vigor of their fame and power, obeyed with alacrity the signal of war, prepared their arms and horses, and assembled under the standard of their aged king."[7] A mirror to Attila, Aëtius, as a child, had lived as hostage among the Huns in exchange for Attila. The two had met before Attila departed for Italy and may have been friends.

The Hun army numbered about 30,000, while the allied field force was nearly 50,000. The mass of Gallic tribes reinforcing the Romans was a surprise. Attila had not expected a dynamic response. The allied force was well balanced and fielded a vast amount of first rate cavalry. Attila's operational raison d'être was movement, and he quickly abandoned Orléans. A series of sweeping maneuvers concluded with both forces meeting near Châlons-en-Champagne. The battlefield was dominated by a ridge, and the battle was a seesaw struggle for control of that ground of tactical importance. Aëtius and Theodoric deployed first as Attila waited and watched, secure inside his wagon laager. Whether in accordance with Hun custom or being simply superstitious, the normally sophisticated Attila summoned a shaman to examine the entrails of his sacrifice to the gods. The omens were dark, foretelling a debacle, but divined that one of the Roman leaders would die in battle. Attila decided it was to be Aëtius and gave orders. He had delayed until the afternoon, allowing the enemy the advantage. When his reconnaissance reported the Roman force deploying upon the high ground, he dispatched his first echelon of horse archers. They raced the French cavalry to secure the ground.

With thunderous advance, each side established opposing flank positions and then fought for the center crest. The alliance cavalry was quicker and secured the ridge before the Huns. In the fierce struggle, both sides took heavy casualties. Aëtius attempted a double envelopment, hoping to roll up Attila's flanks. King Theodoric, wounded in a running melee, was ridden over and trampled to death, proving the diviner's forecast correct. His son, Thorismund, led the cataphract cavalry and counterattacked, retaking the key terrain. The Huns withdrew, confused and demoralized. Aëtius ordered the pursuit. Cataphract cavalry intercepted Attila's own Guard cavalry and engaged them with such ferocity that Attila was forced to retreat to the safety of his camp.

Faced with certain defeat, Attila ordered a cavalry funeral pyre (a mound of saddles) and determined to "cast himself into the flames, that none might have the joy of wounding him . . . [that he] might not fall into the hands of his foes."[8] Finally, realizing Aëtius had no intention of rushing his camp, Attila took a chance and conducted a breakout battle. The Huns did what they did best—maneuvering, dispersing, and regrouping elsewhere. It worked. The horse army managed to extricate themselves and retreat to the Danube. The Roman Empire was euphoric. The battle's most important result was that it demonstrated the Huns' vincibility. Gibbon identifies Châlons as "the last victory which was achieved in the name of the Western Roman Empire."[9] In hindsight, Châlons fame rested in that simply, Attila had been defeated for the first time. Aëtius's conduct of the campaign drew deserved criticism, for he failed to follow up his victory and permitted Attila to escape. Attila licked his wounds and rebuilt his cavalry. The next year he returned. The Huns ravaged Italy, laying waste to Venetia, sacking Milan, and then descending on Rome. However, Attila spared the city, evidently moved by the brave piety exhibited by Pope Leo I who advanced barefoot in snow to beg the Hun emperor to show mercy for the eternal city. Other accounts suggest that the pope arrived at Ravenna with a flock of priests, and they negotiated on horseback. This time the Romans caved in. Ambassadors visited Attila's camp and, amidst the intimidation of snorting horses and archers, offered ransom, including Princess Honoria. Interestingly enough, Attila declined. Honoria was abandoned, forced to marry a senator, and disappeared from history.

Within a decade the empire collapsed, leaving the Huns to become a dim nightmare. This did not, however, end the Roman Empire's attraction for Asiatic horsemen. The last great horsed invasion by equestrian barbarians occurred in the thirteenth century when Mongol riders ("the Devil's Horsemen") thundered into Western Europe.

THE PERFECT WEAPONS SYSTEM—NOMADIC
CAVALRY ARMIES OF THE GOLDEN HORDE

> The Mongols are by nature good at riding and shooting—they took possession
> of the world through the advantage of bow and horse.
>
> —Chinese maxim

> The greatest pleasure is to vanquish your enemies and chase them before you,
> to rob them of their wealth and see those dear to them bathed in tears, to ride
> their horses and clasp to your bosom their wives and daughters.
>
> —Genghis Khan[10]

Eight hundred years after Attila, Asian cavalry again appeared in the west as
a mounted horde led by Genghis Khan. The conquest of Europe by a cavalry
army composed of nomadic Mongolians retarded the development of Russian
and Ukrainian states. It also shook up the remaining part of the old Roman
Empire—the Byzantine realms of Constantinople. The term *Golden Horde*
(Russian, *Zolotaya Orda*—"Golden Rule" or "Government") refers to political
divisions of the Mongol Empire (The Golden Horde, The Blue Horde, etc.).
The Asiatic method of describing cardinal directions: blue (east), red (south),
white (west), and yellow or gold (north) may have also accounted for the nam-
ing of hordes.

The nomadic Mongols comprised a moving flood, a sea of horses that like
an irresistible tsunami, swamped empires, washing away opposing armies
in a torrent of hoofs and arrows. They are further described in a passage
from *The Golden Horde*: "A numberless multitude swept across the hill
crests and like waves of a black ocean did they sweep down upon us. Their
arrows fell like clouds of biting flies from the darkened sky. The death screams
of our warriors were o'erwhelmed by the drumming of infinite hooves so that
only the endless thunder was heard at the last."[11] The Great Khan poured
out of the eastern Siberian plains onto the steppes of the Ukraine and in
short order sacked all the major commercial centers of Eastern Europe and
the Greek Christian cities of Byzantium along the Black Sea. The Mongol
cavalry, numbering more than 200,000 light horse archers, fought battles
against heavy European cavalry, often outnumbered. Their defeat of Teutonic Knights and powerful Polish cataphracts brought them to the gates of
Vienna.

The Devil's Horsemen slaughtered over 80 percent of the Slavs in their initial invasions. The Kyiv Empire never recovered but continued a loosely organized rebellion led by their own indigenous steppe cavalry—the Cossacks.
The steppes of the Ukraine became a struggle between Christian Cossacks and
the seigneurs of the Golden Horde, the Tartars. The Cossacks pronounced it
Tatar [tah tarr], the term said to reflect the initial terror all cavalry bestows, the
pounding rhythm of advancing hooves: tatar, tatar, tatar.

Subsequent Mongol campaigns invaded the Middle East, defeating the great Caliph and capturing Baghdad. Parthian and Scythian tactics were chaff before the whirlwind that was the Mongol mounted assault. About the only thing that thwarted the Mongol cavalry was geography. The rock-strewn terrain of Syria initially hindered the Mongols who did not use horseshoes. When the Mongols reached Egypt the Mamluks burned their pastures, delaying the inevitable. The Mongol tide was stopped by an imperial death and a resulting civil war. Genghis Khan's death in 1227 (appropriately, he fell off his horse) did not remove the Mongol presence from Eastern Europe, but it did introduce a new foreign policy. Subsequent Mongol rulers were far more interested in China than the backward barbaric Christians or Arabs that comprised the west.

Nomadic by temperament, the Mongols concentrated on sacking, devastation, and massacre. They were content with tribute and a general indifference to local religions. Nonetheless, they eventually established an efficient feudal state administered with some skill. The Mongol cavalry was often at least as barbaric as those they conquered and had no difficulty terrorizing their more sophisticated opponents. Despite their cruelty and no-quarter philosophy, the Mongols apparently did not seek to torture or mutilate their enemies: "The Mongols did not partake in the gruesome displays that European rulers often resorted to elicit fear and discourage potential enemies—none of the stretching, emasculating, belly cutting and hacking to pieces . . . The Mongols merely slaughtered, preferring to do so at a distance."[12] Conversely, Mongols unlucky enough to be captured in battle could count on humiliation and the most excruciating death, all for the amusement of their Christian or Islamic captors.

The Mongols are credited with introducing examples of stirrups, which was an advantage in mounted battle, as valuable a tech improvement as steel versus bronze. The stirrup offered stability and permitted the archer to stand in the saddle while shooting—even at the gallop. The stirrup's origin is, however, debated. The Sarmatians or Scythians are credited with working stirrups in the first century. They settled along what is Ukraine and Caspian Russia and evolved into various Cossack tribes. Sarmatian heavy cavalry used a long heavy lance and wore armor: "[they] were probably the first troops to charge bodies of infantry in the accepted cavalry fashion."[13]

The standard stirrup was probably Asian, perhaps perfected by the nomadic Turkil tribes bordering China.[14] The victory of Gothic cavalry over Byzantine legions at Adrianople in A.D. 378 is sometimes credited to the use of the stirrup. The Mongol armies likely used both the early loop stirrup (toe loops at the end of a strong cord) as well as wood and metal combinations attached to leather straps fastened to a saddle. The stirrup was finally introduced to Europe around the eighth century and, coupled with the storm of horse archers, inaugurated an era of cavalry dominance. Horse armies, Mongolian archers, and heavy cataphract formations dominated warfare into the medieval period.

Europeans were shocked at the power, range, and penetration of the Asiatic composite bow. It was easily the equal of the Welsh longbow. The composite reflex bow originated on the Asian steppes. Unstrung, it looked like an inverted art deco *C*; when forced back and made taut, it became a bow much more familiar to modern westerners than a longbow—it was the embodiment of the stylized Cupid's bow. The enormous tension and energy created from bending the bow inside out created a weapon of formidable range and penetration. The bow was a combination of select wood strips sandwiched between elastic sinew and horn bone bonded, then laminated, with fish glue, which imparted strength yet resilience and protection from moisture. Bowstrings were made from horsehide, which was supple in very cold weather.[15] Bows were custom made; construction including fitting and compressing, curing and drying and took at least a year, making acquisition of a Mongol bow equivalent to purchasing a good car.

The bow's dynamic power catapulted arrows about a football-field length beyond that of the longbow: 350 yards versus 250 yards average distance. Skilled archers exceeded this; Mongol cavalry delivered punishing barrages from at least 200 paces and began to penetrate armor at 100 yards.[16] Horse archers shot using the Mongolian release, "a special ring on which the string is hooked before release. This thumb ring . . . is typically made from Chinese jade or agate, but leather, metal and bone is also known to have been used."[17]

Mongolian cavalry included women. Chinese and Persian chronicles note women were part of the cavalry army and were trained for military campaigns: "[Chingis Khan] ordered women accompanying the troops to do the work and perform the duties of the men, while the latter were absent fighting."[18] Marco Polo tells of Kublai Khan's nephew and rival Kaidu's daughter Aigiarn ("Shining Moon") who was famous for her "unparalleled feminine beauty as well as her immense strength of body . . . so strong that she surpassed every male Mongol warrior in physical strength and skill. Consequently, she accompanied her father on his campaigns and took great pleasure in the thrills of fighting."[19]

The Mongol warriors wore rough campaign dress but preferred Chinese silk shirts. Silk was a tough fiber and used as part of a *cuirasse*. Latin arrows shot from a great distance did not easily penetrate, and if an arrow pierced flesh, the silk generally held so that the arrow could be drawn out by twisting then pulling, thus preventing poison from entering the bloodstream. Mongol body armor comprised a composite wood, leather, and silk, treated with resilient fish glue lacquer. The result was impervious to most arrows, swords, and knives and was comfortable on the march. Mongol warriors also wore metal and leather helms: "Each rider had a sharpening stone for keeping the metal arms in top shape. Since self-sufficiency was the order of the day, in addition to the indispensable knife, an awl, needle and thread were carried by each rider, to enable quick and effective repair of almost any type of equipment in the field."[20]

The Mongol army was a superlative *Glubokii boi* ("deep battle") force. The advantage of being able to cross any terrain in the most adverse weather with no baggage gave the Mongols incredible advantage and defined the concept of maneuver warfare. Offensive maneuver featured extensive recce and advance along a central axis by the main body in a loose crescent formation much like a Zulu *impi*. The core of the crescent threatened the enemy while each "horn" attempted to flank or encircle. If the enemy answered with creative maneuver, the Mongols adopted a feigned retreat known as the *mangudai*. Mongol doctrine emulated the Parthian and Hun tactics of maneuver and shooting on the move. This included tactical ruses and contrived retreats, for staged routs induced the foolhardy into pursuit. The aristocracy of Europe and the Middle East was only too keen to test their mettle against light cavalry but invariably discovered tactical reality within a cunning killing zone. After volley fire, the horde closed on a disorganized foe to deliver a withering penetrating fire at less than 100 yards. Each horse archer carried two types of arrows: crippling barbed ends or small-tipped armor-piercing tips. Adventurer Giovanni da Pian del Carpine recorded, "Everyone must have at least these weapons: two or three bows or at least one good one, and three large quivers filled with arrows, a battle-axe, and ropes for dragging machines. . . The length of their arrows is two feet . . . the heads of the arrows are very sharp and cut on both sides like a two-edged sword."[21] Arrow assault was followed by a devastating melee. Close-quarter fighting featured aggressive horses and awesome hardware.

The two preferred melee weapons were the *Zhanmadao* or "horse chopping sword" (developed in China) and the Mongol saber, a heavy slashing weapon that could cut deeply into the muscles of man or mount. The horse archer carried his saber wrapped in a rough fur scabbard, next to his quiver and tied to his wrist to prevent loss in close-quarter action where swords were either knocked out of grasp or stuck in the flesh of the enemy and had to be yanked out.

Genghis Khan imposed force unity by breaking up ethnic or tribal affiliations and mixing his troops into teamlike subunits. The Mongols were intuitively metric, and their army was organized in multiples of 10: initial family-like groupings of 10 archers, troops, then 100 warrior squadrons *(jaghun)*, 1,000 strong regiments *(mingghun)*, and 10,000 man brigades *(tjumen)*. Transfers between units were not permitted, and discipline was ruthless and uncompromising. Essentially a nomadic nation on horseback, the Khan's cavalry was used to harsh winters and long-distance travel.

They also excelled at sieges and mass river crossings, and the Danube, Prut, Dnieper, or Volga proved no obstacle. The Khan was practical enough to include Chinese and Arab engineers in his specialist formations. While the Chinese invented gunpowder, and the Mongols introduced it to the Middle East, it was the Arabs who refined the chemical compounds to create a stable and effective explosive that could service siege artillery and, eventually, firelocks. Mongol engineers astonished Christian and Islamic cities with sophisticated assault incorporating modern siege engines to destroy fortifications and conquer walls.

Their greatest weapon was terror. The psychological effect of an approaching Mongol horde was often enough to break an opposing army. They advertised their own barbarity by ensuring that select survivors were freed to spread the tales of the slaughter they had witnessed.

The Mongol warhorse was half-wild, unshod yet sure footed, impervious to harsh climate and little fodder. It was a shooting platform, an attack vehicle as well as transport. On campaign the horse was a source of protection, warmth, and sustenance. Its milk was gathered for drink or turned into yogurt on the march. Poured into a bladder and tied to the saddle, the milk was churned into a sustaining beverage. In emergency, a starving rider made a small incision in the neck and drank his horse's blood to give him enough energy to carry on. Crippled horses or battle casualties provided meat and rawhide. Bone marrow enriched the diet. The Khan's mounts were allowed to go shaggy for warmth, and sported a variety of color. Dark brown or black were standard, although grey and *Chagaan* (white) were much prized. Mongol horses were hardy but diminutive (4 feet high at the withers) and resembled modern ponies. The best example is Prezwalski's horse, a surviving species of Mongol horse discovered in Asia in 1879: "Their horses are fed upon grass alone and do not require barley or other grain. The men are habituated to remain on horseback during two days and two nights without dismounting; sleeping in that situation whilst their horses graze . . ."[22]

Mongol horse furniture included a bridle and stirrups secured to a leather and wood saddle kept snug with sheep's fat. Mongolian horse blankets, actually horsehair pads, were particularly effective in that they did not "sweat" and gave protection to the horse's back in the most foul climate. The *Terlik*, or Mongol horse pad, was made at the beginning of winter when the horses did not need long tails to swat away flies. Attached saddlebags carried hard rations, water, and yogurt pouches. The Mongols enjoyed *Kumis*, a drink made from fermenting mare's milk in a horsehide pouch. The result was mildly alcoholic and could be further distilled into a serious spirit called *Araka:* "It leaves a taste of milk of almonds on the tongue, and it makes the inner man most joyful and also intoxicates weak heads, and greatly provokes urine."[23] The Mongols' diet gave them operational superiority over their opponents who required grains and constant resupply from depots or well-organized forage collection. One legacy of the Mongol cavalry style may be steak tartare. Legend has it the scrupulous horsemen cut off a share of meat from any tough, stringy carcass available, whether beef, goat, or horse, and slapped it under their saddle: "They give it a kind of cooking by placing it between their own thighs and the backs of their horses."[24] After a day's ride the meat was tenderized and made piquant with a natural vinaigrette made from the horse's sweaty flanks. The final product made for a quick meal *à la russe* or briefly warmed over a fire. The modern version tastes better with chilled vodka or champagne.

The traditional Achilles' heel of a marching army, the "logistic tail," did not exist. Horse milk and horse blood were staples of the Mongolian cavalry diet. Anything beyond what was carried on horseback was foraged and taken as plunder. Like members of a particularly savage *Bushkazi* team, each Mongol archer owned one extra horse—most averaged three to five spares. According to Marco Polo: "Their horses are so well broken in to quick changes of movement, that upon the signal given, they instantly turn in every direction."[25] The total dependence on their mounts led to Mongol shaman bestowing spiritual denotation and including horses in precampaign ritual. The horse was both a symbiotic comrade in battle and a sacrosanct artifact. Mare's milk was scattered before battle, and in some cases, horses were sacrificed to ensure transportation to heaven.

The cavalry invasions of Europe gave impetus to social, economic, and military reform on the continent. The evolution of trading leagues, technological change, or tactical doctrine ambled along with almost a casual pace. Change was gradual. The central problem was stable government and nothing as efficient as Roman rule emerged from the Dark Ages. Eventually, a political system, based on hereditary monarchial rule anchored on Catholic mysticism, produced demonstrable social and political change with an affected graciousness. This transformation was centered on the horse.

Chapter 4

Warhorse: **"Surely we are not about to charge Peasants?"**

The Medieval Cavalry

The history of the use of the horse in battle is divided into three periods: first, that of the charioteer; second, that of the mounted warrior who clings to his steed by pressure of the knees; and third, that of the rider equipped with stirrups.

—Lynn White, *Medieval Technology and Social Change*

I speak Spanish to God, Italian to women, French to men, and German to my horse.

—Attributed to Charles V, King of Spain and Holy Roman Emperor, 1500–58

The Hundred Years' War found the warhorse triumphant and the center of the operational art. By the time the last arrow hit the ground at Agincourt, it was a spent force relegated to the role of "supporting arm" in a martial world dominated by infantry and gunpowder. The conduct of the war on the medieval battlefield may appear less bizarre if certain aspects are considered: the knight's equipment and heraldic advertisements, and, his drive train, the great feudal warhorse. The specifics of the mounted attack in time and space must be explained vis-à-vis the technical characteristics of what proved to be the warhorse's greatest opposition—the longbow. Finally, a review of two battles that challenged the dominance of chivalry—Crécy and Agincourt—is appropriate to trace the warhorse in its devolution.

The concept of *chivalry* or *knighthood* originated with the French. Chivalry and *chevalier* (*cheval* means horse) refers to mounted aristocracy within the feudal or medieval period. European feudalism extended from early references in the eighth century to a violent termination in France in the eighteenth century. Aspects of feudalism remained; *seigneurialism* was practiced in French Canada until the 1830s, and Czarist Russia was essentially an autocratic feudal society at the time of the revolution. Chivalry was based upon reciprocal obligations coupled with exaggerated class values that included the concept of *courtly love* and ideal *knightly virtues*. Its most durable and most romantic symbol is the knight and his warhorse—an aristocratic symbiotic relationship. The Catholic feudalism advocated an absolute system of faith and politics; thus it was only logical that its noblesse should adopt an absolute system of tactics. Cavalry served as a resplendent icon of fighting aristocracy as well as the acme of martial influence. Chivalry epitomized the trinity of maneuver warfare (armor, mobility, and shock) that would remain the goal of cavalry into the new millennium.

THE ARMORED CAVALIER

> No other Knight in all the land
> Could do the things that he could do.
> Not only did he understand
> The way to polish swords, but knew
> What remedy a Knight should seek
> Whose armour had begun to squeak.
> —A. A. Milne, *The Knight Whose Armour Didn't Squeak*

The mounted knight, clinquant in steel and heraldry, dominated the field of battle, and his mere appearance reduced infantry to also-ran status. The distinctions between the two traversed social, economic, and martial strata. The warhorse and armor were simply unaffordable, as was the time required to produce a competent warrior. One cavalry officer compared it to running a Formula 1 racing team—"buying the beast, training, maintenance, and keeping the driver at peak condition."[1] A suit of armor retailed at between £8 and £16. A year at Oxford, with tuition, board, and clothes, cost £8 (a *pound* or *livre* was equivalent to a pound of pure silver). A good warhorse cost about £80, which was equivalent to a Ferrari. Unmatched in weapon craft, riding skill, or protection, the knight concentrated on combat with the only opposite worthy to challenge him—another knight. This social distinction, with its attendant mannerisms and styles, influenced the conduct of medieval warfare:

> A young knight from France, called sir Tristan de Roye, who was desirous of displaying his courage. . . . He sent a [herald] to the English army, requesting, that since peace had put an end to the combat, some one would have the kindness to tilt with him three courses with the lance before the city of Badajos. When this request was brought to the army, they consulted together, and said it ought not to be refused. A young English squire then stepped forth, called Miles Windsor,

who wished honourably to be created a knight, and said to the herald, "Friend, return to thy masters, and tell sir Tristan de Roye, that to-morrow he shall be delivered from his vow, by Miles Windsor, before the city of Badajos, according to his request."

On the morrow morning, Miles Windsor left the army of the earl of Cambridge, and went towards Badajos . . . well accompanied by friends . . . there were upwards of one hundred knights on the spot, where the tournament was to be performed. Sir Tristan de Roye was already there, accompanied by French and Bretons.

When the combatants were completely armed, with lances in their rests, and mounted, they spurred their horses, and, lowering their spears, met each other with such force that their lances were twice broken against their breast-plates, but no other hurt ensued. They then took their third lance, and the shock was so great that the heads of Bordeaux steel pierced their shields, and through all their other armour even to the skin, but did not wound them: the spears were shattered, and the broken pieces flew over their helmets.

This combat was much praised by all the knights of each side who were present. They then took leave of each other with much respect, and returned to their different quarters, for no other deeds of arms were performed.[2]

For professional warfighting, the feudal army required a main battle tank; this was, by mid-fourteenth century, a mounted knight in plate armor and the subject of apotheosis in song and chronicle. Style and color formed an important part of the knightly image. The martial art, and here is meant *heraldry*, was an eccentric combination of the effete and the macho. What was considered militarily in 1346 today borders on the laughable—a smorgasbord of decor and family tree devices. Tournament attire comprised a splash of colors and symbols, which included fantastic papier mâché or leather creations atop helmets, from lions to swans. Many knights' helmets included a *torse* (a twisted cord or wreath) representing Christ's crown of thorns—a fashion brought back by crusaders. Armor was polished or blackened steel since black armor collected less heat than shiny metal. The knight's outfit was layered against the elements, searing sun or rusting rain. Combinations varied. Western knights used chain mail, leather (hardened in boiling wax as *cuir bouille*), scale, plate armor, or creative bricolage; full plate did not dominate until the end of the fourteenth century. The ensemble included the *gambeson*, a thick padded garment worn under mail. The main armor, in custom-fitted sections, was meticulously forged for comfort and flexibility. The complete suit included the helm, *pauldrons* (shoulder plates), gauntlets, gorget (a neck protector), breast-plate or *cuirasse*, and greaves, the equivalent of shin guards. This was covered by a knee-length fabric chemise or *surcote*.

The *surcote* was as important as armor. Adorned with the knight's heraldic arms, it clearly identified him in a sea of faceless metal. This prevented friendly fire from archers or an errant bash from a comrade in the heat of melee. *Surcotes* helped squires rescue their masters from a throng of mud-spattered bodies or distinguished the bearer as someone worth sparing for ransom:

> The pathetically quixotic Duke of Brabant, whose loyal retinue had left him on his own for fear that by crowding around him in his captivity they would draw attention to his rank and riches. His captor had removed his helmet, but seeing nothing in his features, nor in the eccentric makeshift surcoat he was wearing over borrowed armour, to indicate the value of his prize, had decided he was not worth preserving and cut his throat.[3]

Once the ensemble was strapped on and adjusted, scratching an itch or quashing a biting flea became impossible. The old saw of a flea in the knight's ear was all too true. Personal comfort, including toilet duty, was difficult, if not impossible. Genitalia were protected with a codpiece, the precursor to the modern athletic support. Made of metal or chain mail, affixed with leather straps to ensure a snug fit, the contraption made relieving oneself, scratching, or sudden passion an irritating challenge in or out of the saddle: "Already in a rage of lust, mad after a wife, and vehemently hot upon untying the codpiece-point; I itch, I tingle, I wriggle."[4]

Resplendent nobles in flashy accoutrements drew archers' attention, but then martial vogue was supposed to attract attention. Most knights flew personal banners or *guidons* (corruption of *Guide Homme*—"Guide Man"). A banner was a square reproduction of heraldic arms and colors and a particularly accomplished knight might have a *schwenkel* streaming from the end of his banner. Very accomplished knights were permitted two, which was the origin of the swallow-tailed guidon used by modern cavalry. A red *schwenkel* was a mark of great honor; they were particularly long, and three or more feet was not uncommon. A retinue of the rich and famous could surround a king with a virtual forest of banners, pennons, guidons, and flying *schwenkels*. *Pennons* were more personal displays, depicting the primary "charge" or a badge of the bearer. They were long, always tapered to a single point, and restricted to royal peers and knights who displayed them on lances.

The knight's armor was relatively thin (about 60–80 pounds) and finely articulated: "the helmet and cuirasse of one Knight, Ferry de Lorraine, weighed ninety pounds."[5] Tests conducted at the Tower of London confirmed an armored knight could mount, kneel, stand, and certainly fight in his suit of armor, which was evenly distributed proportionately over his entire body as opposed to the harness and rucksacks of twentieth-century soldiers, which constituted a dead weight on their backs and shoulders. The battle-ready version of the knight was streamlined for action. Excessive paraphernalia was discarded, but the kaleidoscope of color and heraldic devices remained, if only to discourage fratricide. The final product, an explosion of color and thundering hooves atop a powerful horse with flying pennon, was a larger than life force and a daunting spectacle that intimidated opponents. It was as much a mind game as a bloody sport.

THE WARHORSE AND ITS FURNITURE

Armored combat demanded a powerful war engine: "the great horse" or *destrier*. Percherons, Belgians, Clydesdales, and shire horses, including modern day draft horses are descended from the destrier and trace their lineage to jousting requirements, which was far more exotic than pulling a beer wagon. The destrier was twice as large as a riding horse, and its iron shoes were reinforced with hobnails for support and additional clout against infantry. Horseshoes were de rigueur for the Western warhorses; Asiatic horses appear to have had tougher hooves as the Mongols conquered their empire with horses au naturel. For pleasure or utility, the knight rode the *palfrey*, a shorter legged horse with a longer body and a comfortable ride; for speed and delivery of communiqués, feudal breeders developed the *courser*, forerunner of the modern racehorse. Coursers carried Arabian and Turkish stock; they were lean, athletic, spirited, and pretty to look at but unsuitable for heavy metal warfare. An average knight, with armor and saddle, could weigh close to 300 pounds—hard duty across rough terrain for any horse. The Arabian horse had endurance and was nimble, often outmaneuvering his opposite number. It was assumed the Moors had brought horses with them when they invaded Spain. It is now believed that while some light *barb*-type horse was introduced by the Moors, the majority of their fighting horses came from indigenous stock already in Spain. Western knights preferred the "cold-blooded European" warhorse, while their Moor opponents used "warm-blooded" chargers developed from Arabian and Spanish barb breeds. Although biologically analogous, the smaller Spanish barb and Arabs are referred to as warm blooded; cold-blooded horses include large draft horses. The warhorse's size and weight created the shock of the charge with *lance couchée*. Equipped with solid horse furniture (high-backed saddles with accoutrements) and buttressed by stirrups, the knight presented a cohesive armored attack weapon.

A brief examination of the saddle and stirrup may be appropriate. Historian Lynn White has argued that "few inventions have been so simple as the stirrup, but few have had so catalytic an influence on history . . . The Man on Horseback, as we have known him during the past millennium, was made possible by the stirrup."[6] A parallel case has been made for the saddle as decisive cavalry kit by Ann Hyland: "It became clear that this saddle must have revolutionized cavalry warfare, bringing it to a stage not thought possible until the advent of stirrups. The front horns permitted putting considerably more poundage behind the lance thrust than was possible with a pad saddle. Lateral sword slashes were more effective due to horn security."[7]

Modern medievalists have jousted with this thesis. The couched lance technique is the normal method of delivering shock and has been practiced since Alexander. The debate evolved beyond speculative theory as sports jousting increased in popularity in Europe and North America and experienced riders experimented with attack techniques. Medievalist Richard Alvarez contends that while saddle and stirrups improve the joust, "shock combat" without saddle or stirrups was possible: "One of the biggest misconceptions about shock combat is that the combined weight of horse and rider is directly translated to the lance, as if somehow the horse, rider, and lance were one rigid mass. In fact . . . *they react as separate units* [emphasis added]."[8] A lance tucked under the armpit did not withstand the shock of impact any better if the bearer's legs were firm in the stirrup; maintaining one's seat, particularly during a melee, still required the sine qua non of the equestrian art—the thighs and knees. Stirrups and saddles were less important than fitness and proper training. The crash at full gallop was potentially devastating to both attacker and victim. A downed rider or horse became a rolling bowling ball, knocking opponents over like 10 pins as well as an obstacle to following comrades.

MEDIEVAL TACTICS

There were two parts to the cavalry attack: first, the approach and charge, and second, the shock of contact with subsequent melee. The galloping destrier was fearsome to behold, but the attack of heavy cavalry was most effective en masse. Knights were often grouped in "banners"—a troop of 15–20 horses, commanded by a bannerlord. The group's most effective formation was a square, four horses across, which maximized the armored punch of each knight and ensured enough depth to absorb casualties, exploit a break, or dominate in a melee. The presence of disciplined infantry forced the attackers into a wedge formation, a large triangle with the heaviest, best-armored destriers at the front. After crashing into the enemy, the flying wedge immediately lost momentum and caved in on itself as foot soldiers quickly surrounded the horses.

Three or four banners would constitute a "battle," which was the standard tactical unit of chivalry. The average strength was about 60 warhorses. Individual knights were dubbed a *lance garnie* (French: "garnished, all dressed") and brought their entourage to battle. A "lance" comprised the fully armed knight and included his squire and two horse archers. Well-heeled knights brought pages, men at arms, grooms, and supplementary warhorses to be used as fresh replacements, much like a polo match.

The charge of cavalry was deafening and expeditious. A mounted assault could cover 300 meters in just over a minute. The tactics were deceptively simple in theory but complex in execution. The cavalry attack was an orchestrated affair divided into specific sequences with accelerated tempo: the walk, trot, canter, and, finally, the gallop. The maneuvering trot was a stable approach permitting control and a homogeneous formation. Another efficient pace was at the extended trot or collected canter. The gallop was reserved for the final stage, but this varied with conditions and disposition. Much was dependent on collective discipline and training. Richard Alvarez noted that "it is the time taken to 'dress ranks' that eats up distance."[9] Ideally, the mass of chivalry advanced at a systematic cadence, sorting out ranks and maintaining a solid, phalanx-like frontage. The intent was to conserve energy. Speed was not the primary factor, for a trained warhorse could move from a standing start to canter in about three strides, roughly three horse lengths. Alvarez analyzed the conduct of a mounted attack against archers:

> All that is asked from the horse is for a "Canter Depart" . . . the time and space needed to get a horse to a "Charge" is negligible—probably under ten yards . . . At three hundred yards, I would start a walk, *dress* after fifty, trot for the next fifty. With the departure of the first flight [of enemy arrows] I would move to an "Extended Trot" or "Collected Canter" (the speed is the same, only the gait is different). It is more important to hold the line together . . . I would hold this for the next fifty yards, then "Charge" the remaining hundred and fifty.[10]

Measured across one football field or 100 yards, a cavalry attack required 26 seconds at the trot (8 miles per hour) and 18 seconds at the full trot or canter (12 mph). The full canter and gallop, at 25 miles per hour, takes 8 seconds.[11] The canter is a controlled, three-beat gait; the gallop is very much like the canter, except that it is faster, covers more ground, and has a four-beat gait. It is the fastest pace of the horse, averaging between 25 and 35 miles per hour, and is the most logical choice when confronted with a hail of arrows. The last bound before physical contact will depend on the state of mind of horse and rider as both are savaged by disciplined archers. A storm of arrows invariably hastened the pace, but veteran captains continued to insist on the maneuvering trot to maintain control. Cavalry charged "boot to boot" until the Great War.

A mélange of contributing factors determined the success of the mounted attack. Alvarez cites size, endurance, sex (animal's sex influences its temperament), and age and considers temperament most crucial. Culture and regional sexism determined the choice of mount: "The European Knight considered it *unmanly* to ride into battle on anything other than a stallion. This preference lasted at least until the sixteenth century. Conversely, eastern horse cultures thought the *mare* more suited to combat."[12] Attack pace was further affected by the condition of the horse and weight of armor. Canter and gallop encouraged competition, and not all horses are as fast as each other; this is most apparent at the gallop, which is essentially a horse race. The spirited charge destroyed control, and the uniformity of the attacking line was lost. The inevitable melee required horses that were not blown from a long frenzied dash. Again, this is theoretical as the cavalry battle was completely unpredictable. Success depended on psychological ascendancy—to break the will of the enemy before he broke yours. The physical effect of a charge created the psychological shock of a ground-shaking, menacing approach followed by catastrophic impact. The best and most common effect of a good charge was that the enemy broke and ran.

The real killing began in the melee. The term *melee* is from the medieval French *pêle-mêle*, which meant "mingled disorder" and aptly described a brawl between armored warriors. Given a steady enemy, the melee was a perilous affair. Being mounted was an advantage but hazardous against trained infantry. Knights preferred individual combat against other knights, with squires to drag them away and prevent spearmen from getting in a cheap strike. Combat against a crowd of infantry was to be avoided—this was more practicality than upper-class snobbery. At close quarters, the horse could be wounded or disemboweled by any vile spearman: "These pikemen can also approach and attack cavalry from the side and pierce them right through, nor is there any armor, however good, that they cannot pierce or break."[13] Pole arms hooked onto the knight's armor and dragged him off the horse where his social bearing or training held little advantage against mob attacks from men bent on ransom or revenge.

The attack of the lance itself was secondary since impact usually shattered the wooden poles and were quite useless at close quarters. Broadswords were heavy smashing weapons whose aim was to crush. Well wielded, they broke bone and tore muscle. A sharp point appeared as incidental as a sharp edge, although there was a continuous argument. The ready example was a battle at Tagliacozze, Italy, in 1258 where French chivalry confronted German knights. Charles of Anjou commanded a host clad in chain mail; the Germans were in plate and mostly unaffected by the French clanging away at their new armor. Finally, it was realized that their opponents exposed their armpits when they raised their arm to strike. The French cry became "Give point! Give point!" and the Germans were defeated. The "point" influenced chivalry to the extent that by 1500, many swords were simply long steel skewers with very sharp ends. The cavalry debate between the edge and point—to slice or to stab—was not concluded until the turn of the twentieth century. Tactics frustrated doctrine and the operational art. Most chivalry, particularly French cavalry, became obsessed with the assault (a precursor to the *Attaque à outrance*) and were too impulsive to adhere to disciplined doctrine. The horse's role in all of this was to deliver the goods and then join in as a butting, biting, and kicking complement to the melee.

THE TOXOPHILITE OPPOSITION

> Philologus: What is the chief point in shooting, that every man laboureth to come to?
>
> Toxophilus: To hit the mark.
>
> —Roger Ascham, *Toxophilus*, 1545[14]

The most effective opposition to the mounted charge, other than a counter-charge, proved to be the Welsh longbow. Its legendary status is based on its war record as a knight killer. Archer historian Hugh Soar called it the "charismatic standoff weapon."[15] The English archer was an elite within an army of elitists and rated higher than infantry. His wages were six pence a day, which was four times better than a laborer or plowman, and half the wages of armored men at arms.[16] The British preferred their "war bows" over crossbows, yet crossbows dominated the European battlefields. The difference was essentially economic; it took a good decade to train an archer but days to produce a crossbowman. Archery demanded skill and practice; the crossbow merely required a soldier to cock, aim, and shoot. The losses of crossbowmen were quickly replaced.

The real debate was the longbow versus the Mongol composite reflex bow. Although composite bows gave cavalry the means to defeat most armies, particularly a force with inefficient cavalry, they were not a match for a mass of professional archers armed with longbows. Their respective attributes are still argued by historians; it is probable that the longbow would more than hold its own against the Mongol bow, not because of range and penetration, but because of *doctrine*. A steady formation of longbowmen delivered devastating volleys against any attacking cavalry, including mounted archers. Thus, while horseback archery was the more mobile, it was not as consistently accurate as the fire of planted archers.[17] Forced to melee with heavy cavalry, the horse archer was doomed, particularly if retreat was cut off. This occurred during the Crusades at the Battle of Dorylaeum (A.D. 1097) when Arab horse archers were surprised and surrounded by French knights. They were slaughtered to the man.

The longbow was a "self" bow because, unlike its Mongol opposition, it was made of one wood. It equaled the average height of the medieval yeoman soldier and "was as tall as themselves or a fraction taller."[18] The trained archer took at least 10 years to develop and required a good eye as well as strength (bow draw weights ranged from 80 to 120 lbs.). Although the effective killing range was 200 yards, the best range against plate armor was circa 50 yards. Rate of fire was brisk and greatly superior to the crossbow:

> At the effective range the archer would only get around three arrows off at a mounted man . . . it cannot be regarded as an accurate weapon compared to the

modern compound bows but at fifty yards the English archer would be picking off individual men at arms and at twenty yards he would be aiming at specific weak parts in the armor.[19]

The war bow's range was not equaled until the introduction of the Baker rifle during the Napoleonic Wars. Its rate of fire was not bested until the invention of repeating rifles in the second half of the nineteenth century.

The longbow delivered two types of attack: "plunging" barrage from overhead that drenched a preselected area (a killing zone) and "direct" shooting against selected targets that at the right angle or intimate range pierced armor. At best battle range (approximately two football fields), the intent was to cripple and kill the destrier in large numbers: "The archers, having no aim in battle beyond the desire to win, committed the unthinkable atrocity of aiming at the horses . . . hundreds of horses being shot down."[20] There were two main groups of warheads: barbed and nonbarbed. The barbed broadhead was particularly savage against the warhorse, and like a modern harpoon, it was impossible to remove without tearing the flesh: "The [barb] wound measured three inches long by two inches wide and six inches deep."[21]

The bodkin nonbarbed arrowheads were the true war arrows, designed to remain in the body if the shaft was pulled, making removal complex and usually killing or crippling the victim. A special surgeon's instrument was required to remove arrowheads without further tearing the wound. There is ongoing debate as to whether the warheads were "glued" on or were just a tight fit: "evidence points to *not* gluing the heads on."[22] The bodkin arrowhead was used by the Romans as well as in the medieval period; there were two types—the triangular bodkin, and the war bodkin, the most common. The socket size varied between 5/16 inch and 1/2 inch in diameter. It could penetrate chain mail at medium and short range.[23] The Gerald de Berri chronicle describes Welsh longbows piercing two inch oak "their heads protruded an inch clear of the door on the inside."[24] This is supported by modern tests. Master arrowsmith and archaeological blacksmith Hector Cole participated in a series of experiments conducted at the Ministry of Defence College, Shrivenham. Arrows were fitted with medieval heads and shot from a 140-pound drawweight longbow at "flesh simulating targets" faced with iron plates of differing thickness and composition. Cole concluded that "the English war bow will penetrate *light armor* at over 100 yards."[25]

The warhorse versus longbow results were determined by the rate of shooting: "twelve arrows in one minute is possible, but that such a rate of shot is not possible for subsequent periods. Practical experience points to a rate of shot of about five to six arrows per minute as being feasible over a period up to ten minutes"[26] Archers were grouped into loose companies (much like guilds) and controlled by a captain archer. Shooting was conducted in volleys by successive groups, which ensured a continuous but directed weight of arrows at designated targets. Alternating trajectory contributed to the cavalry's confusion, *plunging fire* in the approach, then in the final bound, shooting *direct* from the flanks.[27] A good suit of plate, barring lucky hits, defeated broadheads and deflected bodkins until close range. Froissart suggested that French armor was invulnerable to the English arrows, which either shattered or ricocheted. This seems to be supported by the fact that large numbers of the French reached English lines. But it has also been demonstrated that bodkins can pierce plate armor. The key was angle of attack. If a war bow's bodkin hit armor at close to a 90 degree angle, at 100 yards, it would likely penetrate. The warhorses were partially protected with armor on their faces and chests, but their great bodies were lightly shielded with only an extended blanket, adorned leather, or linen cover. Their legs, the engine of propulsion, were particularly exposed. They were targeted the moment they entered the killing zone. The aim was to create a rout of tumbling crazed horses causing broken limbs in crumpled armored pileups during the approach to battle. The English bow was as much artillery as machine gun.

Interestingly enough, field artillery was very much available. Gunpowder weapons were increasingly used throughout medieval Europe, appearing during sieges and major battles (Saint-Sauveur-le-Vicomte, 1375, and Kosovo, 1389). *Artillery* stems from the Old-French *attillement* meaning "apparatus or equipment." The artillery available to feudal generals was modestly formidable, save for the unstable quality of gunpowder. Tests conducted with a fourteenth-century Loshult gun determined it could fire a lead or stone ball "as far as 945 metres (and reaching speeds up to 200 m per second), compared to a distance of 1100 metres for the commercial gun powder."[28] The great artillery weapon of the Middle Ages was still the catapult—specifically the trebuchet, which could batter stone walls with reasonable accuracy from a 300-yard distance. The trebuchet used a counterweight to hurl anything from rocks to diseased cadavers.[29] Medieval artillery was ponderous and required clear fields of fire and a sufficient time to compute, measure, and load. Whatever guns accomplished against castle walls, they could not manage in open combat and served as a psychological rather than physical threat. It was not the range (a maximum of 900 yards) as much as attitude. Tactical use of artillery was not the forte of European nobles; it was esoteric, and its common status and noisy delivery earned it disdain.

FEUDAL CAVALRY IN THE ATTACK: THE BATTLE OF CRÉCY 1346

> Before the rain there came flying over both battles a great number of crows for fear of the tempest coming. Then anon the air began to wax clear, and the sun to shine fair and bright, which was right in the Frenchmen's eyes and on the Englishmen's backs.
>
> —Jean Froissart[30]

The Hundred Years' War included an extension of the Mongolian operational art: the cavalry raid. The *chevauchée* (French, literally, "a horse ride") reintroduced attrition warfare by a mobile corps. Raids ruined the countryside rather than besieging castles, caused carnage and chaos, broke the morale of the peasants, and denied the feudal lords income and resources. It was extensively practiced by Edward III whose cavalry excelled at pillage and slaughtering the populace. Its conduct was more analogous to "total war." The *chevauchée* heralded a sobering reverse to the romantic concept of chivalrous warfare. For the French, who still told legends of Châlons and Attila, it was déjà vu.

In the 1346 Crécy campaign, Edward raided Normandy, sacked Caen, and maneuvered creatively to draw out French forces and then ambush them on ground of his choosing. However, he underestimated Philip's determination and industriousness. Facing unexpectedly large forces, the English avoided Rouen, skirted Paris, and side stepped Abbeville trying to reach Calais. The principle of the *chevauchée* is to ransack a geographic area and avoid a formal battle via mobility. But the fourteenth-century English army were not a horde of horse archers; they were essentially heavy cavalry, supported by light infantry. They were outmaneuvered. Cornered at Crécy, Edward was forced to

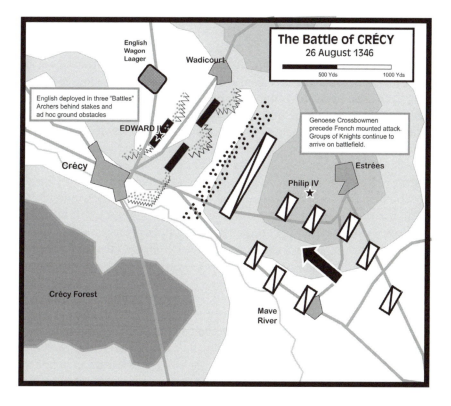

The Battle of CRÉCY
26 August 1346

English Wagon Laager

Wadicourt

500 Yds   1000 Yds

English deployed in three "Battles" Archers behind stakes and ad hoc ground obstacles

EDWARD III

Genoese Crossbowmen precede French mounted attack. Groups of Knights continue to arrive on battlefield.

Crécy

Estrées

Philip IV

Crécy Forest

Mave River

stand and fight a superior mounted force. Losing the initial operational contest, his tactical solution was to fight on foot.

Crécy is the first great battle of the Hundred Years' War and a classic example of cavalry shock combat versus missile fire. It was suggested that just before Crécy, dozens of Norman foot soldiers mooned English archers, exposing their backsides in open contempt of their enemy's skill, ". . . turn up their tails and cry 'shoot English!'"—but they immediately and deeply regretted the act as the English introduced France to the longbow: "the breech of such a varlet has been nailed to his back with an arrow."[31] The lesson, however, appears to have been lost on French nobility.

Crécy is often used as a benchmark for the end of chivalry. The contest displayed the warhorse at its tactical peak against rude infantry; the English army of about 12,000 confronted Philip IV's force of about 40,000 (crossbowmen, spearmen, and at least 12,000 knights). Accompanying Philip was the archetypal cavalier, the valiant king of Bohemia, Charles of Luxembourg, leading several thousand of his own knights to aid the French cause. He was more or less blind yet insisted on riding into battle, instructing his companions to bring him forward so that he could strike one stroke with his sword. Czech knights pressed on either side: "they tied all their reins of their bridles each to other and set the king before to accomplish his desire, and so they went on their enemies."[32]

King Edward found a piece of ground that gave him protected flanks and rear, as well as higher contours offering a better view. He deployed "two up" with his knights dismounted in two forward "battles"; each phalanx was made up of 1,000 dismounted armed men about six ranks deep and about 250 yards long.[33] The term *phalanx* is not inappropriate, for the knights brought their lances and set them before their front ranks like Greek hoplites to discourage mounted attack. Their flanks were protected by archers who were in turn protected by Welsh spearmen.[34] The second line was another "battle" of men at arms,[35] with archers and spearmen on the flanks. There was a small mounted reserve of knights behind the center, ready to counterattack to seal off a French penetration. The position was anchored on the right by a large windmill that overlooked the Maye River and served as a lookout tower; the left rested on Wadicourt village. Edward's impedimenta and supplies were stored in a wagon laager (referred to as "the baggage") set in dead ground, to the rear of the last battle: "within the park were all their horses, for every man was afoot; and into this park there was but one entry."[36]

The French enjoyed the higher ground, but it was of little consequence to the tactical battle. From Philip's position, the terrain gradually fell away to low ground, then rose gently to the ridge occupied by Edward. The approach was approximately 1,000 yards; at the midpoint, the French would have to advance 500 yards up the slight rise to reach the English. It was hardly an uphill approach, but enough to take away momentum and require extra exertion from the horses. The second line of British defense was in slightly "dead ground," not quite a reverse slope position but offered the wagon park cover and some security for archers scuttling back for more arrows. English depth was incidental to the main military problem facing the French of an open approach exposed to continuous observed shooting.

It should be presumed that English veterans "used the ground" and took advantage of folds, pits, and shallow ditches to improve the obstacle and offer nasty surprises that horse or rider would not spot until the last moment. The horses would naturally, instinctively, refuse to ride through obstacles threatening to rip open their bellies, just as they had refused to throw themselves onto the spears of a Greek phalanx. Convention (C.W.C. Oman et al.) has the English archers deployed in three wedges along the line of battle, behind a screen of obstacles of six-foot stakes embedded into the ground and caltrops (forged stars of sharp iron spikes that crippled horses' hoofs). Each archer carried two sheaves (48 arrows) as well as a dozen in his quiver, worn at the hip.[37] Before battle another four sheaves were placed before each archer.

The French arrived languidly, without reconnaissance, in a seemingly endless fanfaronade of chivalry. Philip's cavalcade behaved more like a hunting party than professional cavalry, which was after all, their vocation. The King tried to stop the parade to rest his army. His knights were ebullient and completely insubordinate: "The lords and knights of France came not to the assembly together in good order, for some came before and some came after in such haste and evil order, that one of them did trouble another."[38] Philip gave

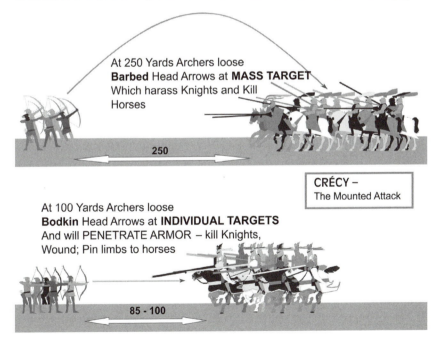

At 250 Yards Archers loose
Barbed Head Arrows at **MASS TARGET**
Which harass Knights and Kill
Horses

250

CRÉCY –
The Mounted Attack

At 100 Yards Archers loose
Bodkin Head Arrows at **INDIVIDUAL TARGETS**
And will PENETRATE ARMOR – kill Knights,
Wound; Pin limbs to horses

85 - 100

up and permitted a hasty attack. Impetuosity as much as bravura brought ruin to the flower of France.

His opening gambit, pushing his crossbows forward, was accompanied by the sound of musical instruments brought to scare the enemy or perhaps amuse his unruly court. In addition to the new technology of the war bow, Crécy was probably the first European battle where gunpowder weapons were used. An artillery barrage inaugurated the contest: "The English remained still and let off some cannons that they had, to frighten the Genoese."[39] The Genoese crossbowmen were an immediate tactical disappointment; they were outranged and almost impotent, for a persistent rain had wet their bowstrings. The English archers simply stepped on their bows, unhooked the string ("good hempe . . . fine Flaxe or Sylk"[40]), and stowed it under their helms until the rain stopped. The weather left the ground wet and slippery. The exhausted Genoese gingerly approached the English, too aware of their technical disadvantage; worse, each crossbowman's *pavis* (a heavy oblong shield worn across the back to give protection while reloading) had been left on the baggage train. They halted 150 yards short of the English position and delivered their first salvo of bolts. It had little effect, save to annoy the longbowmen who returned a devastating barrage supported by artillery fire: "English archers stept forth one pace and let fly their arrows so wholly [together] and so thick, that it seemed to snow."[41] The cannon balls buried themselves into the ground; had the terrain been hard enough to create bounce, they might have plowed through the following French multitude like vengeful croquet balls.

The Genoese were between a rock and a hard place—arrows and artillery to their front and plate-clad knights pushing from behind. They panicked and tried to flee, disrupting the French vanguard, which spurred their horses and rode them down. This met with the approval of Philip who was livid at his mercenaries' failure:

> He said: "Slay these rascals, for they shall let and trouble us without reason." Then ye should have seen the men at arms dash in among them and killed a great number of them and ever still the Englishmen shot whereas they saw thickest press; the sharp arrows ran into the men of arms and into their horses, and many fell, horse and men.[42]

The initial French attack was met with repetitive volleys and soon littered the slope with horses and knights. The aristocracy, partly by elitism, but mostly by tactical prudence, refused to melee with mere archers as long as British chivalry stood formed and dangerous. English knights were a "fleet in being"—as long as they remained intact, they posed the critical threat. If the French ignored the archers, they risked brutal losses; if they ignored the knights, they courted certain defeat. Subsequent waves included the intrepid King Charles who pressed forward gallantly and actually reached the English lines: "they were there all slain, and the next day they were found in the place about the king, and all their horses tied each to other."[43] Charles' personal device (three white ostrich feathers) and motto *Ich Dien* (German, "I Serve") was seized by the Black Prince as a battle trophy. It continues to be used by the present Prince of Wales.

The French approached with the audacity of royal lemmings. Fifteen separate charges were delivered as fresh forces continued to arrive on the battlefield. According to Jean Froissart, "The sharp arrows ran into the men of arms and into their horses, and many fell, horse and men . . . and when they were down, they could not relieve again, the press was so thick that one overthrew another."[44] The battlefield was littered with bodies and screaming horses—over 10,000 French were lost, including 1,200 knights and a half-dozen princes. The English lost between 300 and 500 combatants. Fighting ended "about evensong time," and Philip, himself wounded, ordered the retreat. The more fortunate knights had been rescued by their pages. After the battle, English spearmen and archers went forward to loot the bodies. Those near death were dispatched by *misericordias* ("mercy givers"): "among the Englishmen there were certain rascals that went afoot with great knives, and they went in among the men of arms, and slew and murdered many as they lay on the ground, both earls, barons, knights, and squires."[45]

The warhorse's mastery of the battlefield had been successfully challenged and initiated the *Götterdämmerung* of martial aristocracy. Almost a third of France's nobility was cut down at Crécy. The mass execution by peasant infantry who delighted in slaughter, not ransom, produced a psychological shock. Like all revolutions in warfare, this was not immediately appreciated. This was not simply the French being stubbornly obtuse but rather reflected the reality that the longbow was a defensive weapon. Campaigning required an armored punch, as well as the mobility that cavalry offered. The main enemy remained the armored warhorse. The magnetic attraction of armor for armor was to be repeated, with the same devastating effect, in the Western Desert when British armor sought cavalry battles and discounted the deadly 88 mm antitank gun, the longbow of the Second World War.

CHIVALRY'S LAST HURRAH

> Owre kynge went forth to Normandy,
> With grace and myyt of chivalry . . .
> —Anonymous, *The Agincourt Carol*, fifteenth century

> Then call we this the field of Agincourt.
> —Shakespeare, *Henry V*

On August 11, 1415, King Henry V invaded France purportedly in reaction to raids on the English coast but more likely to avoid domestic woes as well as reinforce his claim to the French throne. Henry's disciplined army faced a disordered France under a weak, allegedly insane king, Charles VI. The prolonged siege at Harfleur ruined the English army. Sleeping rough and drinking contaminated water and calvados, soldiers were soon suffering from colds and dysentery. After a series of attacks ("Once more unto the breach, dear friends, once more"[46]), the town finally fell, but Henry's force was in no shape to continue, with a third of his men casualties and most of the remainder sick. He set his sights on Calais where he had a port, a fortress, and supplies. The army had less than eight days' rations. Essentially a cavalry force despite its archers and spearmen, the English managed to force march 80 miles in five days (October 8–13). They were tormented by French cavalry who preyed on them as Cossacks ("the enemy by craftily hastening on ahead and laying waste the country before us, would weaken us by famine"[47]). By October 24, the force had marched 73 miles in four days and was within two days of Calais, subsisting on raw vegetables, hazel nuts, and bits of hastily roasted meat. However, late in the afternoon, Henry's recce patrols returned to inform him that a French army had crossed his line of march and blocked the road to Calais. The operational flexibility of the feudal warhorse was the converse of Mongol cavalry. Burdened with armor and impedimenta, the armies of chivalry plodded, rather than cantered, about the countryside. The fifteenth-century warhorse was very much like the Tiger tank—fearful to behold and devastating in the attack, but best at short tactical rushes and incapable of extensive operational maneuver.

The French circumvented the English and forced them to give battle at a disadvantage. This time they did not permit the English king to select the tactical ground, and yet they could not have been more accommodating. The ground did not favor Henry, but it did offer secure flanks.[48] Henry prepared for battle by ordering strict silence and, in the darkness, deployed away from his camp, leaving the fires burning to fool enemy *piquettes*. The English spent a miserable night near a favorable battle position selected by the king. The confident French stayed up late drinking and blustering; a group painted a horse cart to parade the captured English king through Paris.

The final battle of the Hundred Years' War trinity, Agincourt, was fought almost 60 years after Poitiers—a sort of Desert Storm after the Battle of the Bulge. Unlike Desert Storm, there was no new technology or warfighting philosophy; with no Guderian or Starry to inspire doctrine, the French remained staid and traditional. Their interest in the new revolution in military affairs, gunpowder, specifically, field artillery, was casual.

Agincourt was fought on October 15, 1415, St. Crispin's Day; Shakespeare immortalized and lionized the outnumbered English army in *Henry V*: "We few, we happy few, we band of brothers; for he to-day that sheds his blood with me shall be my brother."[49] The actual statistics are debated; historian Anne Curry suggests a nationalist spin may have been infused in histories of the

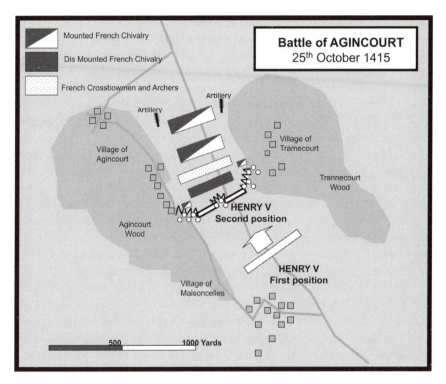

Mounted French Chivalry

Dis Mounted French Chivalry

French Crossbowmen and Archers

Battle of AGINCOURT
25th October 1415

Artillery

Artillery

Village of
Agincourt

Village of
Tramecourt

Trannecourt
Wood

HENRY V
Second position

Agincourt
Wood

HENRY V
First position

Village of
Maisoncelles

500   1000 Yards

battle: "The English were undoubtedly 'happy' but by no means 'few'. They had between 8,500 and 9,000 at the battle whilst the French army had only a few thousand more at most."[50]

The tactical situation was a virtual redux of Crécy and Poitiers with worse terrain. Days of rain had turned the farmland into a morass that discouraged attack by heavy cavalry. Further, the French, loosely commanded by the constable of France, Charles d'Albert, proxy for an ailing King, accepted battle in a defile where their cavalry's mobility could not be of any use save in a frontal attack through kill zones.

Operationally d'Albert did the right thing by blocking the route to Calais. Tactically he permitted Henry a secure location with untroubled flanks; the position was a bowling alley, 500 yards wide and 1,500 yards deep. When morning arrived, the French spent their time organizing. Henry, after waiting the better part of the day for d'Albert's army to sort itself out, decided to force the issue before his weakened army further succumbed to dysentery and hunger. Sir Thomas Erpingham, marshal of the army, satisfied the ranks were in correct order, raised his baton and shouted: "Nestroque!" ("Now, Strike!").[51] This was answered with a loud roar from the archers. Henry's host marched toward the enemy.

The opportunity to tear apart the English at a comfortable distance with their artillery may have been pooh-poohed by the French because the soft ground eliminated that most deadly of artillery techniques, bouncing fire. The artillery was a potential factor simply because the English maneuvered first by quietly marching closer to the static French chivalry consisting of an arrogant mob in metallic haute couture. D'Albert's army comprised about half men at arms; a third were knights, and the remainder were archers, crossbowmen, and artillery. They were massed in three large battles: the first two were on foot, the third mounted, for exploitation. Two horsed squadrons of knights were positioned along the flanks, as vanguards.

The English halted in bowshot of the French; the archers quickly planted their six-foot stakes to create the all too familiar salients; the men at arms were grouped in three battles, in line. King Henry commanded the center mass; there was no reserve. The taunt proved too much for the French nobility who promptly attacked. It was an imprudent endeavor, and by now the French should have known better. They had no missile support; their artillery was masked by the crowds of men at arms. The crossbows had been placed between the first two battles of armored infantry, where they had no clear field of fire.

The first longbow volleys dealt with the mounted attack. It was rudely dispatched. Some knights were trapped under horses in the muddy ground; others bolted through the ranks of their forward division. Many knights were pinned to their horses by arrows that took them through the thigh or calf: "they rode straight at the fences of stakes . . . and having done so, their horses were immediately impaled upon the sharp points and threw their heavily armoured riders at the feet of the archers who soon clubbed them to death."[52] Survivors reported that the area was so littered with fletchings from the arrows, that in places it resembled a snowfall.

The rich attire of the French aristocracy was in direct juxtaposition to the dress of English archers: "Many of them were barefoot and some of them according to one account based on uncertain authority, were naked, without even the hat of boiled leather."[53] Suffering from intense dysentery, the longbowmen were forced to relieve themselves at their battle posts. English lore holds that the rude two-finger flip originated with archers at this battle. It may have been noted during an earlier siege, but Agincourt, where the archers stood half-naked and defiant is as good a battle as any. The longbowmen held up two fingers to the enemy knights, much like a V for Victory sign, to taunt them, as the French promised to cut off the drawing fingers of captured archers.[54]

The leading French battle managed to survive the withering cascade and reach English lines. One reason may be that actually killing a knight was more difficult than knocking him off his horse. In the confused melee, clear shots were difficult, and, after 60 years, armor may have been improved. Hector Cole recalls that during the Shrivenham experiments "when we put some 3 mm plate on the test bed and shot at it—the arrow bounced off. However when we measured how far the plate was pushed into the 'putty' we were told that if it had been an armored knight he would have had three broken ribs and a rup-tured spleen."[55] The French chronicler Enguerrand de Monstrelet recorded: "The French stooped to prevent the arrows hitting them on the visors of their helmets."[56] This may indicate *Bascinet* helmets, which had thinner, perforated face pieces, or simply an instinctive reaction—soldiers in the Great War were described advancing into devastating machine-gun fire "with chins tucked down as if walking into a blizzard."[57]

The elite of France were packed 40 deep. It was a hard slog as armored men struggled through ankle-deep mud, deep enough in places to suffocate the wounded. The French pressed the attack; Henry in particular was the object of sorties by enraged nobles. His archers had shot all their arrows; the English front was now a single desperate line of battling armored men. Henry managed a last ditch counterattack by ordering his longbowmen into hand-to-hand combat. They attacked "with side arms, small arms, hammers, mauls, knives, daggers and short swords."[58] This relatively fresh addition decided the battle. Unencum-bered by armor, the archers had the advantage over mired plated men.

Great numbers of the French were killed or made prisoner. Fallen knights had great difficulty in getting up, and many a wounded knight was saved by his squire. Successive battles trying to reinforce the melee did not fare better. When the nobles leading the third division had been killed or wounded, the French broke. At one point, fearing a mounted counterattack to his rear, Henry ordered the prisoners executed. This was both brutal (certainly unchivalrous) and unpopular as vast ransoms were anticipated. When his knights protested, Henry ordered his archers and spearmen, who had no reservations, to conduct the slaughter. The French losses were terrible and made worse by the butchery of captured men. The constable of France, 3 dukes, 5 counts, and 90 barons were among the dead. The victory permitted Henry to fulfill his original cam-paign goals, and he was recognized by the French (Treaty of Troyes, 1420) as heir to the French throne.[59]

THE WARHORSE TRIUMPHANT

> Know ye not Agincourt? ...
> Where England cloth yard arrows
> Killed the French like tame sparrows
> Slain by our bowmen
>
> —John Stow, *The Annals of England,* 1580

Agincourt was a defeat of dismounted cavalry. It helped cement the status of missile firing infantry, but it did not "break the French noblesse of its love for an obsolete system of tactics."[60] There were more battles, and the last important contest was fought at Verneuil in 1424. It featured a mounted breakthrough, but the undisciplined French knights did not linger to attack the English from the rear and continued their charge toward the baggage train and promise of rich plunder. The Duke of Bedford rallied his troops and won a near-run hacking contest. It was a bloody battle, described as a second Agincourt. Cavalry's partial redemption was trashed by its greed.

In retrospect, the battles of the Hundred Years' War featured no "classic" feudal contests. The use of the mounted charge against other mounted knights did not occur. The English behaved splendidly in what was to be their forte for the next six centuries—dogged defense. The longbow technology did not openly crush chivalry, gunpowder would accomplish that; but it did signal the return of infantry to a place of ascendancy on the battlefield and created social rumblings in the ruling class.

The longbow was too couth a weapon to endure against the simplicity of gunpowder. The elegant ballet of notching arrow, estimating wind and distance, and then intuitively computing the essential trigonometry was challenged with simple drills that poured premeasured powder into a barrel and then pointed, not aimed, in the direction of the enemy. Accuracy was relegated to mass volleys that were bound to hit something. An arquebus could pierce armor. In the battle of Pavia (1525), 3,000 arquebusiers defeated 8,000 French knights and truly signaled the end of chivalry and heavy cavalry domination in Europe. While a dead knight was a catastrophe, dispatched commoners were easily and relatively inexpensively replaced. The extensively trained feudal lord could be felled with a shot by one of his swineherds, a product of less than a week's drill.

Ironically, it was the horse, not the archer that survived the feudal wars. The deliquescence of archery was pressed by gun and pike: "By the sixteenth century those styled as archers in the musters could be armed with bills, pikes, bows or handguns. In the musters taken in York in 1543 of the 108 able men the town assembled to serve in the war against Scotland only eight were noted as 'tried archers.'"[61] Agincourt hastened the end of chivalry. Heavier armor was not satisfactory against longbow or gunpowder for it denied the mounted arm its greatest assets: maneuver and the ability to melee. Suits of comprehensive plate were soon relegated to jousting tournaments. The feudal interpretation of the classical warrior code accepted honor within the tactic of riding down commoners and the shattering impact of horse against inferior infantry. The longbow, followed shortly by gunpowder, did away with class advantage on the battlefield. Cavalry pundits will argue that the Hundred Years' War proved nothing; two of the three major battles were fought on foot, and all things considered, there was still no arm that could deliver shock and, most important, had the mobility of cavalry.

One Charger to the other: "Near as I can figure it — theirs is not to reason why..."

Chapter 5

Into the *Aufklärung:* Cavalry and the Lace Wars

> Good cavalry makes you master of the land. Two or three sudden attacks, which succeed, one after the other, suffice to intimidate the enemy to the point where he no longer has the courage to stand before you.
>
> —Frederick the Great[1]

The intellectual change accompanying the Renaissance mostly influenced the aristocracy and burghers of prosperous towns, the mass of Europe remained little affected. Military changes were less a rebirth of classical thought than a period of doctrinal transition. Warfare evolved with the same propitious tempo as Medici-sponsored frescos. The transition from heavy metal warfare to the lace wars required two centuries. What began as an armored "lance," often equipped with hand cannon, materialized in the Age of Reason (the Enlightenment), as a cloth-costumed, sword-swinging dragoon.

This version of cavalry would endure with little basic alteration until the end of the Second World War. The distinct types of cavalry were formalized in the eighteenth century and endured, in name at least, well after the arrival of tanks. Enlightenment operational art did not showcase cavalry operations, although Frederick the Great's classic battle of Leuthen did use cavalry as an operational feint to both draw away and then destroy the enemy's operational reserve. The standardization of cavalry, in mission and mode, was forged in the eighteenth century and established the basic material that provided Bonaparte the means to an empire. It is charming that the German word for Enlightenment, *Aufklärung,* is the same term used for cavalry reconnaissance.

The appearance of professional "regular" armies began with the French. Charles VII, who after successfully challenging the English via the divine nationalistic ardor of Joan of Arc, decided that to hold France he required a permanent paid army. The decision led to the establishment of fifteen *companies d'ordonnance,* or gendarmes, all cavalry. The cuirassier (simply an armored cavalier) appeared circa 1490 in France and Austria. The gendarme companies comprised 100 lances, and their horse archers soon evolved into heavier versions of Mongol cavalry, capable of dismounted skirmish. According to Denison, "Each lance consisted of six men: the man at arms, three archers, a *coutillier* or squire, and a page or valet. . . The *lance fournie* at this time had 13 horses, the man at arms had four each, each archer two, the *coutillier* two, and the page one."[2]

As feudal duty was replaced by paid service, monarchs found raising large bodies of cavalry prohibitive. By the mid-sixteenth century, mercenary troops armed with the arquebus were attached to gendarme companies. The mounted knight was augmented and then supplanted by heavy infantry (particularly by the Swiss cantons and German *Landsknecht*) and their weapons, the arquebus and pike, "enabled [the Swiss] not only to keep off the horse but very often to break and defeat them."[3] Facing a solid wall of pikes, halberds, or bayonets, the horse often refused to attack at all: "The infantry ought to be more esteemed than cavalry. . . It is difficult to make horses preserve the ranks, and when they are disturbed impossible to reform them. . . Well-disciplined infantry can easily break the cavalry but only with difficulty can they be routed by them."[4]

The great hedgehog phalanxes defeated any cavalry or standard infantry but could be foiled by gunpowder weapons, particularly artillery; as wry observers noted, "artillery against pike squares is a lot like bowling." Oman noted that the art of war had become "a matter not of tradition but of experimentation."[5]

The seventeenth century army was a matter of finance and a drill sergeant's bark. In the new military, discipline—something quite anathema to aristocratic cavalry—was de rigueur. The army depended on rote drill, mindless obedience, and, of course, the lash. By the Enlightenment (1700–1789), military service was a brutal experience for other ranks; the professionals (sergeants and commoners as officers) performed all the real work for modest pay, while the senior officer class seemed little different from the self-centered elitists who appeared at Crécy or Poitiers. Aristocrats still ruled the military.

The epoch of cavalry armies had passed. The equestrian world was turned upside down as horse cultures were challenged and then trounced by sedentary farmers. The Tatar rule was broken on the Ukrainian steppes, and Mongol hordes no longer threatened Russia or Europe. The Ottoman Empire, which was founded by Turkish horsemen, dominated the Middle East, but its success was spurred by gunpowder and siege technology. The Ottoman threat to Europe was broken at the end of the seventeenth century by Christian armies that relied on disciplined infantry. The bodkin *might* penetrate armor at 100 yards; the musket ball *would* kill at that distance. The cavalry, lighter and maneuverable, entered the modern age prepared to take on cannon and musket with the old standard—flashing hoofs and steel.

TYPES OF CAVALRY

By the end of the Renaissance, save the odd cuirasse, troopers went into battle wearing cloth. By the mid-eighteenth century, the cavalry had settled on three basic types of fighting horse—heavy cavalry (cuirassiers), medium cavalry (dragoons and carabineers), and light cavalry (light dragoons, hussars, and lancers). The heavies were big men on big horses measuring 16–18 hands, with cuirasse and helmets. The straight bone-crunching sword was the weapon of choice and continued to be carried into the 1940s.

The dragoon was a practical solution to mobility and a restoration of the horse as so-called battle taxi. The idea was to raise bodies of infantry armed with gunpowder weapons and give them the means to quickly deploy in key areas of the battlefield. Cavalry had made use of the *petrone,* a type of hand cannon that rested on the pommel of the saddle. By 1515, the *arquebus-a-rouet* (wheel lock) was invented. It was a cavalry weapon and soon called the "pistol," which could have originated in its point of first manufacture (Pistoja) or, as suggested by the French historian Daniel, derived from *pistallo,* which means "pommel."[6] Cavalry was eventually equipped with both pistol and its derivative, the carbine, a heavier, longer pistol. James II ordered carbines made for the British army in 1688, and they continue to be associated with the cavalry well into the cybernetic era. The U.S. Cavalry adopted its most recent version, the M4 carbine, in 1997 and carried it into Iraq and Afghanistan.

The advantage of the carbine was that it weighed less than the musket and could be comfortably carried in a leather bucket fixed to the saddle. The most common practice was to sling it via a cross belt with a *karabenierbaker* ("carbine hook"). The explosive fiery result of the weapon's discharge inspired the term *dragoon.* It was soon applied to any cavalry that carried muskets. Dragoons were at great disadvantage against trained cavalry and continually coveted the status of being real cavaliers, preferring to *hack and slay* rather than *shoot and scoot.* By the 1740s, thanks to Frederick's constant raising of cheap replacement cavalry, *dragoon* came to refer to all medium cavalry.

Perhaps the most romantic cavalry type is the hussar—a dashing ubiquitous corsair who combined stealthy reconnaissance with reckless assault on anything before him. The word *Hussar* [huh-Tsar, or, HaZar] is perhaps Serbian (*Gussar:* "a brigand") and morphed from the Hungarian *huszár* to the French *hussard.*[7] By tradition, the hussar is traced to the *Puszta*—a barren wilderness, a grassy kind of semidesert. This central European "steppe" was a natural horse farm, and the indigenous inhabitants created a particularly efficient light horse, which prospered through careful breeding and acquired renown as frontier cavalry that dueled with Turkish and Tatar raiders.

The accomplishments of the Hungarian light cavalry were admired in the West. When the Turkish juggernaut finally crushed the Hungarian kingdom, remnants sought succor from the Hapsburg Empire. Economic necessity soon saw cadres in *codottieri* service. France's chief minister, Cardinal Richelieu, contributed to their fame in 1635 by hiring a complete regiment, *la Cavallerie Hongraise,* for the French army. These horsemen arrived dressed in the Magyar and Croat tradition. The unit wore large handkerchiefs around their necks, which beguiled Parisian society. It soon became the fashion at court to wear a kerchief "a la Croate" and led to the *cravatte* or necktie.

All Hapsburg light cavalry raised in the eastern part of the empire were hussars. There was a serious attempt to make them "German" yet retain the rakish Hungarian style and cocky swagger. Hussar regiments became popular, and a large number were raised by Frederick the Great. German hussar regiments were often used as mercenary units by France and England. Hessian hussars were hired by the British for service in North America during the War of Independence. Although the Poles raised unique hussar regiments, eventually creating a distinct alternate version of the type, the "Hungarian" hussar became the model for European light cavalry.

The fur-trimmed pelisse is perhaps the most noticeable and distinct part of the uniform. It was a rococo garment worn loose over the shoulder and left to fly free as the hussar galloped. The style included the tight-fitting dolman or "Attila" jacket. The rough Magyar cap was replaced by a cylindrical shako, which looked very much like an overturned flower pot. Its attraction was the trailing cloth called the *flamme* (French: "blaze" or "banner"), which followed the hussar like a *schwenkel.*

Perhaps more interesting is hussar fixation with hair. Moustaches were de rigueur, and men whose facial hair was too fair or sparse were allegedly ordered to blacken their lip hair or paste on horsehair for formal parades. Even more bizarre is the fancy for plaits (braids and pigtails). The traditional eighteenth-century army queue (a long braid) was replaced by four braids, one at each temple and one behind each ear. Some hussar regiments, it is claimed, added pistol balls into the ends of plaits to allow a good vertical hang. It was allegedly tradition to cut off a braid if one killed a man in combat. Braid fashion was mostly Continental and did not appear in the British cavalry, although long hair remains as a cavalry trademark.

The hussar was a romantic rascal and no matter how dashing or sophisticated his officers might be, the hussar was considered a rough, hard-drinking, womanizing rogue who looted anything not nailed down and was callous, if not cruel, to civilians. Jean-Martin De La Colonie noted that "the Hussars are, properly speaking, nothing but bandits on horseback, who carry on an irregular warfare; it is impossible to fight them formally ... when they might be thought to be entirely routed and dispersed, they will reappear, formed up as before."[8] A good hussar regiment required tough sergeants and unforgiving officers ready to order pitiless discipline. Frederick made them professional. Hussars were little different from the rest of the light cavalry but simply more glamorous.

POLISH HUSSARS AND ULANS

> While the hussar keeps his lance the Pole shall remain master of the field, when the lance dies so dies Poland's virtue.
>
> —Aleksander Fredo

Polish cavalry attained fame in the frontier campaigns of the Polish-Lithuanian Commonwealth, which, at its greatest, extended from the Baltic to the Black Sea. Its enemies included Tatars, Swedes, Austrians, Ottomans, Muscovites, and Ukrainian Cossacks. The most persistent foes were the Teutonic knights and the devastating Mongol horde. The Poles developed efficient cavalry to deal with their varied enemies: cataphract squadrons against Germans, and mobile, hard-hitting light horse against the Tatars.

Although mostly employed on eastern borders, Polish cavalry was prominent in some western campaigns, most notably King Jan Sobieski's timely attack against the besieging Turks, credited with saving Vienna in 1683 and keeping Western Europe Christian. The Poles' victory provided them with new breeding stock. Arabian horses were difficult to acquire in numbers, but the Turks left large numbers. This campaign had long-reaching effects on Western society; one of these was the discovery of dark beans in Turkish camps and the subsequent introduction of coffeehouses! Additional culinary firsts are the creation of the first croissant and bagel. A popular legend has the city saved by an early rising baker who heard Turkish miners digging a sap beneath the walls. In commemoration, the baker is said to have introduced a new roll, formed as a Turkish crescent—the first croissant. Finally, another grateful Viennese baker, aware of the Polish monarch's fondness for horses, produced a small bread in the form of a stirrup or *Bügel*.

The mostly colorful representative of Polish cavalry was the *Husaria,* or winged cavalry. The winged hussar (sometimes called *pancerni,* or armored cavalry) was an interesting mix of armor and eccentric embellishment; it was often confused with the Hungarian hussar but in fact was a completely different type. The Polish version was more cataphract cavalry and, in reality, a feudal force. The Husaria uniform included two huge "wings" made of eagle or crane feathers fixed in a row onto wooden laths fastened to the back of the cuirasse or the saddle in great wooden arcs. The fledged extensions appeared behind each shoulder and rose nearly two feet, very much like the war bonnet of American Plains Indians. At the gallop, the contrivance resembled a pair of fearsome outstretched wings. The result was both daunting and majestic; it was a psychological attack par excellence, producing a distinct whirring resonance that frightened enemy horses and added to the terrible splendor of the hussar attack.

> They wore the skin of a tiger or leopard as a cloak. Their harnesses, saddles and horse-cloths were embroidered with gold and gems and their long lances were painted with stripes like a stick of rock and decorated with a five-foot-long silk pennant . . . They even sometimes painted their horses red and white.[9]

The Poles crossed Turkish and European breeds to produce horses with speed and endurance and "rode on eastern saddles in order to place less strain on the horse. Because of these factors they could cover tremendous distances (up to 120 kilometers a day) without killing their mounts."[10] The eighteenth-century version of the Husaria were known as "Ulans" and continued to attack with *lance couchée.*

Polish Ulans remained the custodians of a medieval tradition that would be resurrected throughout the Continental military at the turn of the nineteenth century. The lance provided a distinct advantage in the first impact of the charge, creating shock and effective in melee against pikemen or boxes of bayonets, something that sworded cavalry could not hope to do. According to Sikora, "the front rank carried an astonishing lance of up to twenty feet in length [4.5 to 5.5. meters]."[11] For close melee, they carried carbines but depended on the *Koncerz,* a five-foot-long thrusting sword hung from the left side of the saddle, as well as the *Palasz,* a cutting sword three and a half feet long. The Husaria attack used distance to gain maximum psychological effect:

> The hussars charged from about 375 m. It crossed the first 75 walking (*stepie*), the next 150 trotting (*klusem*), then a canter (*cwale*), breaking into a gallop. The charge is completed at a canter for the final 30 meters. Only the leading ranks galloped, the back ranks proceed only at a canter . . . Sometimes the second rank moved forward to double-up with the first . . . It made up for losses in the first rank but more importantly it doubled the density of the line.[12]

In a prolonged melee, the advantage quickly shifted from lance to sword as lancers required room to wield their weapons. Like longbowmen, lancers were an expensive commodity requiring time to train properly and difficult to replace. The deadly lance became a cumbersome tool in the hands of an amateur, and by the end of the Seven Years' War, it had virtually disappeared from the European battlefield.

CAMP FOLLOWERS

Aufklärung military discipline advanced beyond strict to brutal and was often needlessly vicious. The aim, as Frederick the Great suggested, was that the soldier "fear his officers more than the danger to which he is exposed."[13] It is a matter for thorough psychological analysis to determine if in fact it was *cruel* discipline (gauntlet, lashing, beating, imprisonment, mutilation) or whether soldiers were motivated by rigid *fair* discipline as well as efficiency and professional pride. An officer in Frederick's army described the Prussian system:

> Every incident was punished as if it were a crime. A slip in the manual exercises, an improperly polished button on the uniform, or water spots on spatterdashes [leggings] would draw down a severe caning. Caning in fact became so common that it was regarded as part of the service, and no drill passed without one.[14]

The soldier was given uniform, rations, powder, and shot but had to provide most everything else. He was followed by sutlers and traders, prostitutes and peddlers. By the Seven Years' War (1756), most European armies allowed women (not necessarily courtesans), and eventually children, to accompany an army on the march. Simply referred to in the orderly books as "Women," they were common-law wives of senior soldiers such as sergeants and corporals. Women made extra money by providing varied services such as laundry, cooking, and uniform repair. Widows would instantly remarry within their companies to maintain their ration status for themselves and their children. Some military women were actually taken *on strength*: "a total of six normally permitted in each company (i.e., on the regiment's establishment and, therefore, entitled to rations) . . . [regiments] were permitted to have up to 84 women on their ration strength (not including children)."[15]

Surgeons and veterinarians were indispensable yet in short supply. There was no support staff; trained nursing instruction did not exist, but regimental women were often experienced nurses, learning their craft on the campaign trail. The regimental surgeon was a commissioned officer and ideally a "doctor of medicine" from a recognized university; he was assisted by a warrant officer surgeon's mate, orderlies (usually musicians), and regimental women. On the battlefield, triage was swift but perfunctory. A surgeon would typically stuff wounds with bandages moistened with wine or brandy, and, if infection and suppuration threatened, antiseptics such as tincture of myrrh, hot turpentine, balsam of Peru, or camphor were sometimes applied. Trephining was the routine procedure used for head injuries, as was the cauterization of blood vessels after amputation.

Treatment was unintentionally brutal; orderlies held down soldiers, and the fortunate ones received brandy or opium. A skilled surgeon could cut through muscle, saw through bone, and remove a limb in under a minute, if his instruments were sharp. The greatest killer was shock and disease—gangrene, putrid fever, lockjaw, and dysentery were common. Infection was often prevented with gunpowder sprinkled into the wound; when ignited the flash would burn off infecting debris and cauterize the wound. Most dangerous was simply disease; armies lost more men to infections, colds, pox, and simply poor hygiene than all the battles and campaigns combined. This was to be the case until the twentieth century.

By the end of the Enlightenment, the term *farrier* had morphed from "horse doctor" to someone who shoes horses—a blacksmith. In fact, the cavalry farrier was a wealth of knowledge and expertise, specializing in horse remedies rather than shoeing. *Farrier* comes from the Latin *faber ferrarius*.[16] Their official military status in western armies may be traced to the 1796 Adjutant General's Report: "A person properly educated and having received a certificate from the medical committee of the Veterinary College shall be attached to each regiment having the name of Veterinary Surgeon."[17] Veterinarians and farriers spent much of their time with the navicular bone and treating laminitis; both diseases dealt with the inflammation or degeneration of the coffin bone and subsequent effects on the cannon bone and, eventually, the hoof. It was all about the legs, and the hoofs were the first element to connect the horse with terra firma.

LACE WARS STYLE AND MANNERS: "GENTLEMEN NEVER FIRE FIRST!"

The art of war was best practiced by the experienced professional, but in reality campaigning was in the hands of amateurs. Command was monopolized by aristocrats whose appointments of significance were determined by connections in court. There was no war college system available, save for the rigors of warfare; acquiring a competent commander required good luck or a full purse.

The aristocrat at war presented a splendid sight: carefully tailored uniform and silk hose to show a well-turned calf. Only officers had culottes (half trousers), while soldiers wore trousers or canvas leggings. Long pants were the mark of the peasant who became known as the *sans culottes* (literally, "without short pants"). Officers sported powdered wigs, and everyone wore the tricorne, or three-cornered hat, made of felt produced from beaver pelts, which was another reason for the much-contested North American fur trade. Aristocrats' faces were powdered since a pale complexion denoted social status and only commoners became tanned. Minor facial makeup was fashionable; beauty marks were emphasized or drawn in; some even applied eyeliner, rouge, and lip color. Although this sort of complete court makeover was less likely on a hard campaign, it would not be unusual in armies with vast tented camps only a few days' march from garrison cities or capitals. The overemphasis on breeding rather than talent produced questionable leadership on both sides. The Battle of Fontenoy (1745), though a French victory featuring grand cavalry attacks, became memorable for the battlefield affectation of Lord Charles Hay, commanding what are now the Grenadier Guards. He purportedly recognized that their equivalent, the *Gardes-françaises*, were opposite, walked in front of his regiment, bowed, and doffed his hat to the French commander whom he may have met at a ball in London a few years before. He then invited the French Guards to fire. Their commander bowed, doffed his hat, and called back: "Messieurs les anglais, vous tirez les premiers" (English gentlemen, you may fire first). Hay accepted, ordered "Give fire," and badly cut up King Louis' favorite regiment. The biography of Marshal de Saxe (who was present at Fontenoy), argues the popular story, first related by Voltaire in his *Reign of Louis XV,* is apocryphal and supports another version of the event:

> [Hay] took out a silver hip flask, bowed to the French officers, drank with a flourish, and called out "I hope, gentlemen, that you are going to wait for us today, and not now swim the Scheldt as you swam the Main at Dettigen." And one of my Lord's sergeants . . . murmured: "For what we are about to receive, may the Lord make us truly thankful."[18]

The lace wars' style emphasized courtly elegance and aristocratic panache. It must be appreciated that the fashions exhibited by the officers of the period were no less ornate than the heraldic livery of their predecessors who rode to Crécy, although the medieval knight's outfit may well be considered the more practical.

CAVALRY ATTACK

Enlightenment cavalry tried "charging at the trot" and practiced the first rank to perform as "pistol firers while charging." European cavalry was conditioned to attack via a constrained approach to fire pistols or carbines followed by a pause or withdrawal to reload. This often was abandoned for the reckless galloping charge if enemy fire proved telling or discipline was slack. The caracole (Spanish for "spiral" or "twisting") was designed to permit cavalry to advance at the canter and then deliver a volley at packed masses, withdraw to safe ranges, reload, and repeat until the enemy was disorganized enough to invite a charge with sword. This exercise is still repeated in dressage.

The problem of keeping your powder dry or ready in the pan was doubled aboard a trotting horse. The caracole, last used at the Battle of Minden (1759), ultimately proved ineffective: ". . . when the first rank opens fire with its forty carbines, there is frequently not a single hit."[19] Saddle volleys forfeit the cavalry's greatest attributes of maneuver and speed. Frederick the Great noted: "They were besotted with the idea of firing off their pistols. I finally had to make some straw dummies and I was able to show them that all their pistol shots missed, whereas they cut down every single figure with their swords."[20]

The warhorse was the largest target on the battlefield. The charger's head protects much of the rider; in a frontal attack the trooper presents mostly knees and part of his head to musket fire. Infantry close-range fire smashed the horse's chest, legs, and head; canister (a cluster of musket balls) was worse. The best method for cavalry to deal with pikes or squares was to wait for the artillery to blow them apart. The cavalry attack had found a new friend—the horse artillery—a slightly psychotic arm that exhibited all of the dash and élan of cavalry (it adopted the hussar costume) and delivered the most brutal of consequences. Horse artillery acquired a flamboyance that was much admired, for they fancied themselves a hybrid elite. The arm had been developed by Gustavus Adolphus and reached prominence under Frederick II, who spent time and money to create a mobile force capable of long-range and indirect fire.

Cavalry stalked the battlefield, carefully preserved for "the right moment." The charge more than ever demanded the mutual cohesion of rider and horse. Deprived of extensive armor and facing musketeers with bayonet or pole arms, or worse, supported by artillery, a fighting horse was forced to endure much to engage in melee. Frederick the Great insisted on two main characteristics for the cavalry attack: it must be impetuous and quick. By the eighteenth century, Continental cavalry offered little substantial difference in tactics, equipment, or effect. Austrian and Prussian heavy cavalry carried the cuirasse, but the French and English did not. Although household guard regiments existed, the main mounted effort depended on the dragoon, which by 1760 was mostly line cavalry as opposed to mounted musketeers. The European dragoon, in calico or cotton, wore the tricorne and brandished the broadsword; minor differences were training and quality of horse, which varied and reflected the strength of the kingdom's treasury as well as its breeding farms.

The real difference lay in doctrine. Massed cavalry was severely limited by tactical restrictions; it was useless in closed terrain, urban areas, or against fortifications. It could not hold ground or stand against artillery. In order to create the havoc it promised, cavalry had to survive fire at increasingly longer ranges. Cavalry sat on the wings of battlefield drama and hungered for its lost status as the arm of decision.

THE THIRD GREAT MANEUVER: LEUTHEN, DECEMBER 5, 1757

My father left me a bad cavalry, in which there was hardly an officer who knew his profession. The troopers feared their horses and scarcely ever rode ... and the effects in our first war were so bad that I saw that I had to remake the entire corps.

—Friedrich der Grosse, *Die Politischen Testamente*[21]

Leuthen was the most complete of all Friedrich's victories; two hours more of daylight, as Friedrich himself says, and it would have been the most decisive of this century.

—Thomas Carlyle[22]

The architect of Continental, certainly Germanic, operational doctrine is Friedrich der Grosse (Frederick the Great). Military historian Robert Citino has observed: "There is indeed a German way of war and ... it had its origins within the Kingdom of Prussia ... the war of movement on the operational level (*Bewegungskrieg*)."[23] The quintessence of *Fingerspitzengefühl* flows from Frederick's management of war. The reinstatement of cavalry as a dynamic factor may be traced to his development of the arm. After the Seven Years' War, the organization and use of cavalry reached a more professional status than it had enjoyed since chivalry or the Mongol horse armies. Frederick not only revitalized Prussian cavalry but gave it the tactical clout it always sought: its own mounted fire support. Horse artillery was first employed by Frederick (in fact he preferred howitzers to guns) and quickly became an elite force, emulated by Europe's armies.

The French military philosophe Jacques-Antoine de Guibert wrote: "In all his camps, at all his reviews, wherever Frederick sees his cavalry, it is to these important charges in large numbers that he gives the most attention, these that he values most highly."[24] The warhorse's restitution was the result of Frederick's

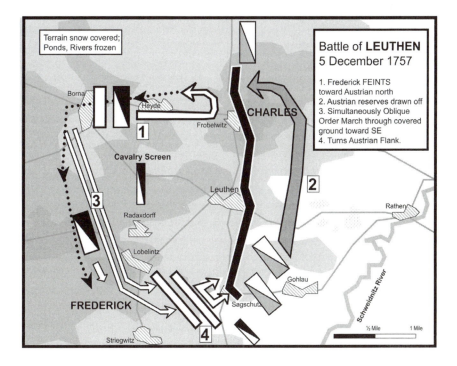

Terrain snow covered; Ponds, Rivers frozen

Battle of **LEUTHEN**
5 December 1757

1. Frederick FEINTS toward Austrian north
2. Austrian reserves drawn off
3. Simultaneously Oblique Order March through covered ground toward SE
4. Turns Austrian Flank.

Borna

Heyde

Frobelwitz

CHARLES

1

Cavalry Screen

Leuthen

2

Rathen

Radaxdorff

3

Lobelintz

Gohlau

Schweidnitz River

FREDERICK

Sagschut

4

Striegwitz

½ Mile   1 Mile

determination to create an instrument that would assist him in defeating empires. He ensured an aggressive esprit de corps simply by insisting upon it: "The King hereby forbids all cavalry officers, under penalty of being cashiered, ever to allow themselves to be attacked by the enemy in any action. Prussians must always attack the enemy."[25] Frederick's military zeal prompted Mirabeau to observe: "La Prusse n'est pas un État qui possède une armée; c'est une armée qui a conquis une nation."[26]

The European segment of the Seven Years' War (1754 and 1756–1763) featured Prussia (allied with England) taking on, mostly single handedly, the three Continental superpowers of France, Austria, and Russia. It was perhaps the first real "world war"; campaigning was initially launched in the forests of North America where it was called the French and Indian War. Prussian diplomacy was Machiavellian. Frederick grumbled that the Seven Years' War was essentially a war against three angry women: Maria Theresa of Austria, Catherine the Great of Russia, and Louis XV's mistress, Madame de Pompadour. The king had snubbed the influential but common-born marquise and then openly insulted her by referring to his pack of greyhounds as his "marquises de Pompadour."[27]

Prussia's central position made her Europe's doormat, and Frederick's successes simply invited more wars of revenge. The king's military legacy includes the restoration of operational maneuver. The oblique order (the tactic of refusing one's flank) was made famous by the Theban general Epaminondas in the Battle of Leuctra (371 B.C.). It was next put to good use by Alexander at Arbela in 331 B.C., trouncing Darius. It is perhaps the best way a smaller force can hope to attack a larger force:

> You march towards [the enemy] but keep him uncertain as to how you will attack; then do on a sudden march up, not parallel to him, but oblique, at an angle of 45 degrees,—swift, vehement, in overpowering numbers, on the wing you have chosen. Roll that wing together, ruined, in upon its own line, you may roll the whole five miles of line into disorder and ruin, and always be in overpowering number at the point of dispute . . . none but Prussians, drilled by an Old Dessauer, capable of doing it. This is the *Schräge Ordnung*.[28]

Despite his austere, caustic demeanor, Frederick was beloved by the rank and file, particularly the cavalry where he was called *Vater Fritz* ("Father Fritz") to his face:

> That same evening Friedrich rode into the Camp; the first regiment he came upon was the Life-Guard Cuirassiers . . . the men, in their accustomed way, gave him good-evening, which he cheerily returned. Some of the more veteran sort asked, ruggedly confidential, as well as loyal: "What is thy news, then, so late?" "Good news, children (*Kinder*): to-morrow you will beat the Austrians tightly!" "That we will, by___!" answered they . . . "Well, I will see what you can do: now

lay you down, and sleep sound; and good sleep to you!" "Good-night, Fritz!" answer all.[29]

The Leuthen campaign began when the Austrians surprised Frederick by laying siege to Breslau, Silesia's capital. Frederick force-marched 170 miles with such dispatch that he surprised the Austrian's forward bakery and fed his army. On November 28, 1757, the day Breslau fell, he reached Parchwitz, a few miles from Leuthen. The Austrians had about 65,000 men deployed against his own 33,000 with 210 guns versus 167 Prussian cannon, though Austrian guns were of lighter caliber. After a careful appreciation of the situation, Frederick decided he could not afford *not to fight.* He was familiar with the area, a site he had used for autumn war games, and the murky weather would mask any extensive maneuver.

Frederick gathered his officers in Parchwitz where he delivered a famous before-battle speech and, though not quite the stuff of *Henry V*'s "we happy few, we band of brothers," it achieved the same result: "I fully recognize the dangers attached to this enterprise, but in my present situation I must conquer or die." He then paused, and in measured pace, quietly and emphatically added:

> The Cavalry regiment that does not on the instant, on order given, dash full plunge into the enemy, I will, directly after the Battle, unhorse, and make it a

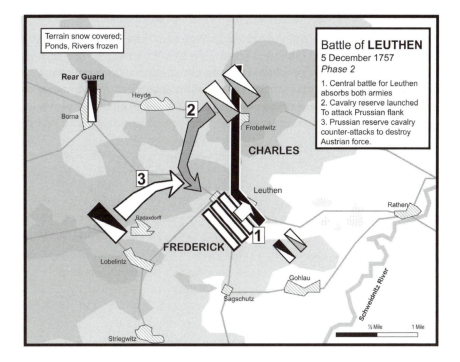

Terrain snow covered; Ponds, Rivers frozen

Rear Guard
Heyde
Borna
Frobelwitz
CHARLES
Leuthen
Radaxdorff
FREDERICK
Lobelintz
Gohlau
Sagschutz
Striegwitz
Rathen
Schweidnitz River

Battle of **LEUTHEN**
5 December 1757
Phase 2

1. Central battle for Leuthen absorbs both armies
2. Cavalry reserve launched To attack Prussian flank
3. Prussian reserve cavalry counter-attacks to destroy Austrian force.

½ Mile   1 Mile

Garrison regiment. The Infantry battalion which, meet with what it may, shows the least sign of hesitating, loses its colors and its sabres, and I cut the trimmings from its uniform! Now good-night, Gentlemen: shortly we have either beaten the Enemy, or we never see one another again.[30]

The Prussians faced a familiar opponent, Prince Charles Alexander of Lorraine, who was not particularly keen to fight but resolute about holding Silesia. He was anchored to a long ridge near the town of Leuthen. Concern about Frederick turning their flanks resulted in a front line almost six miles long. This did not dissuade Frederick from bold maneuver; his bravura was made possible by an intimate knowledge of the terrain and the discipline of his near robotic army. He planned to feint with his left to draw off Austrian reserves while he marched his entire army across the Austrian front where he then attacked Charles' flank.

The Austrian left (the south) rested on Sagschutz village and then fell off to plashy low ground and the Schweidnitz River, both near frozen. The center, on slightly higher ground, incorporated Leuthen while the right flank rested on the highest feature incorporating the village of Frobelwitz, covered by cavalry screens extending about another half mile northwest.[31] *Der Alte Fritz* played his opening gambit where he pushed forward an infantry vanguard and the bulk of his cavalry, which emerged from low ground to advance menacingly toward Frobelwitz. The entire battlefield was shrouded by thick fog, and from his observation post in the tower of Leuthen church, Prince Charles saw nothing.

Prussian cavalry attacked the Austrian screen and drove it onto its supports, then chased the fleeing squadrons toward Frobelwitz, finally halting just before the crest, in sight of the Austrian center. It was the sort of cavalry operation Friedrich liked to see: *kurtz und vives* ("short and lively").[32] The maneuver mesmerized the Austrians for the better part of the day. Prince Charles reacted as Frederick hoped and moved his cavalry reserve to the north, behind Frobelwitz. But within a half hour, the Prussians had disappeared.

Contained by the mist, Frederick maneuvered, using ground like a *Jägermeister.* The terrain west of Leuthen gave away to a natural approach that led south, skirted into dead ground, and then went through a draw to reappear less than a mile from Sagschutz, overlooking the Austrian southern flank. German historian C. F. Barsewisch noted that, "our army advanced with sounding music, as if on parade. Its order was as magnificent as at any review at Berlin, for it was marching under the eyes of its great monarch."[33] The operation was supported by Prussian artillery, leapfrogging from one battery position to another.

Marching in *Schräge Stellung,* Frederick's force completely turned Charles' flank. His army, where it should not have been, stood deployed in attack formation: his center and right in contact, his left flank refused. The left-wing cavalry division, commanded by Lt. Gen. Wilhelm von Driesen, covered his open flank. Austrian temerity abetted this intrepid maneuver, which was destined to be studied ad nauseam in staff colleges. Consternation and desperate repositioning followed as Charles' staff tried to swing the army to face imminent assault. Battalions force-marched to create a new line of battle, crowding into Leuthen.

By one o'clock, as the sun burned off the last of the fog, the Prussians went smartly into the attack, clearing Sagschutz with the bayonet. Pounded by heavy 12 pounders, Charles' left flank collapsed: "[the front] beswept by those ten *Brummers* and other batteries, till bullet and bayonet can act on it, speedily gives way."[34] Frederick's battalions rolled up the Austrian line and then stormed Leuthen with a coordinated artillery and infantry assault. The fighting was furious; "behind the Windmills they are a hundred men deep."[35]

As the battle for Leuthen raged, Prince Charles was presented an opportunity to restore the situation. His mass of cavalry was intact and still north of Leuthen. Austrian cavalry considered itself an elite, and this was a splendid opportunity to prove it. Prussian momentum had waned; the battle was now a firefight between staggered battalions. Frederick's left flank was "in the air" and unprotected save for the battery of *Brummers* the Prussians had brought up to pound Leuthen. At five o'clock, as the low December sun began to turn hillcrests blood orange, Charles finally gave the order. General of Cavalry Count Lucchese had marshaled seventy squadrons including cuirassiers, dragoons, and hussars.[36]

This majestic body swept forward, boot to boot, an irresistible sea of flashing steel, kicking up a billowing surf of powdered snow as it neared Frederick's flank. Von Driesen coolly allowed Lucchese to ride across his front; then he in turn charged the Austrians with "thirty-five squadrons of cuirassiers and the ubiquitous Bayreuth Dragoons. Thirty further squadrons hastened up from the Prussian reserve to join in the fight."[37] The shock of the charge dissipated into furious melees that reeled into Leuthen. When Lucchese was cut down, the Austrian cavalry gave away, fleeing into the alpenglow. The Prussian horse then charged Charles' infantry, which finally broke.

Leuthen featured audacious operational maneuver and dexterous tactics: hard-hitting infantry, supported by aggressive, advancing artillery. It was in the end, an *all-arms* battle that was initiated and finally won by the cavalry.

THE ROOTS OF *AUFTRAGSTAKTIK:* CAVALRY COMMANDERS

The cavalry leader is a unique charismatic type, better known for passionate action than deliberate planning. The following Mess anecdote has been circulating for years and shows the difference between an infantry officer and a cavalry officer. An infantry officer and a cavalry officer are both asked, "What is the sum of one and one?" The infantry officer pauses, quietly uses his fingers beneath the table, and says "Two." The cavalry officer slams his fist on the table and shouts "Three!" Quick, decisive, and, close enough for government work. This goes to illustrate the point made by Patton: "Success in war depends upon the Golden Rule of War: Speed—Simplicity—Boldness."[38] No cavalry record could be complete with acknowledging the officer who resurrected the hussar and the light cavalry mystique—"the Hussar King," Baron Hans Joachim von Zieten. He was a man of small stature and frail voice, which led to a trigger temper and 74 separate duels. Von Ziethen became Frederick's favorite cavalry general and possessed "wisdom with courage, contempt of danger with perseverance, and dexterity with presence of mind, and activity with the most perfect command of temper. He conceived his plans with the progressiveness of the rising storm and executed them with the rapidity of the thunderbolt."[39] Ziethen died in bed after 70 years of service at the age of 86. Conversely, his compatriot, the larger than life Seydlitz, died in recompense for living life to dangerous excess and bravado: "Seydlitz was noticed by his sovereign as one of the few cavalry commanders who used his own initiative."[40]

THE WHORING HUSSAR—FRIEDRICH WILHELM, FREIHERR VON SEYDLITZ

Under Frederick William I, the concept of *Prussian obedience* became endemic to the Germanic military, and yet it is also clear that at the operational level, it was not an obedience that was merely blind. While Frederick the Great may be the creator of the *Prussian militarism*, it is Seydlitz who epitomizes the essence of *Auftragstaktik*—a particularly "cavalry" system of warfare, for it appeals to the free spirit of the mounted officer to be creative and respond from the saddle. Seydlitz demonstrated the fundamental spirit of cool initiative at Zorndorf in 1758. When Frederick ordered him to attack the Russian *front*, Seydlitz, about to deliver a paralyzing blow to the Russian *flank*, replied: "Tell his Majesty that my head will be at his disposal after the battle, but that as long as the battle lasts I intend to use it in his service."[41] Before the battle of Rossbach (November 1757) Frederick put the 36-year-old von Seydlitz in command of the entire cavalry, superseding two senior commanders. When the passed-over generals raised brooding eyebrows, von Seydlitz snapped: "Gentlemen, I obey the king, and you obey me."[42]

Von Seydlitz was the complete cavalry commander; he excelled at all military virtues and petty vices. He embraced base temptations as recklessly as he faced danger. The outspoken, heavy drinking officer was a rogue's rogue as well as a cavalier's cavalier. His absence from duty after Rossbach was less due to a sustained saber wound than because "he had caught the pox in Silesia from a lady of high birth but lowly conduct."[43] Von Seydlitz had read Count de Rochefort's *Idées Practiques sur la Cavalerie* and confided to King Frederick that he could not conceive how an officer of cavalry could be made prisoner if his horse was not killed. The king was struck with his remarks and decided to test them. The opportunity presented itself when the king was crossing a bridge. He stopped and turned to Seydlitz, the commander of his escort, surrounded by cuirassiers and senior officers:

> You pretend, Monsieur Seydlitz, that an officer of cavalry ought never to be made prisoner; certainly it is the idea of a brave man, nevertheless there are occasions where one could surrender without dishonour. Suppose for instance, that we were enemies, you would not attempt to pass by force. What would you do then?[44]

Seydlitz, prompt as thought, drove in his spurs and threw himself with his horse into the torrent, and without suffering any injury, returned to the retinue near the king, whom he saluted, saying, "Sire, behold my reply."[45]

Seydlitz was soon promoted to major general and awarded the *Orden Pour le Mérite*.[46] Between wars, Seydlitz concentrated on training the cavalry; he believed an officer "must be in a position to show [his men] how it ought to be done and do it in an exemplary style."[47] He would leave in the morning by jumping his horse over the gates of his estate and insisting his staff do the same. Seydlitz demonstrated complex traits; he ordered the cavalry regiments to abandon most corporal punishment, but he was unforgiving and ruthless in training. He maneuvered large masses, riding the regiments at full gallop over broken ground where it was common for troopers to be hurt or killed. Frederick once took him to task for the number of deaths during training. "Seydlitz coolly answered, 'If you make such a fuss about a few broken necks, your Majesty will never have the bold horsemen you require for the field.'"[48] Although Seydlitz was outspoken and Frederick did not particularly care for honest talk, it was his personal conduct that annoyed the king. By the end of the Seven Years' War, Seydlitz was considered a liability because he was susceptible to recurrences of his syphilis. The disease consumed him, destroyed his marriage and ended his career.[49] Seydlitz died at the age of 53; this was a loss for Prussian cavalry, which went into a state of sad decline, not recovering until Blücher.

The technology that revolutionized tactical conduct for the infantry could not be efficiently adapted for work in the saddle. Further, it put the horse in unnecessary danger; conversely, massed assault was decisive. Cavalry, completely dependent on the warhorse, sought to discover a weapon with which to conduct warfare in the Age of Reason. In the end, it was left with the sword.

The Hussar: "I suppose *Shock* is alright if you have no finesse or panache..."

Chapter 6

Napoleonics, Part I: Cavalry Becomes an Operational Arm

> Charges of cavalry are equally useful at the beginning, the middle and the end of a battle. They should be made always, if possible, on the flanks of the infantry, especially when the latter is engaged in front.
>
> —Napoleon Bonaparte [1]

The French cavalry was seriously disheveled by the Revolution. Most regiments were sympathetic to the Bourbons, and the majority of the aristocratic officers fled to avoid the Terror. Two regiments, the Hussards du Saxe and the 15iéme Cavalerie (Royal Allemande), defected en masse to the Austrians. Republican army cavalry was formed from scratch and given the fewest resources. By the time Napoleon held his first command at Toulon, the revolutionary forces comprised 26 heavy cavalry regiments.[2] Their actual strength was about half of the required establishment. One of Napoleon's military accomplishments was to turn a ragtag mounted force with a lineage of defeat dating back to Louis XIV into the most feared cavalry in Europe. Further, he raised this force beyond tactical parameters into the heady business of operational warfare and strategic maneuver. By the time Bonaparte had redefined operational warfare, a regiment or brigade of cavalry was mere bagatelle.

Comparatively, French cavalry remained the weakest arm of the imperial army, although generally superior to competing cavalries. All the armies used dragoons and put their best heavies into body armor except France. Bonaparte changed this. Austrian heavy cavalry was consistently rated outstanding, and both cuirassiers and hussars were superb. The Austro-Hungarian breeds were much admired—particularly the Lipizzaner horses, which descended from Roman cavalry. The breed was created by Archduke Charles who imported Spanish stallions and established what is today the "Spanish Riding School." After the Austerlitz campaign, Napoleon demanded large numbers of Austrian mounts to refurbish the French cavalry. The Lipizzaners were evacuated and hidden from the emperor, but after the 1809 campaign, France again demanded horse levies. The Austrians once more concealed their prized mounts in Mezöhegyes, Hungary, where the climate almost ruined the breed. They were restored to their prized status after 1815.

Prussian cavalry continued the styles and techniques instituted by Frederick. Their cuirassiers were well regarded because of the robust Holstein horse—a long-winded animal that endured extended gallops over hard ground and then could melee. Oddly enough, Frederick preferred the ancient race of English horses and paid top prices for strong, tall mounts, which he provided for his generals.[3]

British cavalry was regarded as the best mounted in Europe but suffered from poor discipline. English cavalry earned its Napoleonic spurs in the Peninsula. Sir Charles Oman considered the Sahagun fight (December 21, 1808) "perhaps the most brilliant cavalry exploit during the whole six years of the war."[4] Individual regiments were courageous and exhibited excessive élan but were difficult to control. Most historians recall Wellington's acerbic words to censure British cavalry: "Our cavalry officers have acquired the trick of galloping at everything and then galloping back as fast as they gallop at the enemy . . . One would think they cannot manoeuvre except on Wimbledon Common."[5] Historian Ian Fletcher valiantly argued in defense, pointing out that Wellington's crack and subsequent historical reaction is "not only unfair to them but is totally inaccurate."[6]

Yet the English cavalry's performance in Waterloo was as inconsistent as the duke suggested: from brilliant to disappointing. Despite some impressive wins, Wellington never completely warmed to his cavalry. As late as 1826 the Duke wrote: "I consider our cavalry so inferior to the French from want of order, although I consider one squadron a match for two French squadrons . . . I could not use them till our admirable infantry had moved the French cavalry from the ground."[7] Ian Fletcher theorized:

> [Wellington] grew to distrust his cavalry. However, this mistrust certainly appears to have had an adverse effect on the cavalry which can, perhaps, be demonstrated by the fact that many of the fine victories gained by the British cavalry were achieved in Wellington's absence.[8]

Despite careful doctrine, cavalry ployment invariably resulted in a mad charge, which often succeeded because of troopers' bravado rather than careful tactics. Even British cavaliers admitted their cavalry was a juxtaposition of "unbelievable brilliance and bravery, tempered by frequent rashness and incompetent handling."[9]

A melee with the British was nasty business. The 1796-pattern light cavalry saber was heavier than nineteenth-century counterparts; it was a curved saber designed for slashing and cutting that swelled at the point like a machete quite capable of chopping off limbs or chunks of horseflesh or cleaving bone:

> A corporal of the 13th had killed one of his men [a French Colonel] was so enraged, that he sallied out himself and attacked the corporal . . . both defended for some time, the corporal cut him twice in the face, his helmet came off at the second, when the corporal slew him by a cut which nearly cleft his skull asunder, it cut in as deep as the nose through the brain. The corporal was not wounded.[10]

Russian cavalry was considered competent: "The [Russian] cavalry was fine and commanding. . . . The heavy cavalry are undoubtedly very fine; the men gigantic, the horses good, the equipment superior and in perfect condition. The light cavalry are less striking."[11] In 1812, after a series of defeats, Czar Alexander I added 58 regiments to the regular cavalry, 6 of them cuirassiers.[12] The Czar's heavies were poorly directed above the regimental level. Russian regiments were not grouped into operational bodies; their generals preferred to spar in attritional contests rather than maneuver. Cossack regiments, or *sontas*, formed the bulk of Russian light cavalry. The Cossacks generally operated in great swarms: "a hardy and vigorous race of horsemen, such as are not to be met in any other country of Europe."[13] The French thought little of them until the 1812 campaign:

> These rude horsemen are ignorant of our *divisions,* of our regular *alignments,* of all that order which we so overwhelmingly estimate . . . They spring from a state of rest to a full gallop . . . they move with extraordinary rapidity, have few wants and are full of warlike ardour.[14]

The Cossacks were a mix of Tatar and Ukrainian steppe tribes and were particularly ruthless foes who often impaled or skinned prisoners. They were not particularly liked within their own cavalry and vice versa. A captured marauder complained to Bonaparte: "It is the Cossacks who do all the fighting; it is always their turn. While the Russians sleep the Cossacks keep watch."[15] Some regiments, certainly the Cossacks of the Guard, were first rate and capable of sangfroid as well as wild abandon. Czar Alexander watched his Lifeguard Cossacks charge French cuirassiers and noted they approached the enemy as if they were coming to a wedding. After the campaign they adopted Mendelssohn's "Wedding March" as their regimental tune.

The Russian warhorse was respected for its endurance, particularly in bad weather and winter, but rated as not heavy enough, for the muscle and bones did not produce the required shock in combat. The Russian cavalry tended to favor European mounts, which were larger and purchased from Prussian stud farms. Horses were bred with Arabians, Karabakh, Turkish, Danish, and horses from the Don basin—unattractive yet capable of enduring great hardships. The light horse was taken from southern Ukraine, which had developed a particularly hardy breed after centuries of combat against Turks and Tatars. Russian cavalry mounts were of average size; line cavalry regiments varied from 13 to 14 hands, but the Guard Cuirassiers horses were large, stout beasts.[16] When Grand Duke Constantine required a horse during combat, he was offered a replacement by one of his troopers. The Duke quipped "Well, Mirkovich I see you are already riding on an elephant!"

Compared to the Continental cavalry, French mounts were substantial, averaging 15 hands throughout, while British cavalry was comparable at 15 hands or more. The most exotic additions to European cavalry were by the French who incorporated Egyptian Mamluks into the Imperial Guard. Napoleon insisted they keep their Byzantine dress, which included a turban, billowing red *saroual* pants, and a scimitar. They were an exclusive outfit and attracted French officers who led them in battle wearing the same costume, sporting a traditional Turkish moustache. They were beguiling but tough and fought with savage determination from Austerlitz until the bitter end at Waterloo.

THE RETURN OF THE LANCER

These gallant horsemen [at Somosierra] can hardly be paralleled in the annals of war.
—Sir William Francis Napier, *History of the Peninsular War*, London, 1828

Napoleon was smitten by two Polish treasures—foremost was the Countess Marie Walewska, second were the Polish lancers. When Napoleon entered Warsaw in 1807, he was escorted by an honor guard of Ulans who so impressed the emperor that he commanded a squadron of Polish *Chevau-Léger* be attached to the Imperial Guard, initially without lances.

The French cavalry also included line regiments of Polish Ulans, dressed and equipped in their national style. They were sent to Spain where they impressed English cavalry: "very large men, well mounted; the front rank armed with long spears with flags on them, which they flourish about, so as to frighten our horses, and thence either pulled our men off their horses or ran them through. They were perfect barbarians, and gave no quarter when they could possibly avoid."[17] After Wagram (1809) it was decided to issue the lance to the Polish Guard Regiment for it was, after all, their national weapon. They were renamed *le Regiment de Chevau-Léger Lanciers Polonais de la Garde Impériale.*[18] Their blue uniform was imperial blue offset by lapels in a color unique to this regiment, Polish crimson, a cross between scarlet and royal purple. They wore their distinctive headgear that was to become the style for all lancers across the world—the square topped bell shako known as the *czapka*.

After the war, the Duke of York, who had been mightily impressed by lancers at Waterloo, ordered the raising of British lancer regiments dressed, of course, in the Polish style. After 1812 lancers often supplanted dragoons as mediums for standard work, and the cuirassiers for a heavy punch. This worked well in the attack, and it became suggested that all cavalry should have their front ranks charge with the *lance couchée*—an advantage in the first shock of attack, useful to stick infantry in squares or a gunner hiding behind gun trails. Still, once the melee started, the saber reigned supreme for it required a well-trained Lancer to wield a 12-foot weapon in a closed set-to: "Lancers looked well and formidable before they were broken and closed by our men, and then their lances were an encumbrance."[19]

THE CAVALRY UNIFORM: UTILITY VERSUS SEDUCTION

> Cavalry Uniforms follow certain peculiar lines of their own. They strive for gorgeousness and display, and frequently develop decorations which make it impossible for their wearers to function as cavalry.
>
> —James Laver, *British Military Uniforms* [20]

James Laver, distinguished costume historian and a past Keeper of the Robes at the Victoria and Albert Museum, suggests that there are three key principles that dictate the evolution of military fashion: hierarchy, utility, and seduction. It is argued by Laver that utility always surrenders to the principle of seduction,[21] which attempts to emphasize physique and exaggerates posture by the use of tight waists, stiff high collars, and gaudy accoutrements.

Hair was a great burden in the eighteenth century; by the beginning of the Napoleonic era, in a rare display of common sense, short hair was permitted. Queues were discontinued from December 31, 1806. "Short hair" meant touching the collar; some cavalry regiments continued to plait their sideburns, but most were glad to be rid of combing, plaiting, and hair wax. Moustaches for all ranks were de rigueur in most cavalry regiments save for Prussia where German hussar officers disdained to adorn the upper lip like the lower ranks.

National uniform color was simply tradition. At a distance, an army's colors proved incomprehensible save for the Austrians who wore white and the British who wore red. At cannon shot, Prussian blue was much like French blue, and the Russian green was not distinguishable from either of them. Cavalry regiments were particularly difficult to distinguish at longer range, and friendly fire was a constant threat from enthusiastic gunners.

A classic example of Napoleonic fashion slavery was headgear. The Polish *czapka* was copied throughout, and the bearskin became the signature of elite units, particularly British and French. Bonaparte's *Grenadiers à Cheval* (the elite of all European Guard heavies) and the British Scots Greys fought wearing bearskins. The *Grenadiers à Cheval* were larger than life and known as "The Gods": ". . . the exclusive privilege of that character and that steadiness . . . The general expression of his figure was the coldness."[22] Napoleon normally wore the uniform of a chasseur colonel, perhaps because he felt at home in their presence. The average chasseur was "small in size and slightly squat; his short neck is almost lost in his shoulders . . . an enormous moustache decks his upper lip; in his ears broad silver rings are hanging . . . one of the best riders of the Guard . . . *durs à cuire* ["hard to cook": a tough man]."[23] Elite squadrons in French light cavalry were issued the *Colpack,* a shorter type of bearskin with a large flap—the remnants of the old *Hussaren flamme.*

The whole look was quickly copied by British cavalry who had their *Colpacks* made in London by the firm of Busby and Sons. It soon became known as "the Busby"; the *flamme* became a "Busby bag," and the hat was continually confused by civilians who referred to it as a bearskin, which was vexing to the cavalry who exhibited hubris over their *Colpacks* or Busbys.

Most heavy cavalry sported variations of the classical Minerva helmet with its flowing Kublai Khan mane, an *aigrette* or plume or both. The British heavy dragoons changed their helmet manes to bouffant pompadour crests. Suffering for fashion was de rigueur: the helmets "heated up a horseman's head as if it were inside a brass cooking pot and upset his balance."[24] High headgear affected balance; a victim was none other than the Duke of Wellington himself: "The Duke fell from his horse the other day at the Review in consequence of having on his head the extravagant Grenadier cap with which . . . in a high wind, it is impossible to balance yourself."[25] *Colpacks* and Busbys were only marginally better, and it is a wonder how cavalry cantered or attacked at all.

Doctrinal Epistemology.
The Cavalry: "**Damn thin red line – if we edge in another 100 yards, we can charge.**"
The Infantry: "**Damn cuirassiers – if they edge in another 25 yards, we'll have to form Square…**"

Chapter 7

Napoleonics, Part II: Ulm to Waterloo

> Without cavalry, battles are without result.
>
> —Napoleon Bonaparte[1]

In the cavalry attack, control rests in a resolute leader's personal demonstration of élan from the front and by trumpet command—never by bugle, an item relegated to the infantry. Nerves were on edge as regiments formed; adrenalin pounded, horses' ears perked and followed the sounds of jingling bits as lines moved forward. As soon as the *advance* was given, the thrill for man and horse was difficult to describe. The pounding of a massed canter eclipsed all. Ground shook and the thunder of hoofs, as raucous as artillery yet more menacing, totally dominated the field of battle. The call to charge made the blood boil. Entire regiments were often swept into an attack because the riders could no longer control the bloodlust of the warhorses. During the battle of Waterloo at least two brigades of French cavalry broke forward to join in Ney's ill-timed charge.

Napoleon's tactical variations on a theme were seemingly simple and perhaps obvious: fix the enemy's attention by pressing against a particular area, feign an attack to draw off reserves then smack them in the flank or front with a superiority of artillery and assault forces. Overwhelming fire was an essential component of maneuver; as he explained: "In battle, skill consists in converging a mass of fire upon a single point," however, he cautioned, "infantry, cavalry and artillery cannot do without one another."[2] The essentials were a strong reserve, effective artillery capable of rapid *groupement* and inspired command. Nevertheless, it was Napoleon's management of operations, as much as grand tactics, that brought the French victory.

The plodding Royalist army was re-formed and subdivided into mini armies, or corps, each capable of all phases of war and, more importantly, creative maneuver. The corps system was a bona fide revolution in military affairs emulated by all Western armies and the basis for Clausewitz's guiding principles on the operational art. Each corps had a complete headquarters and support services.[3] A gifted corps commander had the opportunity to develop the situation, maneuver, and practice his own particular *Fingerspitzengefühl*. A good marshal could deliver victory; conversely, an inept corps commander could bungle instructions and waste his divisions.

The best example of the corps system at work is the Ulm-Austerlitz campaign (winter 1805) where thanks to timely intelligence reports and semaphoric communications, Napoleon redeployed his army from the Channel port of Boulogne to dissect the Austrian-Russian coalition before they could invade France. The Allies' ponderous approach permitted Napoleon to maneuver aggressively. The Austrian advance was premature, and their communications with their Russian allies scandalously inept. Napoleon dispatched his cavalry corps, led by the madly intrepid Marshal Prince Joachim Murat, to block the passes through the Black Forest; he then maneuvered his remaining

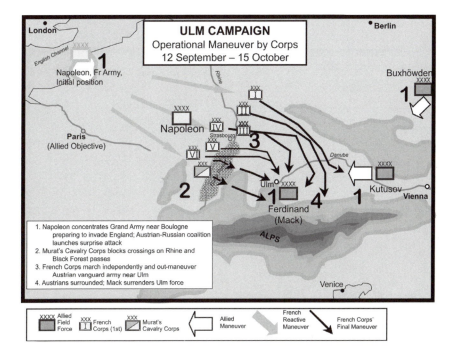

corps to outflank and surround General Baron Mack von Leiberich at the
fortress town of Ulm, northwest of Munich. Marshals Mamont, DeRoi, and
Bernadotte slammed the door shut, preventing any reinforcement or counterattack from Vienna.

The corps system permitted a wide approach followed by a decisive concentration since roads were not clogged with material: "[Napoleon] assigned each
corps an independent line of march, thus ensuring that only a single formation would have to live off the countryside in any given area. He reduced supply trains to a minimum and ordered engineer officers to scout the German
roads."[4] Ulm demonstrated maneuver that smacked of Mongol horse armies
and would not be repeated in style until the blitzkrieg campaigns or Patton's
breakout in Normandy.

FRENCH CAVALRY AT EYLAU, FEBRUARY 7–8, 1807

> Heads up, by God! Those are bullets, not turds!
> —Commander of the Grenadiers à Cheval, during the Battle of Eylau

One of the grandest cavalry charges of the epoch was conducted by
French horse at Eylau, East Prussia, during a terrible snow storm. It was a
see-saw battle, rife with errors as corps commanders lost units in snow flur-
ries and corps were misdirected. Bonaparte, with only two uncommitted
forces (the Guard and Murat's Cavalry Reserve) realized he was in danger

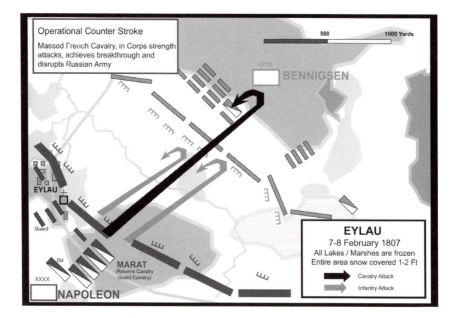

of losing his first important battle. Desperate, Napoleon ordered Murat to attack.

This imposing force, about 10,000 sabers, formed behind the center of the army and then advanced in a menacing parade. The well-known painting by Simon Fort is particularly useful. It avoids romantic portrayal and depicts a cavalry counterstroke in all its drilled complexity. The "charge" resembled rush hour around the Arc de Triomphe. The regiments squeezed together boot to boot, plodding through three-foot snow at a walk or a maneuvering trot at best. This was a professional cavalry charge, all business and emphasizing masse and cohesion over speed.

> At this moment the Emperor, wishing to strike the final blow, ordered Murat with ninety squadrons to advance between Eylau and Rothenen. The terrible weight of this mass broke the Russian centre, upon which it charged with the sabre, and threw it into complete disorder. The brave General d'Hautpoul was killed at the head of his cuirassiers, so also was General Dahlmann, who had succeeded General Morland in the command of the chasseurs of the guard. The success of our cavalry made victory certain.[5]

The snow prevented the Russians from seeing the terrible destruction that rolled toward them; most regiments were swept through and cut up before they could form squares and in some cases squares were broken by Murat's cuirassiers: "The brave phalanx of infantry was soon leveled to the earth like a wheat-field swept by a hurricane."[6] Murat's mass continued, attacking in echelon, hitting the flank of a Russian cavalry division and destroying the entire formation. Murat then advanced upon the main Russian line and overran the artillery, sabering the gunners as they stood by their pieces. The horses and troopers had advanced nearly three kilometers, fighting at regular intervals. Captain Baron Marcellin de Marbot recorded how his charger Lisette was the symbiotic battle partner within the melee:

> The Russian grenadier with redoubled fury made another thrust at me, but, stumbling with the force which he put into it, drove his bayonet into my mare's thigh. Her ferocious instincts being restored by the pain, she sprang at the Russian, and at one mouthful tore off his nose, lips, eyebrows, and all the skin of his face, making of him a living death's-head, dripping with blood. Then hurling herself with fury among the combatants, kicking and biting, Lisette upset everything that she met on her road. The officer who had made so many attempts to strike me tried to hold her by the bridle; she seized him by his belly, and carrying him off with ease, she bore him out of the crush to the foot of the hillock, where, having torn out his entrails and mashed his body under her feet, she left him dying on the snow . . . She continued her rapid course, and went through a hedge. But this last spurt had exhausted Lisette's strength; she had lost much blood, for one of the large veins in her thigh had been divided,

and the poor animal collapsed suddenly and fell on one side, rolling me over on the other.[7]

The attack reached the Russian reserve, broke it, and in a tribute to the high state of training and discipline, re-formed to attack again. The regiments responded to the trumpet call, and charged back through the Russian army, retracing their original approach march. When they reached French lines, they again calmly re-formed. It was an outstanding bit of derring-do and an exemplary operational cavalry attack—controlled, delivered at a tight maneuvering pace, grouped for shock, in succeeding echelon to maintain momentum, and a classic operational piece of war. The maneuver cost Murat 1,500 horsemen but saved the day. This attack is sometimes chastised as a misuse of cavalry. However, criticism ignores the opportunities of cavalry at the corps level. Chandler noted, "Napoleon had good cause to be grateful to his cavalry arm, which now came indisputably into its own as a finely tempered and practically irresistible battle weapon . . . [he had] transformed the French mounted arm from a laughing-stock into a very redoubtable weapon"[8] and, equally important, Bonaparte had transformed the offensive doctrine that governed its employment as a *force de chasse,* an instrument of maneuver warfare, and a *force de rupture.*

BORODINO, SEPTEMBER 1812

> Among all my battles, the worst one was on Borodino field. My army showed that they deserved the Victory; and the Russian Army got the right to be called invincible.
>
> —Napoleon

Borodino's scale and numbers seem to defy mere tactics. The battle required corps-level and army-level resources.[9] Borodino incorporated zones of protective fire connecting dominating strong points much like a *web defense.* Behind the Russian front lay divisions of cavalry and brigades of Cossacks, ready to pounce on isolated units or raid into the French rear areas. They were essentially the same horde of muzhiks that had tormented Frederick 50 years earlier. Cossacks radiated a threat quite out of proportion to their ability or tactical creativity; nevertheless, they worried Bonaparte throughout.

Borodino began with bland maneuver and attacks on the flèches, V-shaped minor redoubts. An ambitious counterattack by Russian cavalry scattered French infantry and savagely handled supporting cavalry; their enthusiastic pursuit was finally checked by Bonaparte's artillery which fired canister into the Russian mass. The struggle for the Raevsky Battery was Borodino's bloody center piece: a giant earthworks incorporating 27 guns and defended by two infantry divisions. The redoubt was captured, lost, and counterattacked.

Bonaparte then launched a great attack with six complete cavalry divisions supported by three divisions of infantry against the Raevsky Battery—referred to by the French as "the Great Redoubt." This was the antithesis of accepted doctrine as cavalry did not attack fixed defenses and certainly not trench lines supported by dug in artillery. It was, technically, *maneuver* in the Alexandrian sense—a frontal attack, taken to bizarre extremes—that smacked of desperation, impulsive logic, and a cruel waste of a maneuver force, for the battlefield was already a charnel house.

The bloodletting was so terrible that by the end of the day both armies were approaching battle exhaustion and on the verge of neuropsychological shock.[10] The Czar's commander, Prince Mikhail Kutuzov, architect of the scorched-earth strategy, remained consistent with his own doctrine: live to fight another day. With the French 700 miles deep inside Russia, Kutusov ordered retreat. In some ways the conduct of Borodino is an awkward precursor to the 1943 Battle of Kursk. The French had learned that Frederick's bitter comment, made after the battle at Zorndorf, was all too true: "It's easier to kill the Russians than to win over them."[11] The Czar's troops had to be beaten down man by man; mortally wounded Russian soldiers would drag themselves a few feet toward the east, simply to be closer to Mother Russia when they died.[12] Brig. Gen. V. J. Esposito and Col. J. R. Elting contend that "Borodino has been magnified—largely through Tolstoy's fiction—into an apocalyptic struggle. Losses were heavy—between 28,000 and 31,000 French and more than 45,000 Russians—but actually Wagram was a greater and more sternly contested battle."[13] But Borodino was decided by a cavalry attack.

THE LAST ACT: CAVALRY AT WATERLOO, JUNE 18, 1815

> War is a strange art: I have fought sixty big battles and learnt nothing beyond what I knew already at the first.
>
> —Napoleon

Napoleon's conducting at Waterloo was no better than his direction at Borodino. His health was much worse, causing him to be absent during key tactical instances of the battle; he also exhibited lapses of operational judgment. In fairness, that the French army arrived to fight a major battle is a tribute to Napoleon, and certainly the general staff he recreated. Facing a determined coalition of four major powers, the emperor's solution was to strike north and engage the Prussian army (Field Marshal Blücher), then turn on the British army (Wellington) and drive it into the Channel. He could then pirouette and snarl at the approaching Russian and Austrian forces. Experience advocated that if the Prussians and British were crushed, the war-weary eastern Europeans would agree to a compromise. All Bonaparte required was time.

La Grande Armée struck north, appearing in Belgium and smartly brought the Prussians into a battle—not particularly decisive, but nevertheless a victory and one that rattled the European parliaments and stock exchanges. The problems began with the operational follow-up. The pursuit was uninspired; Napoleon did not unleash his army to devour Blücher, and he did not instill a sense of urgency into Marshal Grouchy, who was more content to follow the Prussians rather than ride them down. With Grouchy was nearly a third of Bonaparte's army[14]—a force he would desperately need at Waterloo but which would not figure in the battle in any context.

Wellington had decided to defend on a gentle ridge that was prominent enough to give his artillery a slight edge. In front of this position lay a series of walled farms and châteaux that the duke ordered occupied and prepared for defense. A heavy rain during the night made the ground unsuitable for maneuver. Napoleon lost most of the morning waiting for the fields to dry. He had a simple plan—a left hook against Hougoumont to occupy Wellington's attention and draw off his reserves, followed by an attack at the left center with D'Orlon's Corps, which should crush the Allied army. Napoleon ordered a *Grande Batterie* formed directly behind D'Erlon's front. The cannonade was devastating, and British regiments were ordered to lay down to avoid the fire.

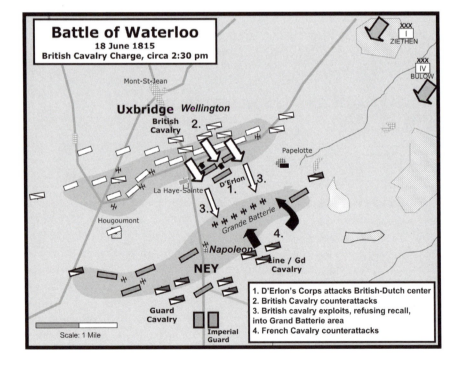

D'ERLON AND *LE FEU DE BILLEBAUDE*

Finally, when the ground had dried somewhat, Bonaparte ordered D'Erlon forward, supported by Milhaud's 4th Cavalry Corps including eight regiments of cuirassiers. This attack was conducted in the best French tradition of *feu de billebaude*. The corps advanced with a noisy, nerve wracking determination: drums beating the *pas de charge*, skirmishers forward, random shooting from the packed columns, and the constant shouts of *Vive l'Empereur!* British infantry, most of them veterans of the Spanish campaign, had seen it before and coolly waited until the French closed range and then began a lively platoon fire. D'Erlon's brigades paused but did not stop. Supported by batteries of 12 pounders, a second effort by the French would indeed create *une rupture*. It was then that they heard the trumpets and the awful pounding of hundreds of horses. Veterans of Salamanca quickly understood that it was the British cavalry charge.

Wellington had unleashed the Earl of Uxbridge's heavies. Seven regiments of British dragoons (Somerset's Household Brigade and Ponsonby's Union Brigade) moved forward progressing from walk to trot to canter. In the center, D'Erlon's left, the Household Cavalry (Life Guards, Horse Guards, and Dragoon Guards) swept over the crest, surprising the 1st Cavalry Brigade (Dubois) and cutting it apart. The cuirassiers broke and Somerset's regiments went after them, sabering coincidental infantry. A few squadrons actually reached the *Grande Batterie*, overrunning two troops. Ponsonby's Union Brigade advanced through its own infantry. Even though the Scots Greys, in distinctive bearskins and mounted on impressive alabaster gray horses, were not in the Household division, they certainly behaved as elite cavalry. "Ces terribles chevaux gris! Comme ils travaillent!" (Those terrible grey horses, how they strive!) groused Napoleon.[15]

Despite Lady Butler's famous painting, the Greys approached the French at a very controlled trot—some suggest at a walk. They lunged forward and began to hack away until the French broke. Exuberance did them in. British cavalry, notoriously brave but undisciplined, ignored a series of recalls ordered by Uxbridge. They cut down all before them until Napoleon had enough and ordered Baron Jacquinot (1st Cavalry Division) to send in a brigade of lancers. Then the party ended. A vengeful hurricane of fresh *lanciers* tore into the British dragoons, sticking senior officers and troopers as they attempted withdrawal. Wellington lost almost a third of his cavalry, 2,500 horsemen; his heavies were not to play any further role in the battle. The French lost 3,000 men and two Eagles, which were the only Eagles taken during the entire Waterloo campaign.

The British charge was judiciously ordered and perfectly executed; its pursuit, however, was discomfiting. The cavalry heard *recall* several times but

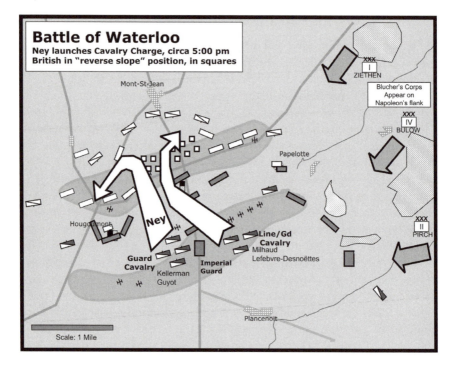

Battle of Waterloo
Ney launches Cavalry Charge, circa 5:00 pm
British in "reverse slope" position, in squares

refused to comply. A brilliant counterattack turned into an uncontrolled rampage that was the converse of how veteran cavalry should behave.

CAVALRY DOCTRINE CONSIDERED

In terms of cavalry doctrine, this was a tactical event with operational consequences, for it delayed the battle, forced a change in Napoleon's operational plan, and caused a complex third stage of operations. It doubled the pressure on Bonaparte and likely induced his physical discomfort. The emperor was already aware that Blücher was marching toward his flank, for Prussian vanguards were appearing in the far distance. Grouchy, obstinately and doggedly following Napoleon's instructions to the letter, opted to ignore common sense as well as his own staff's pleas and steadfastly refused to march west. He could have cut off Blücher as well as arrived to turn Wellington's flank.

In hindsight, Wellington's reaction was small potatoes compared to Eylau, and had the British been better disciplined and, more importantly, had the cavalry attacked in echelon, Napoleon may have been swept off the battlefield well before the Prussians appeared. Wellington did not appear to have the inclination or the force to order an operational counterstroke, but he certainly had the opportunity. With 11 cavalry brigades (32 regiments) and 44 horse guns under Uxbridge, Wellington had the means to organize a *force de rup-*

ture. He had roughly the same resources available to his opposite number, the equivalent of three corps of cavalry or 14,500 warhorses against Napoleon's 15,500.[16]

Bonaparte became focused, if not desperate, and ordered a coordinated assault on the British center. It worked well. Having savaged the British by *la Grande Batterie,* which systematically destroyed British artillery in counter-battery fire, he then went on to shatter battalion after battalion with round shot and canister; the allied infantry fell back before well-supported attacks by the French brigades. By 3 P.M. Wellington had had enough; he ordered the allied line to withdraw 300 yards north and occupy a new position behind the ridge in dead ground. This was the origin of the much emphasized reverse slope position taught in war colleges. The theory is simply that a crest prevents direct observation and accurate fire. If the enemy advances, he is surprised by the defense, subject to directed fire while his own forces are incapable of giving support. This is as true of tanks versus anti-tank guns or missiles in the Middle East and Normandy as it was in Belgium in 1815.

NEY'S CHARGE

> There ensued a most terrible silence; then, all at once, a long file of uplifted arms, brandishing sabres, appeared above the crest, and casques, trumpets, and standards, and three thousand heads with gray mustaches, shouting, "Vive l'Empereur!" All this cavalry debouched on the plateau, and it was like the appearance of an earthquake.
>
> —Victor Hugo, *Les Misérables*

> La Cavalerie parait, de toutes les armes, la plus difficile à manier. (Cavalry seems, of all the arms, the most difficult to manage.)
>
> —Jacquenot de Presle

The causes of this most famous charge are mostly speculative. Bonaparte was ill and indisposed; when he finally realized there was a charge taking place, his only reported comment was that it was "an hour too early." Other explanations include Marshal Ney's personality and state of mind; he was furious at the success of the British cavalry charge and misinterpreted Wellington's tactical repositioning for a general British retreat. There appeared, as well, to be a clear gap in the center of the allied line. It should be appreciated that though the allied army fell back the equivalent of three football fields, the ridge crest was still covered by swarms of skirmishers, keeping in contact with the French. It should also be noted that Ney simply ordered one of Milhaud's brigades forward to test the situation. However, in rebuttal, in a display of *Fingerspitzengefühl* gone awry, he also ordered a cuirassier brigade to charge, hoping to instigate a British rout.

Herein lies an alternative explanation of this lamentable horse drama: as Milhaud's cuirassiers escalated from walk to canter in what should have been a relatively minor brigade escapade, the one act drama spiraled into a Wagnerian production: "Division after Division was drawn into the battle. Lefebvre-Desnouettes followed Milhaud's cuirassier Corps, and by 4 P.M. all of 5,000 French cavalry, both heavy and light—were pounding towards the crest, towards the Allied right center."[17] As the French tidal wave broke over the crest they were presented with a daunting panorama of the British, not in retreat but formed in steady squares, bristling with bayonets. The thunderous French assault was delivered at the trot, perhaps a controlled canter, though some regiments may have been at the gallop; this would have been difficult because of the soft ground and sunken road near the crest of the ridge. The French rode into a prepared kill zone: "For a full hour surge after surge of French cavalry beat like twelve waves against the lines of squares—unavailingly, for, despite mounting losses, they stood firm."[18]

In *Les Misérables,* Victor Hugo made much of a deep-set road that was yet another culprit in foxing the cavalry attack:

> Unexpected, yawning, directly under the horses' feet, two fathoms deep between its double slopes; the second file pushed the first into it, and the third pushed on the second; the horses reared and fell backward, landed on their haunches, slid down, all four feet in the air, crushing and overwhelming the riders . . . horses and riders rolled there pell-mell, grinding each other, forming but one mass of flesh in this gulf: when this trench was full of living men, the rest marched over them and passed on. Almost a third of Dubois' brigade fell into that abyss. This began the loss of the battle.[19]

A sunken lane did exist but, as David Chandler noted, it has been "elaborated into a hidden ravine".[20] The French cavalry gave it a solid effort, but finally exhausted by their ride and the demonic reel around the squares, inadvertently accompanied by Scottish piping, they stopped: "The horses of the first rank of cuirassiers, in spite of all efforts of their riders, came to a stand-still, shaking and covered with foam."[21] To their credit, the regiments rallied, re-formed, and prepared to do it all again, even as the subsequent waves approached. The attack was joined by the rest of the cavalry reserve, as well as the guard cavalry, which included a squadron of the *Lanciers Polonaise,* the only French cavalry units to have charged in full dress uniform.

CAVALRY VERSUS SQUARES

> The horses resisted all attempts to force them to charge the line of serried steel.
> —Capt. Rees H. Gronow

Waterloo, like Russia and Spain, was another graveyard of horses. For decades visitors were sold helmets and cuirassiers by local farmers; horseshoes from the battlefield adorned hundreds of portals throughout the Lowlands and England. The issue of repeatedly charging steady squares is cited as an example of wasted bravado, frustrated desperation, and useless doctrine. Nothing could be further from the reality of cavalry warfare. The essence of the *coup d'oeil* or *Fingerspitzengefühl* is the ability to read the enemy. Some regiments are ready to be broken; their posture and the look in their eye betrays a brave facade—a nudge and they collapse. Secondly, a determined assault by zealous cavalry can destroy confidence, wreck morale, and cause a rout:

> Not a man present who survived could have forgotten in after life the awful grandeur of that charge. You perceived in the distance what appeared to be an overwhelming, long moving line, which, ever advancing, glittered like a stormy wave of the sea when it catches the sunlight.[22]

Eylau, Borodino, and a host of other examples show that squares were broken by cavalry as a matter of course. This is best done with supporting horse artillery firing canister but is also effected by lancers using their weapons with determined skill. A 12- to 16-foot lance has the advantage over musket with bayonet. Further, once the musket has been fired the infantry must either reload or stand firm and in either situation they risk being stuck or killed. Courageous lancers can break a square, and so can aggressive heavy cavalry; at Hof (1809) General D'Hautpol's cuirassiers "smashed all resistance by brute force, jabbing at the enemy faces with their sword-points, breaking down an infantry square, pressing their powerful horses through the line of guns and riding down the gunners."[23]

It is moot to comment on Bonaparte's inability to control this battle, although Wellington dryly noted, "Napoleon did not maneuver at all. He contented himself with advancing in the old style, in columns, and was driven off in the old style."[24] Napoleon allegedly stated once that the only real influence a commander has on the conduct of a battle is where and when to use his reserve. Bonaparte watched his cavalry ride away, frittered away his Guard and then in the end, sent but a portion of it into his last counterattack. He had also glibly quipped, "Never interrupt your enemy when he is making a mistake," which Wellington accomplished, if only by a strategy of reaction. Napoleon's subsequent analysis of Waterloo offered two reasons for his defeat:

> The chief causes of the loss of that battle were, first of all, Grouchy's great tardiness and neglect in executing his orders; next, the 'grenadiers à cheval' and the

cavalry under General Guyot, which I had in reserve, and which were never to leave me, engaged without orders and without my knowledge; so that after the last charge.[25]

THE NAPOLEONIC CAVALRY GENERAL

> In victory, you deserve Champagne; in defeat, you need it.
> —Napoleon Bonaparte, *Mémoires*

The profitable ployment and manipulation of cavalry depends on a delicate mix of leadership, doctrine, and warhorse. Cavalry particularly requires spirited, dynamic leadership from the front. It is not simply a case of preparedness to die heroically; the leader must ride well and inspire his command. A poor cavalier cannot be a tactical leader and should be kept at a discrete distance from his troops. Napoleon was better off at his *quartier général* than at the head of the Guard cavalry: "Napoleon rode like a butcher . . . whilst galloping, his body rolled backwards and forwards and sideways, according to the speed of his horse."[26] Nonetheless, Bonaparte conducted his own reconnaissance, often accompanied by only a half squadron of *Chasseurs à Cheval*. Napoleon's coolness under fire and the willingness to go forward and risk danger magnified his reputation within the ranks. Cavalry commanders are as unpredictable as their horses and their conduct includes terms like courageous and brilliant as well as "stupid but lucky."

Joachim Napoléon Murat, Marshal of France, Grand Duke of Cleves, and King of Naples, was a splendid warrior obsessed with Napoleon and elaborate costume—his uniforms bordered on the outrageous. He would have ended as an object of ridicule were it not for his surreal bravery (he once led a corps charge brandishing a riding crop) and string of victories. Murat was well understood by his imperial mentor:

> He was a paladin in the field but in the cabinet destitute of either decision or judgment; he loved, I would rather say, adored me; he was my right arm, but without me he was nothing. In battle he was perhaps the bravest man in the world; left to himself he was an imbecile without judgment.[27]

The archetypal cavalier, Antoine Charles, Comte de LaSalle, was a complex mélange of passion and fashion.[28] LaSalle led from the front and saw combat in 29 battles, including Austerlitz and Wagram. He received a dozen wounds and was captured twice: "A man of surpassing talent; his mind and learnings are no less deep than brilliant."[29] LaSalle benefited from genial publicity—the painting of him by the academician François Flameng is regularly selected to depict the nonchalant officer of hussars. LaSalle's quips have become legend: "Un hussard qui n'est pas mort à trente ans est un jean foutre" (Any hussar who isn't dead by 30 is a wanker). Despite this caveat, LaSalle lived to the age of 34, dying at the head of his cavalry, leading a gratuitous charge at the end of the battle of Wagram in 1809.

The important aspect of the battle is that cavalry is foremost a physical force dominated by psychosomatic obsessions. While it may be a tactical or operational arm, it is also a mercurial creature and affected by psychological as much as technological or tactical principles. Like its generals, it is often unpredictable.

Chapter 8

The Industrialized Warhorse: From Balaclava to Gettysburg

> In a charge, the trooper is merely a projectile, the saber its point.
> —2nd Lt. George S. Patton, Jr., Master of the Sword, 15th Cavalry, 1914[1]

The Romantic movement was very popular in the cavalry. The emphasis on emotion and aestheticism appealed to the temperament of the horseman. The military found comfort in any epistemology that advocated tradition and uniformity. The significance of historical and natural inevitability ornamented with heroic models nicely buttressed the style and mannerisms of the cavalry. The second Industrial Revolution (ca. 1850) did in Romanticism and forever changed the conduct of warfare. The most obvious and impressive aspect was the steam engine, which led to railroads and the opportunity for tightly planned strategic deployment. In 1853 Capt. Claude-Etienne Minié invented an elongated bullet that expanded in the barrel upon firing, filling rifled grooves and dramatically improving infantry's lethality. Loading was easier and faster but the great technological improvement was range and accuracy.

> This was the second great blow that the cavalry received through the introduction of gunpowder . . . this second invention trebled the range . . . the rapidity of fire has been increased fourfold, so that a body of cavalry charging upon infantry would now have to run the gauntlet of at least ten shots, well aimed, where in the time of Frederick the Great or Napoleon, one volley alone could be fired.[2]

The Minié rifle was first used against Russian troops in the Crimean War where, despite the increasing influence of industrialized military technology, European cavalry gave the eighteenth century one last tumble. It was a bitter-sweet experience and became the stuff of legend.

BALACLAVA: *C'EST MAGNIFIQUE, MAIS CE N'EST PAS LA GUERRE*

> Ah, steeds, steeds, what steeds! Has the whirlwind a home in your manes? Is there a sensitive ear, alert as a flame, in your every fiber? Hearing the familiar song from above, all in one accord you strain your bronze chests and, hooves barely touching the ground, turn into straight lines cleaving the air.
>
> —Nikolai Gogol, *Dead Souls*

The Crimean War is a worthy study for modern staff officers struggling with coalition warfare in a desolate place. The Charge of the Light Brigade cannot be ignored, if only to serve as a splendid bad example. It survives because of a bizarre cavalry nostalgia that chooses to revel in the glory of a disciplined body of horse that followed the orders of its commander despite the coercion of common sense. Notwithstanding the effects of industrialism, the cavalry appeared with all the bling and accoutrements any romantic could hope for.

The tactical situation on October 20, 1854, was that a successful Russian probe had caught the allied command napping, secured a dominating piece of ground, and surprised several redoubts, capturing the guns. This was embarrassing. Confusion and imprecise orders resulted in two separate charges on either side of the captured ridge. This dearth of command control is mocked by the fact that the senior staff sat on a good piece of ground and could observe the maneuver terrain at leisure. The two British cavalry brigades watched the events with both anxious hearts and rising anger at the inactivity of their commanders, visible behind them, arguing over what was to be done.

THE OTHER CHARGE: CAVALRY VERSUS CAVALRY

> Russian officers said the extraordinary unhurried deliberation displayed in the movements of the tiny British force had done much to shake Russian morale.
>
> —Cecil Woodham-Smith of the Heavy Brigade, *The Reason Why*

> The most difficult position a cavalry officer can be placed in is in command of cavalry against cavalry; for the slightest fault committed may be punished on the spot.
>
> —Captain Lewis Edward Nolan, 15th Hussars

The Charge of the Light Brigade was preceded by the Charge of the Heavy Brigade; both attacks advanced on parallel lines, bisected by the ridge that guaranteed tactical isolation for each group. The stationary Heavy Brigade was suddenly approached by a mass of Russian cavalry. The brigade's commander, General Scarlett, owned eight squadrons or about 500 horses but was faced with a multitude of 4,000 mounted Russians. Scarlett decided he would charge.

The heavies' attack was nattily delivered; the disciplined regiments advanced at the walk, trot, canter, and then gallop. Scarlett's impetuosity resulted in his reaching the Russian mass well ahead of his brigade, which had to pick their way through vineyards before forming attack lines. The Russians, perplexed by the sight, stopped. They then watched as the British "crashed furiously into the Russian mass, and the wild sound of their battle cries floated up to the heights, the Irish yell of the Inniskillings and the fierce growling 'moan' of the Scots Greys."[3] The Greys, now sporting even larger bearskins, were called by the French cavalry *les grenadiers à cheval*. It was a compliment, and if not initially intended as such, soon proved correct. The Heavy Brigade hit the Russians with enough force to create confusion, then panic.

"It was a heavy Dragoon's dream of a lifetime come true," one participant recalled: "I never in my life experienced such a sublime sensation as in the moment of the charge. Some fellows speak of it as being demoniac."[4] The result was an unexpected triumph and often described as one of the greatest feats of cavalry against cavalry in the history of Europe. This success infuriated James Brudenell Lord Cardigan, the commander of the Light Brigade. He was given command because of his political clout and conducted himself in the most spoiled style. Cardigan lived aboard his private yacht while his regiments endured the severe Crimean weather. It is believed the chilled Brudenell ordered his sweaters tailored to allow them to be used as a coat; this front-buttoned apparel became known as the *cardigan*.

Brudenell now faced a classic situation; a sudden savage pursuit by light cavalry, judging by Russian confusion, could have broken the front. A steadfast adherence to orders, or the dearth of them, became the handy explanation by senior commanders both immediately after the action and in subsequent libel trials in England. The British cavalry argued, with some logic, that the unfortunate battle was due to confused directives. When the Russians began hauling away British guns as war prizes, Lord Raglan ordered the Light Brigade to stop them. However Lord Cardigan's attention was fixed on the valley to his front, which featured a large Russian battery. Instead of turning right to rescue the English guns on the redoubts, or follow up Scarlett's success, he advanced unflinchingly into the jaws of death.

THE LIGHT BRIGADE: *C'EST MAGNIFIQUE, MAIS . . .*

> Death loves a crowd.
> —Colour Sergeant Timothy Gowing, Crimea, 1854

The attack, by the most splendid-looking cavalry in the world, defied logic, certainly broke every cavalry doctrine imaginable, and most astounding,

Cardigan's force actually reached the guns. The Russian battery comprised 12 unlimbered cannon; there were 14 more guns and cavalry on the Fedioukine Hills on the left flank. The approach, a mile across an open valley dominated by enemy on either side as well as on the objective, was swept by fire:

> The guns on our front were playing on us with round-shot and shell, so the number of men and horses falling increased every moment. I rode near the right of the line. A corporal who rode on the right was struck by a shot or shell full in the face, completely smashing it, his blood and brains bespattering us who rode near. . . We were now fully exposed to the fire from all three batteries, front, right, and left, as also from the infantry on our right. . . As we drew nearer, the guns in the front plied us liberally with grape and canister, which brought down men and horses in heaps.[5]

The brigade was not up to strength: "cholera and dysentery having taken their toll—the five regiments could muster only about seven hundred all ranks, both regiments in the first line, the 17th Lancers and the 13th Light Dragoons were led by captains."[6] The advance was a model of controlled precision; even when the first artillery fire fell around them, the brigade continued in good order, at a steady trot, increasing speed to canter, and then as canister riddled their ranks, into a final desperate charge. One French observer described it as a terrible and bloody steeplechase. A captain in the 13th Light Dragoons noted, "The men behaved splendidly. The last thing I heard before I went down was one man saying to his neighbour, 'Come on; don't let those b—ds [the 17th Lancers] get ahead of us.'"[7] As the thinning lines approached the Russian guns one command was echoed: "'Close in! Close in!'"[8] The brigade's effort would have been bloodier had not the 4th *Chasseurs D'Afrique* delivered a supporting charge.

General Bosquet was forced to utter his immortal critique: "C'est magnifique, mais ce n'est pas la guerre" (It is magnificent, but it is not war).[9] The five regiments thundered into the battery and "fell upon the gunners with a frightening savagery and massacred them with the ferocious excitement of Samurai."[10] The astounding success was short-lived as there was a formidable body of three squadrons of lancers to the rear of the guns. At first the Russians were awestruck, then their officers recovered and with a simple *Davai!* (Give it to 'em!) counterattacked.

As the Light Brigade fell back along the line of retirement they were harassed by Cossacks engaged in pillage and killing dismounted and wounded men. In all, over 500 horses were killed. Of the 673 men who had charged down the valley less than 200 had returned. The Russians were much moved even though Gen. Pavel Liprandi at first thought the English cavalry were all drunk. He later told the brigade's survivors, his prisoners, that they were noble fellows, and that he was very sorry for them. Pemberton's analysis of the charge bears citing: "For the Light Brigade it was less a test of courage than discipline.

Courage can stem from an instinctive resolve to live or can be inspired by rage ... Discipline on the other hand is never instinctive: it can be acquired only the hard way."[11]

AMERICAN INDUSTRIALIZED CAVALRY

The Army of the Potomac made only five cavalry charges during large battles before 1864, all of them very small by Napoleonic standards. It was therefore unsurprising that they won little success with this particular tactic.

—Paddy Griffith

The scope of the Civil War was beyond anything European, save for Bonaparte's far-flung campaigns. The general staffs of both armies conducted concurrent operations on several fronts in addition to naval campaigns. Nevertheless, the European strategist of the nineteenth century, *Generalfeldmarschall* Graf von Moltke, sneered that the Civil War was not worth study by the Prussian general staff, since it was nothing but "two armed mobs chasing each other around the country, from which nothing could be learned."[12] Despite a condescending attitude, the European armies kept a close and interested watch. Mobs of aristocrats and government pooh-bahs attended the headquarters of both Union and Confederate armies and duly sent off detailed reports.

The Civil War resurrected a devastating medieval tactic: the *chevauchée*. The carnage and chaos wrought by Confederate, but particularly Union, expeditions served to both break the rural morale and deny governments vital resources. They were conducted with the same cruel enthusiasm that marked the Black Prince's forays into the Loire valley. The Continental dismissing of Union cavalry operations as nothing but a series of armed raids appears contrived. While raiding was perhaps too great an occupation and acquired legendary status via General Sherman's march to the sea, there were cavalry battles of note. The Continental sniff at American cavalry was perhaps based on its apparent rude origins and enthusiasm for practical weapons like pistols and Spencer rifles vis-à-vis the saber or lance. Available technology made the battlefield deceptive; a panoramic view would suggest little had changed, tactically or physically, from the armies of the Napoleonic era; historian Paddy Griffith correctly describes the U.S. Civil War as "the Last Napoleonic War." The Union soldier was better off than any Napoleonic grenadier: tinned foods, waterproofed ground sheets, canteens, and well-soled boots. Conversely, he faced deadlier conditions on the field of battle.

The American cavalry did not emulate European cavalry. Republican virtues and Yankee practicality resulted in no uhlans or hussars, and certainly no cuirassiers. There was no dominant saber tradition; the American weapon was the gun—from the Revolution's Kentucky long rifle to buffalo gun to Winchester. American cavalry was raised as carbine toting dragoons.[13]

The cavalry weapon of choice was the Sharps New Model 1859 carbine. The shorter breech loader was ideal for mounted use. In the early years of the war, Southern cavalry was as well armed as the Union, and many regiments went to war with sawed off shotguns firing buckshot, preferred for the melee. By the end of the Civil War, Union cavalry had a decided advantage over the South. Low industrial capability and naval blockade introduced technological imbalance—a situation unknown in Napoleonic campaigns.

Despite the penchant for rifles and pistols, the saber continued to be widely used even though experience proved that *l'arme blanche* was less effective than hand guns in the mounted attack. Records show that fewer than a thousand saber wounds were treated in federal hospitals during four years of combat. Confederate cavalier Col. John Mosby, whose prowess in raiding caused Lincoln to dub him "the Gray Ghost," commented: "We had been furnished with sabers before we left Abingdon, but the only real use I ever heard of their being put to was to hold a piece of meat over a fire for frying."[14]

ORGANIZING AMERICAN CAVALRY IN THE CIVIL WAR

> If you want to have a good time, jine the cavalry! Jine the cavalry! Jine the cavalry!
> If you want to catch the Devil ... If you want to smell Hell, Jine the cavalry!
> —Confederate cavalry song, Gen. J.E.B. Stuart's favorite

In 1861, although the continent appeared crisscrossed with railroads, the horse was still an operational requirement. Compared to Europe, which was thoroughly settled with vast agricultural regions, the American landscape was a wilderness. The eastern states, although cultivated, did not enjoy the complex road network of Western Europe; operational maneuver would require immense wagon trains to support the movement of industrialized armies.

The enormous numbers of horses and mules essential to operations resulted in rapid expansion of quartermaster depots and an assembly-line process of acquisition, training, and delivery of warhorses to fighting regiments. There were only three qualified veterinarians immediately available for the Northern cavalry. The Revolutionary War allotment of one farrier per squadron (1791) eventually became the Veterinary Corps. Military farriers were temporarily abandoned after 1812 and redesignated when regular cavalry regiments were reconstituted in the 1830s. Private ownership had been encouraged early in the war but proved impractical. The Confederacy ended the practice in 1863. In the first half of the war, Union mounted assets were managed badly by masses of hurriedly mobilized men who did not properly care for the horses. Rail transportation was crude and often caused injuries. Physical breakdown, exhaustion, and disease were common. After the Gettysburg campaign, en masse procurement resulted in additional veterinary problems, even in the agricultural South. A serious glanders epidemic ("the great glanders epizootic") killed an enormous number of horses. In just over a year the Lynchburg Quartermaster's stables lost 5,875 horses to disease—3,000 died, and another 450 were shot, leaving 1,000 for the cavalry.

THE WARHORSE IN OPERATIONS

> Will you pardon me for asking what the horses of your army have done since the battle of Antietam that fatigues anything?
> —Abraham Lincoln to Gen. George B. McClellan, 1862

European dismissal of American cavalry operations as a series of raiding campaigns is harsh but is not completely unfair. Northern cavalry did not evolve into an effective force until 1864; prior to this it had been playing catch-up to the Confederacy, which had stressed major cavalry operations from the outset. Southern cavalry demonstrated competence and near reckless bravado. The regiments were grouped into brigades and permitted considerable independent initiative. Confederate operational maneuver groups conducted deep raids into Union rear areas augmenting reconnaissance with captured supplies. Even more valuable was the psychological effect on political leadership and civilian centers. Raids by Gen. J.E.B. Stuart drew Washington's attention away from strategic goals and diverted large bodies of troops away from the front to conduct rear area security operations and chase Confederate regiments about the countryside.

The prelude to the decisive Gettysburg campaign featured a gradual evolution to excellence by Union cavalry and intrepid holding actions by Confederate horsed formations, which were initially the better strike force. The battle at Brandy Station (June 8–9, 1863) was the largest cavalry action of the Civil War and considered the opening engagement of the Gettysburg campaign. Union cavalry, commanded by Maj. Gen. Alfred Pleasonton, gamely took on the crème de la crème of Southern horse commanded by the legendary Gen. James Ewell Brown (J.E.B.) Stuart. The battle marked a turning point; the Confederate horse passed the zenith of its command of the battlefield, and the Union horse was on the ascendancy.

Hubris, it may be argued, preceded the fall. Prior to the campaign Stuart reportedly requested a review of his mounted force by Gen. Robert E. Lee; it was a splendid affair. At the walk and again at the canter, 9,000 horsemen with batteries of horse artillery paraded past their commander in chief. This proud procession was observed by Union scouts, reconnoitering for Major General Pleasonton's field force of 8,000 cavalry, just across the Rappahannock. What they actually saw is speculative; neither Stuart nor Lee was imprudent enough to concentrate their entire operational reserve for a theatrical display.[15] The Union commander immediately schemed to make two crossings to envelope then annihilate the Confederate force, trapping them between his two pincers. The maneuver caught Stuart off guard. The audacity demonstrated surprised his command psychologically and physically; Stuart's headquarters were overrun, and his rear areas penetrated. Reinforcements appeared in time to force a 12-hour battle where fortunes appeared and ebbed. The furious fighting included attack and counterattack with rifle, pistol, and sword.

> We dashed at them, squadron front with drawn sabres, and as we flew along— our men yelling like demons—grape and canister were poured into our left flank and a storm of rifle bullets on our front. . . . many of our horses and men piled up in a writhing mass in those ditches and were ridden over. . . . we dashed on, driving the Rebels into and through the woods, our men fighting with the sabre alone, whilst they used principally pistols. Our brave fellows cut them out of the saddle and fought like tigers, until I discovered they were on both flanks, pouring a cross fire of carbines and pistols on us, and then tried to rally my men and make them return the fire with their carbines.[16]

Finally, Pleasonton withdrew across the river giving Stuart a tactical but discomforting victory. He had been surprised and temporarily outmaneuvered. These were cardinal sins for a force of cavalry.

The Gettysburg Campaign (July 1–3, 1863) is carefully studied by modernists for it is both an example of maneuver, and, it may be argued, a version of deep battle. This was the second demonstration of an audacious operational style by Lee. In 1862 he penetrated into Maryland and won a series of engagements culminating with the battle of Antietam.

Gen. Robert E. Lee's military skill was both enhanced by the questionable tactics of his opponents and diminished by the inept conduct of some subordinates, including his cavalry commander. Penetration into Union rear areas boldly outflanked the Rappahannock-Potomac lines and Washington itself. Unfortunately, Lee's cavalry conducted itself as a grand *chevauchée*. It did not provide the first duty of an operational force of cavalry—complete reconnaissance and sterile screening. Lee was left blind, feeling for the Northern forces with infantry fingers. The criticism of Civil War cavalry—that it was primarily a raiding force—seems apropos in this campaign. However, the performance of Union cavalry established them as a force to be reckoned with. The regiments, rejuvenated and retrained after earlier disappointing efforts, did yeoman work as a delay force, flank guard, and finally as a *force de frappe* in a cavalry versus cavalry effort.

Brigadier General Stuart's cavalry did not contribute until the second day of the battle. He had taken Lee's best maneuver force (three good brigades) on an inconsequential raid around the Union right flank. The dashing Stuart galloped out of contact, then finally reappeared leading a lumbering cavalcade of liberated Union supply wagons. He was given an acerbic reprimand. The vexed Lee ordered Stuart to screen his left and to threaten the Union flank and rear areas. This mission could have played havoc with communications and demoralized the North, already flustered by the Confederate threat to the capital. Worse, Stuart's cavalry was depleted (less than 3,500 sabers and 13 guns); the horses and troopers were fatigued after their too long and ineffective *chevauchée*. It is a matter of speculation what might have transpired had Stuart coordinated his maneuver with General Lee's intent and struck at the rear of the federal army in concert with frontal assaults.

Maj. Gen. Alfred Pleasonton's Cavalry Corps was the maneuver force for Gen. George Meade's Army of the Potomac. Two divisions were available for the battle; approximately 3,200 Union cavaliers confronted Stuart, who had become the antithesis of the Confederate cavalry maxim on mounted victory: "Git thar fustest with the mostest." The maxim is properly attributed to Confederate *beau sabreur* and perhaps the best cavalier of the war, Gen. Nathan Bedford Forrest. He credited his mounted successes because he "got there first with the most men." Gettysburg was a cavalry juxtaposition of fortunes: the Union's best day and the South's least productive mounted effort. Not only were Stuart's troopers beaten in the field, his flamboyant horse artillery was bested by Union horse gunners in a battery duel.

EAST CAVALRY FIELD

Action in the East Cavalry Field (July 3, 1863) simply confirmed what Brandy Station had implied—Union cavalry had come of age. Even more important was the technological factor. Northern cavalry, armed with Spencer repeaters, easily held their own in a skirmish line or cavalry-versus-cavalry duels. Valiant charges and countercharges were conducted. Days before the battle, General Meade promoted George Armstrong Custer to brevet brigadier, making him one of the youngest generals in the army at 23.[17] Custer established himself as the too brave, near reckless cavalier. But it was exactly that sort of example that the horse brigades needed in a big-time cavalry contest: "As the two columns approached each other the pace of each increased, when suddenly a crash, like the falling of timber, betokened the crisis. So sudden and violent was the collision that many of the horses were turned end over end and crushed their riders beneath them."[18] The battle was indecisive but its strategic implications were significant. It ensured no chaos in the Union rear areas, no Confederate operational maneuver group to cause panic in Washington.

A second cavalry action (South Cavalry Field) took place on July 3, 1863, after the infamous Pickett's Charge had been defeated in the central part of the battlefield. It was essentially a reconnaissance in force. A series of ill-conceived charges against Confederate infantry wasted a first-rate force of cavalry. It was an unfortunate conclusion to a campaign that was virtually won and had previously demonstrated accomplishment for Union horse. Union cavalry operations would take on a more dramatic and strategic tone after General Grant took command of the Union armies and brought with him Gen. Philip Sheridan to lead the Union mounted force.

THE ADVENT OF GRANT: SHERIDAN UNLEASHED

Come tighten your girth and slacken your rein;
Come buckle your blanket and holster again;
Try the click of your trigger and balance your blade,
For he must ride sure that goes riding a raid.

—Civil War soldier's ditty

The change in the Union's operational art included elevating the cavalry art. The primary missions of reconnaissance and screen were set aside in favor of creating an operational strike force that could deliver strategic results. General Grant gave Sheridan authority to strike south in Attila tradition. Sheridan promptly invaded Virginia with 10,000 horses, savaged Stuart's depots, and enticed the Confederate cavalry commander into battle (Yellow Tavern, May 1864). It was the gallant Stuart's last action, for he was mortally wounded, appropriately, in a cavalry charge led by George Custer.

Grant then directed Sheridan into the Shenandoah Valley *chevauchée* where Union troops successively destroyed crops and livestock which was devastating for Lee's armies. The key action was the Battle of Opequon (also referred to as the Third Battle of Winchester, September 19, 1864). Sheridan's two corps initially caught Gen. Jubal Early's divisions dispersed, but the two commanders soon concentrated east of Winchester. The cavalry actions were conducted with inspired élan in the bloodiest traditions of any Napoleonic action:

At the sound of the bugle we took the trot, the gallop, and then the charge. As we neared their line we were welcomed by a fearful musketry fire . . . [the] officers cried out, "Forward! Forward!" The men raised their sabers, and responded to the command with deafening cheers. . . In a moment we were face to face with the enemy. They stood as if awed . . . and in an instant broke in complete rout, our men sabering them as they vainly sought safety in flight.[19]

Sheridan called the battle a splendid tactical victory. His initial frontal was followed by a left flanking while his cavalry tormented the Confederate right. Finally he unleashed two cavalry divisions into the Confederate left rear:

At this time five brigades of cavalry were moving on parallel lines; most, if not all, of the brigades moved by brigade front, regiments being in parallel columns of squadrons. One continuous and heavy line of skirmishers covered the advance, using only the carbine, while the line of brigades, as they advanced across the country, the bands playing the national airs, presented in the sunlight one moving mass of glittering sabers.[20]

The left-right blows staggered Early and continued to pummel him until the Confederate army was in full retreat. Sheridan's Shenandoah campaign became known locally as "the Burning," and again contributed to the notion that the Civil War was mostly cavalry raiding. In fact, the campaign was a gambit with strategic implications. Further, Sheridan's bag of booty was as immense as the bounty his army destroyed.[21]

The Union cavalry now held a decided technological advantage, for by 1864 all regiments were equipped with Spencer repeating rifles. The introduction of the seven-shot repeating Spencer rifle has been called the turning point of the Civil War. Its 56/56 caliber used the most powerful cartridge in any repeating rifle of the Civil War. Hand guns and carbines did not completely redefine the *arme blanche*. Regiments in Confederate Gen. Lunsford Lomax's cavalry division were equipped with repeating rifles but issued no sabers. They soon discovered they could not engage in close melee and were at a tactical disadvantage in open terrain when facing large formations of rapidly advancing, saber-brandishing cavalry. It was massed horse, an officially designated cavalry corps, which raised the American arm to international strata.[22]

In the spring of 1864, Gen. William Sherman was made supreme commander of the Union western armies. Grant ordered him to "create havoc and destruction of all resources that would be beneficial to the enemy."[23] He struck out with the equivalent of an army group consisting of 99,000 troops and 254 guns. By May he was at the gates of Atlanta. Sherman's deep battle was the stuff of Mongol horse armies.

CIVIL WAR OPERATIONAL ART: WILSON'S KONARMIYA

> The next moment we rode right through them, some of the men trying to cut them down with the sabre and making ridiculous failures, others doing real execution with the gun and pistol.
>
> —General Duke, *History of Morgan's Cavalry*

The U.S. Civil War circumvented the question, what is the proper role of cavalry? The debate was represented by two camps. The light cavalry school held that the best role for industrialized cavalry, whether tactical or operational, was to scout and raid; the heavy cavalry school sought breakthrough and decision, arguing that the proper tradition of cavalry was shock. Deploying massed cavalry to decide a battle in the Napoleonic style proved risky in the face of rifled muskets, repeating rifles, and improved artillery. Save for the serendipitous opportunity on the battlefield, the boot-to-boot saber charge was not seriously planned for by veteran general staffs—Northern or

Southern. The Napoleonic wars[24] perfected the all-arms *groupement tactique;* cavalry brigades often fought much like infantry with skirmishers forward, horse artillery deployed, and a main maneuver force.[25]

> Union Cavalry did much of its fighting on foot, it never ceased to be cavalry properly speaking, capable, and proud of it, of charging the enemy with the saber, mounted. The same regiments that advanced on foot, with their carbines blazing to attack and breach the Selma fortifications on April 2, 1865, had charged with the saber, mounted, and driven back Confederate infantry and dismounted cavalry deployed behind field fortifications at Montevallo on March 30 and at Ebenezer Church, April 1.[26]

The raid by Brig. Gen. James Harrison Wilson into Alabama was a notable exception. It was heralded as "one of the most remarkable cavalry operations of the war" in Col. George T. Denison's *History of Cavalry.* The campaign is a show piece of mounted accomplishment, significant enough that Stephen Starr began his classic history, *Union Cavalry in the Civil War,* with Wilson's foray into the Deep South: "Sheridan in the East and Wilson in the West demonstrated for all to see the capabilities of the kind of cavalry that four years of war had brought into being."[27]

James Wilson, a brevet brigadier general at 27, remains the youngest field commander in American history. His spectacular progress included fortuitous service under Grant at Vicksburg and Chattanooga. Grant liked what he saw, and the young engineer was soon appointed Chief of the Cavalry Bureau. With demonstrable military skills and Ulysses Grant at his back, Wilson's meteoric rise was assured. Wilson commanded a cavalry corps in the Franklin-Nashville campaign (fall 1864, concurrent with Sherman's march to Savannah); his decisive attack stopped Forrest from turning the Union flank and was credited with assuring victory. Grant recommended he be permitted to make a sortie against Tuscaloosa and Selma. Wilson soon convinced General Thomas that a mere "demonstration" would be a waste: "I would not only defeat Forrest but would capture Tuscaloosa, Selma, Montgomery and Columbus, and destroy the Confederacy's last depots of manufacture and supply and break up its last interior line of railroad communications."[28] Wilson then persuaded Thomas to award him "the latitude of an independent commander."[29] The young corps leader had parlayed himself into achieving mission command and, given the distances involved, virtual independence.

On the other side of the hill, the situation was less propitious, despite Bedford Forrest's best efforts. His cavalry was indifferently mounted, many regiments unhorsed, and he faced a Spencer-borne technological disadvantage. His vast area of responsibility forced him to disperse his brigades to effect a viable *écran* against Union probes. The Confederate commander was a bona fide legend and an accomplished cavalry general—a *Zeiten* to Lee's *Friedrich.*

Wilson and Forrest shared some tactical and administrative traits but were otherwise complete opposites. Wilson was considered urbane and sophisticated, while Forrest was deplored for being capitalistic, rude, and temperamental—he had once been shot by an angry subordinate after a brawl. Forrest achieved fame and notoriety for his ability to organize formations and conduct punishing raids. By the summer of 1863, he commanded a corps. Personality clashes and disputes with his army commander resulted in Forrest being transferred to Tennessee and made mikado of a minuscule body of cavalry. Through energy and initiative, he built the force into an annoying thorn in Sherman's side.

In March 1865, Wilson set out on his month long *chevauchée* to lay waste to the agricultural and industrial centers in the heartland of the South. His immediate objective was the Confederate arsenal and industrial works at Selma. The strategic goal, to irrevocably knock the Confederacy out of the war, was as ambitious as Sherman's. He had forged a corps of three well-led divisions. Forrest's corps consisted of three weak divisions and some horse artillery. Wilson invaded Alabama with a remarkably balanced *Konarmiya* (cavalry army):

> 12,000 horsemen with artillery and 1,500 dismounted men to guard the trains, and to be mounted as fast as horses could be obtained. . . . Every trooper carried five day's light rations in haversacks, twenty-four pounds of grain, 100 rounds of ammunition, two extra horse shoes. . . . Pack animals . . . supply train numbered only 250 wagons and it was considered that, with what could be gleaned from the country, the column had a sufficient supply for a campaign of sixty days. They also had a light pontoon train of thirty boats, transported by fifty wagons.[30]

His initial ployment had successfully prevented Forrest from concentrating his force "then began a running fight that did not end until after the fall of Selma."[31] After a series of peripheral skirmishes, the two cavalry forces confronted each other near Ebenezer Church, some 19 miles outside of Selma. Forrest hoped to impose a delaying action; it was the best he could manage; his force, less than 3,000, was a third of Wilson's corps (Upton's division had 4,000 sabers, and Long mustered 5,000).

The battle was initiated by dragoon action. Long's division broke the Confederate left flank and began to roll up the front. This was followed by a mounted attack in the center. Forrest instructed his troopers to countercharge with saber in one hand and pistol in the other. It was a cavalry melee in what had now become an American tradition. In a testimony to both the effectiveness of pistol over saber and the ongoing cavalry debate of *slash* versus *point*, Forrest became engaged in a personal confrontation:

> Captain Taylor of the Seventeenth Indiana recognized Forrest, made for him and assailed him so fiercely with a shower of saber strokes aimed at his head

and shoulders that for a moment it appeared he would kill Forrest. However, the Confederate leader managed to spur away sufficiently to turn and shoot him from the saddle.[32]

Forrest later allowed, "If that boy had known enough to give me the point of his saber instead of its edge, I should not have been here to tell you about it."[33]

The pursuit ended at Selma, a hastily fortified city that required formal assault. Wilson attacked in three columns: "Dismounting two regiments from each of the brigades of Colonels Miller and Minty, General Long and those two officers gallantly leading their men in person, charged across an open field . . . sweeping everything before them."[34] The city fell, but Forrest managed to escape. Selma's capture yielded enough horses to saddle the corp's dismounted men and replenish supplies. Destroying his surplus wagons, Wilson trotted into Georgia, capturing Columbus, the last great Confederate storehouse, on April 16, 1865, a week after General Lee had surrendered to General Grant. His force added a postscript to the Civil War when it arrested Confederate President Jefferson Davis fleeing through Georgia.

General Wilson's campaign was notable for several reasons. It captured five fortified cities, 288 cannons, and 6,820 prisoners; it had a low cost of about 700 Union casualties against Forrest's 1,200; it resulted in the destruction of rail centers, arsenals, mines, and factories at the heart of the Confederacy; and the operation was not tainted by the excessive destruction and pillage of civilian property that is associated with General Sherman's campaign. Granted, the two marches had different operational goals. Sherman imposed a total war objective—the savage destruction of the general population's confidence and morale in order to end war.

Wilson sought practical military targets and although every raid or operation included a certain *La Maraude* feature, he limited collateral damage via tight control and rapid movement. Sherman noted admiringly that Wilson's cavalry could cover 100 miles while his (Sherman's) could only cover 10 miles. Denison was effusive:

> It was not a mere raid or dash, but an invading army determined to fight its way through. Its success was greatly. . . . It is certainly one of the most extraordinary affairs in the history of the cavalry service, and almost recalls the romantic episodes of the Crusades, where the armies consisted almost solely of knights.[35]

This operational success appears to have been ignored and certainly dismissed by the European military who went on to extend a myopic metaphor about American cavalry and raiding. Nevertheless, cavalry conducting deep battle again emerged as a viable doctrinal approach. The key aspect of the American cavalry evolution, doggedly resisted by the European powers, was that although industrialized cavalry maintained the two traditional roles of heavy and light, its realistic mission had changed from *beau sabreur* to rifled dragoon. Cavalry, armed with modern repeating weapons, was the key to winning maneuver contests. The caveat was that this new age cavalry, because of its temperament and the vicissitudes of war, had to be equipped and trained to use the saber.

Chapter 9

The Warhorse versus Technology: From Mars-La-Tour to Little Bighorn: From the Sudan to Manchuria

First there is the Cavalry Officer.
Then there is the Cavalry Officer's Horse.
Then there is nothing...
Then there is the Infantry Officer.

—Prussian cavalry maxim, circa 1870

Strategy belongs primarily to the realm of art...tactics belongs primarily to the realm of science.

—Carl von Clausewitz, *Vom Kriege*

The wars of German unification are remembered as empire gambits engineered through the political shrewdness of Prince Otto von Bismarck, King Wilhelm's "Iron Chancellor," and forged through the military savvy of the chief of the Prussian general staff, Field Marshal Helmuth von Moltke. Von Moltke applied Clausewitz with a cold Prussian efficiency and Junker detachment. While Bismarck practiced grand strategy, von Moltke excelled in the operational Art. He encouraged *Auftragstaktik,* which permitted German generals to exercise that rare gift of Mars, *Fingerspitzengefühl.*

More importantly, Prussia acquired a general staff and a supporting war college to administer a modern nineteenth-century army. The Prussian general staff was designed to provide professional counsel. The system taught selected Prussians how to think; it did not impose rote solutions but rather "institutionalized excellence."[1] Von Moltke regarded strategy as a coterie of options: "War is a system of expedients."[2] Bismarck's strategy required a popular unification of German states under a Hohenzollern Kaiser. He could not accomplish this without the defeat of the two empires that would not accommodate the rise of a new Prussian led superpower in central Europe—France and Austria. Bismarck solved this with blood, iron, and von Moltke's planning: "In the long run luck is given only to the efficient."[3]

The first major war dealt with Austria. The opening battles confirmed a technological advantage. Although dated, the Prussian "needle gun" (a rifled breech-loading musket) gave the Prussian infantry a decided edge in that it allowed rapid fire and the ability to lie down or kneel behind cover while the Austrians had to stand to reload. The bolt-action Dreyse delivered six aimed shots for every one fired by the Austrians. In addition, Prussian breech-loading artillery wrecked enemy infantry formations and engaged their guns in counter battery fire. Austrian cavalry was superb but not well directed by its commander who demonstrated temerity, if not overt pessimism. The opening thrusts of the Battle of Königgrätz (or Sadowa, July 1866) included a gallant cavalry charge by Colonel Wilfried von Bredow's 5th Cuirassier Regiment against an Austrian battery:

> Bredow, under cover of some undulating ground, formed his regiment in echelon of squadrons for the attack on the guns. . . The squadrons . . . within a few hundred paces from the battery, they broke into a steady gallop. . . All the time of their advance the gunners poured round after round into them. . . The flank squadrons, made for either end of the lines of guns in expectation of finding there some supporting cavalry. . . The two center [squadrons] went straight as an arrow, against the guns themselves and hurled themselves through the intervals upon the gunners. . . Of the eighteen captured guns, seventeen were conveyed to Prosnitz . . . [the] colonel placed himself at the head of his first squadron and charged [Austrian cavalry] to cover the retreat of his regiment's spoils.[4]

Von Bredow's handling of his regiment showed he had a knack for charging impossible targets, something which would serve him well in his next war.

Despite the disappointment of Königgrätz, Austria managed a cavalry victory to salve the army's pride on the Italian front in late July. The *Trani Uhlanen*,[5] commanded by the fanatical Colonel Maximilian Rodakowski, seemed transported from another century. Recruited from Poles living within Habsburg lands, they used a peakless version of the *czapka* with a tall eagle feather secured to the top brim. Officers and men wore baggy trousers and hung their *Uhlanka* tunics from their shoulders like hussars.

The regiment was screening an Italian advance. Ordered to do a little aggressive reconnaissance, the overzealous Rodakowski promptly got himself involved in a losing melee. Rodakowski went berserk. He delivered a fiery oration striking his long, straight-bladed *pallasch* against the uhlan's hoisted lances, exhorting them into battle fury: "Follow me! And when you can no longer see the regimental standard, look out for the feather of my *czapka* to see where the action is. . ."[6] He then spurred his charger and galloped for the nearest Italian regiment, his dolman and mustachios streaming behind like *schwenkels*. It was all quite mad but very light cavalry.

THE FRANCO PRUSSIAN WAR—A REHEARSAL FOR THE SCHLIEFFEN PLAN

> Moltke looked upon war more as a business than as a science or an art, in which military force represented capital to be invested, and victory the dividend paid on it.
>
> —J.F.C. Fuller, *The Conduct of War*[7]

The Franco-Prussian War would feature an army anchored in technology and reaction facing an army comprised of stoic Lutherans committed to maneuver and a liberal interpretation of orders and tactics. Von Moltke's staff dwarfed its French counterpart, which was less a general staff in the Clausewitzian sense than a cabinet of elder marshals. Supported with superior intelligence and a better plan, Prussian armies overcame the technological surprises of the battlefield—the chassepot rifle and the *Mitrailleuse*, which was the first practical machine gun of the industrial period.

Prussians did not appreciate the possibilities of the *Mitrailleuse*. But then, neither did the French. It was handled as a secret weapon; its size (mounted on a gun carriage with its own caisson) and long range resulted in a doctrine that distributed the gun in single batteries to deserving divisions where it was often treated like artillery by senior officers who had little or no experience with the weapon. It was regularly deployed next to the guns, which was not altogether wrong as the *Mitrailleuse* delivered accurate fire to 2,000 yards at 150 rounds a minute. Its deadly *Tak-Tak-Tak-Tak* became a fearsome staccato for Prussian infantry. However, despite its devastating effects, it required tactical grouping, its own *grandes batteries,* to stop a major assault. Although Prussian artillery was superior, it was the rifle that proved deadlier. The French chassepot was newer, faster loading, and accurate to 750 yards. Seventy percent of Prussian casualties were caused by infantry fire.

THE CAMPAIGN: THE AUGUST ENCIRCLEMENTS

> Their cavalry is much superior to ours, the privates are better mounted than many officers in our army, and they ride better.... I have seen one of their Cuirassier regiments which was something splendid.... Their horses, moreover, are

far less weighted than ours. The Cuirassiers I saw carried less weight on their big
steeds than we do on our small Arabs and South of France horses.
—Capitaine Philippe Jeannerod, on Prussian cavalry

Three Prussian armies pushed into France with a maneuver element total-
ing 133 squadrons of cavalry facing two armies with about 100 squadrons of
horse.[8] The French deployed cavalry divisions with each corps, as well as a
cavalry reserve corps of three divisions consisting of 48 squadrons, 30 pieces
of horse artillery, and 6 *Mitrailleuses.* German cavalry "pressed forward one or
two days' march ahead of the main body of the infantry, keeping the enemy
constantly in view . . . forming an impenetrable curtain or veil."[9]

The Franco-Prussian War was essentially two great encirclements—the first
locking Marshal François Achille Bazaine in the bastion of Metz, the second
an advance to contact against France's remaining field force, commanded by
the emperor himself. Napoleon had his army finally concentrate at Sedan, daring the Prussians to destroy themselves in frontal attacks against *Mitrailleuse*
backed chassepot battalions. Von Moltke swung a fresh army around the flank
of the Sedan force concluding a second deadly envelopment. The emperor and
his army were trapped and, despite valiant attempts to break out, were finally
forced to accept defeat. The crucial aspects of the design to defeat France were
executed within less than four weeks of hard fighting and dynamic maneuver.

There was little to choose between the two armies as each exhibited bravery, élan, and reasonable staff competence at the tactical level. Their weapons' advantages cancelled each other out, and the real superiority was at
the operational level. Prussian maneuver frustrated clumsy French probes.
The Metz encirclement was contested by Bazaine's forces at Gravelotte and
Mars-La-Tour—battles fought to prevent a Prussian scythe across the line of
French withdrawal. Cavalry actions were mostly aggressive recce and skirmishing; marching brigades and artillery decided the final outcome—all save
for the battle of Mars-La-Tour.

BATTLE OF MARS-LA-TOUR—A SERIES OF BALACLAVAS

MAN. You never saw a cavalry charge, did you?

RAINA. How could I?

MAN. Ah, perhaps not—of course! Well, it's a funny sight. It's like slinging a
handful of peas against a window pane: first one comes; then two or three close
behind him; and then all the rest in a lump.
—George Bernard Shaw, *Arms and the Man*

The battle near Vionville (August 16, 1870) is notable because of the results
produced by a mass cavalry charge. This attack had two major effects—the immediate influence on the battle and the doctrinal future of cavalry.

The turning point of the siege of Metz was a rolling action that raged from Vionville to Mars-La-Tour. General Constantine von Alvensleben's 3rd Corps advanced toward Mars-La-Tour preceded by two divisions of cavalry. As the 5th and 6th Cavalry divisions probed toward Metz, von Alvensleben became suddenly aware he had bumped into Bazaine's entire army, and they were about to attack. German cavalry had bungled its primary mission of early warning.

Marshal Bazaine had a tactical advantage because four French corps and elements of the Imperial Guard had the Prussians fixed and flanked. He was presented with the opportunity to crush the Prussian 2nd Army in detail, extricate his force from a potential trap, and, with creative maneuver, surround the 1st Prussian Army that was moving against him from the east. Instead he chose to do the minimum required.

The enthusiasm and *Auftragstaktik* of junior commanders on both sides contributed to an escalating main engagement. In the end, von Alvensleben proved the more assertive. Appreciating his corps was the spearhead of a turning maneuver that could trap Bazaine's entire army, he decided aggressiveness would mask weakness. This proved to be the most audacious command decision of the campaign. Alvensleben's lead divisions wheeled toward the French and went smartly into the attack suffering horrendous losses from artillery, *Mitrailleuse* fire, and the deadly chassepots. The astute veteran Gen. Philip Sheridan, present as an official military observer for President Grant and a guest of Otto von Bismarck, recorded his impression of French firepower:

> As they approached within short range they suddenly found that the French artillery and Mitrailleuses had by no means been silenced, about two hundred pieces opening on them with fearful effect, while at the same time the whole crest blazed with a deadly fire from the Chassepot rifles. Resistance like this was so unexpected by the Germans that it dismayed them, and first wavering a moment, then becoming panic-stricken, they broke and fled.[10]

VON BREDOW'S DEATH RIDE, AUGUST 16, 1870

> C'est un spectacle étrange que celui de ces cavaliers qui vont "se flanquer des gnons" pour leur propre compte dans les régions excentriques de la bataille.
> (It is a bizarre spectacle—cavalrymen seeking individual punch-ups around the periphery of the battlefield.)
>
> —Capitaine F. Canonne[11]

French assaults wore down Alvensleben's force which became a thin balloon about to burst. As the French formed for a last breakthrough charge, Alvensleben ordered his remaining brigade, commanded by the intrepid Friedrich von Bredow, now a general, to thwart the French counterstroke; in effect sacrificing the cavalry to save the corps.

With an annoyed shrug ("Koste es was es wolle" [it will cost what it will]), von Bredow formed up his three regiments (the 7th Cuirassiers, 16th Uhlans, and a contingent of 19th Dragoons) and set forth to make cavalry history. "Von Bredow's Death Ride" battle is notable not because it was a decisive bit of cavalry work ("The boldest charge of the war and the only one that was to a certain extent successful"[12]) but because it probably spared the warhorse from the knacker's yard.

The brigade moved off at the trot in line of squadrons with Bredow's *coup d'oeil* taking advantage of every dip or incline to screen his approach from long-range fire. Finally, just before the brigade crested in full view of the enemy, he ordered his squadrons into line and increased the pace to a canter. The brigade now attracted the interest of *Mitrailleuses* and artillery; the French lines were 1,200 yards away—a two-minute ride through shot and shell.

Von Bredow's regiments tucked in their chins and galloped through, reaching the guns. After an *en passant* slaughter, they charged the French infantry. Carried away by the impetuous fury of their charge, they could neither be rallied nor reformed. The brigade was promptly pounced upon by cuirassiers, spahis, and chasseurs and forced to retreat: "They were very badly handled and suffered great losses, but the sacrifice was well repaid."[13] The costs were surprisingly low for an attack with such colossal consequences: about 385 men and 400 horses, or less than half the brigade. For cavalry, it was more a glamorous than glorious moment. As a Prussian *Balaclava,* it maintained the tactical

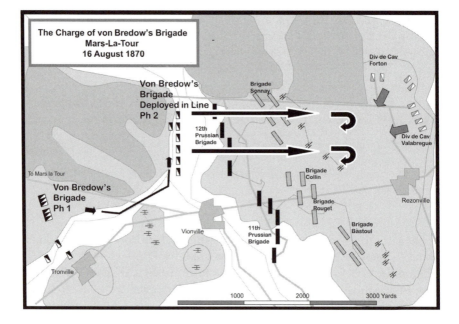

status quo, bought time, and saved the corps, which led to an operational victory—the entrapment of Bazaine's army in Metz.

Sheridan, who had far more experience in cavalry operations than any continental general, summed up his impressions of the war to his president: ". . . there is nothing to be learned here professionally."[14] Technology had made the Napoleonic school, particularly the cavalry, clearly redundant. But von Bredow had changed that. His *TotenRitt* permitted proponents to argue that cavalry remained instrumental in modern warfare—room to maneuver within the industrial era, indeed, into the twentieth century.

PLAINS CAVALRY—AN AMERICAN CHIVALRY

> They have ever displayed a superb courage, which attracts our admiration but does not command our sympathy. It is folly to suppose that contact with white people has made them any more inhuman in their tastes than they have been for ages past . . . what Comanches had been to Texas, these Cheyennes and Sioux are in the north. They are without fear, without faith, and without mercy. . . Killing and stealing form alike their best ideas of earthly honor or of heavenly bliss.
>
> —1st Lt. Eben Swift, Fifth U.S. Cavalry[15]

The U.S. Cavalry, despite its Civil War accomplishments, prefers to be defined by its frontier service. In the new millennium, whether in Fort Hood or Baghdad, the cavalry continued to attend regimental parades in Stetsons. Although the trumpet calls echo Brandy Station or Little Bighorn and its battle honors encompass three centuries, the U.S. Cavalry is besotted by its campaigns in the American West.

Expeditionary forces in deep operations were de rigueur for American cavalry—geography ensured its campaigns easily equaled the breadth and depth of the Golden Horde. To the natives, there may have been little apparent difference. Campaigns against American Indians spanned the pre-revolutionary colonial period to the end of the second Industrial Revolution. The forest Indians on either side of the Appalachians excelled in *la petit guerre,* which comprised mainly raiding, ambush, and surprise skirmishes in closed terrain. The Indians of the plains were horse peoples.

Large numbers of readily available horses first appeared after the Pueblo Rebellion (1680) forced the Spanish ranchers south. Well-bred horses were left behind and taken over by aboriginal tribes for use or trade. By the nineteenth century, the Comanche culture was completely dependent on the Spanish horse and conducted regular horse-stealing expeditions against the ranches astride the Rio Grande; the Comanche liked to boast that they permitted the Spanish to stay in Texas simply to raise horses for them.[16] The European horses reintroduced into North America by the Spanish included Barbs, Arabians, Lipizzaners, and lesser breeds. These bloodlines eventually produced the best-known American horse—the mustang.

Indian cavalry was well mounted, and herds were regularly improved through breeding and raiding. Wild horses were not particularly sought as they were often inferior to carefully raised stock. As noted by Orland Ned Eddins, "Horses were adapted to fit the Indian lifestyle . . . horses did not materially change the Indians hunter-gather lifestyle. Indians still did the same things in pretty much the same ways except now they used horses."[17] Mesmeric adornments were as much a feature of Plains cavalry as in elite European regiments. Indian warriors did not use horse furniture, spurs, or extensive bridles but did add their own heraldic markings to honor their mount.

The horse's *battle scars* (always painted red) and the *pat hand print* (left hand drawn on the horse's right hip) were honors reserved exclusively for the horse who had brought his master back home from a dangerous mission unharmed. Apache and Comanche legends recount a great battle during which a fatally wounded warrior patted his charger's right shoulder, leaving a bloody handprint. Personal honors portrayed enemies killed and horses stolen. Battle colors included an *upside-down handprint* for the men setting out on "do-or-die mission . . . [it was] the most prized symbol a warrior could place on his horse."[18] Preparation for battle included extensive grooming since knotting up the tail prevented the enemy form grabbing it during melee. The mane was braided to prevent obstruction to archery. In a buffalo hunt or a sudden melee, the bow or spear reigned supreme. In close-quarter combat, the tomahawk was as efficient as a pistol and used in much the same way a knight wielded a battle-axe at Crécy. Indian warriors disdained muskets as they were inefficient and cumbersome to reload on horseback. The most prized attack weapon was a Winchester rifle.

Mobility defined certain American aboriginal cultures. The Indians of the eastern forests depended on the canoe, while the Plains nations were completely defined by the horse, and their meanderings were determined by the treks of the great buffalo herds. The horse transformed tribes of hunter-gathers and sedentary farmers who scratched out existence on the periphery of the steppe ocean that was the American prairies. The mounted Indians transformed to a confident, often arrogant and condescending, society that looked down on those who hunted on foot. Plains tribes hunted valor via mounted jousts. The Apache and Sioux offered the most effective resistance to western settlement; led by skilled *hetmen,* they proved masters of maneuver warfare and expert guerrillas. It is moot who the real terrorists were as both sides invariably committed great excesses and the resistance of the indigenous population of the plains was fierce and generally savage.

Indian cavalry combated a political and cultural threat, but specifically, they faced the U.S. Cavalry, which was a homogeneous collection of veterans, former slaves, Confederate soldiers, adventurers from European cavalries, and romantics. While ethnic combinations made the American cavalry unique in many ways, as a collection of cavaliers it was little different from any European cavalry sent to patrol the empire frontiers, whether in India, Manchuria, or the Ottoman border.

The horse culture of the American Indian produced a complex mixture of feudal valor and Mongol doctrine. Initially the Plains Indians demonstrated the same bizarre ethics as French chivalry. Contact by a foe's *coup stick* (French—"to strike") brought dishonor to the victim and exalted the warrior qualities of the victor. Plains Indian historian George Volger noted, "But the solitary warrior in a headlong battle charge climaxed by harmlessly touching an enemy scored a coup; honors were given for the daring required of close contact. . . The surprise nudge from a coup stick would sting in one person's memory."[19] European opponents had long abandoned this equestrian ballet and responded with gunpowder in much in the same way that Welsh longbowmen greeted French knights with bodkins. Plains Indians quickly discarded the chivalrous approach and reverted to ambuscade and raid. The western campaigning soon required infantry skills as much as equestrian competence from both sides:

> The officers and men worked day and night, and with our Indian allies, would crawl upon their hands and knees for long distances over terrible cañons and precipices where the slightest miss-step would have resulted in instant death, in order that when daylight came they might attack their enemy and secure the advantage of surprise so indispensable in this kind of warfare.[20]

Frontier operations demanded long marches on meager rations: "In the year [1876] most of the troops marched over two thousand miles; ninety-three of our horses died of exhaustion and starvation."[21] Cavalry-Indian battles varied from long-range gun duels to violent skirmishes. Traditional cavalry clashes were rare; the preferred method of engagement was to lure American cavalry into a killing zone in rough terrain and then attempt a close-quarter battle. Both sides depended on subterfuge, and night attacks were common: "It was a little after daylight, and a complete surprise. The cavalry was formed in line of troops, in columns of twos, guide right, and so they dashed into the village . . . The Indians rallied and fought desperately hand to hand."[22]

The Comanche were particularly highly regarded as horse archers, and their appearance and manner was not that different from Attila's warriors:

> ". . . in stature rather low, and in person often approaching to corpulence" . . . they were not as large [or] handsome as the Kiowas. . . "In their movements they were heavy and ungraceful; and on their feet one of the most unattractive and slovenly-looking races of Indians that I have ever seen." But the mounted Comanche presented an entirely different appearance. Once on his horse, he continued, "He gracefully flies away like a different being." U.S. Army officers, who fought them, called the Comanche Indians the finest light cavalry in the world.[23]

Despite ability and bravado, the Plains tribes were completely outclassed in operational confrontations, standing no reasonable chance against a sophisticated industrialized society prepared to conduct operations in barbaric style.

A series of wars with the American government were incited by disputes over land grabs, mining rights, and general encroachment on traditional Indian lands. More serious was the systematic slaughter of the great buffalo herds by indiscriminate hunting or cruel sport. The discovery of gold in Dakota and subsequent infiltration of treaty lands by miners prompted the last major war with the Sioux, which is best known for the demise of Gen. George Armstrong Custer and much of the 7th Cavalry in 1876.

U.S. CAVALRY AND THE AMERICAN INDIAN WARS

> When the scouts came back and called out to him to hold on, that the Sioux were coming in large numbers to meet him. He crossed over, however, formed his companies on the prairie in line of battle, and moved forward at a trot but soon took a gallop.
>
> —George Herendon, scout for the Seventh Cavalry[24]

Custer's command penetrated deeply into Sioux (Lakota) territory and fought a series of skirmishes against a Sioux-Cheyenne alliance led by Chief Sitting Bull. Finally, Custer set out to find and destroy their main encampment. The raid was a series of blunders—ineffective reconnaissance was the greatest failure. The 7th Cavalry of the 1870s was not a crack unit. Custer relied on hired Crow Indian scouts and not his own troopers. He tended to suspect the information he did get, and for all practical purposes, he was tactically blind. Custer's skittish command style—quite the opposite of his *beau sabreur* exploits in the Civil War—proved him less adept in maneuvering a single horsed regiment than a brigade of Union cavalry. Brig. Gen. Frederick Benteen, who commanded a reinforced squadron at the Little Bighorn battle, found Custer "vain, arrogant and egotistical."[25]

Sitting Bull caught Custer's force deployed piecemeal. The 7th Cavalry's notorious battle was actually a series of uncoordinated dismounted dragoon actions fought from skirmish lines and, in some cases, rough shell scrapes. Dragoon tactics required sections of five troopers as skirmishers with the fifth stationed to the rear to control the horses. The formation is efficient in temporary rear guards or screen dust-ups but not capable of withstanding a dogged mounted assault from front and flanks: "The Sioux, mounted on their swift ponies, dashed up by the side of the soldiers and fired at them, killing both men and horses."[26] Indian veterans remembered it was "just like hunting buffalo . . . white men went crazy. Instead of shooting us, they turned their guns upon themselves. Almost before we could get to them, every one of them was dead. They killed themselves."[27] Chief Low Dog (*Xunka Kuciyedano*), one of the attacking Sioux, recalled:

I called to my men: "This is a good day to die: follow me." We massed our men, and that no man should fall back, every man whipped another man's horse and we rushed right upon them. As we rushed upon them the white warriors dismounted to fire, but they did very poor shooting. They held their horses' reins on one arm while they were shooting, but their horses were so frightened that they pulled the men all around, and a great many of their shots went up in the air and did us no harm.[28]

Control of the 7th passed to Benteen who managed to extricate the survivors, leading two mounted charges to break out from a maneuvering envelopment. His initial failure to reinforce Custer has been criticized in a battle where no American cavaliers demonstrated *Fingerspitzengefühl*.

The technological balance was interesting; besides battle-axe, spear, and bow, the Indians carried a collection of firearms including Spencer, Henry, and Winchester repeaters, while Custer's men were equipped with single-shot Springfield carbines with copper cartridges which were prone to jamming.[29] The event, sensationalized in blazing headlines, resulted in greater repercussions against the Lakota, many of whom sought sanctuary in the Canadian Northwest Territories where they were better handled by the Mounted Police. In the end they suffered the same fate as all tribes and were reduced to life on reservations. Indian campaigns continued until the last great Apache chief, Geronimo, was captured in 1885. The final Sioux versus cavalry confrontation was at Wounded Knee, in 1890, where the reconstituted 7th Cavalry killed 200 Sioux, including Big Foot, Sitting Bull's brother.

Of the 11 U.S. Cavalry regiments that served in the West, two are particularly favored by history—the 7th and the 10th Cavalry, better known as the buffalo soldiers because Indians claimed the black troopers' hair resembled the mane of the prairie buffalo.[30] The police actions in the West were primarily cultural conflicts; the bizarre action of the buffalo soldiers (former slaves, freed after the Civil War) begs analysis along with the conduct of European émigré refugees seeking a liberal way of life.

CAVALRY AND JIHAD: OMDURMAN

Two hundred and fifty yards away the dark-blue men were firing madly in a thin film of light-blue smoke. Their bullets struck the hard gravel into the air, and the troopers, to shield their faces from the stinging dust, bowed their helmets forward, like the Cuirassiers at Waterloo.

—Winston Churchill[31]

The Battle of Omdurman (1898, The Mahdist War) is sometimes recorded as the last full-scale cavalry charge of modern warfare. This may be presumptuous, given the events of the Great War, the Polish-Russian War, and particularly the operations of the Red Army cavalry during the Second World War. It was certainly the last charge of the Napoleonic century.

The campaign took place in Anglo-Egyptian Sudan and faced a Muslim army commanded by Muhammad Ahmad ("the Mahdi") who had declared a jihad and conducted a war of liberation against Ottoman-Egyptian military occupation. After initial success and the capture of Khartoum, the Mahdi established a government based on traditional Islamic laws. He died within six months; his successor, Abdallahi Muhammad, eventually faced a British relief force commanded by Gen. Horatio Kitchener with 8,000 British regulars and a mixed force of 17,000 Sudanese and Egyptian soldiers. The battle took place near the Nile, which secured the flank and contributed supporting fire from gunboats. Kitchener's force deployed in a wide arc with artillery and Maxims well forward. The cavalry covered the extended flank: "As the sun rose, the 21st Lancers trotted out of the zeriba and threw out a spray of officers' patrols."[32] The Muslim forces conducted a zealous charge but were easily defeated. Kitchener decided to grab Omdurman while the Mahdists were disorganized and ordered the cavalry forward to screen his advance.

> There was a brief conversation—an outstretched arm pointing at the ridge—an order, and we were all scrambling into our saddles and straightening the ranks in high expectation. We started at a trot, two or three patrols galloping out in front, towards the high ground, while the regiment followed in mass—a great square block of ungainly brown figures and little horses, hung all over with water-bottles, saddle-bags, picketing-gear, tins of bully-beef, all jolting and jangling together; the polish of peace gone; soldiers without glitter; horsemen without grace; but still a regiment of light cavalry in active operation against the enemy.[33]

The 21st Lancers soon came upon a rearguard astride a *khor* ("a dry river-bed," or *wadi*). Their commander impetuously ordered a charge; his 400 strong regiment, in a déjà vu of Waterloo, were surprised by the steep banks of the *khor* and its contents of well over 2,000 Mahdists. One participant was Winston Churchill, a lieutenant from the 4th Hussars, a supernumerary officer to the 21st Lancers. His staff duties were primarily as a correspondent, but he contrived to lead a troop in the charge. The battle made a lasting impression:

> two living walls had actually crashed together. The Dervishes fought manfully. They tried to hamstring the horses. They fired their rifles, pressing the muzzles into the very bodies of their opponents. They cut reins and stirrup-leathers. They flung their throwing-spears with great dexterity. They tried every device of cool, determined men practiced in war and familiar with cavalry; and, besides, they swung sharp, heavy swords which bit deep. . . Terrified horses wedged in the crowd, bruised and shaken men, sprawling in heaps, struggled, dazed and stupid, to their feet, panted, and looked about them.[34]

The lancers finally fought their way through: "I remember no sound. The event seemed to pass in absolute silence."[35] To their credit, they reformed for a second charge but wiser heads prevailed. The plain was a mess of riderless horses, lancers "clinging to their saddles, lurched helplessly about. . . Horses, streaming from tremendous gashes, limped and staggered with their riders."[36] The Sudan incident was neither a test of doctrine nor an effective dress rehearsal for the Boer War. The cavalry charge, despite an inordinate amount of popular press, was impetuous and, though brave, a sloppy bit of tactics. Although the French had been kept sufficiently occupied in North Africa, perhaps Omdurman should be correctly remembered as the first modern war against Muslim extremists.

BOER WAR—RAIDING AND RECCE—DRAGOONS AGAIN

And fear came down with a gusty rain of lead on his final bed . . .
Before I turned for cover again, I knew that his life had fled.
My heart is warm for a heart that died in the desert flank attack,
And the white sand surges down to the hide and bones of a faithful
trooper's hack.
                                   —Edwin Gerard, "The Horse that Died for Me"[37]

The war in South Africa was a David-Goliath affair conducted against republics governed by Dutch-Afrikaner settlers, referred to as *Boers* by British press. The advent of formal war between republic and empire resulted in a multinational force joining the British. The additional troops were drawn from the dominions and constituted the first major forays into the business of foreign wars for Australia, Canada, and New Zealand. The Australian government sent two regiments of light horse, and New Zealand provided a regiment of mounted rifles; the Canadians initially sent a ubiquitous contingent named The Canadian Mounted Rifles (CMR). The latter soon evolved into three cavalry regiments, the Royal Canadian Dragoons, The Lord Strathcona's Horse, and the CMR.[38] The force included many western cowboys and volunteers from the Northwest Mounted Police (now The Royal Canadian Mounted Police) who were familiar with prairie operations. Their influence was considerable. The Canadian cavalry even adopted the Mounties' Stetson as headgear. The South African war is continually evoked via cavalry terminology—*trekking* is an Afrikaans term, as is *laager* ([lah gar], not the beer—a wagon encampment). Armored cavalry squadrons continue to form tank laagers for administrative halts or tactical halts into the twenty-first century. Afrikaners wore casual civilian clothes and used terrain to advantage; the British response was to retire the traditional scarlet uniform and dress their army in *khaki*, an Indian word meaning "dust," which the English pronounced as "karkee."[39]

Boer effectiveness in long-range rifle engagements was doubled with the use of new smokeless powder cartridges. "Smokeless powder" is a misnomer—the real advantage was that smokeless powder generated much greater pressures and higher velocities. Equally important, it was vastly cleaner and reduced stoppages.

Although Gen. John French commanded a full cavalry division, there were no traditional mounted actions and yet plenty of campaigning. In 1900 the Afrikaans forces formed mobile commandos to raid British rear areas and assault isolated contingents. Horses were battle taxis again, and the cavalry adopted infantry tactics to deal with continual ambush or quick raids against posts. Conditions were difficult; many horses failed to acclimatize and consequently died of disease. Epidemics followed:

> It was not the severity of the work they had to do which killed them; but it was the wretched conditions under which they did their work. If our horses could have been kept free from sickness, and have been properly fed, they could have done all the Army work with the greatest of ease. As it was, they died like flies.[40]

General French's cavalry regiments rode horses from all corners of the world with little regard to climate or unrealistic demands on their legs and frames:

> Great round-hipped English chargers, light wiry Australians, mongrel Argentines, wonderful little Burmese ponies and last, but not least, the Cape horses; meanwhile, Afrikaner cavalry used Cape horses which proved sturdy and capable of extended maneuver. The Cape ponies were small, weedy, narrow little things, but they are full of 'quality.' Being in their own country, they did not get sick, and they stood more work than any other style of horse, but the great weights they had to carry soon brought them to grief.[41]

A cavalry charge occurred at Klipt Drift (February 15, 1900) when three squadrons attacked a position held by Boer mounted infantry. It was a sudden frontal assault and featured the rare sight in South Africa of lances, pennants, and an attack by a brigade of cavalry. "The charge of the 16th and 9th Lancers, with lance-heads pointed before them, thundering forward in double line with eight-yard intervals between files"[42] unnerved the Afrikaners who wisely mounted and scattered.

The Boer War's finale played out with some similarity to the Iraqi campaign of the twenty-first century. After formal battle ended, there was continued guerilla action that required strong garrisons and regular active patrols. The enmity between the invading force and the conquered peoples grew. The British enforced regional jurisdiction via lines of blockhouses or wire fences to hamper veldt maneuver. Control was sporadic, and if forces did not remain in place and conduct regular aggressive patrolling, the commando guerillas infiltrated back and continued to ambush and raid.

THE CZAR'S CAVALRY MEETS SAMURAI— MANCHURIA 1905

> When the Russo-Japanese War broke out everybody was convinced that the numerous Cossack cavalry ... would cover themselves with laurels, not, of course, on the field of battle, but in the very extensive domain of exploration and reconnaissance.
>
> —Capt. Serge Nidvine[43]

In the summer of 1905, Japanese-Russian imperialistic rivalry resulted in a war fought over Manchuria, an area virtually unknown to Europe. The Czar's quest for a warm-water port found Russian forces on the Pacific facing a recently industrialized Japan intent on expanding her own interests in Korea. The Russians deployed troops into Manchuria; the Japanese dispatched an ultimatum and followed up with a surprise attack against the Russian naval base in Port Arthur—a forecast of Pearl Harbor. They then sent an army across the Yalu River. Despite the construction of the Trans-Siberian railway, Russian leadership exhibited as little competence as it had during the Crimea. The army was continually outmaneuvered, and the cavalry surprised by their Japanese counterparts. The Manchurian steppes were inhospitable, even for hardy steppe horsemen:

> The officers lived largely on rice cakes and took their tea without sugar. The Cossacks subsisted upon roots, and upon grain, which they crushed with stones; and instead of tea they drank hot water . . . the typical young Cossack officer . . . wears the fur cap or helmet according to circumstances but not according to the seasons; a blouse that is rather new; trousers of some dark color; fair leather boots; neither shoulder belt nor cartridge box; a fair leather strap serves for a belt and to it are hung the meal bag, the tobacco pouch and the field glasses. In rear hangs the revolver in a dirty holster. The pipe is thrust into a boot-leg. Finally a tattered map is carried in the blouse over the breast.[44]

Extended maneuver required that squadrons travel light and attempt to live off the land, which was most challenging in Manchuria: "The horses left much to be desired; they were small poorly bred Siberian horses, many of which had just been taken from the plow and they did not promise much in the way of endurance."[45] Cavalry actions were mostly attempts at reconnaissance, which did not bring appreciable results; raids were carried out in Cossack tradition, if not the same dogged style. One Cossack foray attempted infiltration through arduous mountain territory, but they did not know the language and had no guides. They were harassed by Japanese patrols and were obliged to be in hiding in caves and ravines. The first major action took place during March 1904 when Gen. Mitshenko's Transbaikal's Cossack brigade of eighteen *sotnas* (squadrons of approx 100 men) and a battery of horse artillery attempted to screen General Kuroki's advancing field force. After a minor skirmish with Japanese dragoons, the Cossacks fell back.

Kuropatkin continued to send out large cavalry raids into Japanese rear areas to harass convoys, with limited success. Campaigning was hard on men and horses. Nevertheless, the devotion and courage of the cavalry remained surprisingly strong in one action "under a hailstorm of bullets while the trumpets sounded and all the Cossacks sang *Boje Tsaria khrania* (God shield the Czar)."[46] The Manchurian war was a clash of doctrines and the Japanese, acolytes of the Prussian system, faithfully duplicated the best von Moltke principles, save for the crucial one of creating an enlightened politically detached staff college. The Russian doctrine applied the same dated techniques they used against the Turks. It was a mortifying defeat. Things would be different the next time cavalry appeared in Manchuria, in 34 years, near the Khalkin Gol.

Ensemble: **"Ach du Lieber in Himmel!"**

Chapter 10

Cavalry in the Great War, Part I: The Golden Summer

> The rifle, effective as it is, cannot replace the effect produced by the speed of the horse, the magnetism of the charge and the terror of the cold steel.
>
> —British cavalry doctrine, 1907[1]

> In Cavalry action a vigorous attack, ridden stirrup to stirrup, is the sure road to victory.
>
> —German cavalry doctrine, 1913[2]

The Great War constitutes a watershed for the cavalry; it was both an apocalypse as well as, for mechanized visionaries, a renaissance. The actual study of operational cavalry in the First World War is not exhaustive and can be dispensed with in short time as it spans less than two months. The following two chapters will reflect on the complexities of the new century as a technological and traditional smorgasbord. The equipments and styles of the three principal cavalry forces of France, Britain, and Germany will be reviewed, and established doctrine will be considered via an assessment of the first two months of a war that initially featured bold maneuver but ended in dissolute stalemate. The operational conundrum and its mechanical solution will be briefly examined and will conclude with cavalry at the end of the war demonstrating both frustrating limitations as well as unlimited bravado and success at Moreuil Wood and Beersheba.

Twentieth-century infantry had become a deadly killing machine that performed better in the defense than the doctrinally preferred shock of the bayonet attack. Machine guns were improved at an alarming pace—the Maxim introduced a high rate of fire, automatic extraction of spent cartridges, and was a compact size easily carried by three men. A single water-cooled barrel capable of delivering 600 rounds per minute promised quick slaughter to the orthodox assault. Bolt-action rifles were fitted with magazines enabling infantry to lie behind cover or in a trench line and could deliver an astonishing volume of accurate fire. The British used a ten-round magazine compared to the five rounds in a German Mauser. The rate of fire produced was staggering. The record set in 1914 by a British sergeant was 38 rounds into a 12-inch target at 300 yards in 30 seconds. Most infantry could manage 30 aimed rounds during a "mad minute" of volley fire. Europe was no place for a horse.

Despite futuristic exhibits at world's fairs in Paris (1898, the Eiffel Tower) and Chicago (1893, electricity demonstrated), modern armies preferred tradition, a nuance of tactical adjustment, and a soupçon of technology. Science fiction was popular (Jules Verne's *From the Earth to the Moon* in 1865 and H. G. Wells's *The War of the Worlds* in 1898), and the military experimented with futuristic machines to deliver dispatches or peek across a border. In 1885 Karl Benz built the first car using an internal combustion engine; by the turn of the century, 700 heavy trucks had been built in the United States, and by 1914 production had reached 25,000 while heavy tractors were extensively used for farming. This had next to no effect on Western armies—particularly the cavalry. The adamant contention of any general staff was that cavalry must continue to serve operationally as a reconnaissance and screening force. Motorized transport was resisted as being impractical, mechanically unreliable, incapable of cross-country maneuver, and limited to a paucity of suitable highways.

The war that is synonymous with unimaginative frontal assaults began and ended with creative maneuver. The Schlieffen Plan attempted to put into grander scale the methods demonstrated by the elder von Moltke; its *chef,* Count von Schlieffen, was the essence of the Germanic warrior spirit in that he was prepared to take risks.[3] The bold hook through Belgium (Liddell Hart called it "a conception of Napoleonic boldness") depended on a perfect execution of a delicate timetable. If the massive German right wing advanced smartly and wheeled around Paris, France would be forced into surrender, with plenty of time left over to deal with any Russian push toward Berlin. Unfortunately for the Kaiser, von Schlieffen died, and the recipe for victory was trusted to a *sous-chef*—Helmut von Moltke the younger. As knowledgeable generals warned, and history proved, he was not capable of managing a war. Court wags quipped that the Kaiser simply wanted *his own Moltke,* just like his dad.

In 1914 there were still cuirassiers in European cavalry: 10 regiments in the German army, 12 French, and 3 Russian, all in the Imperial Guard. The French army appeared physically unchanged from 1870: "clad in old red caps and trousers which a parsimonious democracy dictated they should wear . . . the gallant officers who led them were entirely ignorant of the stopping power of modern firearms, and many of them thought it was chic to die in white gloves."[4] However, the French problem was not dress, but doctrine. Post 1870 analysis determined the army had lacked an aggressive spirit, but this was perhaps more true of the most senior commanders than of the regiments. France adopted a doctrine with cultural roots: "Attaque à outrance" (attack to the last extremity, at all cost).

The French command argued that victory would fall to the side with the greatest élan and determination. The philosophy has been criticized as senseless human wave tactics, but this ignores the main reasons for what became a very European doctrine: the challenge of armies of reservists and conscripts within industrialized war. Attacks in successive dense lines could absorb the casualties modern weapons promised to create and still bash through. The Allied general staffs argued that while *Attaque à outrance* caused large casualties initially, in the long run it produced lower overall casualties. The most practical solution, of course, was not to attack, but that was simply not a political option. The Great War inaugurated an era where effective operational maneuver depended on the telegraph, telephone, and airplane. The cavalry's most significant involvement with the Great War would last just about six weeks.

FRUSTRATED BRAVURA—THE CAVALRY OF FRANCE

The fanfaronade of French cavalry included both the insouciant demeanor of hussars as well as mustachioed cuirassiers who had little changed from the Napoleonic *grognards* observed by the artist Haydon a hundred years earlier: "the look of thoroughbred, veteran, disciplined banditti. Depravity, recklessness, and bloodthirstiness were burned into their faces."[5] Regimental tunics flaunted traditional piping, including the very French *Aurore*—a haunting pink that resembles a dawn sky.[6] Within a year they would all be wearing *le bleu-horizon* of trench warfare.

Many modern armies had adopted neutral colors for field work; the Americans and British were in khaki by the end of the nineteenth century, and the Germans wore *Feldgrau* (Field Grey) by 1910. Whatever survived Napoleon and Bismarck was diminished. Headgear was made of cloth or leather, gave no protection against bullet or shrapnel, and provided little defense against rain or sun. German *Uhlanen* carried high-tech lances made of thin rolled steel but, nevertheless, lances. All cavalry continued to carry the saber as the weapon of choice, augmented by the bolt-action carbine, the weapon of common sense.

Of all the cavalries that were to see combat in the Great War, France's *arme blanche* appeared the most perplexing; it presented a combination of the bizarre traditional as well as the practical. While the Germans and British adopted muted earthen hues and misty weaves, the French went forth boldly in republican blue and mordant red. In a curious attempt to deflect criticism over the rather obvious colors, the word *red* had been banned by Paris, and the French resolutely insisted their army wore *bleu-cerise* ("cherry blue"). Everyone was armed with the *Sabre de troup, modèle 1882* to add dignity to their main weapon, the carbine.[7]

Ployed behind bocage or formed in wheat fields, the regiments mirrored Bonaparte's cavalry massing before Waterloo. The cuirassiers had changed little, with breastplates of gleaming steel or copper and plumed Grecian helmets with trailing Kublai Khan manes. Before battle, the cuirasses and helms were made *camouflé* beneath grey or cerulean covers. Many regiments simply stopped polishing their breast plates; one practical colonel adopted a brusque method to diminish the metallic patina. He ordered the cuirasses placed in the caserne's courtyard and told the men to relieve themselves.[8]

Cynical accounts of the cuirasse suggest the worst aspects of Crécy. But it should be made clear that the cuirassier uniform was the most practical of the early Great War costumes. In a campaign deluged by shrapnel showers and torrents of bullets, body armor, no matter how thin, and metal helmets made more sense than felt caps and leather *Haubes*. The cuirassier's surcoat was no different from that of his German counterparts who covered the *Pickelhaube* to eliminate glint and thwart detection. Flash (from bayonets, swords, telescopes, binoculars) is what betrays position.

Color, part of the principle of seduction, is a relatively innocent cavalry obsession and has little real bearing on long-range detection. The things that attract attention are movement (or a fluttering pennon), size, shape, and shadow. Putting a large pink elephant in a wheat field will likely be obvious on a clear day, but intelligent use of ground and cover will prevent even psychedelic pachyderms from being discovered. French cavalry dress was certainly no less bizarre than British armies sending their Scottish regiments into battle wearing kilts to eulogize the manly warrior tradition, then ordering the apparel covered with a canvas apron.

France's technology was a match for any European power; their quick firing 75 mm field gun, *le soixante quinze* ("the 75"), would become the emulated standard of modern field artillery. The cavalry carbine was considered efficient, and the small arms and machine guns of the infantry were on a par with modern armies. New technology meant the ability of a cavalry division or corps to force breakthrough was irrevocably passé in Europe. It would take both the Cavalry and the General Staffs a while to accept it, but the warhorse was neutered as a combat arm.

France met the Schlieffen Offensive with 10 cavalry divisions supporting its five armies deployed from the Ardennes to Alsace.[9] Seven divisions were attached to the field armies, two with the First and Second Armies, while the Third, Fourth, and Fifth Armies had a mounted division each. The Army commanders distributed cavalry assets to formation headquarters.[10] For operational maneuver, Paris created a GHQ Reserve comprising a cavalry corps commanded by General Jean-François Sordet.[11] Between August and September 1914 the French had available, for varying periods, five *corps de cavalerie* but principally maneuvered with the two corps led by Generals Sordet and Conneau.[12]

BRITISH CAVALRY

> Cavalry are always rather independent cusses and don't care much for people from outside and object to superior commanders and staffs and such like.
> —Capt. L.A.E. Price Davies, observations about British cavalry, 1914[13]

The British cavalry was very much the living embodiment of the clever cartoon that appeared in *Punch* circa 1892; a young monocled *cavalwy* officer lounging with gin and tonic is accosted by a Gilbert and Sullivan major general: "Mr. De Bridoon, what is the general use of Cavalry in modern warfare?" The classic reply, "Well I suppose to give Tone to what would otherwise be a mere Vulgar Brawl!"[14] The glamour of the London season was mixed with polo and occasional tactical riding. The men were trained hard while the officers were expected to look good and not interfere with the troop sergeants. Most officers joined because they simply liked a life with horses. Despite a casual decadence, the British produced a very professional cavalry—at least at the regimental level.

British cavalrymen wore the same khaki service tunic as their infantry colleagues and a soft cloth hat that offered less protection than their forefathers enjoyed at Waterloo or Balaclava. Their 1908 saber was allegedly the finest cavalry weapon devised and specifically designed to *give point*. It still receives mixed reviews: "With its slim tapering blade and its pistol-grip hilt, it is a thrusting weapon, originating more from the experiences of the gymnasium and drill-square than those of the battlefield. [However] it replaced a thoroughly bad sword, the 1890 pattern."[15] The attack sword was augmented by the .303 cavalry carbine SMLE (Short Rifle Magazine Lee Enfield, or "Smelly" as the troopers dubbed it) carried in a "rifle bucket" strapped to the saddle. The Lee Enfield Mk I infantry rifle with five inches cut off the barrel was a compromise and declared suitable for infantry, mounted infantry, and the cavalry. It proved to be unpopular:

> The subsequent introduction of Mk VII ammunition, with a velocity of 2,440 feet per second resulted in the lighter rifle developing a quite unpleasant kick. . . . Millions of infantrymen were now landed with a rifle that was unpleasant to shoot, all in the cause of the standardization of weapons between them and a comparative handful of cavalry![16]

The lance was an on-off affair often influenced by continental vogue. All British lancer regiments lost their raison d'être weapon in 1903; the steel-tipped, steel-shod bamboo version was regulated to ceremonial use only but was suddenly restored to active duty in 1909. This was considered a political success for "the lance lobby."[17] Another tactical debate concerned stirrups. British military equitation had been heavily influenced by the "Old German Seat" and troopers were trained to ride with long stirrups and straight legs. Combat experienced officers argued that, esthetics aside, a bent knee should be used on operations. Veterans prevailed and in 1914 the British cavalry entered France "with short stirrups and a bent knee, taking rough country in their stride and able to lean forward, sword thrust out in the straight arm engage, to gain a slightly longer reach than a continental lancer."[18]

The British Expeditionary Force (the BEF) arrived in France as a very professional army of four infantry divisions buttressed by a rather fulsome cavalry force of five brigades (one more than regulation), known simply as "the Cavalry Division." After the war, General Haig, a devoted cavalier, was asked why the British needed four brigades in a cavalry division. He replied "But you must have four. For the Charge, two brigades—first line; one in support, and you must have a reserve!"[19] The additional fifth brigade was a very old-boy arrangement; it was an independent brigade, commanded by Maj. Gen. Sir Philip Chetwode but without a complete headquarters. Chetwode reported to Allenby, who reported directly to Sir John French, commander of the BEF. It was a mighty host and, as it proved, was more than its commander Gen. (later Field Marshal) Edmond Allenby could handle.

The Cavalry Division, with its fifteen regiments,[20] was a monster compared to its German and French counterparts whose divisions comprised three brigades of two regiments apiece. Allenby's force was the equivalent of a German cavalry corps, with artillery to match consisting of five batteries: twenty 13 Pdr (approximate 75 mm) horseguns. A German cavalry corps owned 24.

British horseguns were served by selected crews and officers from the Royal Horse Artillery, considered a *corps d'élite* within the artillery. Dale Clarke noted that, "a junior officer would not be considered for service with the RHA ('earning his jacket') until he had completed at least six years service with the Royal Field Artillery and was an accomplished horseman."[21] The Cavalry Division's training emphasized performance as a *force de rupture* or a *force de manœuvre;* the bulk of entire doctrinal schooling had been dedicated to mass shock with only 10 percent of the training syllabus devoted to reconnaissance skills.

By the end of the Great War, the British had raised 12 divisions of cavalry, 6 of which served on the western front. The remainder saw action in the Middle East against Turkish Armies in Gallipoli, Palestine, and Syria.[22] This European force spent most of its time in anticipation of breakthrough and pursuit. Offensives became nightmares of artillery preparations mixed with noxious gas; prospects for mobile action became bleak. The front lines were turned into muddy porridge with shell craters that could easily drown a horse; where progress was possible, the torn earth made advance an awkward crawl. Regiments that were not disbanded or reorganized (the Life Guards were converted to a machine gun corps) were augmented with squadrons of automatic weapons; the cavalry brigade machine gun squadron proved far more useful than a brigade of dragoons.

THE KAISER'S CAVALRY

> Concentrate your energies, for the immediate present, upon one single purpose, and that is that you address all your skill and all the valour of my soldiers to exterminate first the treacherous English and walk over General French's contemptible little army.
>
> —Kaiser Wilhelm's "Order of the Day," August 19, 1914[23]

Although the Kaiser's army is synonymous with the bland field grey uniform, the Germans were as committed to their military traditions as the British and perhaps even more so. The German Empire adopted the M1907 *Feldgrau* in 1910, but their cavalry did not abandon distinctive styles. The *Uhlanen* continued to wear their Ulanka tunics and were conspicuous in their traditional square-topped *czapka,* albeit with gray cover. Hussars still wore the *Pelzmützen* (Busby) and Attila jacket, in *Feldgrau* weave. The German army of the Great War was not a homogeneous organization. Four German kingdoms that existed prior to unification in 1871 (Bavaria, Prussia, Saxony, and Württemberg) each retained their own army, with the Prussian being the largest. They maintained certain distinctions and attributes with strong regional ties and elements of dress; Bavaria, for example, raised four corps and its own *Bayerische Kavallerie-Division*. The only pan-Germanic cavalry was found in the *Garde Korps*.

Unlike their French counterparts, the 12 *Kürassier* regiments no longer wore the metal cuirasse. These units traced lineage to Friedrich der Grosse and commemorated historic roles or famous commanders or historical incidents. The *Graf Wrangel* regiment was popularly known as the "Porcelain Kürassiers" stemming from 1808 when the Elector of Saxony offered 600 dragoons to Frederick William I in exchange for a cabinet of china. All 10 regiments wore cream frockcoats and were called *die Weiß Kürassier* (white cuirassiers). The *Garde Kürassier Regiment,* Kaiser Wilhelm's favorite, had a remarkable *Metalhelm* made from Tombak (an alloy of copper and zinc); the result was a dazzling golden bronze with silver adornments, topped by an overwhelming rampant silver eagle. The uniform was often worn by the Kaiser and regularly portrayed in savage caricatures, emphasizing the *Metalhelm* with its extraordinarily ambitious avis. The regiment's motto, emblazoned in silver on the helmet's front was *"Suum Cuique"* (Latin: "to each his own"). It was more than appropriate for a unit in white kirsey, sporting a lurid bird of prey, to adopt an aphorism, which was, in essence, *chacun à son gout*. Frederick the Great selected *"Suum Cuique"* as his personal motto, but in his case, it held decidedly sexual connotations.[24]

German heavies used a menacing *Pallasche* while the light cavalry carried a shorter saber.[25] Allied reconnaissance reports were regularly confused, reporting an inexhaustible supply of *Uhlanen;* this was because all German cavalry regiments were armed with the lance; great for poking into infantry squares but at considerable disadvantage against a Lee Enfield or Vickers machine gun.[26] In 1914 Kaiser Wilhelm owned 11 divisions of reserve cavalry designated for operational missions as cavalry corps and a further 9 divisions of line cavalry assigned to infantry corps for tactical work with field divisions.[27]

The mass of cavalry that preceded the Schlieffen maneuver was tasked with one imperative: speed. Two cavalry corps led the invasion into Belgium. They were to be used as a *force de manoeuvre* but not in concert.

CAVALRY BATTLES IN 1914: DOCTRINE VERSUS TECHNOLOGY

> To make war always means attacking.
>
> —Friedrich der Grosse[28]

The North German plain is a vast pampas that sweeps through Belgium and into France, continuing onto the Seine. In 1940 and 1944, generals would call it "good tank country"; in 1914 it was an ideal theater for a cavalry performance. Initial operations seemed to be exactly what the Paris Expo promised— romanticism wrestling with no-nonsense twentieth-century physics. The heretofore cavalry task of deep reconnaissance was augmented by a scattering of airborne resources that gave the summer landscape a Wellsian *War of the Worlds* appearance. Lance toting uhlans trotted over manicured French valleys escorted by a Zeppelin poking past clouds. In turn they were observed by *Hussards* and a Blériot XI dipping its wing to take note of columns along the *route nationale*.

Like their fathers in 1870 and grandfathers in 1815, *Uhlanen* squadrons quietly crossed the Our River the night before the offensive began and seeped into Belgium. Both supreme commands were not quite sure what the other was up to: "The German cavalry which spread over the country . . . was merely a screen, which defective air-work failed to penetrate, and the frequent engagements were merely the brushes of outposts."[29] The BEF had brought along two dozen reconnaissance airplanes, mostly BE 2s (*Blériots Experimental*); France purchased 25 *Blériot XIs* just before the war; the Kaiser's army boasted an aerial cocktail of zeppelins and Rumpler *Tauben* ("Dove"): "A German aeroplane came soaring down close to us and startled us with the sharp crackling of its

The Warhorse versus Technology

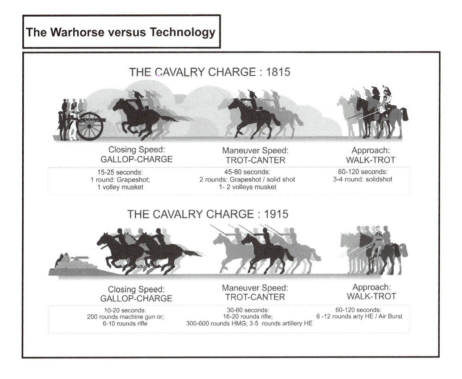

THE CAVALRY CHARGE : 1815

Closing Speed:	Maneuver Speed:	Approach:
GALLOP-CHARGE	TROT-CANTER	WALK-TROT
15-25 seconds: 1 round: Grapeshot; 1 volley musket	45-60 seconds: 2 rounds: Grapeshot / solid shot 1- 2 volleys musket	60-120 seconds: 3-4 round: solidshot

THE CAVALRY CHARGE : 1915

Closing Speed:	Maneuver Speed:	Approach:
GALLOP-CHARGE	TROT-CANTER	WALK-TROT
10-20 seconds: 200 rounds machine gun or; 6-10 rounds rifle	30-60 seconds: 16-20 rounds rifle; 300-600 rounds HMG; 3-5 rounds artillery HE	60-120 seconds: 6 -12 rounds arty HE / Air Burst

motor. It took a good look at us and then went its way."[30] There were four zeppelins assigned to the skies over Belgium and France, another two patrolling the North Sea, and a pair in Prussia. It was zeppelin reconnaissance that reported the progress of the Czar's army before the battle of Tannenburg. The "combat bird-like" *Taube*[31] shared the skies with its Allied counterparts in an affable execution of recce duties. This chivalrous accommodation would not last.

The airplane, with the tank, were kindred specters of a revolution that would eventually conspire to remove cavalry from modern war. But in 1914 one was nonexistent while the other appeared innocent enough. Aircraft recce was limited by weather; headquarters staffs began to take an increased interest in meteorological reports. In addition, there was the Luddite factor since the airplane was considered more complex and less reliable than cavalry. Pilots were not trained for this sort of work (although many flying officers were from the cavalry) and generals suspected that air crews sometimes confused or exaggerated what they saw; there is little difference between *Feldgrau* and khaki from 500 feet. One *Taube* pilot reported seeing troops running around in discernible panic, while in fact they were playing soccer. The threat of fratricide was a universal hazard on the ground and in the air: "French troops were firing more and more at their own airmen: a flying machine was a target they could not resist. Like victims of the drug habit, the more they indulged their craving, the less were they able to resist it."[32]

The real problem was communication, particularly from air machines; early methods were weighted bundles dropped near headquarters, followed by signals, which were invariably misinterpreted. The final solution, adopted in 1915, was the Morse code. The telephone and telegraph provided more timely battlefield information than mounted couriers and by the end of August, everyone was forced to use the radio or wireless, which however were not secure and permitted the other side to listen in:

> The rapidity of the advance frequently made it difficult to maintain the telephonic cables leading to the rear, which were often destroyed by the inhabitants or by fire, sometimes accidentally by our own troops... Communication with the Supreme Command had therefore to be carried on mainly by wireless stations, which again were overworked in keeping touch with the Cavalry Corps.[33]

Zeppelins had large crews and used on-board telegraph, while *Blériots* and *Tauben* flew a pilot and an observer who would record and sketch what he saw. Cameras were mounted on recce aircraft by the winter after it was suggested that photographing the enemy was better than rendering portraits.

The German invasion was a complete strategic surprise. The Supreme Headquarters (GQG "*Grand Quartier Général*") discovered that two gargantuan armies, over half a million Germans, were pushing toward Brussels and the French border and were expected to reach the Somme within three weeks. The main attack was conducted by the 1st Army, commanded by Gen. Alexander von Kluck, and the 2nd Army commanded by the fellow he disliked most, the well connected Gen. Karl von Bülow. Facing this grey flood was the small Belgian army, the promise of the BEF, Lanrezac's 5th Army, and General Sordet's Cavalry Corps.

The French responded to the German invasion by sending General Lanrezac into Belgium to meet von Bülow. On his left, protecting a vast open flank and about to confront von der Marwitz's Kavallerie Korps, were Sordet's three *divisions de cavalerie,* including one cuirassier brigade: "Our Corps suddenly ran up against a curtain of cavalry, a vast mass the Germans had thrown up to cover the advance of their Corps; thus we had no inkling of what was unfolding behind them."[34]

Early probes by advancing reconnaissance squadrons were bold ("The Germans tried to ride through the enemy by sheer dash and daring"[35]). A *Kürassier* brigade routed the 1st Belgian Lancers and trotted toward Brussels. Corps reconnaissance soon developed into firefights and skirmishes, which generally resulted in carnage. Vanguards discovered the obvious: cold steel and élan could not overcome rapid fire from bolt-action rifles and machine guns.

The first cavalry battle of the war took place on August 12 at Haelen. It was not a large scale engagement, but since it was a Belgian victory, Allied

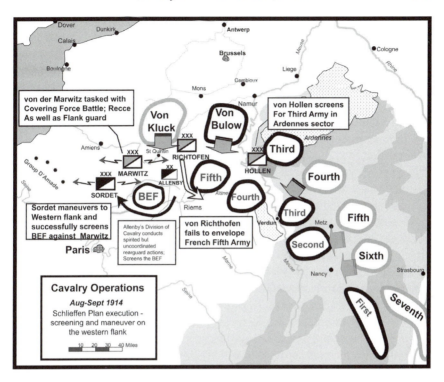

newspapers made much of it. German cavalry encountered a rearguard about 40 miles east of Brussels. There followed a series of skirmishes locally known as "the Battle of the Silver Helmets," which offered ominous portent of future cavalry operations. Repeated attacks by uhlans, hussars, and Kürassiers simply produced a slaughter of cavalry: "our retreat was . . . paralyzed by the number of riderless horses roaming about, and by the stragglers of the 2nd Kürassiers and 9th Uhlans who had been cut up by machine-guns."[36] The Belgian cavalry had dismounted and fought as dragoons, behind cover. Nearly 1,000 casualties, 300 prisoners of war, and 400 horses were lost. The Belgians lost half that number. The American ambassador to Belgium drove in to see for himself: "We had no difficulty in locating the field of battle. . . The ground was strewn with lances and arms of all sorts, haversacks, saddle-bags, trumpets, helmets."[37] Belgian resistance enraged the Germans. Lieutenant General von Poseck, author of a definitive history of German cavalry in The Great War, bitterly noted: "Many a good cavalryman had become victim of the bullet of a cowardly assassin in ambush."[38] The invaders seemed to miss the point. The Germans often behaved badly toward civilians; even von Moltke admitted that their advance through Belgium was brutal. This was intentional. Psychological warfare or *Schrecklichkeit* ("terror-frightfulness") was part of the operational plan, calculated as "an instrument of the invasion" and was meant to disarm or destroy any civilian resistance to the advance of German armies.[39]

As von Kluck's irresistible host pushed into France, it simultaneously created a considerable open western flank. The gap between its right hand corps and the English Channel was scantily covered by a cavalry screen about 30 miles wide, which in turn had its own flank hanging in the air. The mounted vanguard comprised the robust 2nd Kavallerie Korps commanded by the debonair General Georg von der Marwitz, and the 1st Kavallerie Korps under General Richthofen (no relation to the another famous cavalier who became a flying ace). The 4th Kavallerie Korps, under Lt. Gen. Baron von Hollen, was assigned to the forested confines of the Ardennes—a waste of cavalry. The remaining armies had either a division or brigade of cavalry attached.[40]

Cavalry operations included a medley of distinct activities: reconnaissance, maintaining contact between advancing armies, and finally, preparedness to act as a *force de manoeuvre* to exploit victory. As it turned out, von der Marwitz had to do all three, which soon dissipated his force of three cavalry divisions, which comprised nine brigades, or a total of 18 regiments. Their progress was bothered by an ad hoc mix of *Territoriales* (two divisions of older reservists) and the odd cavalry patrol, which formed *le Group D'Amade*, thrown in front of von Kluck as speed bumps.

German cavalry was confronted by Joffre's maneuver force—the GHQ cavalry reserve "under its dapper, hard working, loyal little General, Jean-François Sordet."[41] Sordet promptly launched his own *Chevauchée* into Belgium, a 150 mile romp ("un magnifique raid, faisant des randonnées de 130 kilomètres en vingt heures"[42]). His advance was stymied at Gembloux, astride the infamous Gembloux Gap, which would haunt French cavalry until 1940, and he was forced back. The reconnaissance in force had a devastating effect on Sordet's Corps:

> Unfortunately the torrid heat and strenuous work wore out our regiments. The horses were exhausted; the men weary, uneasy and discouraged. They had seen the enemy everywhere, attacked and tried to make him flee but with no effect; they had been completely frustrated in their attempts to defeat the invader. Enthusiasm fell. The reconnaissance mission had been a complete failure.[43]

The French had failed to penetrate the German screen, and no one was certain as to the specific locations of von Kluck's corps. When opposing cavalry did clash, the type of unit and size of warhorse determined the outcome:

> A squadron of the French 10th Hussars, the captain well in advance of his men, came on at full gallop. "Charge" shouted Captain von Ploetz and the two squadrons came together with a mighty crash. It was an unequal contest, the big Kürassiers on their heavy horses and the little southern Frenchmen on their

cat-like Arab horses. The collision of the heavy Irish charger of Captain von Ploetz rolled over the little thoroughbred of the French captain. Even as he fell he gave his adversary a sabrecut in the face. There followed a hand to hand encounter in the roadway, the long German lances against the keen sabers of the Frenchmen.[44]

The results were much the same when cuirassier met *Hussaren*. However, sabers and lances were the exception. Mounted skirmishes became conservative; cavalry regiments quickly adopted the tactic of falling back upon their machine-gun-equipped Jaegers and horse artillery batteries. As defensive fire slowed cavalry operations, the marching brigades actually caught up and "units rather intermingled."

Sordet fell back to the Meuse, attempting to cover Lanrezac's left, now an enormous maneuver area leading directly to Paris. It would require another army to hold along the Meuse. Luckily, the British were on their way. The BEF landed at LeHavre on August 10. Marshal French's introductory meeting with the fellow he was to support, Lanrezac, was a disaster: "The two commanders met alone, and having only the vaguest knowledge of each other's language, it was plain when they reappeared that each thought the other a fool."[45] The BEF marched north to Belgium; Allenby's regiments fanned out, trying to make contact with French and German alike. Sir James E. Edmonds noted, "as the Cavalry Division drew off, it was followed by a German airship."[46]

Von Kluck discovered the BEF at the Mons canal on August 22. The Germans immediately foxed a combined army-level attack. Both battles resulted in German victories, the abandonment of the Meuse line, and Allied retreat. Allenby's cavalry, although it won initial skirmishes and supposedly acquired "a moral superiority which was never lost,"[47] was not operationally vigorous. The hard fought successes by individual squadrons and regiments were dissipated by uncertain direction. The most unforgivable cavalry crime imaginable occurred directly after Mons. The cavalry was discovered to have abandoned its infantry and left them exposed.

Allenby's recce patrols reported no enemy to their front and he assumed the area was clear: "By 1130 this whole body of troops which could have covered the left of the 5th division had fallen back behind it, congratulating themselves they had eluded the enemy."[48] It was at this point that the German IV Corps appeared and threatened to roll up the British flank. Allenby immediately retraced his steps. The oversight was embarrassing for an officer who held a reputation for "an obsessive concern with regulations . . . spectacular tantrums when directives were ignored . . . earned him the nickname of 'the Bull.'"[49] Spirited actions restored the situation, but at a price.

Gen. Henry De Beauvoir de Lisle, commander of 2nd Cavalry Brigade, rode up to Lt. Col. David Campbell, commanding the 9th Lancers, advising "the safety of the 5th division depended on the cavalry delaying the German attack and that if necessary, he would have to sacrifice his regiment to effect this." He later reflected "I failed to explain my intention as clearly as I should have done."[50] As historian John Terraine glibly observed "British cavalry rarely need urging to dash at the enemy."[51] The 9th interpreted "delay the attack" into "charge the Germans." The subsequent efforts brought to mind Wellington's "galloping at everything" comment. The rescue of the 5th Division involved a series of sanguine actions. The 9th Lancers and 4th Dragoon Guards "charged towards the enemy with little artillery support and without the benefit of reconnaissance";[52] they were thwarted by a wire fence, badly shot up, and forced to retreat.

The force eventually withdrew in good order, but the incident pretty much forecast the tactical and operational conduct of the Cavalry Division for the next few weeks. Although he commanded an outfit that matched the cavalry opposite him, General Allenby did little to impose his will on the enemy; in fact, he had some difficulty exercising command: "The retreat began in the early hours of 24 August and almost immediately Allenby discovered he had lost control over nearly all his brigades."[53]

Weakened by heat and forced marches and harassed by stalking German cavalry, the BEF was a mass of very tired men trying to push south through mobs of French refugees. The last straw was when Allenby informed the commander of II Corps, Sir Horace Smith-Dorrien, he could not promise to cover his withdrawal: "I am afraid I cannot intervene effectively in the fight."[54] Smith-Dorrien, in a classic demonstration of *Fingerspitzengefühl* and *Auftragstaktik*, decided to stop, reorganize, and order a "stopping blow." The attack (the Battle of Le Cateau) surprised and momentarily staggered von Kluck; however, the action also created a hole in the center of the BEF between his II Corps and Douglas Haig, which infuriated his boss.

MANEUVER AND COUNTERSTROKE

> The great towering cuirassiers, clumsy and massive in helmets and breastplates, sat impassive on their horses. Not a man dismounted…There was something stoical about these men that was very striking, terribly reminiscent of one of the well known pictures of the Franco-Prussian War of forty-four years ago.
> —Maj. Gen. Sir Edward Spears, liaison officer
> to the 5th French Army, August 1914[55]

Under Von Kluck's continued pressure, Smith-Dorrien found himself separated from Haig's 1st Corps. The internal breach was hurriedly duct taped with more cavalry. Allenby was quickly using up his five plucky, but now extremely fatigued, brigades. Dusty marches were accompanied by swarms of insects; the horses wore fringes to keep flies out of their eyes, while the troopers rolled down neck covers to protect against the burning sun.

The scattered brigades had difficulty managing flank guards as well as covering the withdrawal. Allied cavalry action should be criticized. After all, Allenby had 15 regiments of cavalry, Sordet's corps owned another 18, and together, this combined mass of cavalry could have and should have ridden circles around von der Marwitz's 18 regiments. It will be correctly pointed out in rebuttal that there was no effective joint headquarters nor a visionary commander of Allied cavalry to order this.

Nonetheless, there were operational maneuvers of consequence conducted in August that were accomplished by the French and, principally, General Sordet. His efforts to assist the BEF were not applauded by its commander who thought Sordet reminded him of a piece of Dresden China. Field Marshall French demanded immediate compliance, and his post factum ruminations were less than effusive:

> [On the 24th] I visited General Sordet, and earnestly requested his co-operation and support. He promised to obtain sanction from his Army Commander to act on my left flank, but said that his horses were too tired to move before the next day. Although he rendered me valuable assistance later on in the course of the retirement, he was unable for the reasons given to afford me any support on the most critical day of all.[56]

Field Marshall John Pinkstone French was an experienced cavalry officer; his criticism should be cited even though he was considered fatuous by both his corps commanders. Smith-Dorrien's opinion of Sordet's cavalry differed substantially from French's:

> To my mind this was a very opportune action on Sordet's part, as he had got outside the German flank—and their subsequent advance gave us no trouble at all. Prior to [the] action at Le Cateau the German Cavalry outflanked us via Tournai and Denain, and was a very serious menace.[57]

French was miffed because Sordet had hampered his army's withdrawal by marching across the British lines in order to get to Smith-Dorrien. On the morning of August 26, the roads south of Le Cateau were "still full of British transport . . . after protracted delay owing to the passage of General Sordet's cavalry corps across them."[58] Smith-Dorrien's rearguard had lost most of its artillery and was about to be outflanked when "Sordet's Cavalry Corps with its quick-firing '75s arrived on the British left."[59] The Germans paused to recce this unexpected threat, losing an afternoon's pursuit. But Sordet had been run ragged. It has been suggested it was his own doing:

> The French cavalryman of 1914 sat his horse beautifully, but was no horsemaster. It did not occur to him to get off his horse's back whenever he could, so there were thousands of animals with sore backs, the smell of some units, owing to

this cause was painful. A sixth of General Sordet's command had already melted away."[60]

Sir Edmond Spear's criticisms merit notice; as liaison to GHQ Fifth Army he saw all of the French divisions, particularly Sordet's. This invites speculation; the French had successfully managed cavalry for over a millennium, and there was nothing they did not know about horses or horsemanship. But it should also be noted that the French themselves were critical of Sordet's handling of horses: "he was blamed for not letting the horses drink in the hottest summer days."[61] This, as well as personal exhaustion, may explain his being relieved of command in September.

Serious gaps remained in the Allied front. The Cavalry Division had skirmished at Le Cateau and then, as far as GQG was concerned, disappeared. A British colonel commanding one of the regiments called British GHQ via a village telephone seeking his brigade; he was told by the staff officer, "We have heard nothing of any of the cavalry for two days, Can you tell me where any of them are?"[62] Allenby's regiments were out covering the BEF or ploying in reserve, but as bits and pieces, not a mobile strike force.

By the end of August, Sordet's corps have virtually ceased to exist as a viable unit: "A very hard month. Despite the cruel forced marches and useless developments the troopers prevailed simply because their morale was good but their horses were either dead or in no condition to campaign, burnt out and in poor looking shape."[63] However, Sordet's screening forays had come closer to the mark than they imagined; one squadron nearly bagged all of von Kluck's army headquarters. The general recalled:

> At dusk an audacious detachment of French cavalry had attacked an aeroplane station south of La Ferte Milon, just as the line of cars of Army Headquarters was approaching the scene of action. All the members of the Staff seized rifles, carbines, and revolvers, so as to ward off a possible advance of the French cavalrymen, and extended out and lay down, forming a long firing-line . . . the French squadrons had been apparently shot down, dispersed, or captured by troops of the IX or another Corps. These bold horsemen had missed a goodly prize![64]

Meanwhile the BEF and Fifth Army's retreat to the Marne threatened to cause a domino effect on the entire front. British historian John Terraine felt Lanrezac had largely lost his nerve. During the withdrawal across the Aisne, the general could be heard proclaiming loudly: "Nous sommes foutus! Nous sommes foutus!"[65] Joffre demanded Lanrezac attack von Bülow to slow him down. The subsequent Battle of Guise took place on August 29, led by the dynamic Gen. Louis Franchet d'Esperey. He rode to the head of one of his brigades and personally gave the order to advance. As the long lines of French infantry smartly advanced, d'Esperey, a second-generation cavalry officer, called out to one of his brigadiers, the future Marshal Pétain, a former instructor at the staff college: "Eh bien, Monsieur le Professeur à l'École de Guerre, que pensez-vous de ce movement?"[66]

The attack jolted von Bülow; he demanded that von Kluck come to his assistance. Whatever his failings as a commander, Lanrezac should at least be remembered for his influencing von Kluck to stop and change direction. On August 31, von Kluck, despite being unsure of the actual location of the enemy, headed toward Château Thierry, closer to von Bülow. This pretty much put paid to the Schlieffen Plan.

This was of course not known to Marshal Joseph Joffre. One of the great rules of war is that the first thing a commander must do after he has used his reserve, is to create another reserve. The day after the Mons battle, Joffre issued General Order No. 2, which created a new French army, the Sixth. It was the stuff of strategical temper, ruthlessly gleaning divisions from the armies on the east of the Allied line; Joffre would build a new force in Paris, where he knew the German attack must end. But von Kluck was now moving southeast, skirting Paris. Von Kluck, von Bülow, and therefore von Moltke, were strategically blind, completely unaware that the French 6th Army was forming on their open flank. Reconnaissance reported the British and French in full retreat—incomplete information from a diminishing cadre of *Tauben*. A few days later, the same pilots reported: "the advance of four long enemy columns towards the Marne."[67] In both cases they had been correct.

By September 1, von der Marwitz, operating to the southwest of von Kluck, had scattered the *Group d'Amade* and threatened the BEF's left flank via a series of bloody actions against Allenby. He was now responsible for an ever-increasing front as von Kluck marched away from the Channel. Meanwhile, Richthofen's cavalry was moving into the open area between the BEF and Lanrezac. The war was now a matter of marching to keep up. One of von Kluck's staff officers wrote: "Our men are done up. For four days they have been marching 24 miles a day . . . The men stagger forward, their faces coated with dust, their uniforms in rags, they look like living scare-crows. They march with their eyes closed, singing in chorus so that they shall not fall asleep on the march."[68] It was little different in British and French divisions mixed amongst throngs of refugees and jams of wagons: "If Napoleon's Grande Armee had withdrawn from some African Moscow, in torrid heat instead of through snow, the conditions would not have been dissimilar."[69]

Joffre, aware of Sordet's pitiful state, now ordered GQG to issue *Instr. Generale No. 4* to form a new cavalry corps to cover the chasms between Lanrezac and the BEF, and more importantly, to confront what now appeared to be two German cavalry corps maneuvering into the area. He appointed Louis Napoléon Conneau "a splendid cavalryman, gaunt, huge, dark skinned, with hair *en brosse*. He looked like a centaur on the big thoroughbred he liked to ride."[70] General Conneau was given control over his own and Sordet's divisions; he noted proudly: "Murat himself never had such a command."[71] The Allies now deployed seven cavalry divisions around Paris. They were met in kind. As von der Marwitz and von Bülow neared the Marne, they too were covered by seven German cavalry divisions, the elements of three corps, for von Hollen was maneuvering southwest. But it was von Richthofen who merited most concern, advancing toward Lanrezac with vigor. Richthofen was regarded as peculiar and quixotic, even for a cavalry general:

> A will o' the wisp just escaping the grasp of Kluck or Bulow. The wireless was constantly vibrating with the plaint of the German wireless: "Where is Richthofen?" trailing off, when no answer was received into a querulous note: "But where on earth does Richthofen now lie?" . . . [he] appeared to us in the light of comic relief; we saw him as a butterfly of war, flitting away gaily when Kluck or Bulow seemed about to bring their nets on him.[72]

He came close to providing a definitive example of envelopment. As the Allied left front tottered, Richthofen's Corps suddenly appeared inside the gap. Marching 35 miles, scattering cavalry screens, Richthofen seemed about to cross the Fifth Army's line of communications—an event of cataclysmic proportions. It was not to be.

Richthofen, allegedly unaware of the situation to his front, stopped short when he reached the crucial crossings of the Aisne River. Additional effort would have severed Lanrezac's retreat, but Richthofen was content to spend the night on the north bank rather than exploring south into victory. By the next morning the opportunity had slipped away. The significance of this failed maneuver was assessed by Sir Edmond Spears:

> The Fifth Army owed its extraordinary escape partly to a lucky accident and lack of initiative of the German Cavalry . . . Owing to the heat of the day and the fatigue of the troops, the British had not retired so far as had been intended . . . The Germans wasted time reconnoitering its outposts on the river instead of advancing into the undefended country . . . when night came [Richthofen] withdrew westward to rest tired horses. If the German Cavalry had had real dash and been well led, it is difficult to see how the Fifth Army could have escaped without serious loss.[73]

German cavalry was burned out; perhaps Richthofen did not have the "right stuff." Clearly he was neither given the whip by his superiors nor supported. Another cavalry corps in echelon, something Murat did out of instinct, did not appear. Von der Marwitz was preoccupied with the western flank. The insertion of von Hollen's corps might have ended the campaign in German favor. It is all quite speculative. Richthofen's horses were literally off their legs: "The German Guard Cavalry Division reported that its horseshoes were almost completely worn out, begging that three or four lorry loads be sent . . . but above all that nails for shoeing were to be forwarded immediately."[74]

Fortuitously for the Allies, the German strategic concept fell apart in a series of Moltkian fumbles. At 4 A.M. on the 31st, he suddenly ordered all three divisions of von der Marwitz's cavalry corps to reconnoiter *toward* Paris. By September 2, the Paris Stock Exchange had shut down and the government had moved to Bordeaux as *Uhlanen* patrols reached Paris suburbs, eight miles from the Eiffel Tower. At midnight, von Kluck received a radio message from his supreme commander with a new plan. Von Kluck's army was to follow von Bülow in echelon; his mission was to protect the open flank. Esposito noted, "Thus the spearhead of the Schlieffen Plan was to be merely a security detachment!"[75] By the time von Kluck began to smell a French trap, the battle of the Marne had begun. The Allied counterstroke caught the Germans completely off guard.

The Battle of the Marne defeated the principal armies of maneuver, forcing them into hurried retreat. Allied pursuit was professional but not vigorous. The shoe-worn cavalry was spent and the troopers exhausted.[76] The new mission became to anchor the western flank on the English Channel, securing as many of the channel ports as possible. Joffre sent Conneau north, reinforcing what is often called "the race to the sea." The campaign was a series of attempted envelopments and saw the Germans surrender much of the territory von Kluck's army had taken in August. The determination of the Germans to make amends for their embarrassment at the Marne and salvage at least a superior strategic position, drove them to desperate efforts: "it was 'incomprehensible' that they could not get the better of the French."[77]

Von Moltke ordered a strong offensive near Arras which included three cavalry corps—a grand aggregate of eight cavalry divisions.[78] It was, on paper, an impressive overwhelming mass. Von der Marwitz commanded a cavalry army consisting of the I and II Kavallerie Korps with five divisions, while the IV Korps, under Baron von Hollen, deployed three cavalry divisions. They were expected to sweep across Flanders; von Hollen's orders were "to ride round the flank and rear of the enemy opposite the right wing, thoroughly destroy the communications, particularly the railways . . . and at the cost of the last horse and man . . ."[79]—a last ditch *chevauchée.*

Marwitz, reinforced by the *Garde Korps Kavallerie Division,* headed toward Calais, but was promptly checked by Conneau's three cavalry divisions.[80] The appearance of yet another French cavalry division on their left was enough to convince the Germans to withdraw north. Not only was their cavalry stopped, but it found itself outflanked and facing elimination. It had to be rescued by the XIV Infantry Corps, which arrived in time to extricate the warhorses.

Marwitz was turned back by an Allied horse army, which included Allenby's Cavalry Division, Conneau's formations, and a newly created French cavalry corps under General de Mitry. For the Germans it was a forlorn last act for a force that had languished on tales of Mars-La-Tour and from whom so much had been expected.[81]

The front settled into a positional stalemate. This was expected and predicted after the American Civil War as well as the Russo-Japanese War, but "none of the belligerents entered the war prepared for trench warfare on a large scale."[82] The *shovel,* a tool that would become synonymous with the combatant of the Great War, was an item stowed somewhere back in B Echelon.

One auspicious skirmish occurred at Dunkirk on September 26. A probe from the 9th German Cavalry division bumped the 63e Chasseurs who were supported by Rolls-Royce armored cars. Dubbed "Churchill's Toys," they had been dispatched by the First Lord of the Admiralty to support Royal Marines. Armed with a medium machine gun, the vehicles carried 9 mm armor, and their tires were practically bullet proof. The Germans promptly withdrew. The incident had rattled the German horses and gave them a glimpse of the future.

THE 1914 CAMPAIGN POST FACTUM

On the western front, the study of cavalry as an operational arm begins and ends in 1914. It centers on the maneuver of four corps, two French and two German, and a fifth, if one considers Allenby's Brobdingnagian Cavalry Division of 1914. Despite the heroic efforts of individual cavalry formations, cavalry accomplishments were incidental, evoking that unfortunate apothegm "Lions led by donkeys." Both sides conducted gallant attacks at the regimental level. Operationally, German cavalry failed to accomplish what was expected despite an area of operations that was superb cavalry country: "In spite of the exhausting marches it was called upon to carry out, brought in little or no information of value."[83] Spears decided that Allied supreme headquarters had:

> but little idea of what could be expected of cavalry, or what horses could or could not do. A criticism that can be legitimately leveled at Sordet himself is that he carried out the orders he was given with his whole force, instead of whenever possible detailing a single squadron or even when necessary a division for the duty in question.[84]

The observation may be valid, but also serves as an apologia for Allenby, whose tactics suggested a paucity of resources, when the opposite was true. Sordet's use of mass may have been excessive, but experience suggests it was worth the risk to the horses' health. Arriving with a full corps to prevent envelopment is preferable to arriving with a squadron or feeding in bits of brigades. In cavalry maneuver, mass precedes shock.

Of the armies in conflict that late summer, the French cavalry was the better used. Its conduct resulted in key rescues and timely maneuvers when the Allies needed them most. The British cavalry had been led with little inspiration from Allenby despite the accomplishments of its regiments. It reacted rather than imposed dynamic maneuver. General Phillip-Howell concluded: "The [Cavalry] Division was never a unit; it was a collection of Brigades."[85]

The race to the Channel anchored the left flank to the coast in Flanders and established a long front line stretching to the Swiss border. Fighting paused. The armies were worn out, nearly out of ammunition and short of provisions. Both sides dug in, trench lines and barbed wire covered the front. With no open flanks and the front a continuous wall of machine guns, rifles, and quick firing artillery, the cavalry was sent to the rear, to await a breakthrough. They had four years to wait.

"I hear it's a good Mudder..."

Chapter 11

Cavalry in the Great War, Part II: Tactical Stalemate and Quest for Breakthrough

It became obvious that special support was required to achieve any sort of meaningful result on the western front. Carnage sown by artillery *rafales* sobered everyone up. The cavalry regiments needed little convincing: "We were asked to gallop through the 'G' in 'Gap'. They might as well have aimed for the dot in 'Futile'."[1] Cavalry could not advance until the suppression of enemy fire. French officers observed lancers forming to support a tank-infantry attack quipped: "They're holding all these fellows back for the breakthrough that we've been waiting for two years—you know there's nothing like a lance against machine guns."[2] The challenge was achieving penetration at corps level: "Breakthrough always remains the most difficult form of a decision."[3] The army required a new type of shock weapon. The need for protection and mobility suggested an armored machine that could traverse trenches and ditches, flatten barbed wire, and defeat strongpoints, particularly machine-gun emplacements. Experiments with armored cars indicated that a tracked vehicle based on the agricultural tractor may well be the solution.

The tank pioneer, Major Ernest Swinton, sponsored by a visionary Winston Churchill, produced a successful prototype for the Landships Committee. Despite the enthusiasm of Sir John French, the navy, not the army, created the first tanks: "Little Willie," "Big Willie,"[4] and finally, "Mother." Testing had begun in September 1915. The Navy referred to tracked armored vehicles as "landships"; the great secrecy that surrounded construction resulted in a cover story: the vehicles were called *water-carriers,* later *water-tanks,* and finally, tanks. Factory workers were advised they were constructing tracked water transporters for the Middle East.

Meanwhile, French general Jean Baptiste Estienne also experimented with caterpillared armor and may have developed the tank first. The French initially built furniture vans (St. Chamond, Schneider) but finally settled on a diminutive but successful design, the Renault tank. Despite the disadvantage of a two-man crew, the vehicle sported a turret and proved popular. Renault FT-17's were available in numbers to counterattack Hindenburg's last offensive and were soon dubbed *le Char de la Victoire.* The American army built Renaults in the United States after the war, and the French army continued to employ them straight into the Second World War.

Rhomboidal tanks were first introduced into battle by the British at the Somme in September 1916. They shocked the enemy, but despite pleas from Swinton,[5] were not used in mass—surprise was wasted. There is speculation whether this attack was a bold, calculated venture or the British trying to outdo the French. The most fervent tank missionary, John Frederick Charles Fuller, argued for overwhelming astonishment (shock and awe): "If a Commander sees an invention or a new weapon which strikes at the root of his main problem and difficulties he is justified in taking the risk and employing it as a surprise and banking on it."[6]

Fuller's arguments made little impression until strategic offensives had failed catastrophically. A massed tank assault was finally attempted at the Battle of Cambrai (November 20, 1917). The vehicles stunned German front line troops and enjoyed a spectacular tactical success: "[we] must admit our efforts to stop these tanks are ineffective. We can do nothing against them."[7] German knee-jerk reaction was premature; the tanks' operational performance as well as their tactical triumph was, upon sober reflection, inconclusive. Mechanical breakdown, ditching, and damage from German artillery contributed to preventing penetration wide enough to introduce cavalry for exploitation. The tank did not vanquish trench warfare, but its effects suggested great promise if used in echelon and supported by fast-moving infantry. The key was "mass." Infantry requirements suggested a few tanks at a time were sufficient to help platoon/company groups penetrate, isolate, and destroy machine-gun blockhouses. Tank philosophers argued vehemently that the answer was a *tsunami* of armor: hundreds, thousands of tanks.

Surprisingly, the imperial German army was slow to adopt the tank. Low priority in construction eventually resulted in about 20 first-generation panzers reaching the front; they were uninspired, boxy affairs, resembling armored sheds. The first tank-versus-tank duel took place in April 1918 when three German A7Vs met three British Mark IV tanks. It was indecisive—few imagined that this was the vehicle that would both define modern war in 20 years and doom the cavalry to the knacker's yard.

THE CAVALRY-TANK TEAM VERSUS
THE SAVAGE RABBITS

> Messieurs, la victoire appartiendra dans cette guerre à celui des deux belligérants
> qui parviendra le premier à placer un canon de 75 sur une voiture capable de se
> mouvoir en tout terrain.
>
> —Gen. Jean-Baptiste Eugène Estienne[8]

The Great War produced a multitude of technological and tactical innovations from advanced platoon tactics to air support. Artillery had become ever more scientific, incorporating sound ranging, counter battery fire, flexible fire plans and a mix of munitions, including smoke and gas that disrupted enemy defense. Initially developed by the French army, the "creeping barrage" schemed that infantry would advance behind a wall of fire that kept pace with their attack until it reached the enemy trenches. The phased "set piece" attack created a doctrinal environment dominated by artillery generals and continued until the Germans introduced *Stosstruppen* and *Hutiertaktik*.

By 1918 doctrine called for fast-moving platoon teams intimately supported by tanks to advance behind shorter but well-planned barrages. As enemy machine guns came to life, they were dealt with by the tanks, which crossed trenches, ignored small arms fire, and could engage defenders by frontal or flanking fire. Success, again, was varied for tanks got bogged in giant shell craters, broke down, lost a track, or were knocked out; conversely, terrain or enemy fire could slow or stop infantry progress, leaving individual tanks to fend for themselves. German infantry, armed with grenades, charges, and flamethrowers, lay in wait for the isolated tank: "small groups along the front, hidden away but ready to pounce on the enemy when he passed by—like 'Savage Rabbits' as they were known."[9]

Theory held that a series of waves would break through successive lines of defense. Follow-on mounted regiments would be supported by faster "cavalry tanks." The western front was a smorgasbord of tank types and models; the British alone had several main battle machines—the lighter cavalry tank was called the *Whippet*.[10]

Combat experience proved that although the tank's armor stopped machine guns and shrapnel, it did not defeat direct engagements by artillery; surprisingly, gunfire created more casualties than mechanized breakdowns. The solution reached was to resurrect itself later in the Normandy *bocage*. The infantry-tank combat team introduced during the Great War became the basis for all future mechanized tactics: "From Amiens on, tanks were to follow, not precede the infantry to try to reduce tank casualties."[11]

"Following the infantry" was the antithesis of the cavalry doctrine. The creep over torn ground morphed tanks into ponderous testudos instead of dynamic weapons of breakthrough. The aim became to reach "the green fields beyond," which appropriately became the motto of the tank regiment[12] after the war. Once beyond the lines of defense and barbed wire, the cavalry would be set loose. The British and French generals preferred to scatter their tanks in democratic soupçons.

Cambrai, Amiens, and Soissons, are celebrated as the first "tank battles"; the British effort at Cambrai encouraged tank philosophes led by Fuller and Estienne. Fuller, an infantry officer totally besotted with the tank, had planned the tank attack at Cambrai and the autumn 1918 tank operations. His "Plan 1919" envisioned a complete mechanized assault with thousands of tanks but was never implemented.[13] The correct use of tanks continued to be debated well after the war. Fuller's "expanding torrent" excited the tactical mind as a concept but was not the formula to overcome a defense in depth. All agreed that once a breach was secured, infantry and tanks "should go through and push straight ahead so long as it is backed up by the maneuver body of the unit."[14] Until the late thirties, this meant a division of cavalry.

American battle experience was based on British and French training and British and French tanks.[15] The initial force comprised three groups, the 344th and 345th Battalions and Patton's 304th Tank Brigade.[16] The American force experienced serious mechanical breakdown and "ditching"; at St. Mihiel, out of 49 American tanks lost, only three were attributed to enemy fire.[17] This was to remain a constant factor in the cavalry-infantry debate over the operational role of tanks.

French doctrinal influence, started in the Revolutionary War, continued as the American tank corps adopted French kit. American artillery became thoroughly French; the 75 mm and 155 mm guns formed the basis of the army's direct and indirect fire for the balance of the century. Like the French, the Americans disbanded their tank corps by 1920 and placed the remnants under infantry command. Military critics scoffed at the tank: "a freak development of trench warfare which has already outlived its usefulness."[18] When the Great War ended, the warring states reduced their armies, which quickly reverted officers to substantive ranks and looked forward to frontier garrison duty. Sir John Hackett wrote of meeting a friend who said to him on the day of the Armistice: "Thank God, the war is over. We can get back to real soldiering."[19] By war's end, Western armies were anxious to rid themselves of large and expensive organizations that were really only good for killing Germans.

THIRD BATTLE OF GAZA

> It was the bravest, most awe inspiring sight I've ever witnessed, and they were … yelling, swearing and shouting. There were more than 500 Aussie horsemen … As they thundered past my hair stood on end. The boys were wild-eyed and yelling their heads off.
>
> —Trooper Eric Elliot, Beersheba, 1917

The Great War was a bleak period for cavalry, except in the Middle East. The Third Battle of Gaza (October 31–November 7, 1917) found Gen. Edmund

Allenby, promoted and even more dangerous, attacking Turkish armies advised by German officers. Allenby commanded seven divisions divided into two corps and a respectable maneuver force comprised of three cavalry divisions: the Anzac Mounted Division, Australian Mounted Division, and Yeomanry Mounted Division. The "Desert Mounted Corps" was led by Gen. Henry Chauval. The more exciting things in this campaign were Col. T. E. Lawrence's mounted guerrilla actions in the rear of Turkish lines and the splendid cavalry charge conducted by Australian light horsemen against Beersheba.

The Turkish army was commanded by a Prussian, Gen. Kress von Kressenstein, who had defeated the British in the two previous Gaza battles. The Turkish line, particularly weak on their open left flank, was anchored in the desert town of Beersheba. The British scheme was to feint against von Kressenstein's center, then maneuver against his flank and roll up the Turkish army, cutting off rail and road communications and moving on to Jerusalem. Beersheba was the key.

After initial artillery and infantry probes against the outer defenses, the Anzac Mounted Division advanced out of the desert. They were held up by small-arms fire from a well-constructed redoubt and artillery. Chauvel ordered the Australian 4th Light Horse Brigade to conduct a mounted charge. Two regiments (4th Victorian and 12th New South Wales Regiments) advanced at a steady trot, then broke into a furious gallop that became the antithesis of the Charge of the Light Brigade.

> The country was quite open and there was no cover so there was only one way to go at it. We raced across the open and soon the Turks started a barrage of shells but we never stopped. I think our sudden dash at them made the gunners shoot very wild.[20]

The Australians crossed four miles of open ground under steady fire from rifles, machine guns, and howitzers. Horses were hit, but the charge was not checked. Their saving grace was cavalry élan; the sheer audacity of the attack rattled the Turk infantry who did not adjust their rifle sights while supporting Austrian artillery misjudged the rate of the Aussie advance and fired *where they were,* rather than at *where they would be.* It was an audacious effort with three waves of cavalry, 500 yards apart.

> The clouds of dust of the charge may have made picking a target near impossible . . . About half-a-mile from the town, the Brigade began to overrun fugitive troops and guns. Some surrendered but others elected to fight and Light Horsemen here and there dismounted to capture them by rifle and bayonet. Led by two ground scouts about 80 yards ahead, the charge swept on . . . Some Light Horsemen raced through to the town to capture objectives. Others dismounted at various trenches or had their horses shot from under them and dazed or not, 'got to work with the bayonet'.[21]

The brigade overran the redoubt, decimated the gunners and swept on to take Beersheba. Their unlikely venture produced few casualties. The Gaza line fell, 12,000 Turks were captured, and then Allenby went on to take Jerusalem. Military history is breathless with "the last great cavalry" episodes; however, Beersheba was certainly the last great British Commonwealth cavalry charge and perhaps the only Mounted infantry charge, but this would ignore the exploits of Soviet cavalry circa 1943–45.

KAISERSCHLACHT—CAVALRY IN MOREUIL WOOD, MARCH 1918

Bullets have little stopping-power against the horse.
— Field Marshal Douglas Haig[22]

Dramatically reinforced by divisions from the eastern front following the unexpected Bolshevik Revolution, the German army launched a final effort to secure victory in the west before the appearance of a half million American troops under General Pershing. The dynamic duo of Hindenburg and Lundendorff cobbled together Plan Michael—the *Kaiserschlacht* (Kaiser's Battle), the last German offensive of the Great War. Three armies attacked the most vulnerable sectors of the Allied lines on March 21, 1918. Using quick barrages and *Hutiertaktik* (elite "storm troopers" trained to bypass, penetrate, and create headquarters shock, a forerunner of blitzkrieg), the German army accomplished what it had failed to do since the summer of 1914—it broke through. There was good reason to believe that the German offensive might reach Paris and, more dangerously, separate the French armies from the British, perhaps negotiating a favorable armistice. A German corps pushed southwest toward the River Avre, which hugged the Amiens-Paris railway—by morning, March 30, the vanguard of the 23rd Saxon Division reached Moreuil Ridge overlooking the Avre.

The only readily available force in the area was the 1st Canadian Cavalry Brigade, commanded by an officer with propitious initials: Col. (later Brig. Gen.) J.E.B. Seely. John Edward Bernard Seely, 1st Baron Mottistone, was British but commanded a brigade of veteran Canadian horsemen, many of them wearing Boer War ribbons. His three regiments, The Royal Canadian Dragoons, The Lord Strathcona's Horse, and The Fort Garry Horse, were a collection of The Royal Northwest Mounted Police, cowboys, and farmers brigaded with urban workers from the east. Thus far, they had spent most of the war in rear areas, engaged in minor skirmishes. Seely was instructed to delay the enemy advance as much as possible. Before dawn the brigade was ordered "Stand to your horses!" and the three regiments crossed the Avre. It became clear Moreuil Wood was already occupied by German infantry. Seely's from the saddle decision was simple and quick: two regiments would rush the woods, clear it in dragoon fashion; the remaining regiment, the Strathconas, would circumvent the woods (positioned on a bluff overlooking the river) and isolate the Germans.

The initial phase was a smart gallop to the woods where the Fort Garries and Dragoons quickly dismounted and began skirmishing in the closed terrain "mostly ash but not yet in leaf." Despite surprise, the first assault was checked; the Canadians regrouped and went in again with the bayonet: "The Boche had . . . machine guns, the lighter ones of which were up in trees . . . After we got into the wood we had to practically walk because it was very thick and many of our horses were shot and killed."[23]

The Germans had brought up reinforcements including a 77 mm gun troop, which began to engage two of Seely's squadrons: "[the horses] went calmly on with their grazing and paid no attention whatever to the shelling, while I saw others lay down and scream when a shell came particularly close."[24] Strathcona recce patrols probed the flanks and were savagely handled; one was virtually destroyed, a second badly shot up: "Sergeant Watson of 'C' Squadron rode up. His horse was seriously wounded; Watson was a mess. He looked at the Colonel and said 'Sir, the boys has all gone.'"[25]

Seely decided to launch his reserve. This was comprised of three troops commanded by a subaltern with an unlikely name for a bold cavalier, 33-year-old Lt. Gordon Muriel Flowerdew. Flowerdew advanced his squadron and soon discovered a large body of infantry, a howitzer, and several machine guns 300 yards to his front. He turned to his men: "It's a charge boys, it's a charge."[26] The trumpeter began to sound the attack but instead became the first casualty.

The Strathcona attack has been described as "surreal" and splendidly captured by the great equestrian painter, Sir Alfred Munning, who was with the brigade at the time.[27] The charge pitted sabers against rifles and machine guns. The initial shock dissipated into a frenzied melee: "the shouting of the men, the moans of the wounded, the pitiful crying of the wounded and dying horses."[28] One sergeant, leading the first troop had 59 wounds in one leg alone. Flowerdew was killed leading the charge, shot through the chest and legs. Of the 120 men in the squadron, fewer than half returned.[29] The attack was a gallant sacrifice that served to distract the Germans. The battle, including Flowerdew's charge, had operational consequences. Progress was stymied, the Germans stopped to organize a counterattack, and the thrust toward Paris petered out as Operation Michael ran out of steam.[30]

The assault was not done in complete isolation. Squadrons from the 3rd British Cavalry Brigade protected the brigade's right flank; the Royal Flying Corps had dropped over a hundred bombs and conducted dozens of strafing runs, resulting in serious German casualties. Flowerdew was awarded a posthumous Victoria Cross, and the Allied armies got on with the war. The action's significance was placed in context when Marshal Ferdinand Foch visited New York in October 1921. Reviewing a grand parade, the Allied supreme commander appeared delighted to recognize Canadian cavalry in the march past, which prompted an emotive accolade:

> Moreuil Wood. That is where the Canadian Cavalry Brigade saved the day. Those wonderful men held the borders of the wood and even regained ground under the command of gallant General Seely. Yes, they were the Royal Canadian Dragoons, the Lord Strathcona's Horse and the Fort Garry Horse—I shall never forget them.[31]

Considering the spectacular accomplishments of the Canadian infantry corps under Gen. Sir Arthur Currie, this commendation to the cavalry was high praise indeed. Any propitious action was welcome balsam for cavaliers. Moreuil inspired an arm that finished the Great War decidedly in the shadow and unaware of greater mechanical threats to come.

CAVALRY IN THE GREAT WAR—THE FINAL RECKONING

> It is pointless to single out any arm for special praise; the infantry won glory that can never be taken from them; but the artillery and cavalry also maintained standards almost unbelievably high.
>
> —John Terraine *Mons, The Retreat to Victory*

Terraine's praise may be effusive but in the case of the cavalry, exaggerated. The fault lies not with tactical acumen or individual valor, but rather with the success of cavalry as an *arm*. This is as true of the Germans as it is of the British, although French corps, as colossal fire brigades, performed notable missions of rescue early in 1914. The frustrations of cavalry in modern war were well illustrated by the regimental commander of the Russian 1st Sumskii Hussars; forced to dismount, then pinned down by German fire, the enraged colonel stood up and shook his fist at the enemy: "If we could only get to you!"[32]

The study of cavalry in the Great War requires an open mind and thick skin for those sympathetic to the warhorse. Criticisms of cavalry proliferate and often include sarcastic digs and trying repetitions of the obvious. It must be admitted that despite a surfeit of valiant self-sacrifice, the Great War was apocalyptic for cavalry. Within the chronicles of campaigns the heroic horse tends to swamp the operational and strategic horse. There was no Eylau and certainly no facsimile of the Ulm campaign. The use of mass to create shock became simply unacceptable. Gen. Maximillian von Poseck ended his definitive *The German Cavalry, 1914 in France and Belgium* with a quote from von Bernhardi's *Cavalry Service,* written before the Great War: "The times of Seydlitz are in a sense irrevocably past. No battle will be won again as he helped to win them."[33] The best example of the relegated status of cavalry is the

Kaiserschlacht. This final statement in the evolution of German doctrinal thinking featured nine tanks (German A7Vs and five captured British Mk IVs) divided amongst three corps. There was no cavalry per se; individual squadrons were allocated per division for minor recce and liaison duties. The German cavalry now consisted of but three divisions, and these were kept stationed in Russia, where their performance had been rated as disappointing.

Worse, the clear superiority of the airplane in reconnaissance had became unassailable. In order to survive, the cavalry had to wrap itself in mystique and invoke poignant examples of deeds of sacrifice or serendipitous victories like Beersheba. The airplane, however, was a servant of mechanics and weather, while the tank was an imperfect, plodding creature of trench warfare. And there were still empire frontiers to police. As long as air machines needed bases and tanks needed to operate next to logistic arteries, the horse, it was argued, still had a military future.

Schommer's romantic painting captures the essence of Bucephalus, the archetype warhorse, the *anthropophagous*—a man-eater. This portrays the embodiment of the stallion in battle: intimidation, size, slashing hoofs, and an indomitable aura. *Alexander taming Bucephalus*, F. Schommer, late 19th century.

The terror of the Mongol horse army is dramatically captured by De Neuville in a romantic work. The weapons mix shown is decidedly feudal (lance, battle-axe, mace and chain) and does not feature the dreaded "horn bow." Horse furniture is gaudy but the efficient stirrups and complete control of the rider illustrate the technique that created an operational mobility. *The Huns at the Battle of Chalons*, A. De Neuville (1836–1865).

Modern jousting. The beginning of a charge from a standing start. Note the *torse* atop the helm. The lack of protection for the horse is juxtaposed by a well-armored rider and demonstrates the vulnerability that broke up attacks at Crécy. Photo courtesy Richard Alvarez, 2007.

Medieval reenactment by master horseman and historian Richard Alvarez. Modern experiments show a properly fitted knight could conduct melee both mounted and dismounted. The plate armor, evenly distributed over the body (unlike heavy rucksacks) permitted the rider to dismount, kneel, and rise on his own. A dismounted knight was formidable but eventually fought with a disadvantage against a lighter opponent who could maneuver. Photo courtesy of Richard Alvarez.

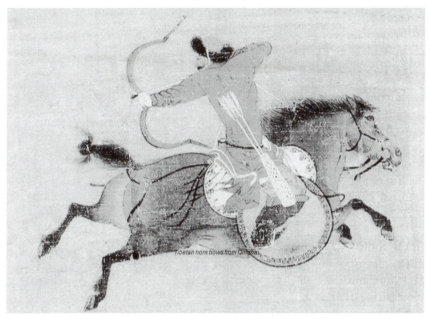

Ancient print of Mongol horse archer depicting the classic "Parthian Shot" as well as the glued and layered Mongol warbow. This design is more familiar than the English longbow because it has been depicted as "Cupid's Bow." The archer uses silk armor and a loose harness, but depends on sturdy stirrups—without which shooting the Mongol bow with any accuracy was quite impossible. Chen Juzhong, *Horse Archer*.

Husaria. This Polish cataphract cavalry was a complex combination of lancer, knight, and hussar. The addition of feathered "wings" created an awesome spectacle of sight and sound—the whirring frightened enemy horses. The Husaria symbol was used as heraldic device marking all vehicles and tanks of the 1st Polish Armored Division, part of Montgomery's 21st Army Group in 1944–45 (insert). Władysław Teodor Benda, *Polish Winged Hussar,* 1911.

Napoleonics: Polish Lancers in Spain. This work by Wojciech Kossak captures the violent shock of a cavalry attack. Note the Polish *czapka*—destined to become universal lancer head dress in the 19th and 20th centuries. The savage cut of a saber caused awful wounds, but shortly after this victory at Somosierra (1808) Bonaparte permitted the Poles to use their favorite arm, the lance. Their success led to a renaissance of the lancer in all European armies. Wojciech Kossak, *Szarża w wąwozie Somosierry*, 1907.

Civil War orderly with horse, at Antietam, 1862. The simple uniform and sensible saddle illustrate the influence of the principle of "Utility" over "Seduction" in military dress. Common sense dominates during wars, and then uniforms become gaudy again. Note the saber (based on the French Napoleonic model)—the length is a distinct advantage in the melee and perhaps might outreach a determined bayonet. The preferred and more effective arm was the carbine. Courtesy of Library of Congress, LC-B8171-0619DL, MHI.

This photograph of a Civil War cavalry melee reenactment ("Battle of Olustee") captures the favored close quarter battle: pistols, shotguns, or carbines. The trooper in the center holds a *Spencer* 52 caliber seven shot repeater—the most advanced shoulder firearm of its day. Its main criticism was the dense smoke it produced when fired, though it did give some cover to cavalry skirmish lines. Confederates were reluctant to use captured *Spencers* because supply of cartridge ammunition could not be assured. Photo courtesy of Kathy Heitman, T.General@att.net.

Captain George A. Custer (on left) with General Alfred Pleasonton. Custer graduated last in his West Point class (1861)—within a few years he was a brevet general, commanding a cavalry brigade. He wears the most common head gear of the Civil War—a version of the French Army *Kepi*. Courtesy of Library of Congress, LC-B8171-7551 DLC, MHI.

Seduction triumphs. 17th Duke of York's Royal Canadian Hussars, circa 1905. The uniform was a duplicate of its sister regiment, the 13th British Hussars. By the end of the 19th century, all Hussar regiments looked similar, particularly with the Busby head gear which was the final evolution of the French *Colpack*. The Busby continued the use of the attractive, but completely useless *flamme* or "Busby bag." The cross-belt was, and is, de rigueur for cavalry costume. Note the carbine bucket—a more useful refinement of lessons learned from the U.S. Civil War. Courtesy of the Directorate of History and Heritage (DHH); Dept. of National Defence (DND)/Library and Archives Canada.

Troopers from the first Canadian Mounted Rifles, in the South African veldt. The influence of the Northwest Mounted Police is evident via the Stetsons and the western-prairie style. This soon influenced most Boer War cavalry. Note the carbines and indifference to the saber. Courtesy DHH; DND/Library and Archives Canada.

The final stage of "Seduction" principle in cavalry costume: a Prussian Garde Kürassier *Metalhelm* (cast in Tombak), circa 1900–1914. The ostentatious helmet was more practical than the infamy it acquired from western cartoonists. Note the motto: "*Suum Cuique.*" The eagle was removable, the helm then fitted with a canvas cover, which offered better protection than the cloth caps of Allied Commonwealth-Empire Cavalry. Photograph used with permission of Tony Schnurr: www.kaiserbunker.com.

British and Commonwealth Cavalry, circa 1918. Trooper from the Lord Strathcona's Horse (Royal Canadians) regiment dressed for combat in khaki and a steel helmet, adapted from the infantry. The short Enfield carbine is stashed in its bucket accompanied by feed bags, rain capes, a bed roll, and an extra ammunition bandolier around horse's neck. The kit includes a gas mask for the rider and the 1908 saber, touted as the finest cavalry weapon devised. Courtesy DHH; DND / Library and Archives Canada.

The charge of the 4th Australian Light Horse Brigade at Beersheba. This photograph is sometimes represented as the actual charge but in fact was a reconstruction. It constitutes a better portrayal of a cavalry charge, despite the rather perfect lines. Note the distance between squadrons—over 500 yards—a better defense against artillery and plunging fire. The grouping is relatively tight and illustrates the aged debate over maneuver *space* versus *mass* for shock effect. Many of the Australians attacked with a practical alternative to the lance or saber: carbines with fixed bayonets. Courtesy MoD, Archives. Australian War Museum, A02684.

Charge of Flowerdew's Squadron, March 30, 1918 by Alfred Munnings, a war artist specializing in equestrian studies. This depiction of the charge captures the drama and blur of a mounted assault. The lines are perhaps too straight but accurately show that in the last year of World War I, cavalry still preferred to attack with saber—even when facing machine guns and rifles. A. Munnings, Courtesy DHH; DND/Library and Archives Canada.

Origins of the *Konarmyia*. Trotsky's poster translated "To Horse, Proletariat!" The charger is less a typical Russian breed but properly menacing and heroic. The revolutionary cavalry depended on rifles and quick firing guns as much as sabers. Lithograph, A. Apsit, 1919.

Mechanization and the warhorse. U.S. Cavalry during the Louisiana Maneuvers, circa 1940. This section advances a machine gun at the canter, demonstrating the cavalry's accommodation for modern technology. Anti-tank guns were also grouped with cavalry regiments by 1939. The troopers wear the British World War I helmets and gas masks. Note the gas masks attached to the chargers. Courtesy Military History Institute Carlisle Barracks/Library of Congress.

Konarmyia versus *Panzerarmyia*. The Red Army fought throughout World War II with a comfortable mix of horse and armor. Cavalry Corps went into action as late as 1945 with a mélange of mounted units, tanks, artillery, and even *Katyusha*. This photograph appears contrived but nevertheless demonstrates the "combined arms" team of 1941: cavalry, tanks, and fighter ground attack. Note the brandished sabers and a very early T-34 tank. Sovfoto, 1941.

Western Cavalry, World War II. A *Humber* Mk IV armored car of the 17th Duke of York's RCH (the 7th Reconnaissance Regiment) in Normandy, July 1944. Two months of stalemate kept Allied mechanized cavalry dismounted and patrolling on foot, or holding defense lines. In August, after the *Cobra* breakout, recce regiments burst out to conduct "proper" long range romps. Unlike the Red or German Army, all western cavalry had paid off their horses by 1942. Courtesy DHH; DND / Library and Archives Canada.

Polish *Cromwell* recce tank from the 10th Chasseurs Regiment (the Poles continued their Napoleonic traditions) passes a brewed up *Panther* during *Operation Totalize* in 1944. Polish armored cavalry maintained its *Husaria* roots: cataphract squadrons with a long deadly reach. The *Cromwell* was the fastest Allied tank in Normandy and a serious contender for the *best cavalry tank* honors. The British actually built cavalry tanks as well as infantry tanks during the war. Courtesy DHH; DND / Library and Archives Canada.

American Cavalry squadron's breakout of Normandy, July 1944. The Cavalry (Mecz) squadrons were assigned a modern mix of weapons: light tanks, armored cars, and tracked vehicles, including assault guns. This photo shows an M-8 Motor Gun Carriage, probably of the 113th Cavalry Group passing a knocked out or abandoned German *Panther* tank. Courtesy Military History Institute, Carlisle Barracks/Library of Congress.

The *Sherman* of the millennium army: the M1 *Abrams* became the main American battle tank of choice, equipping Cavalry Regiments, Army Tank Battalions, and Marine Tank Companies. Better compared to the *King Tiger*, it quickly won admiration and battlefield respect. A heavy tank, virtually invulnerable but impressively fast, the *Abrams* dominates any battlefield—no M1s were lost to enemy tank or anti-tank missile action in both Iraqi wars. The photograph shows an M1A2 in desert livery. Insert: M4 *Sherman*—the standard Allied tank of World War II. *M1* photo courtesy General Dynamics Land Systems; Insert *Sherman* courtesy DHH, DND/Canadian Archives.

Cavalry dress in the cybernetic era. These two men are the Squadron Leader and the Battle Captain of a cavalry regiment in Afghanistan, spring 2007. Major Trevor Cadieu and Capt Mark Lubiniecki, B Squadron, Lord Strathcona's Horse (RC), stand before a Leopard C2. Compare dress to the regimental riding troop (insert), demonstrating 19th century cavalry drill. Photo from Canadian Forces Image Gallery, http://www.combat cameraforces.gc.ca, courtesy of the Department of National Defence.

Cavalry special-to-arms skills. A trooper from the Lord Strath-cona's Horse demonstrates "tent pegging": sticking low wooden pegs from a cantering charger. A large number of modern states, particularly British Army's *Horse Guards*, and France's *Garde Républicain*, maintain full time mounted cadres to preserve cavalry traditions and display horsemanship skills. Photo from Canadian Forces Image Gallery, http://www.combatcamera.forces. gc.ca, 2007, courtesy of the Department of National Defence.

Mounted officers and men of The Life Guards & The Blues and Royals. The combined squadron, stationed at Knightsbridge, regularly maintains guard at Horse Guards Parade and conducts royal escorts—troops are rotated through the tactical regiment that conducts normal operations and has participated in Afghanistan and Iraqi campaigns. Sergeant Mike Harvey, mod.uk.

The endurance of the warhorse even within high-tech asymmetrical war is acknowledged in this model of the proposed monument commemorating U.S. Special Forces. It depicts a soldier mounted and conducting operations with the style and *espirit* of a classical warrior. Courtesy U.S. Army, JFK Special Warfare Center and School, Fort Bragg.

Millennium Cavalry. Tank squadron with a vehicle from the recce troop: *Leopards* C2s, with mine plows attached, ployed alongside a *Coyote* reconnaissance vehicle (a variant of the *Stryker*). The cavalry squadron has become a robust fighting force augmented with the very high tech *Coyote* sporting a sophisticated suite of electronic surveillance equipment including radar, video, and infrared surveillance devices. The vehicle contains a 10-meter telescoping mast that can peek out from behind a hill or building. Photo from Canadian Forces Image Gallery, http://www.combatcamera.forces.gc.ca, 2007, courtesy of the Department of National Defence.

"Raiding and pillage sounds so declassé – I much prefer *chevauchée* ..."

Chapter 12

Mechanization and the Cavalry: Toward an Epiphanic Moment

My legs are bowed from riding on a 'orse when in the ranks
They took away my 'orse and spurs and shoved me in the tanks
I've spent me life with 'orses and I loved the work and toil,
But I can't stand these new fledged beasts that live on gas and oil.
—Lt. Col. C. E. Morgan[1]

In 1918 Gen. J.F.C. Fuller attended a tank demonstration for the British general staff and opined: "They reminded me of the heathen gods assembled to watch the entry of the new Christian era. They felt it was better than their own epoch and left determined to destroy it." Fuller, as reformer, was convinced his opposition was an "equine Tammany Hall which would far rather have lost the war than have seen cavalry replaced by tanks."[2] Mechanization divided the veteran armies of the Great War. The impetus to mechanize was less an argument over improved mobility than a struggle for survival, charged with Shakespearean drama and misfortune, intertwined with subplots that encouraged, nay, demanded nothing short of extermination. In Europe, Socratic dialogue was either brushed aside or purged; in the United States, doctrinal wrangling ended in the cold blooded dispatch of the mounted arm. The chief of cavalry called it betrayal; some called it murder.

This chapter will review the doctrinal struggles that divided the military in some countries and threatened the cavalry in all. The wedding of the warhorse to the tank was an unnatural fusion, yet at once the most obvious solution to the horse's travails, endured since the longbow, and made terminal with gunpowder. Attempting to explain the warhorse as a comrade warrior rather than an implement of battle is challenging but perhaps will be made clearer via the chronicle of Commodore's death. Doctrinal solutions varied but were most dramatic within the French army which, despite an avant-garde façade, began both of its twentieth-century wars with a cavalry corps. The most intricate operational melding of the barbaric with the sophisticated was conceived in, of all places, the Soviet Union, which evolved horse-army technique to vistas beyond Attila. A review of Polish cavalry is required if only to set straight the misconceptions of the warhorse and blitzkrieg, which persist into the new millennium. Finally, the proper end to an examination of cavalry mechanization must be France 1940, the apparent last hurrah for horsed cavalry. The Second World War acquired a different tone and methodology after the fall of France, which this history maintains was an epiphanic moment for the cavalry and a restoration of the stature that mounted troops enjoyed only in the medieval epoch.

GREAT WAR EPILOGUE: BOLSHEVIK CAVALRY VERSUS POLISH ULANS

> The problem is harder where horses are concerned... In the East our armies are entering steppe regions where horses are plentiful... The Soviet Republic needs cavalry. Red cavalrymen, forward! To horse, proletarians!
>
> —Leon Trotsky

After the Great War, Russia was ravaged by civil war against the Bolsheviks. The occasion permitted the new Polish government to retrieve lands wrenched from its grasp by Mongol armies and the defunct Tsarist Empire. Tim Taylor noted in *Red Star–White Eagle*: "The Red Army's counterattack began with the Soviet 1st Cavalry Army [*Konarmiya*]. These anachronistic Cossacks eliminated the Ukrainians, provoking Polish forces into headlong flight."[3] Fighting eventually drove the Poles and nationalist Ukrainian forces west until the Bolsheviks reached the outskirts of Warsaw. Polish operations were bold and incorporated dynamic maneuvers which left an impression on the Soviet commander of the western front, the complicated and flamboyant cavalier, future marshal of the Soviet Union, Mikhail Tukhachevsky.

The crucial battle at Komarów featured political shenanigans between the *Konarmiya*'s commander, the rude and ambitious General Semyon Budyonny and Tukhachevsky. The *Konarmiya* attacked the Ukrainian city of Lviv instead of supporting the main battle against Warsaw. Tukhachevsky was left without his prime mass de maneuver just as he was being decisively outfought by Polish General Sikorski's 5th Army, which used mechanized units (tanks, armored cars) in an almost blitzkrieg-like manner.[4] The Polish-

Russian campaign is particularly interesting for it featured the last legitimate all-horse actions of the twentieth century.

The Battle of Komarów (August 1920) was heralded as the biggest cavalry battle since Napoleon. The operation reached its climax southeast of Lviv. Budyonny brought up four cavalry divisions (17,000 sabers), supporting infantry, artillery and even a few armored cars against about 6,000 Polish Ulans and supporting brigades. He then ordered his troops to envelope the city from the west. As his cavalry attempted to skirt the Polish line they were themselves taken in the flank. The Polish cavalry commander, interestingly named Juliusz Rommel, broke through Bolshevik flanks and surrounded the *Czaritsan* force. Isaac Babel, assigned by Trotsky as a journalist-cavalier embedded in Budyonny's headquarters, recorded a war of bizarre military collectives:

> Bullets buzz, artillery fire chases us from one place to another, miserable fear of airplanes . . . Nothing to feed the horses with. I see now what a horse means to a Cossack or a cavalryman. Unhorsed cavalrymen on the hot dusty roads, their saddles, in their arms, they sleep like corpses on other men's carts, horses are rotting all around, all that's talked about is horses, the customs of barter, the excitement, horses are martyrs, horses are sufferers—their saga, I myself have been gripped by this feeling, every march is an agony for the horse.[5]

In the succeeding phase Budyonny's brawny 6th Cavalry Division penetrated Polish encirclement then formed a defensive screen near the forested Wolica Śniatycka. Rómmel ordered two regiments into a frontal assault and maneuvered the 1st Ulan Regiment against their left flank. After a 30 minute melee, the *Konarmiya* was in retreat. Poles lost no prisoners, suffered about 500 casualties (700 horses), and savaged the Bolshevik Cavalry Army, which suffered at least 3,000 casualties. Its morale collapsed—the *Konarmiya* was a spent fighting force.

Komarów's effects were two fold; the more unfortunate was it gave false hope to cavalry diehards throughout the modern world. Its second result was its prodigious effect on Tukhachevsky and deep battle doctrine. The lessons of the Polish front made little impression on Budyonny. Perhaps his most lasting tribute is that a soviet horse breed was named for him—the *Budyonny* or *Budennovsky*.[6] Appreciated for its size, strength, endurance, and ability to endure the rigors of campaign the *Budyonny* equipped many of the Soviet cavalry regiments in the Great Patriotic War.

THE KONARMIYA FRATERNITY AND MARSHAL TUKHACHEVSKY

> As for me, I get all I ask for.
> —Tukhachevsky to Marshall Gamelin, Paris, 1935

> If some among them are innocent, it is expedient that they should be assayed
> like gold in the furnace and purged by proper judicial examination.
> —Royal letter opening an Enquiry into the Templar Order of Knights, 1307[7]

Glubokii Boi or "deep battle" is the ultimate cavalry offensive, incorporating shock, armor, and maneuver on a gargantuan scale—a protean exploitation by tank and mounted formations causing shock and paralysis. Deep battle is a sophisticated, technical evolution of Golden Horde tactics; its tactical technique is essentially the Mongol attack without the Parthian maneuver; its operational style is nothing less than a cavalry tsunami that floods, then drowns its opposition. Deep battle also incorporates large raiding forces (operational maneuver groups—OMG) that are perhaps the ultimate *chevauchée*. This simplistic précis of deep battle will be criticized as cavalier by doctrinal technocrats but that merely reflects its inherent dichotomy. Deep battle is apparently one-dimensional: simply the act of overwhelming yet it is also a sophisticated operation, seemingly well beyond the means of a proletarian army. Remarkably, it was a result of practical experimentation by the Soviet high command—the Russian character seems to be suited to operational art.

Soviet doctrine benefited from a dynamic duo: Tukhachevsky and V. K. Triandafilov.[8] The initial concept (cavalry operations as a mechanized juggernaut) was conceived by Tukhachevsky, the most prestigious doctrinal guru of the past half century. His stature is likely greater in the U.S. Army War College at Carlisle than Camberley, the Parisian *l'École supérieure de guerre,* or in Hamburg's *Führungsakademie.* Tukhachevsky's popularity amongst martial cognoscente blossomed during the cold war and continued to grow. Deep battle, embellished and perfected by subsequent Red Army practitioners, introduced a strategic concept that dwarfed Fuller and reappeared within the Amerikanski *AirLand Battle.* Tukhachevsky's inspired vision grew out of the chaos within Budyonny's cavalry army.

The Tsaritsyn Cavalry Group, raised in a city destined to be Stalingrad, was the nucleus of Budyonny's *Konarmiya.* The great Bolshevik fraternity and who's who of future Kremlin power consisted of: Stalin as their devoted political commissar; Marshals Timoshenko, Kulik, and Meretskov as squadron leaders; General Krivoshein as a troop leader; Marshal Voroshilov as a staff officer; and even employed Marshal Zhukov as a sergeant. Attacking the *Konarmiya* was regarded as ultimately an attack on Stalin himself. Ironically, this force is popularly associated with Leon Trotsky as the embodiment of his *proletarians to horse* vision.

Stalin's stint in the *Konarmiya* gave him a cavalry bent but he was primarily Machiavellian. He readily embraced any arm that promised victory and offered a faithful cadre that saw him, not the remnants of a Czarist general staff, as the font of operational wisdom. Armored cavalry promised to do that. Factory workers made tanks and farmer's sons could be quickly shown how to drive them. Tukhachevsky was made chief of staff of the Red Army, then deputy commissar for defense. The Wehrmacht resurrection pushed Stalin into a desperate program of building a tank park that would match Hitler's. Tukhachevsky became Stalin's Guderian.[9]

Tukhachevsky's influence abruptly terminated when he was tried and executed in 1938, one of the many victims of the infamous Stalin Purges, which killed off the higher echelon of the officer corps.[10] The political cleansing left three types of "acceptable" senior officers: the original Bolshevik veterans who learned their trade under the czar, the loyal albeit German trained staff officers (the few who survived soon met their former teachers during Operation Barbarossa in 1941), and finally, Stalin's comrades from the *Konarmiya* who survived best. Service in the cavalry paid off.

After the state trials, Tukhachevsky's seminal document, Field Service Regulations *PU-36—Deep Operations,*[11] was purged from the Red Army. Old guard Konarmyists regarded Fuller's mechanization theories as "simply too un-proletarian" and "bourgeois."[12] German invasion would shock the Soviet Union—the Red Army would relearn and ameliorate its warfighting technique through two years of bitter struggle. Relearn but not reinvent.

UNDERSTANDING THE CAVALRY: THE DEATH OF COMMODORE

> [The Cavalry Officer] must have a passion—not simply a liking—for horses, for nothing short of an absorbing passion can make him take the necessary interest in his mount . . .
>
> —Maj. George S. Patton, Jr., 3d Cavalry, *The Cavalryman,* 1921[13]

After Versailles, the initial question of tank custody was solved in different ways. The Americans gave the tank to the infantry, the French gave certain tanks to the infantry but allowed that the artillery also had an inherent right as *artillerie d'assaut,* the Germans were not allowed tanks, the Russians could not initially afford tanks, and finally, the British, who inherited lots of tanks, found the young Tank Turks insufferable and created a separate outfit called the Tank Corps (soon renamed the Royal Tank Regiment—the RTR).[14] Its ensuing zeal was annoying to the establishment who referred to them as "tank maniacs" or "military bolshies."[15] The great nuisance of the RTR was that from earliest appearance, they preached salvation by way of the track.

The tank magi, particularly Gen. J.F.C. Fuller, ardently argued that *tank armies* (not "combined arms") would win future wars, which of course eliminated the need for infantry, artillery, and particularly the cavalry. Gen. Jean-Baptiste Estienne, "*le père des chars,*" a gunner, and the nominal head of the French tank force (ominously called *l'Artillerie Spéciale*) prophesied "with the tank appears a new infantry, *armored infantry* [emphasis added]."[16] But it was a renegade solution that the establishment found absolutely outrageous. It was argued that the tank was so revolutionary, so unique that it should be recognized as a separate *arm* and controlled by wise philosophes who understood its capabilities. The army became increasingly concerned that Fuller's philosophy could lead to a doctrine that subordinated the other arms to "tank control." Tanks' limitations were lambasted in professional journals:

> The tank, with her limited fuel supply, is in infinitely greater measure the child of her base. The faster she moves, the greater her consumption of that fuel which is her life blood; the slower she moves, the less her mobility.[17]

Of the European "Apostles of Mobility,"[18] only Heinz Guderian, a Fuller acolyte, envisioned panzer corps composed of all-arms, all-mechanized panzer divisions that employed *Kampfgruppen* (battle groups, combinations of arms). He taught an operational doctrine that exploited an all-arms breakthrough with panzer formations romping to strategic objectives, incorporating air force support to augment creative inspired maneuver by bold commanders. In an army raised on *Auftragstaktik* and *Fingerspitzengefühl*, conversion would not prove difficult. The Soviet doctrinal philosophes, Mikhail Tukhachevsky and V. K. Triandafilov, were mostly unread.[19]

There was uncertainty if the tank's role was tactical, operational or strategic. Actually, it was all three but this was not immediately understood.[20] The late 1930s were chockablock with challenges to mechanization and predictions of the tank's demise via the antitank gun.[21] Cavalry generals continued to resist morphing the horse into a modern armored fighting vehicle, a *machina ex equus*. This could resurrect traditional heavy cavalry doctrine of armor, mobility and shock. However this meant *ipso facto* terminating the horse.

The cavalry was not a stick in the mud regarding technology. The normally decisive rebuttal of ready provender versus fuel supply was becoming anemic by the thirties. Postwar reforms included roles for aircraft and motor transport but these were solely to augment the horse. Large trucks ("portees") were used to transport cavalry regiments to save a mount's legs. This was reasonable and coincided with the operational missions given the British and American cavalry of border security, policing rebellious tribes and guarding vast frontiers, India-Afghanistan or Mexico. However these were logistical, not doctrinal answers.[22] The cavalry remained essentially unchanged in the same manner that all infantry will forever refuse to surrender the bayonet because cold steel is the essence of shock to the close quarter attack.

Cavalry's opposition to mechanization has been dismissed as hopeless romanticism or criticized as short-sighted parochialism. In fact, its reticence was buttressed by two realities; the first, noble and fundamental: a commitment to the horse. The second considered the rather nebulous doctrinal and mechanical status of the tank. Mechanization offered no quarter in demanding the removal of the raison d'être of the mounted arm from the order of battle. The debate may have centered on doctrinal interpretation but it was tinged with a certain smug revenge.

Cavalry acceded to a legacy of perceived aloofness. Cavalry was distinct; it was kept apart from the army administratively and protected in the order of battle to deliver the decisive strike against the selected *point d'appui*. It exuded palatable difference, an exaggerated style and mystique both admired and resented. Cavalry symbolized the ultimate symbiotic partnership in battle, and proclaimed its innate superiority:

> Cavalrymen require to be more intelligent and better drilled than in the other forces. On outpost duty, patrolling, and reconnoitering, the men are often obliged to be self-reliant and to use their own judgment. This does not occur to anything like the same extent in the infantry or artillery.[23]

The warhorse menagerie was a Byzantine corporation and not easily dispensed with. Despite much modernization, cavalry found it difficult to see past hoofs and stables. The U.S. Army Quartermaster Corps performed much as it had since the Revolutionary War providing chargers, draft, and pack animals. The army contributed importantly to equestrian bloodlines and even included the first Triple Crown Winner (1919), Sir Barton. After the Great War, the army continued to scour the horse farms of the continent, evaluated the offspring and included them in their breeding depots. A determined breeding began in 1919 with the creation of the Remount Board that had complete responsibility for horse breeding. The simple fact remained that despite the impetus toward mechanization and mass production of Model T cars and trucks, until 1943, the world's armies remained mostly horse drawn.

The cavalry, unlike the infantry, was founded on a *partnership* with a living thing. The relationship between horse and trooper was both tactical and familial; training required veterinary skill and Freudian talents to work with a partner whose personality could vary from aggressive to cantankerous, lazy, skittish, or creatively mischievous. Personalities of horses were as dappled as their riders; tempers flared and spats, even brawls, occurred. A daily regimen ("Reveille 0500, Breakfast 0600, Move out 0730, Light Lunch 1300, water, remove saddle, dry back, feed, oats, hay. Stables 1430; Water / feed 1730, troops hot dinner 1800; Water / Hay 2030; Bed down 2100"[24]) was mandatory. The actual rate of advance (7–10 mph) was more representative of cavalry mobility than the endless gallops presented in films. Mobility came at a price:

> Sore backs were common with the hardships of campaigning, and one of the first lessons taught the inexperienced trooper to take better care of his horse

than he did of himself. The remedy against the recurrence of sore backs was invariably to order the trooper to walk and lead the disabled animal.[25]

The cavalry mostly walk-marched; a normal pace in an hour was to trot for about twenty minutes, halt for ten and walk the remainder of the time, the remaining time was divided between mounted and dismounted walking: "It must be remembered that the troopers wore riding boots—not as comfortable as the infantry boot in a route march."[26]

The horses were looked after first and like athletes, they had to be kept fit for game day. Training had to be not only rigorous but also interesting and imaginative: "[The] horses seemed to realize that something unusual was afoot, as they soon were moving along very steadily, with ears pricking and nostrils sniffing the new territory with great interest." Field bivouacs were always lively: "Stable Piquet was doubled in strength for the first night [and the duty troopers] had a difficult task, as the horses took the opportunity to settle many old scores with one another."[27]

An example of tank-cavalry divergence was the death of 12-year-old Commodore: a standard-bred thoroughbred cross, 16 hands 1 inch in height and weighing 1,100 pounds. Commodore was entered in the 1923 Colorado Endurance Ride by Captain Donald S. Perry, 13th Cavalry. At the end of the 48th mile, Commodore slowed up and started bloating slightly; thus far it had been a normal ride, averaging just over seven miles per hour. Captain Perry noted, "Twice on the way I stopped at water and sponged out the horse's nostrils, dock, and between hind legs. Once he drank but not much." At noon stop Commodore would not eat his oats but did eat some grass and drank a little water. Noticing bloating, Captain Perry became concerned and immediately dismounted:

[I] led him to some grass at the side of the road where I unsaddled him . . . requested the veterinarians to come up immediately. . . . The latter did not arrive for about 40 minutes. Soon after he was unsaddled *Commodore* fell down on his side, at about 2:10 P.M. he was dead. An autopsy was made.[28]

Throughout the following year, the *Cavalry Journal* published an entire series of articles concerning Commodore's death including professional debates and analyses of endurance ride organization. It illustrated perfectly the complete distinction between the cavalry and the tanks. It would be difficult to imagine this type of concern over tank hull TD 54059 dropping its suspension or burning its engine. Tankers like to create anthropomorphic relationships with their vehicles; squadron sergeants have been heard referring to a particular tank as an "ornery b__ch"—but it's not quite the same thing.

PLATO AND THE TANK: THE CHALLENGE OF
NEW TECHNOLOGY—WHAT IS A TANK?

I'm an Oil Can, I'm an Oil Can
On a muddy armored car
But I'd rather be an Oil Can than a 17th Hussar
They ride 'orses, pretty 'orses
While we drive our armored cars
But I'd rather be an Oil Can than a 17th Hussar
> —Sung by 6th Duke of Connought's Royal Canadian Hussars (RCH) at their
> horsy Montreal rivals, the snooty 17th Duke of York's RCH, circa 1938[29]

Lumbering trench-crossing tanks did not concern the warhorse, but subsequent technological improvements did. The most promising post war tank design was a private venture by American engineer J. Walter Christie that became mired in personality conflicts and parochial rear guards. Christie was larger than life, a bona fide, albeit abrasive, genius. Though his tank was the slickest, fastest, and most practical model available, his fanaticism alienated the army staff and the ordnance corps.[30] His invention was inspired and well ahead of its time. The *Christie* maneuvered at 42.5 miles per hour on tracks and 70 mph on wheels (the tracks could be removed for a road march); it boasted sloped armor and a superior suspension system. Christie's tank was refused for quantity purchase because it was allegedly too expensive, despite funds being allotted by Generals Fuqua and Army Chief of Staff Douglas MacArthur.[31] The army eventually built a few under duress then directly placed them in storage, its aversion to Christie juxtaposed by its acclaim for the French army's mechanized vogue.[32]

The Christie incident would be trite trivia were it not for its epilogue. In 1930 a secret agreement with the Soviet technical mission based in New York, arranged for two Christie models to be purchased from the U.S. and shipped to the Soviet Union as tractor and machine parts. This was soon followed by the appearance of *Bystrokhodnyi* (BT) tank series, a dead ringer for the Christie, from sloped armor to the ride system, eventually internationally recognized as "the Christie suspension." Remaining stored Christie models were purchased by England and soon inspired copy cat versions.[33] The British built over 10,000 cruiser or cavalry tanks based on the Christie system. In Russia's case, the Christie became the prototype for a generation of successful tanks, the prewar BT series, and most dramatically, the revered T-34, generally considered the best all-around tank of the Second World War.[34] By 1945, almost a hundred thousand Christie types were built, but none in the United States.

Xenophobic squabbles over budgets and control resulted in American tanks being ghettoized in Fort Benning under infantry control, the folks least likely to create panzer divisions. The tank was unwelcome in the traditional arms. General Willis D. Crittenberger, an American *apostle of maneuver,* recalled: "'Tank' was *verboten* in the cavalry."[35] The new commander of *cavalry tanks,* Colonel Adna Romanza Chaffee (subsequently "Father of U.S. Armor") adopted the term "Combat Car" for all cavalry armor since assignment of tanks to cavalry would have required Congressional approval. The armored debate should have centered on Platonic *first principles:* what is a tank? The key difference in definition was therefore between *tank* and *tanks.* One was a ubiquitous tactical adjunct that afforded support to infantry and dominated its immediate area; the second described tanks in *mass.* One was multifaceted, the other complex and severely limited. Massed tanks were simply not viable in cities, forested areas, mountains or against fortified lines. Tanks were a shock weapon capable of strategic results but conversely required specific conditions and efficient care. General Jean Baptiste Chedeville said it best in 1918: "Le Char est très délicat."[36]

SAVING THE CAVALRY—A FRENCH SMORGASBORD VERSUS GERMAN *BLUTWURST*

> We congratulate ourselves at not having succumbed to the lure of a cavalcade of tanks.
>
> —Revue d'Infanterie, 1939

Saving the cavalry required the very qualities that cavaliers are not noted for: diplomacy, patience, and compromise. The British cut short internecine bun fights for ascendancy by shrewdly accommodating both. The RTR's black bereted Fuller acolytes were parked beside cavalry regiments which adopted tanks but kept their horsy traditions. The French warhorse, fortunate to have very senior officers in positions of influence, embraced modern technology. In a remarkable anthropomorphic transmutation, *la cavalerie Française,* threatened with termination, instead regained tactical and operational dominance: "the cavalry concentrated on the problems of motorization and mechanization, and by 1935, it was easily the most modern of any of the French branches."[37] This was accomplished by Gen. Maxime Weygand, inspector-general of the French army until 1935 and supreme commander in 1940, who, in his attempt to rescue both France and the cavalry, contributed to the downfall of both.

Weygand's devotion convinced him that the horse and the tank could profit from a *marriage de raison.* He created a mixed doctrine that offered something for everyone but did not really address the question of the Fulleresque "shot through the brain."[38] German observers at war games scoffed that French doctrine was "seven minutes of attack and seventy minutes of waiting for the arrival of the infantry." The difference between the two was neatly summed up by the Cavalry Chief of Staff, General Willis Crittenberger: "French are limited to the armored division, while the Germans have created an armored branch."[39]

The Weygand syncretic solution of demi brigades and tank-cavalry formations attempted to meld horseflesh and tanks. Cavalry was enjoined with a bricolage of plate, tracks, tires, and petrol cans. Five new cavalry divisions morphed through various configurations from 1929 to 1939, eventually resulting in *Divisions Légères de Cavalerie* (DLC; Light Cavalry Division). The new look cavalry dispensed with cuirasses and traditional Kublai Khan mane helmet but kept the horse and saber. Each DLC had one cavalry brigade, a total of 1,200 horses. To support the requirements of the brigades and logistic trains, France mobilized over 520,000 horses and mules in 1939.

This horse opera dissipated resources and delayed France's true tank divisions, the heavy *Divisions Cuirassée Rapide* and the quick, robust *Divisions Légère Mécanique* (DLM; Light Mechanized Division). It should be understood that French armor was the *plat du jour* of Western armies, admired and copied. The unveiling of a new French tank was greeted with the same fervor and excited anticipation as the spring shows at Lanvin or Coco Chanel. The SOMUA S35 medium tank (hereafter Somua) and Char B *bis* main battle tank (*bis* as in "repeated," the second model of the Char B series) were proclaimed the best of their type in the world and for a brief period, they were.[40]

The Char B was an immediate hit in the West; the British and Americans both followed suit and produced battle tanks (the *Grant* and the *Churchill*) with the main gun in the chassis, not in a turret. But the Char B was a tank only an engineer could love with its grotesque tracks, high silhouette, and the most complex transmission and hydrostatic steering on the planet.[41] The tank's strong points were its heavy armor (almost thrice that of the heaviest German tank), two deadly guns and, a radio.

The fast Somua "Cavalry Tank" was the first tank to be manufactured from cast steel, boasted more armor than any German tank in service and sported a deadly 47 mm gun; its main weakness was the one man turret, which overworked the crew commander. The French also managed a monster that even dwarfed the surreal behemoths conceived by the Germans later in the war. The FCM Char 2C was initially developed for the Great War; it weighed 69 tons and had a crew of 12. Ten were built, and since they were as big as a province, they were named *Picardie, Alsace, Champagne,* etc., and referred to as *Chars de Forteresse.*[42] Pathé newsreels showed a Char 2C advancing across a field surrounded by a gaggle of light tanks looking very much like Mother Goose, and destined to be a metallic *pâté de foie gras.*[43]

The post-blitzkrieg realization that *Divisions de Cavalerie* were the new Dodo led to doctrinal changes. Almost as a penance, the DLCs were dispatched to the rough terrain of the Ardennes where it was assumed tanks and *Stukas* would not find them. To add insult, a shortfall of horses was made up via bicycles and trucks. Concurrently, the threat of swarms of tanks coupled with air attack jump-started the creation of new heavy armored divisions, the DCRs—*Division Cuirassée Rapide.* Charles de Gaulle had previously suggested creating an army of maneuver and mechanized shock composed of elite personnel but it was ignored.[44] The first DCRs were delayed until January 1940;[45] their motto "Speed Is Not Armor," confused the very nature of mobile war and the concept of *chars de manoeuvre ensemble.* The Army waited till the Spring of 1940, almost a year after Poland, to group DCRs into a heavy tank corps: the *1er Groupement Cuirassé.* The force, with two Char B divisions had no time to conduct maneuvers as a *force de rupture* or a *force de manœuvre* and it proved to be neither.[46]

The final French response to the German tank force (10 panzer divisions) was three heavy armored divisions (DCR), three medium armored divisions (DLM), five armored cavalry divisions (DLC) with 13 independent tank brigades of varying types and value, and three independent cavalry brigades. The warhorse was found within the cavalry brigade in each *Division Légère de Cavalerie* which held two regiments.[47] Five brigades of mounted cavalry were deployed to screen against an anticipated German reconnaissance in force in the Ardennes, unaware that this would be the *Schwerpunkt* of an offensive comprising seven elite Panzer Divisions.

The French system proved to be as good an effort as a democratic army could muster; great tank parks were more easily created in dictatorships. Stalin and Hitler were both wary of established arms which perpetuated traditional doctrines, abetted by a coterie of aristocratic generals to defend them. French experimentation occurred within a new strategic concept which was the direct opposite of *attaque à outrance,* a completely *defensive* doctrine based on fortress complexes connected by fire sacks, minefields, and obstacles and supported by mobile forces. The greatest of these resembled futuristic shopping malls buried beneath the ground boasting their own railroads, hospitals, barracks, cinemas, bronzage parlors, and disappearing gun turrets. This massive project, a Great Wall of France, was funded without reservation and named after its most vigorous proponent, the minister of defense, M. André Maginot. Paris was confident *la Ligne Maginot* would provide sufficient time to mobilize and prepare for war.[48]

MECHANIZATION IN EUROPE: THE RUDE MECHANICALS

Cavalry circles loathed the idea of giving up the horse, and thus instinctively decried the tank. They found much support in the War Office and in Parliament ... it is painfully true that the early battles of World War II were lost in the Cavalry Club.

—Liddell Hart[49]

The German postwar army, resurrected by General Hans von Seeckt, accepted mechanization as a logical solution. Initially the German tank school suffered the same internal opposition and suspicion as the British and American; General Ludwig Beck, chief of the general staff, was completely skeptical, but Adolf Hitler saw tanks as a political, economic, as well as a military solution. In 1935 Guderian, chief of staff, panzer troops, demonstrated a tank regiment to Hitler at Kummersdoff. As the panzers rumbled by, the new Chancellor was smitten: "*Das kann ich gebrauchen! Das will ich haben!*"[50] Six years later, General Fuller attended the Fuhrer's birthday parade as a special guest. After an hour-long procession of the new panzer divisions, Hitler elatedly took his arm: "I hope you are pleased with your children?" Fuller replied: "Your Excellency, they have grown up so quickly that I no longer recognize them."[51]

Although German cavalry was as determined as Western cavalries to survive, it bowed before the inevitability of blitzkrieg doctrine and Hitler's enthusiasm for tanks. By 1939 all of the cavalry had been converted into two types: *army cavalry* and *troop cavalry.* Of the 18 cavalry regiments left over from von Seeckt's reforms, only 1 brigade survived. Seventeen cavalry regiments were converted into 38 recce units (*Aufklärungabteilungen*) for divisional and corps HQs. Jeffrey Fowler, author of *Axis Cavalry in World War II* noted, "Troop Cavalry were partly motorized, partly horse mounted, partly bicycle units which upon mobilization would be dispersed to provide the reconnaissance battalions of infantry divisions; these units took the title Kavallerie Regiments."[52] The cadre of the cavalry brigade were permitted to keep the traditional title of *Reiter* Regiment, signifying they were part of a cavalry formation. The army recce battalions absorbed the bulk of German warhorses, leaving the ones stationed in East Prussia as the remaining army cavalry unit that was capable of operational maneuver. Still, the great mass of the German Army (50 divisions, a third of them on the French border) appeared much as it did in 1914: on foot and horse drawn. The Wehrmacht had mobilized 514,000 horses; of the half million available, less than 5,000 were assigned to the 1st Cavalry Brigade.[53]

Meanwhile, the British were patiently developing a tank doctrine and had gone as far as forming a special experimental mechanized force in 1925. They even considered Fuller as commander but his excessive demands, including threatened resignation from the Army, led to the ignominy of being reassigned. The Experimental Mechanized Force (EMF) began training in August 1927 but soon got bad press and was accused of missing the point of "tanks" as a breakthrough force in lieu of simply "raiding." The armored establishment, including Lt. Gen. Burnett-Stuart, who was instrumental in establishing a viable armored corps, could not shake the vision of tanks as a type of cavalry raiding rear areas after the real work of breaking through had been done.[54]

Nevertheless, by 1939 the British had completely converted to mechanization and managed it through disciplined seduction rather than the garroting of the cavalry as occurred in the United States a year later. After much discussion it was decided to amalgamate the two sides into the Royal Armoured Corps. The Tank Corps became the Royal Tank Regiment (RTR):

> On the 30th of April 1939 all the Cavalry and Yeomanry regiments and the Royal Tank Regiment became part of the Royal Armoured Corps. Henceforth all these units would have to work together. The cavalry units were to retain their identity and their great traditions, but all training and schools and policy was to be centralized so as to gain efficiency and a common doctrine.[55]

This was a remarkably civilized transition that spelled the end of the British cavalry and relegation of the warhorse to secondary duties. It was not enthusiastically received:

> Most of the cavalry regiments have been rounded up and pressed into tanks or armoured cars. They have all the sensations of a saloon-bar person in public bar-bar circumstances. . . The Royal Tank Regiment (the Tank men) is a creation apart: it is composed of the rude mechanicals who despise the horse.[56]

The cavalry grumbled. The Scots Greys hung on to their horses with determined ardor until they were finally corralled and made to conform to the new order in September. In the spring of 1940 the British Expeditionary Force's armored component left for France incompletely fitted to duel with German tank formations; what they needed was more of what they had: *Matildas*. The 1st Army Tank Brigade arrived in France equipped with a complement of the heavily armored, up gunned *Matilda* II, about to be declared "the best tank in the world at the time."[57]

NEW HOPE AND GRAVE WARNING: KHALKHIN GOL

> Tanks stormed like a hurricane,
> Fearsome armor was advancing.
> Samurai were crashing to the ground. . .
> Three tankmen, three cheerful comrades,
> The crew of their combat vehicle—where they live—
> An indestructible family. . .
> —*Tri Tankista*, tanker's song from the Soviet-Japanese War, 1939

The Manchurian plains were not friendly to Russian cavalry or their horses. In the summer of 1939 the Red Army cavalry again met the fellows who bested their fathers in the humiliating 1905 war. It was familiar ground and there was a debt to settle.

Khalkhin Gol incorporated the last important cavalry battles before the Second World War. The mobility of the cavalry was enhanced by battalions of new tanks that were the second generation of armored fighting vehicles and battle proven in the Spanish Civil War. The battle was actually dominated by joint arms: the infantry, artillery, heavy machine guns, and second-generation combat aircraft. Armor's potential inspired the Soviet commander, Gen. Georgi Zhukov, who would use it to great effect in the coming Patriotic War. The contest had something for every determined lobbyist: it demonstrated the warhorse's vulnerability to modern weapons as well as its ubiquitous capability to traverse all terrain; it also documented the tank's dramatic ability to create shock assault, its maneuverability, as well as its mechanical woes and limitations in unfavorable ground.

In May 1939 a squadron of Mongolian cavalry rode into the disputed area on the Mongol-Manchurian border, seeking to graze their horses. The situation escalated until by September, Japanese and Russian armies faced each other across the Hlaha River (also known as the Khalkhin Gol). Zhukov, appointed commander of the Soviet-Mongolian 1st Army group, owned three infantry divisions, considerable artillery, the latest Soviet combat aircraft and five tank brigades: 430 *BT*s and about 425 armored cars. His maneuver force was augmented by two Mongolian cavalry divisions. His opposite number, Lt. Gen. Michitaro Komatsubara, owned two tank regiments (medium tanks and tankettes), five regiments of artillery, two infantry divisions, and an air fleet of 500 combat aircraft.

On June 3, 1939, Zhukov threw a combined Soviet and Mongolian force across the Khalkhin Gol and established a defensive position. A determined air war began and generally continued to the end of the campaign. If this campaign created fuel for cavalry-mechanization fires, it particularly inspired the proponents of air power. Air operations included surprise attacks on airfields, struggles for air superiority as well as reconnaissance and attack on artillery. The ground war began in earnest in July. Komatsubara launched a tank attack which was halted by Zhukov's more numerous tank squadrons. The Soviet's "Christie" *Bystrohodny* tank outclassed Japanese armor. The *BT* was much liked by its crews who christened it the *Betka* ("Beetle") but more popularly, the *Tri-Tankista* ("Three Tanker"). The flotation capability of tracks allowed tanks to go where trucks and cars bogged down (Zhukov had built up a fleet of 2,600 trucks, including 1,000 fuel trucks). Tactical fighting continued for weeks; finally Zhukov launched a major offensive incorporating air and artillery strikes, a foreshadow of techniques he would use in the next war. Khalkhin Gol reintroduced the armor versus gunnery debate. Soviet 45 mm tank guns readily defeated Japanese armor at long range. The Yasuoka Tank Detachment quickly lost half of its armor and had to be withdrawn while Japanese light antitank weapons were virtually helpless against armored assault.

A final desperate attack by Komatsubara was torn apart by a counterattack spearheaded by Zhukov's 6th Tank Brigade. Creative maneuver resulted in the surrounding of most of Komatsubara's forces and the campaign concluded with another mass air battle and Japanese retreat. Zhukov was promoted; his star, already bright because of the *Konarmiya* fraternity, continued to rise.

Khalkhin Gol began with cavalry in forage-reconnaissance and ended with cavalry in the pursuit, as most tanks had broken down. The campaign offered faint hope for the cavalry but shrewd tacticians saw the writing on the wall: the future belonged to the tank and the airplane.

BLITZKRIEG 1939—POLISH CAVALRY GOES TO WAR

> Hey, Hey Ulani, malowane dzieci, nie jedna panienka za wami poleci. (Hey, Hey Ulans, colorful lads, there's not a maiden who wouldn't chase after you.)
> —Polish Ulan's mantra, 1939[58]

The opposing Polish cavalry of 1939 was very much like Weygand's mixed bag solution to mechanization comprising an amalgam of ulans, hussars, and tanks. The Polish army, the one post-Versailles force that could not afford to get things wrong, was inadequate to face a blitzkrieg army. Sandwiched between the Soviet Union and Germany, the Poles looked to the West for doctrinal guidance. Their final decisions, mired in cavalry nostalgia, were slightly better than America's and virtually no different from France's with whom they shared a long involved history.[59] Polish doctrine adopted maneuver warfare based on experiences against Budyonny but failed to create a state-of-the-art force capable of carrying it out. The French had declined to sell their *Somua*, and the Poles acquired a hodgepodge of tankettes and medium tanks which by 1939 were near obsolete.[60]

German blitzkrieg was unleashed against Poland's forces on September 1, 1939. The first actions involved both tanks and cavalry: the 1st German Cavalry Brigade attacked the Mazowiecka Cavalry Brigade on the Ulatkowka River. Although the two formations fought as dragoons—dismounted, supported by machine guns and artillery—nevertheless, some saber-versus-saber melees occurred near forested areas of the Prussian frontier. For the Germans it was the apotheosis of operational cavalry. A single formation perpetuated a cavalry tradition dating back to Friedrich der Grosse: the 1. Kavallerie Brigade joined the offensive with two regiments (1st and 2nd Reiter, each of five horsed squadrons). Like contemporary cavalry outfits, the brigade was augmented with machine guns, antitank guns, artillery, and a mixed recce battalion whose combined strength was 6,200 men and 4,552 horses.[61]

The immediate problem with being part of a blitzkrieg army was that cavalry just did not have the stamina and speed of a mechanized division:

I felt my horse, Herzog, could take no more of it—he was stumbling constantly. I called out to the section commander, "Herzog's had as much as he can take!"— and I'd scarcely got the words out when the poor beast fell to his knees . . . we had gone 70 km on the first day, then 60 on the second. . . All in all, that meant we'd gone nearly 200 km in three days without a proper rest.[62]

German cavalry conducted the campaign with distinction but were dramatically overshadowed by the exploits of *Stuka* dive bombers and panzer divisions. They were dealt insult rather than reward: on September 19, Berlin announced the cavalry arm was abolished and the "mobile troops" (*Schnelle Truppen*) were to be created, replacing all GHQ cavalry, reconnaissance, tank, antitank, bicycle, motorcycle and armored infantry units. Whelmed by an onslaught of technological triumph, the German cavalry was apparently to be sent to the knacker's yard—but this turned out to be merely a hiatus from war.

Surprisingly there were fifteen cavalry actions. Poles fielded 13 cavalry brigades (38 regiments of lancers, chasseurs, hussars, and mounted rifles) and two mechanized brigades.[63] Most battles were conducted with a mix of infantry weapons but at least two charges involved Ulans using lances and sabers. In late September 1939, near Krasnobród, a squadron of the 25th Ulans was countercharged by German cavalry screening the 4th Wehrmacht Infantry Division. After a violent skirmish the Germans retreated and the Ulans swept forward to capture the town and Headquarters of the 4th Division, freeing Polish prisoners.[64]

The command "Trot, march" rang out. The enemy had not yet seen us . . . First we proceeded at a slow trot. The Germans still marched on, apparently unconcerned. Then suddenly our heavy machine-guns, hidden in the woods, gave tongue with a well-timed salvo. It went straight into the enemy column. The command "Draw sabres, gallop, march!" flew down the lines. Reins were gripped tighter. The riders bent forward in the saddles and they rushed forward like a mad whirlwind. . . Sabres and lances went to work fiercely. Some confused German infantrymen pushed off our sabre blows with their rifle butts. Some simply tried to cover their heads with their arms, but our lances reached even those who tried to hide between the wagons.[65]

Polish cavalry claimed 12 victories including desperate *breakout* attacks. Four were meeting engagements and resolved by sudden, unexpected charges. Three formal charges were conducted against defended positions plus the memorable Krasnobród cavalry versus cavalry melee. These battles made for grand war stories in cavalry messes but were, unfortunately, bagatelle in operational contests.

SHAMELESS THEATRE: HORSES VERSUS PANZERS

The famed Polish cavalry threw itself into the path of the German mechanized columns, and was swept out of the way like rubbish.

—*Time* Magazine, August 19, 1940

The cavalry's pious defense of the horse, at first admirable, then irrational, was savaged and mocked. The shock of blitzkrieg launched a sycophantic worship of the tank and a savage condemnation of the cavalry. Like betrayed lovers, the world's armies, spearheaded by an overly imaginative press corps, denounced cavalry actions, ridiculed the commanders, and belittled battles that would have inspired awe in any other conflict. They also got things wrong. The most infamous item of derision was the alleged conduct of Polish cavalry against blitzkrieg panzers in early September. Thanks to Axis propaganda, overzealous newspapers and Pathé newsreels, the campaign left the West with an image of pathetic cavalry hopelessly crashing against the technological future.

The genesis of the tale occurred near the Breda river. As German vanguards exploited a quick crossing, they were surprised by a mixed Polish armored cavalry force. Because few of his tankettes were in running order, the regimental commander of the 18th Ulans, Col. Kazimierz Mastelarz, decided to launch a surprise mounted attack. Maneuvering through wooded terrain to the rear of the Germans, the Lancers came upon a German infantry battalion. Mastelarz ordered an immediate charge; his squadrons galloped out of the woods sabering and lancing with wild abandon—the Germans broke. As the melee wore down, a troop of German armored cars appeared and engaged the cavalry with machine gun and 20 mm cannon fire. Mastelarz and about twenty lancers were killed while the remaining squadrons withdrew to covered ground.

There are conflicting reports, but either German or Italian war correspondents and a kinematic unit visited the scene shortly after, viewed the carnage which included dead and dying horses, and wrote an embroidered report on a futile cavalry charge: lances against Krupp steel. The story caught readers' attention and seemed to perfectly illustrate Western unpreparedness, technological inferiority and obsolete doctrine. The incident was repeated and embellished.

Oddly enough, tank hunting cavalry would be common in the mechanized hotbed that was the eastern front. But before the warhorse could restore its good name, the cavalry had to endure one more humiliation—the Battle of France.

ENFORCED ENLIGHTENMENT: THE CAVALRY'S EPIPHANIC MOMENT, MAY 1940

In my opinion, Colonel de Gaulle's conclusions should be rejected... A new school of opinion has visions of large formations of tanks ploughing up the enemy front in an irresistible onslaught and eliminating resistance in a few hours!

—General Duffieux, to Gamelin, 3 Dec 1939

Today we are crushed by the sheer weight of the mechanized forces hurled against us, but we can still look to the future in which even greater mechanized forces will bring us victory. Therein lies the destiny of the world.

—Gen. Charles de Gaulle, 1940

The "impenetrable" Ardennes was a tank vespiary—the *Schwerpunkt* of the German armored assault. In May 1940 the shrouded roads were a sinuous collective of concealed panzer divisions. Hitler finally approved a variation of Manstein's gambit—less ambitious than Schlieffen's but imminently doable. The key was to lure the BEF and a French army into Belgium, then let loose a pride of panzer formations onto their right flank. The *Sichelschnitt* or "sickle-cut," a Churchillian sobriquet, was an accurate description. The key army group, commanded by Field Marshal Gerd von Rundstedt, included seven of the Wehrmacht's 10 panzer divisions organized into three Panzer Korps. These would burst from the forests, overwhelm French covering units and rush for the Meuse. They were to rumble across the same fields that van der Marwitz and Richthofen had plodded 26 years earlier.[66] Two tank corps were welded into an independent maneuver force named *Panzergruppe Kleist.* Once the bridges on the Meuse were secure, they would be turned loose; their objectives read like a mission statement from the Great War—the Meuse, the Sambre, and the Somme. To make things almost perfect, the BEF was deployed just northwest of Mons.

The plan worked. The thrust through the Ardennes was a shock to French army headquarters and part of a series of techno surprises that caught the West off guard that spring: *Fallschirmjäeger* (paratroops) quickly captured allegedly impregnable Belgian fortresses as well as an experienced Luftwaffe that promptly assumed air superiority, yet benignly permitted the Allied left wing to march into Belgium with scarcely an air strike.

The two panzer divisions assigned to Belgium headed for the Gembloux Gap, just as von der Marwitz had done. There they would meet an echo of Sordet, the only *Corps de Cavalerie* France was to use in the war.[67] This cavalry formation did not have a single warhorse to its name. Commanded by Lt. Gen. René Prioux, it grouped the best tank formations in France's arsenal: three *Division Légère Mécanique.*

Despite the name, the DLM was more powerful than the DCR (190 vs. 150 tanks) and more mobile.[68] Panzer divisions were about 30 percent faster than British or French armored divisions, a problem Great War cavalry never had to deal with. The French cavalry DLMs, however, could easily keep pace with the panzers, had better guns than most of the German tank force and thicker armor than all of them. The disadvantages were crews and communications.[69] Most French tanks had no radio. Control was via hand signal.

The cavalry corps dispatched north to establish contacts with the Belgians as well as imposing delay upon Armee Gruppe B, crossing the upper Meuse with three *Panzerdivisionen.*

CAVALRY CORPS IN COMBAT, MAY 1940

> All truth passes through three stages. First it is ridiculed. Second, it is violently opposed. Third, it is accepted as being self evident.
>
> —Schopenhauer

> At the roots of Alexander's victories, one will always find Aristotle.
>
> —Col. Charles de Gaulle, *The Army of the Future*

The German invasion of France was the first demonstration of "proper" blitzkrieg. Poland had demonstrated panzer attack, but on a wide front; France featured concentrated armored spearheads. There were two cavalry contests. The first featured the elite *Corps de Cavalerie* comprised of the 2e and 3e DLMs and was highlighted by violent tank duels; the second took place in the Ardennes where the warhorses of the four *Divisions Légère de Cavalerie* faced an onslaught of panzers—only to be swept away like so many dry leaves.[70]

The cavalry corps entered Belgium on May 10, and the first French-German contact was déjà vu: Panhard armored cars from the 12 cuirassiers surprised a gaggle of Panzer IIs from the 4th Panzer Division outside Liege. Instead of tilting lances there was an exchange of semiautomatic cannon fire. The Germans lost a tank then bolted. Instead of a zeppelin peering over the clouds, the sky was groaning with enemy aircraft. Prioux wrote that the Luftwaffe was "Entièrement maîtresse du ciel."[71]

Prioux faced a key decision. The XVI Pz Korps, commanded by General Erich Hoepner (known as "Der Alte Reiter"—the old cavalier), was conducting a hurried crossing of the Dyle and Sambre canal systems. He could attack and catch them at their most vulnerable state, or adopt conservative tactics, throw out a screen and wait for infantry divisions to catch up. Prioux opted to fight a series of delaying actions—the battles of the Gembloux Gap (May 12–14). These contests included the first big tank battle of the war pitting two DLMs against two panzer divisions.

The Gembloux Gap is an open maneuver area between Brussels and Liege leading directly to Mons, and then Picardy. The town of Hannut is dead center. In this minicampaign, approximately 700 German tanks working under air superiority were repeatedly checked by about 170 Somua and 60 Hotchkiss light tanks.[72] As the battle continued, the Grand Quartier Général (GQG) became confident the Germans meant to repeat the Schlieffen Plan and therefore content to leave the Ardennes sector in the hands of its horsed divisions.

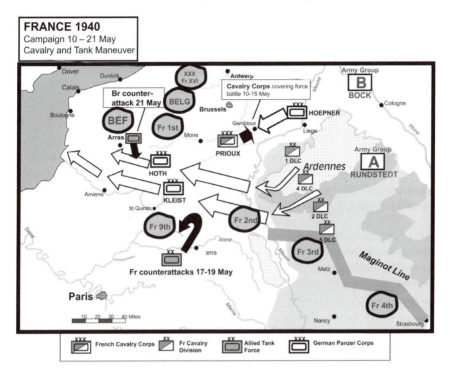

FRANCE 1940
Campaign 10 – 21 May
Cavalry and Tank Maneuver

Liddell Hart described this phase of the German offensive as "the Matador's cloak."[73]

Tactically, the Battle of Hannut was a cavalry disappointment; operationally, it constituted a minor delay. General von Bechtolsheim noted "initially our tanks were outnumbered but that advantage was neutralized by the French lack of maneuver."[74] Despite their edge, neither the DLM commanders, nor Prioux created the formidable masses that could swamp German defense. The Germans thought the French had squandered their advantage:

> During the course of combat we discovered our adversary's weak points: although they had good guns and superior armor, the enemy . . . fought without coordination in isolated, segregated groups, unable to utilize his strength nor his numbers.[75]

The Germans assaulted in bulk and never attacked with less than a tank battalion against French squadrons. The tactical gunfights were unnecessarily difficult for the French because, unlike the Germans, only a select few of their tanks had radios. It was not unusual to see officers scampering from tank to tank, banging on the turrets and shouting orders to the crews. Both the

Germans and the French considered Hannut noteworthy as the first major tank battle in history: *"la première bataille de chars de l'Histoire Panzerschlacht."*[76] French cavalry commanders thought they fought *avec un brio magnifique* [magnificent brilliance].[77]

Meanwhile, to the southeast, the German attack had immediate success and scattered the Cavalry DLCs. The German General Staff, veterans of 1914, were astonished at their achievement and almost cringed awaiting a violent French reaction. It required much argument from Guderian to get them to cancel a *stop order* and unleash their panzer corps to race for the distant Channel.[78]

FRANKFORCE AT ARRAS: COUNTERATTACK

By May 20, 1940, the British Expeditionary Force, under command of Field Marshal Lord Gort VC (he had been awarded the Victoria Cross in the Great War, for conspicuous bravery at the Canal du Nord, not very far from where he was fighting now), found itself in a situation akin to that of 1914: it was threatened with encirclement. By May 21, Kleist's van had reached the Channel, cutting the Allied armies in two, thus accomplishing what von Kluck and von der Marwitz had been unable to achieve.

Lord Gort ordered a counterattack, in concert with French armored forces. The immediate foe was the 7th Panzer Division, commanded by a little-known infantry general, Erwin Rommel. The attack was to be led by Gen. Sir Giffard Le Quesne Martel, an *apostle of mobility* and soon to become director of the Royal Armoured Corps. Martel (known as "Le Q," and alleged to have inspired Ian Fleming) commanded two divisions and 74 tanks supported by a battalion of 60 French tanks from 1e DLM.[79] The *Matildas*, in their inaugural combat, surprised the Germans. "[They were] quite unable to penetrate our tanks,"[80] Martel recalled.

> His tanks were knocked out quite easily by our 2-pdr. Anti-tank gun [mounted on British tanks], whereas our infantry tanks resisted the shell fire of the corresponding enemy 37-mm gun without difficulty. Some tanks were hit fifteen times without having an effect on the tank or the crew.[81]

Rommel was forced to order forward his artillery and the 88 mm *Flak* guns: "I brought up every available gun into action at top speed against the tanks. . . I personally gave each gun its target."[82] The *88* was first used in Spain by the Condor Legion as a tank killer; it now saved Rommel's division and perhaps the German offensive. Sixteen Matildas created chaos in Hoth's Corps. However, as the British attack progressed, its accompanying infantry was shot up and the remaining Matildas moved alone against Rommel's gunline, literally, sitting ducks.[83]

Frankforce, though repulsed, was a limited armored success and gave Gort opportunity to withdraw to Dunkirk, an act which likely saved the BEF but earned him rancor from the French.[84]

DOCTRINAL LESSONS AND EQUESTRIAN EPIPHANY: *MACHINA EX EQUUS*

It is glibly said the Maginot Line was a shield that required a sword. That is not correct. Doctrine, not equipment, sank the French. The German all-arms solution featured mutual support and mass—this defeated better weapons. Stalin was to note a year later: "Quantity is a quality all by itself."[85]

The blitzkrieg campaign was the epiphanic moment for all cavalry. The realization that *tanks are horses* took time to sink in but then cavaliers are as conservative as they are bodacious, as slow to learn as they are quick to charge. More precisely, tanks, as anthropomorphic steeds, presented the cavalry with its first chance to turn technology to its benefit and resurrect lost ascendancy. With a nuance of blasphemy, the cavalry could embrace the tank as the resurrection of chivalrous superiority, a restoration of the qualities that made it the dominant arm of decision: armor, shock, and mobility.

Every general staff made plans to create its own panzer divisions. The warhorse was poised to enter a greater horsy renaissance, or could just as easily be cast into oblivion. After 1940, the cavalry was brutally given the option of *transmutation* or *termination*. This is what happened in the United States. In the best Shakespearean tradition, it was Brutus who struck down Caesar, not the mechanical enemies he feared. The Chaffee-Herr confrontation was the stuff of theater.

The Illuminatus: **"By Jove I've got it! Tanks is 'orses!"**
The Warhorse: **"Good God. He's gone quite mad."**

Chapter 13

Cavalry in the Second World War, Part I: The American Apocalypse

We must not be misled to our own detriment to assume that the untried machine can displace the proved and tried horse.
—Chief of Cavalry, Maj. Gen. John K. Herr, 1938

The horses took the opportunity to settle many old scores with one another.
—Maj. R. S. Timmons, RCD

Bias and branch loyalty garroted the warhorse and hamstrung American armored evolution at the very time that modern armies were adopting mechanization. As panzers conquered Europe, the U.S. Army had no tank force, no modern tank, and, most crucial, no clear doctrine. The U.S. Cavalry comprised 1 mechanized cavalry brigade and 12 regiments of horse, only 2 of which were mixes of cavalry and mechanized squadrons. An additional cavalry regiment served in the Philippines.[1] Perplexingly, both branch chiefs continued to refuse to create their own "panzer division."[2] The Infantry, bequeathed the duty of managing mechanized armor, kept "the tanks" in Fort Benning, while the cavalry tried its best to pretend the rude vehicles did not exist. The central question for the mounted arm was whether the proper definition of *cavalry* was "soldiers fighting on horses" or was *cavalry* merely a generic term for "mounted soldiers." One interpretation demanded tens of thousands of horses, the other required modern equipment.

The American army of the 1930s was a small professional force not unlike the British army. They had the same use for frontier cavalry but by 1931 Army

Chief of Staff, Gen. Douglas MacArthur noted: "The horse has no higher degree of mobility today than he had a thousand years ago. The time has therefore arrived when the Cavalry arm must either replace or assist the horse as a means of transportation, or else pass into the limbo of discarded military formations."[3] The move toward mechanization of the cavalry was imposed despite parochial rearguards. A cavalry-tank experimental unit was formed at Fort Eustis commanded by Colonel, later General, Daniel Van Voorhis. This cadre moved to Fort Knox to eventually become the 7th Cavalry Brigade (Mechanized), the vanguard armored formation in the army. They adopted the term *combat cars* because it would have required an act of congress to assign "tanks" to the cavalry.[4] The vehicles were light T5E2 tanks,[5] twinned with horsed squadrons transported by cavalry portees and augmented with small all-wheel drive reconnaissance-liaison vehicles named "Bantams." They were in fact, the first "Jeep," but originally called the "Peep" by the U.S. Cavalry and continued to be referred to as such throughout the war.[6]

Brigadier Chaffee took command in 1938 and continued his crusade to convert army praetorians to mechanization. His main opponent, appointed chief of cavalry the same year, was "long-legged, polo-playing" Maj. Gen. John Knowles Herr, who was prepared to risk all to protect the warhorse. Chaffee and Herr were West Point graduates; although Chaffee was four years Herr's junior, they were confrères and accomplished cavalrymen but their natural friendship had grown to animosity over mechanization.

Chaffee's earlier efforts to convert the army were rebuffed; when he presented a lecture on mechanization to the Army War College, he was called "visionary and crazy."[7] Criticized that he was sabotaging *cavalry tradition* by advocating mechanization, Chaffee, recognized as the Army's finest horseman, liked to retort: "The tradition of Cavalry is to fight!" He bemoaned his colleagues' reticence:

> They seemed blind to the possibilities of a mechanized cavalry ... that the definition of cavalry now includes troops of any kind equipped for highly mobile combat and not just mounted on horses. The motto of the School says, "Through Mobility we Conquer." It does not say, "Through Mobility on Horses Alone We Conquer."[8]

Herr's apologia invoked the stables: "There is no such thing as Armored Cavalry—remove the horse and there is no cavalry." Chaffee may have been the embodiment of Denison's ideal cavalier: "A Cavalry general should be possessed of a strong inventive genius and be self reliant to strike out a new line and adopt reforms when he sees them necessary."[9] His defining moment occurred at the Louisiana Maneuvers ("first genuine corps and army maneuvers in the history of the United States"[10]). The war games ended May 25, the day six German panzer divisions arrived outside Dunkirk to complete the encirclement of Allied armies entrapping half a million troops. High ranking American officers met in the basement of the Alexandria Junior High School to discuss the doctrinal consequences facing the U.S. Army.

It was near clandestine; the chiefs of infantry and cavalry (Lynch and Herr) were not invited, though both were attending the war games. The implications of the maneuvers and the concurrent campaign in France were obvious; there was no room for horses on a blitzkrieg battlefield—the army required a mechanized armored force. The "Alexandria Recommendations" urged that the unified development of armored units *separated* from cavalry and infantry.[11] It was a centurion's revolt. Herr was the great obstacle, and Chaffee was selected to travel to Washington to bell the cat.

Chaffee was direct and uncompromising: the chief of cavalry *must* convert horsed regiments in order to create the first tank division. General Herr "sat there rather straight in his chair, head down—then he looked up. 'Adna, not one more horse will I give up for a tank.'" He banged his hand on the desk.[12] Chaffee stood his ground: "Johnny, if that's the way you feel about it." He saluted and turned to his aide, Lt. Col. Robert Merrill Lee, an Army Air Corps officer, "Come on Bob, I'm through with him."[13] Herr's emphatic refusal led to Chaffee's critical decision to ditch the cavalry and directly petition the Army Chief of Staff, Gen. George Marshall. Chaffee delivered a bombshell: abandon the cavalry to its own ends and create an independent armored force.

Chaffee had twice before proposed an armored force, but always under cavalry control; his recommendations had been waved off. However with France surrendered and Britain facing invasion, Marshall assented. The U.S. Armored Force was created July 10, 1940; the Fort Knox force became the 1st Armored Division, and Chaffee was appointed chief of the new armored branch: "The Father of Armor."[14] The title *Armored Force* was conciliatory to the infantry who had long resisted the term "mechanized" and the cavalry which absolutely despised the word "tank." Maj. Gen. Robert Grow, destined to become an acclaimed tank division commander, concluded that the chief of cavalry "staunchly refused to give up a horse unit. So he lost it all . . . My firm belief is that had General Herr, from the beginning, taken a strong stand for the mechanization of the cavalry Branch, the Armored Force would never have been created."[15] Chaffee's *lese-majesté* against the warhorse eliminated the cavalry from playing any crucial role in the Second World War. The army called it a new age; Herr saw it as treachery.[16]

In hindsight, the 1930s American debate centered around trivia. The cavalry position becomes brittle when it is remembered the chief of cavalry not only consistently refused tanks but continued to lobby for a return to the *saber* as standard issue. Herr's loyalty to the *arme blanche* is both chivalrous and tragic. His refusal to accept reality even after the British realized cavalry must finally be sent to the knacker's yard was unfortunate; his intractability after the fall of France was irrational.

In the end, the United States produced three mechanized armies: the Armored Force, which fielded complete Tank Divisions; GHQ Battalions,[17] which were "infantry tanks" in style if not design and seconded to infantry divisions; and the Tank Destroyer empire with its dozens of independent battalions, maneuvering much like ambulances about the battlefield. The core of the Tank Destroyer Doctrine ("massed guns kill tanks") is correct. Its fault was rooted in unnecessary branch competition. The self evident solution was that guns do kill tanks, not as artillery but as high velocity armament in main battle tanks. By the autumn of 1943 the Wehrmacht was no longer on the offensive; blitzkrieg was something done by the Red Army. The Allies were doing the attacking and they required well armored, big gunned main battle tanks. There were none to be had.

The AGF profited by the efficiency of Detroit if not by the Ordnance Corps' vision.[18] Despite testing dozens of models, the Americans went to war with one main tank, the M4 *Sherman,* which was the Western version of the T34. Although inferior to German panzers, it defeated them via sheer numbers and a more practical design.

The British and Canadians supplemented their corps with tank brigades, which were independent formations that had a theoretical dual role: maneuver if necessary but not necessarily maneuver. They ended up, like American GHQ tank battalions, being penny-packeted out to support infantry combat, shunted around, much like cavalry reconnaissance squadrons, from division to division and forced to reinitiate complex get-acquainted rituals with the infantry units they supported. Combined-arms combat is all about mutual trust and requires time and often savage mutual experiences. Cavalry regiments were dumped together with tank units and formed the *Armored Brigades* of Commonwealth tank divisions.

ARMORED CAVALRY IN AFRICA AND EUROPE

> Yearly we've ridden the Djebel Stakes
> Yearly fought back on our course,
> Yearly we've made the same silly mistakes,
> Over-ridden a failing horse,
> —*The Djebel Stakes,* a metaphoric analysis of the Desert War, 1942[19]

The one place cavalry regiments felt at home, notwithstanding their nouveau armored status, appears to have been the African desert. The Western Desert was the mother of all military metaphors. Armor deployed as cavalry in *light* and *heavy* brigades; the regiments maintained the studied casual nonchalance that was associated with the horsy set and sought maneuver in fox hunting style. The vexing thing was that the desert was also the antithesis of things cavalry. It demanded maneuver and bold attack, but in a decidedly naval manner.

Alan Moorehead, whose *African Trilogy* is perhaps the best egalitarian account of the cultural, political and military aspects of the Mediterranean war, wrote:

> Desert warfare resembled war at sea. Men moved by compass. No position was static. There were few if any forts to be held. Each truck or tank was an individual as a destroyer, and each squadron of tanks or guns made great sweeps across the desert as a battle-squadron at sea will vanish over the horizon. One did not occupy the desert any more than one occupied the sea.[20]

There were horses and camel cavalry in the desert but they were Bedouin or Berber and did not deploy to fight, even in the most convoluted Weygand style. The desert was fought by mechanized units: steel plate and calibers ruled. This is a dangerous statement since there was much fighting by the infantry, who fulfilled admirably that description put forward by a British general, himself an infantryman, of his arm: "the lice that live in the folds of the earth." He did not mean to be critical.

Meanwhile, the armor units (and there were two distinct social classes: the *cavalwy* and the RTR *Rude Mechanicals*) were much like Crusader cataphracts and maneuvered like medieval armies. The light tanks navigated as fleets but pounced like Mongol regiments. The War in North Africa (1940–1943), considered a tactician's paradise and a quartermaster's nightmare, continued the crucial debate vis-à-vis better armor and guns that could defeat it. Long range tank duels generally went to the side that had the latest up-gunned and up-armored tank. The theater offered almost unlimited opportunity for operational maneuver as there were virtually no towns or indigenous population. Yet the vast desert steppes regularly narrowed by opportune geographic choke points like Hellfire Pass or the Qattara Depression, which determined operational tactics.

The monastic regimental life nurtured old school habits and brought forth a carefree professionalism that was as avant-garde as it was rigidly professional. The desert dress of the armies varied from pith helmet to cloth cap, from knee socks and shorts to winter great coats and scarves. Corduroy trousers, suede desert boots, flashy silk bandanas and neckerchiefs were sported first by cavalry, then all officers. Desert combat, though savage and technological, had elements of tilting and was cited as a chivalrous event between tank crews, or at least often pretended to be. The armies had much in common and the seesaw campaigning had them trade positions and embrace opposing styles, even music. The haunting "Lili Marlene" became the desert soldier's song and was adopted by both armies. An eccentric desert camaraderie existed which meant prisoners were well treated and successful commanders respected.

Desert slang was a mix of cavalry banter. *Swanning* across the desert meant to go on a wasted but not unpleasant tour, a "swan." *Brewing up* could mean having a meal or getting one's tank hit and set afire: *We brewed up after stopping* as opposed to *Harry's tank was brewed up by an 88*. Successful desert technology was copied, the most famous being the German gas container, which was preferred to the flimsy British tin can. It was dubbed "the Gerry Can" and soon served both armies; indeed it continues to be used in the twenty-first century by NATO armies—hard plastic copies, faithful to the Wehrmacht model, still referred to as *Gerrycans.*

ARMORED CAVALRY GENERALS

Our friend Rommel.
—Gen. Claude Auchinleck, summer 1942, the Western Desert[21]

Desert generals are a genre to themselves. A privileged community that somehow has escaped the more horrid facets associated with war and often portrayed as medievalists, jousting for honor across a realm seemingly designed for nothing but war and maneuver. Despite a surfeit of hard-hitting history, a certain romanticism continues to be associated with the desert—from *Lawrence of Arabia* to *The Desert Fox.*

General Sir Richard O'Connor, yet another infantry officer with an intuitive understanding for maneuver, commanded the *Western Desert Force,* responsible for protecting Egypt and the Suez Canal from a bombastic, much larger Italian army poised on the edge of the Libyan frontier. Marshal Rodolfo Graziani attacked in September 1940, pushed to Sidi Barrani, about 50 miles inside Egypt, and dug in. O'Connor, outnumbered five to one, promptly counterattacked. He was confident for he felt he had better commanders and more experienced troops—his force included the 7th Armoured, Britain's first operational tank division and poster child for the cavalry epiphany of marriage between horse and tank. The outfit was initially commanded by the raging bull of the British Armoured Corps, the rude but brilliant Maj. Gen. Percy Hobart, a bona fide "Apostle of Maneuver." It soon adopted the local Jeroba as its heraldic symbol and its men proudly called themselves "The Desert Rats."[22] Although the Italians had hundreds more tanks, the British order of battle included the impregnable *Matilda* IIs. O'Connor blitzed through Graziani's army, inflicting defeat after defeat. The Matildas ruled the desert and thoroughly demoralized the Italians. In January the British struck for the strategic port of Tobruk, captured it, and began to drive the Axis out of Cyrenaica.

O'Connor sent his armor deep into the desert and executed a wide flanking movement, reappearing at Beda Fomm, more than halfway to the Italian capital at Tripoli. His tanks surprised Graziani and bagged the entire army. O'Connor radioed Cairo, in clear for Mussolini's benefit, using a horsy term: "Fox killed in the open."[23]

This splendid victory alarmed Berlin. Hitler, fearing the Axis would lose Africa entirely, dispatched his favorite general, Erwin Rommel, with an elite mechanized group, the *Deutsche Afrika Korps* (DAK). Rommel's cavalry style (his origins were the light infantry) earned him grudging admiration from British troops and adoration from his own Afrika Korps. *Der Wüstenfuchs*[24] handled his three maneuver divisions with the style of Murat and sometimes with the desperation of Ney. "[Rommel] preferred maneuver, chose sweat rather than blood. As a rule he was right, but there are times when the heavy blow on fixed defenses will quickly open up the field of maneuver."[25] His daring and innate *Fingerspitzengefühl* won him great victories; his cavalier attitude toward his quartermaster nearly bought disaster on several occasions. In the British Desert Army a particularly clever piece of work became known as *a Rommel*: "He outwitted, bluffed, deceived, cheated the enemy. It was said that his greatest pleasure was to trick his opponents into premature and often quite needless surrender."[26] Winston Churchill complimented him on the floor of the House of Commons, which endorsed Rommel's international standing: "We have a very daring and skillful opponent against us and, may I say across the havoc of war, a great general."[27] His reputation was such that before El Alamein the 8th Army issued directives forbidding senior officers to refer to Rommel by name in briefings to troops. In the end he was defeated by a general with half his skill but twice his material.

On arrival Rommel immediately counterattacked, driving the British back to Tobruk.[28] Like O'Connor, he swept across the desert, bisecting the Benghazi triangle and appeared at Gazala (April 1941). An open tank battle between the two desert generals did not occur. O'Connor was captured after an audacious recce, made prisoner, and taken to Italy.

Rommel defended against a series of determined British attacks (Operations Battle Axe and Crusader) and again was forced to resort to 88s to stop the formidable *Matildas*. Crusader and its aftermath showed Rommel at his cavalier best and worst. Trapped between two formidable groups, Rommel tried to panic the British by launching a raid. In effect, it was a *chevauchée* that instead of agricultural bounty, sought dumps of gasoline as well as the infliction of chaos. His opponent, Gen. Claude Auchinleck, did not blink. Rommel soon found himself out of supplies and holding vast reaches of empty desert neither capturing dumps of petrol nor denying them to the British. Normally Rommel's personal bravery and feral tactics produced dividends: "[his officers] attributed his immunity to his *Fingerspitzengefühl* that innate sense of what the enemy was about to do."[29] This time he was forced to retreat; maneuver alone cannot forge victory, one has to eventually capture something.

Demonstrably beaten and out-tactic'd, Rommel abandoned Cyrenaica, seemingly a disaster of strategic proportions. But just when the British assumed he was running for Tripoli, he counterattacked. The Afrika Korps enveloped scattered tank units, overran dumps to sustain its drive and bounced Auchinleck back to the legendary port-stronghold of Tobruk. It was a gutsy bit of tactics and met a standard set earlier by O'Connor who had said: "I would never consider a commander completely successful until he had restored the situation after a serious defeat and a long retreat."[30] The remaining campaigns followed the pendulum of the North African war. Rommel again risked everything by attacking the Gazala Line (an extension of fortress Tobruk, reaching twenty five miles into the desert) and again the British held firm. Rommel became trapped on the wrong side of British minefields but instead of letting him wither, the 8th Army attacked. Resolute assaults—only to be shattered like so many knights at Crécy by the longbow of the desert, the 88 mm antitank gun:

> The British advanced to battle with an armoured corps trained and organized according to a haphazard set of wrong principles, led by officers who had never commanded armour in battle before, and who were not tank men . . . the British tried to get at the German armour, ensconced amid its lorried infantry and artillery, in a series of "cavalry" charges.[31]

This time Auchinleck fell back and Rommel quickly captured Tobruk and swept into Egypt seemingly about to capture Suez. In *The Desert Trilogy*, Alan Moorehead noted, "The British Fleet had left Alexandria. The demolition gangs stood ready."[32] The Afrika Korps was stopped at El Alamein, one of the three great battles that turned the tide in the Second World War; the other two were Midway and Stalingrad.

General Bernard Law Montgomery, who had replaced Auchinleck (some thought without cause), was awarded an embarrassment of material, a surfeit of tanks and resurrected the "set piece battle." His offensive (the "Third Alamein," October 23–November 4, 1942) outlasted Rommel, eviscerated his armor, and finally followed him out of Egypt. It was an uninspired pursuit given that Rommel had been strategically outflanked. A British-American force had landed near Casablanca and Algiers, over two thousand miles to his rear and threatened his only port, an impressive piece of Allied strategic maneuver and envelopment.

The American corps was commanded by Gen. George S. Patton who arrived after Rommel rudely handled the novice 1st U. S. Armored Division at the battle of Kasserine Pass (Tunisia, February, 1943).[33] A Rommel-Patton confrontation did not occur—Rommel invalided out to Europe. Within seven months the German-Italian army was surrounded by two Allied field forces. The war in North Africa was over.

The Desert War was a cavalry war in that it emphasized maneuver and acquired a chivalrous repute; despite mordant reality, the campaigns prepossessed a certain romantic patina. The war produced renowned generals, including a plodding infantryman, an ersatz cavalier and a bona fide cavalryman. Field Marshals Montgomery, Rommel, and General Patton reconvened in Normandy where each would have opportunity to exhibit their mettle. Rommel and Montgomery would actually duel in violent but uninspired tank battles; only Patton would demonstrate what armored cavalry was all about.

Les deux: "I understand one of us is obsolete."

Chapter 14

Cavalry in the Second World War, Part II: The Horse within Blitzkrieg

Das Paradies der Erde liegt auf den Rücken der Pferde.
(Paradise on earth is on the backs of horses.)

—German cavalry motto

Actually, the lowly horse played a most important part in enabling the German Army to move about Europe.

—U.S. Army Intelligence Bulletin, March 1945[1]

Perhaps the most interesting aspect of an army famous for its mechanized operations and synonymous with "tanks" is that the German military was so much dependent on the horse. By the end of the war, Western armies were totally mechanized and supported by truck borne logistics; the German armies included cavalry not because it was useful, but because they absolutely had to. The surprising revelation about the German army was that it included millions of horses; the bulk of its infantry and much of its logistic organization used horse power as its only alternative for there were simply not enough trucks to go around. Of the 264 German combat divisions available in November 1944, only 42 were armored or motorized. The great bulk of the German combat strength marched into battle on foot, with their weapons and supply trains propelled almost entirely by four-legged horsepower.[2] The strength of German army horses during the war averaged around 1,100,000.

The 1st Cavalry Division was mechanized in October 1941 as the 24th Panzer-Division (destined to be destroyed in Stalingrad); its logo was a jumping horseman. This caused bitterness; the warhorses, bred and trained for the most flamboyant tasks were dispatched to the infantry to pull artillery and supply wagons. A few senior officers managed to send their chargers back to Germany, but the remaining thoroughbreds were sentenced to "hut slut" duties in the rear areas.

Surprisingly, the Wehrmacht suddenly raised three new cavalry units in 1942 (1st, 2nd, and 3rd Reiter Regiments) but the chargers of the old 1st Cavalry had been dispersed: "pulling old, dirty wagons somewhere in the mud of Russia. So everything else remaining on four legs had to be saddled: little fat ponies, old heavy farming horses and horses captured from the enemy."[3] Reconstruction took time even though a substantial selection still existed. Curt Schulze, Veterinarian General of the Army, controlled 1,250,000 horses, 37,000 blacksmiths, and 125,000 horse soldiers, some of them cavaliers. The panzer obsessed Wehrmacht operated 48 veterinary hospitals and serviced the blitzkrieg armies with 68 horse transport divisions. The veterinary hospitals treated about 100,000 horses a day.[4]

By 1944 the western front became a prolonged slaughter of horseflesh as Allied tactical aircraft shot up any transport or column found on roads. Harnessed horses were easy marks; veterans of the Falaise Gap vividly recall the awful stench of rotting animals, the sight of hundreds of bloated horses crammed into narrow Normandy lanes, victims of artillery and air attack. In an article, Maj. Matthew Guymer stated, "We had to wet our scarves and handkerchiefs to cover our mouths and noses to try to cut out the awful stench . . . rotting crops, the nasty unpleasant all consuming odor of dead men, farm animals and dead bloated army horses."[5] The effects of Allied strategic bombing made the horse a viable and required asset in war, both as fighting cavalry and as part of the logistic trains. However, though *Bomber* Generals Harris and Spaatz crippled motor transport production, they left East Prussian horse-breeding farms alone.

The new German cavalry formations were sent into rough terrain to fight partisans. Horse formations did better than tank outfits in the Balkan mountains or the muddy morass of a rain soaked Ukrainian steppe. Like tanks, warhorses preferred open ground and maneuver; unlike panzers, cavalry could not survive modern guns. A bizarre collection comprised late war Nazi cavalry—it included Wehrmacht Reiters, still sporting yellow piping, Waffen SS, foreign cadres and even Cossack brigades. The zealously independent Cossacks of western Ukraine and the Don-Volga valleys welcomed Hitler's invasion and hoped to secure their traditional homelands from Soviet rule. They were soon organized into the 1st and 2nd Cossack Divisions and fought exclusively against their former masters.[6]

Waffen SS units included the poster boys of the *Schutzstaffel* horsy set, the 8th SS Cavalry Division *Florian Geyer,* and the 22nd SS Volunteer Cavalry Division *Maria Theresa.* They first saw action as regiments in the invasion of Russia; within a year they had become the *SS Cavalry Division,* a solid outfit that endured frustrating actions including Stalingrad, and then expanded into two formations. The *Maria Theresa* had a strong contingent of Austro-Hungarians and adopted the cornflower, favorite of Empress Maria Theresa, as their divisional emblem. *Florian Geyer* went on to fight Tito's partisans and Serbian *Chetniks* in the Balkans before conducting rearguard actions into the *Puszta.* Though referred to as the SS Cavalry Corps, they were never officially grouped but fought their last battles around Budapest.

CRÉCY REDUX: STEEL STEEDS AND OPERATIONAL MANEUVER IN NORMANDY

> We have nothing to fear from Panther and Tiger Tanks.
> —Gen. B.L.M. Montgomery, July 4, 1944

American General Dwight David Eisenhower, Supreme Commander of Allied forces in Europe, controlled four Allied armies. However, he was content to let the more experienced Montgomery control operations. Field Marshal Montgomery's attempts to breakout out of the Normandy bridgehead on his side of the front included two strategic offensives, both failures. In both cases the attacks tested a defence set by Field Marshal Rommel in his last battlefield command. Operation Goodwood (July 18–20) confirmed the leitmotif of the Allied strategic offensive signature—heavy bombers as preparatory artillery. The Red Army used divisions of heavy artillery; the Western Allies bombed. The sight of waves of bombers apparently obliterating the enemy was technologically seductive and popular with the troops. In fact, it produced limited results and often caused fratricide. Despite the claims of strategic bombing advocates, heavy bombers were dramatically inaccurate. In three of the four Normandy offensives there was an aiming error and Allied troops were savaged by friendly bombs.

Goodwood was spearheaded by the redoubtable desert maneuverist General Richard O'Connor. He escaped Italy in December 1943, returned to England, was knighted and given command of VIII Armored Corps that included his old African chum, the 7th Armoured, "Desert Rats." O'Connor arrived in Normandy in June 1944, ready to do battle with the fellow who had bagged him near Gazala, and now defended western France: Erwin Rommel. O'Connor's tanks advanced at the slow trot and were shot to pieces by Panthers and Tigers as they attempted to storm Verrières Ridge. Long range fire shredded three armored divisions and sent O'Connor back to the start line. The disappointing offensive was followed five days later by the great Allied success of the Normandy campaign: Operation Cobra (July 25–31, 1944).

Bradley's attack was presented in two parts: General Hodges' 1st Army as the *force de rupture,* then Patton's tank army as the *force de manoeuvre.* The offensive became gargantuan when Montgomery threw in Dempsey's 2nd British Army (Operation Bluecoat, July 30–August 7) forcing the three British tank divisions into thick bocage. The 21st Army Group comprised two Commonwealth forces—the 1st Canadian Army (General Crerar) and the 2nd British, both near Caen. On August 8, as Major Generals Wood and Grow neared LeMans and Brest, Montgomery had the 1st Canadian Army launch Operation Totalize south of Caen. He was presented with dramatic results. Lt. Gen. Guy Simonds's II Corps broke through, at least initially, and reached Falaise by the end of the month. This created a Cannae effect as American and Canadian armies "closed the gap." Panzer General Fritz Bayerlin wrote:

> The battle of annihilation in Normandy—the breakthrough at St. Lô, resulting in the envelopment, encirclement, and annihilation of the German defenders (Fifth Pz and Seventh Armies)—appears to me to be the greatest strategical and tactical achievement of this war, as well as the most decisive.[7]

Although Falaise was the great Allied maneuver victory, the senior commanders, Montgomery and Bradley, had to be dragged, almost shamed, into triumph by Patton and his romping tank commanders. Internecine arguments, tinged with nationalistic pique spoiled the campaign's elegant execution. Bradley held a smoldering loathing for Montgomery; he came to despise the latter's arrogance, particularly his tactical pontification. Montgomery's affected desert army style, a deliberately casual ersatz cavalry manner, did not impress the senior American staff: "... in his corduroy trousers, his loose fitting gabardine coat and his beret like a poorly tailored bohemian painter."[8] He was considered a prima donna even by his greatest fans; Churchill quipped: "In defeat, indomitable. In advance, invincible. In victory, insufferable."[9] This Allied anomaly was created by Eisenhower himself, a splendid chairman of the board but an ineffective war leader. He appointed Montgomery the tactical *majordomo* in Normandy and therefore overseer of all maneuver. His determination to breakout on the eastern flank near Caen simply wasted tanks. However, Bradley's follow-up at Avranches was equally unenlightened. Even when Patton's progress made the required maneuver self evident, Bradley and Montgomery could not reach cooperative agreement. Eisenhower was content to observe from above. This esurient managerial tempest simply validated George Marshal's astute observation: "A democracy can't fight a Seven Years' War."[10]

The campaign ended with spectacular maneuver warfare. General Patton's armored divisions were amongst the finest formations on any front; their

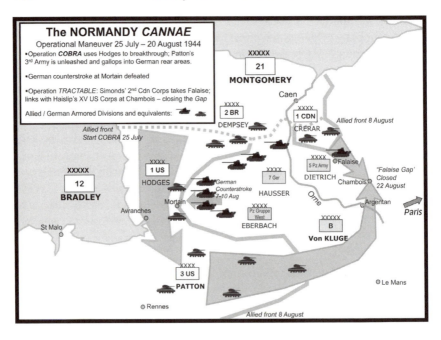

commanders, Maj. Gen. Robert Grow (6th Armored Division) and especially Major General John S. "Professor" Wood (4th Armored Division) demonstrated the fundamentals of mass armor exploitation—shock.[11] Patton's 3rd Army conducted corps sized *chevauchées,* scattering rearguards, causing chaos. Wood completely rattled the commander of the western front, Gen. Hans von Kluge: "The news that an American armored division was in Rennes had a shattering effect, like a bomb burst, upon us."[12]

The Allied pursuit ended in Belgium, near the Ardennes, where it all began in 1940. Desert alumnus, Lt. Gen. Brian Horrocks, advanced his British XXX Corps 250 miles in six days, capturing Brussels and Antwerp. Patton, frustrated by a lack of fuel, reached Lorraine but not the Rhine. His divisions would again demonstrate prowess in Lorraine where its tank commanders, like Colonel Creighton Abrams, would ride circles around experienced Germans in better tanks. Normandy may have demonstrated the American tanks' operational style but Lorraine proved their tactical acumen. It remains a campaign that requires careful study by the armored cavalry.

WESTERN CAVALRY FORMATIONS—IN REVIEW

In 1940, as the German panzers rolled across France, the U.S. Army still included two horse cavalry divisions, two horse-drawn artillery regiments, and two mixed horse and motor transport regiments, with a total authorization of 16,800 horses and 3,500 mules. The last cavalry unit to see combat was the 26th Cavalry Regiment (The Philippine Scouts); it was forced to destroy its horses after the retreat to Bataan. It continued to fight dismounted in the cavalry-dragoon tradition. Of the two cavalry divisions active during the Second World War, only the 1st Cavalry Division fought as a unit, albeit as dismounted dragoons—undistinguishable from "leg infantry." The 2nd Cavalry Division was partially inactivated in July 1942 and became the army's third black division designated 2nd Cavalry Division (Horse) (Colored). African Americans were actively recruited into its four regiments and trained in cavalry operations. When the War Department announced there was no intrinsic need for a second cavalry division, black community leaders, reacting against the criticism of the performance of negroes in combat units, protested the possible conversion of the division. The unit was shipped overseas despite plans for its being stood down. The 2nd Cavalry Division was inactivated on May 10, 1944 off the North African coast.

Neither of the two cavalry divisions took horses overseas; by 1943 the expense and space required made deployment of cavalry units an unnecessary luxury. Thus via logic and economics, the last horsed formation was quietly discarded and the last warhorse abandoned by the army.[13] After the advent of Chaffee, cavalry horses were returned to the remount depots. Less than a half dozen horses were procured during the war. There was an unexpected demand in 1943 from the Coast Guard for 3,000 horses to be used to patrol coast lines as a reaction to German U-Boat activity and the possibility of agent-saboteurs being landed. By 1944 the submarine war had been won and the horses were returned to remount depots.

The unsung ungulate veteran of the war was the war-mule: over 14,000 mules were used during the last two years. Hardy, sure footed and capable of bringing war supplies over any difficult terrain, army mules served in both Mediterranean mountains and Asian jungle. The unorthodox combat unit, "Merrill's Marauders," used approximately 340 horses as well as 360 mules in Burma. Pack mules were used in Tunisia during the winter of 1942–43 and throughout the Italian mountain ranges. In Sicily, the 3rd Provisional Reconnaissance Troop (3rd Infantry Division) quickly adjusted to the rigors of mountain warfare and became mounted by acquiring 143 horses and an additional 349 mules for its pack train. Patton wrote in the Cavalry Journal:

> It is the considered opinion, not only of myself but of many other general officers . . . that had we possessed an American cavalry division with pack artillery in Tunisia and Sicily, not a German would have escaped, because horse cavalry possesses the additional gear ratio which permits it to attain sufficient speed through mountainous country to get behind and hold the enemy until more powerful [units] can come up and destroy him.[14]

The specialized 10th Mountain Division used thousands of mules in the Dolomites—but these were operations with mounts rather than mounted operations. There really was no "cavalry" in the sense of an "arm." The only fighting mechanized cavalry were the squadrons attached to armored divisions and their success again depended entirely on German cooperation or the presence of an armored vanguard from one of the combat commands (CCs), which were formed headquarters, much like holding companies, to control battle groups cobbled together to fight specific missions. CCs were initially conceived by Chaffee with the "stern warning that they were not designed to be bureaucratic compartments but servants of ad hoc tactical creativity."[15]

Of the 16 tank divisions that saw combat, 14 had a "Cavalry Reconnaissance Squadron (Mecz)" attached; the other two were serviced by AGF recce battalions. None of the 54 tank battalions carried the guidon of an established cavalry regiment and certainly not one of the hundred plus independent GHQ tank battalions or tank destroyer units perpetuated the cavalry. Its elimination had been humiliating and complete; indeed, the cleansing may be considered excessive.

Mechanized cavalry units served as the "eyes and ears" of commanders. Cavalry units provided reconnaissance for corps or army headquarters; mechanized cavalry reconnaissance squadrons supported armored divisions, and a cavalry reconnaissance troop worked for each infantry division.[16] Cavalry performed traditional flank security tasks, picketing open flanks and guarding the major river crossings during the Cobra breakout—the 6th Cavalry Group was unofficially dubbed as "Patton's Household Cavalry."[17]

The British and Canadian reconnaissance regiments in armored divisions were different outfits and included main battle tanks. The scheme made sense but in fact there was little appreciable difference because practical consideration overrode traditional cavalry tactics. The tank squadrons in 21st Army group's recce regiments were regularly used as a fourth tank regiment, grouped with infantry and asked to conduct normal operations, though they were careful to use cavalry mannerisms and shibboleths.

CAVALRY AS ARMORED RECONNAISSANCE

Mounted units, schooled in American cavalry doctrine, would have been the perfect solution. Hardened and well trained horseman, possessing mobility and fire power, could have infiltrated through the extended German lines, encircled the delaying detachments, and would have permitted the maintenance of pressure on the retreating enemy main forces by our infantry division in their direct pursuit and would not have given the Germans sufficient time to prepare strong defensive positions to the north. As it was, there was no cavalry available.

—Maj. Gen. John P. Lucas

While German horsed cavalry conducted patrol and security tasks, active reconnaissance was performed by panzer recce units which could fight for information. The panzer reconnaissance battalion reflected combat experience; it outclassed its opponents and its heavy armored cars had an advantage over British and American counterparts. German recce would, however, meet its match if confronted by a British or Canadian corps recce regiment for they sported the impressive Staghound armored car, which was "very advanced for its time . . . preferred by crews due to its reliability, speed, armor protection and low maintenance requirement."[18] The British Staghound's robust qualities were much admired by their American counterparts who were nursing their lighter M8 Greyhounds. The vexing thing was that Staghounds were manufactured in the United States but rejected by the AGF for front line service: "The Stag was to a British design spec and the U.S. Army wasn't about to adopt someone else's design."[19] Their preferred quality was being able to take a hit whether by heavy machinegun or mine; against panzerfaust or tank guns the heavy cars stood the same chance as a Sherman: "We were never bothered by the standard German recce but their eight wheeled cars often mounted 75s or high velocity 50 mm that could stop us. German rearguards were one or two tanks and infantry with *panzerfausts* hiding and sneaking around . . . shabby little men."[20]

The standard American recce vehicle, the M8 Greyhound, was a 6x6 armored car fitted with a 37 mm but not much larger than a *Peep,* or three-quarter-ton truck. The Greyhound was fast, mechanically reliable but road bound. Cavalry units criticized its cross country performance and its light armor. Australian armor authority, Doug Greville, who still drives his restored Greyhound, is blunt in his evaluation:

> It was an antiquated design, grossly underpowered and with an open top turret. Ergonomics of the gunner's position are terrible, no periscopes, just cheap and small episcopes . . . a cheap and nasty design. But worst of all was the sheet metal belly, which provided zero protection to the crew from mines.[21]

Although armored cars are often touted as a more natural extension of cavalry, they are a decidedly urban vehicle; they struggle in sand and mud. The Greyhound held its own in the Far East where its 37 mm gun could dispatch any Japanese tank. The vehicle ended the war much in the shadow of other more intimidating combat cars. Derided and dismissed, the Greyhound had the last laugh for the new millennium found it still in service with several third world countries, a lingering artifact of the mechanized cavalry debate and more a tribute to the vehicle's simplicity than its effectiveness.[22] The British complement to the Greyhound was the Humber armored car, which was the most widely produced recce vehicle with over 3,600 built and boasted decent armor and a 37 mm gun.

Cavalry officers particularly enjoyed the grand pursuit that followed the Cobra breakout. After months of dismounted operations, the reconnaissance squadrons fanned out across the open ground between the Loire and Meuse trying "to catch Jerry." For horsemen who had not been in the saddle since 1939 and had endured Normandy's ultracautious *sneaky-peeky* tactics, it was an exhilarating time. Lt. Col. William Bowen, then a squadron commander in the 17th Duke of York's Royal Canadian Hussars, relished the memories of his Norman Summer:

> Mad, sunny days, tearing down the *routes nationales*—as we came to the end of a map, we flung it over our shoulders—they were British overprints of rather dated French *cartes rouges*. Most enemy contacts were small rearguards near bridges or some sort of mine or tank ambush—normally from the rear.[23]

The American "cavalry reconnaissance squadron (mechanized)" included light tanks and an assortment of supporting arms and scout-infantry, operating much like Great War cavalry sending out recce troops to discover the enemy, ready to fall back upon supports if things got sticky. From August to September the danger was from rear guards and ambush. A shrewd tactical approach required time, dismounted patrols and careful observation but this caused delay and annoyed senior commanders who demanded brazen advance:

> At 1030 the Army Commander, General George S. Patton, came to the head of the column, inquired about the situation, and spurred on to immediate advances. "What I want is audacity!"[24]

The steppe pony: "I was sent to the Cossacks."
The Bolshevik pony: "Really? Well Trotsky sent the *Proletariat* to me."

Chapter 15

Cavalry in the Second World War, Part III: The Russian Warhorse and the Tank

Produmaen Eshche.
[Let's think this over.]

—Stalin instructed Stavka, after *Barbarossa*

The summer of 1944 was the doctrinal and tactical zenith of the warhorse and the tank. Operation Cobra, the best example of Western operational maneuver, was exclusively conducted by tanks; participating cavalry units were strictly armored. The great Soviet summer offensive (Operation Bagration, a.k.a. "The Destruction of Army Group Centre") matched Cobra in length and breadth, but dwarfed it in number of German formations destroyed. The offensive was a masterpiece of the operational art and the pluperfect evolution of *glubokii boi* combining tank armies with cavalry groups and independent cavalry brigades. The Russian decision to attack with warhorse and tank was not simply Slavophile practicality as much as enlightened accommodation.

Stalin permitted a potpourri of doctrines to exist, each well funded and supported by a levee-en-masse mentality that included the horse. At first the cavalry simply fought because Russia was desperate and shaken by astounding losses. The final iteration of the Christie-BT series, the ubiquitous T34, provided the central instrument of Soviet survival and operational success as the perfect cavalry tank.[1]

Despite Stalin's success in industrializing an agrarian state, Russia was hamstrung by a limited rail network, a chaotic mix of primitive highways, and a punishing climate. Deep snows and a muddy spring thaw defied cross-country tracked maneuver and left plenty of room for hardy cavalry. At its peak the Red Army had 10 cavalry corps in varied compositions. Soviet horsed formations included simple mobs of Dragoons and Cossacks that conducted operations in eighteenth-century tradition as independent, ubiquitous outfits. Soviet hybrid Mech-Cavalry divisions would have made Weygand covetous.

Horsed formations did well amidst desperate and disorganized formations; the battle of the Korsun Pocket (winter, 1944) demonstrated cavalry-tank effectiveness. The pocket was a splendid double envelopment and trapped six German divisions. Equipped with creative mixes of sticky mines, antitank guns, and heavy machine guns as well as supporting indirect artillery, the cavalry divisions matched the mobility of tank brigades in rough terrain. A cavalry assault could include any type of tank and supporting arm. In the end, simple kit and plenty of it triumphed on the eastern front as it did in Western Europe.

CAVALRY RAIDS—RED ARMY CHEVAUCHÉE

Before the German invasion Stalin had created 74 stud farms and a well-organized remount service, which he maintained despite a frenzied program of tank construction. By 1945 Soviet cavalry had evolved from a mix of *what was available* to combinations of *what worked.* The cavalry rode proud steeds whose lineage was Borodino, tough Asian ponies, as well as Cossack mounts from the Don and Volga. Red Army cavalry acted in concert with set piece offensives or conducted independent operations. It was specifically used where terrain prevented employment of mechanized formations but was also ordered to perform active reconnaissance and independent incursion. Raids were bold and extensive; one operation included an entire cavalry corps and lasted 135 days. Another pair of corps conducted extended operations 60 miles behind the front, harassing communications and rear area logistics. They maneuvered parallel to the front despite deep snow and temperatures well below freezing. The week long raid traversed 50 miles and destroyed a series of German supply dumps. These operations were similar to American Civil War raids and extended the mounted dragoon technique.

Strategic offensives were more complex: after a *grand strike* by mechanized formations, breakthroughs unleashed Red Army tank and cavalry divisions deep into the German rear areas. These drew away German reserves, interrupted countermaneuver, and created chaos in the soft sectors of armies. Red cavalry overran communication centers, threatened airfields, and savaged second- and third-line repair areas; mechanical engineers required to resurrect damaged tanks often found themselves fighting desperate actions. Particularly disruptive was any mounted attack against artillery. The appearance of cavalry in the gun lines completely rattled headquarters, deprived the front of supporting fire, and used up reserves.[2]

THE LAST CAVALRY BATTLES

The Hungarian Puszta has been the site of great cavalry battles, perhaps none greater than the confrontations between Soviet and Waffen SS Cavalry in the autumn of 1944. In September Stalin ordered Marshal Rodion Malinovsky's already spent force to press on to Budapest, the gateway to Vienna, Hitler's home town. The 6th Guards Tank Army included Mobile Group Pliyev and Mobile Group Gorshkov, two cavalry formations—perhaps the final word in the evolution of the warhorse and its *marriage de raison* with the tank. Malinovsky instructed General Issa Alexandrovich Pliyev's tank-cavalry corps to encircle German forces at Debrecen. Debrecen is the second largest city in Hungary, about 300 km east of Budapest, centered on the Great Hungarian Plain; it dominates the puszta as well as approaches from the Carpathian passes.

Mobile Group Pliyev realized the Weygand dream of a balanced force of cavalry. The group comprised a cavalry corps (about the size of a standard division) supported by as many as four tank regiments as well as attached arms and services, including five regiments of 76.2 mm artillery augmented with 122 mm batteries—over 350 guns. This was further supplemented by *Kathyusha* multiple rocket launcher batteries. Cavalry artillery was generally horse-drawn, but heavier guns could be allotted trucks or tractors if available.

Pliyev's boldness hovered on the impudent as he whipped his warhorses into a dramatic encirclement, advancing 60 kilometers, to link up with the 6th Guards Tank Army. Pliyev's attack then succumbed to the bugbear of all Soviet offensives—he outran his supply trains. Still, the offensive vexed Hitler enough to dispatch six SS panzer divisions, a quarter of the entire Wehrmacht tank strength, to Hungary. Like Malinovsky, German General Johannes Friessner also planned a Cannae encirclement. Success could delay a Soviet offensive against Budapest until the next spring. Both sides' plans were concurrent and concentric and both generals underestimated the strength of the opposition.

The Germans maneuvered against Pliyev and raised the Debrecen siege. Two panzer divisions struck his flank. Determined actions were fought at all ranges, day and night; confusion reigned with neither the Soviets nor the Germans knowing who was surrounding whom. A second pincer movement by General Fretter-Pico brought success. Led by a battle savvy *King Tiger* battalion, an ad hoc force including the *Florian Geyer* Cavalry Division and the *Feldherrnhalle* SS Panzer Corps, Pico surrounded the Soviets. Group Pliyev fought with determination; however, the Hungarian Puszta was no place for a cavalry outfit by the end of the war. Pliyev was chopped to pieces by *Panthers, JagdPan-thers,* and *KingTigers.*[3] A series of desperate counterattacks by Malinovsky and Pliyev's own breakout attempt were beaten back. Finally the besieged cavalry group destroyed their horses, tanks, and artillery then attempted to infiltrate back to their own lines. Pliyev actually escaped and the German victory was short lived. The battles around Debrecen proved to be the last time the German army inflicted a decisive defeat on the Russians; it was certainly the last time the two were to conduct maneuver warfare on even terms.

Pliyev went on to see more action at the very end of the war. Virtually unknown in the West, he is one of the great cavalry commanders and certainly the last modern cavalier to reach a zenith in the cavalry operational art. Pliyev commanded the last Red Army cavalry action which took place in August 1945. Pliyev's Soviet Mongolian Cavalry-Mechanized Group (its mounted component comprised mainly of Mongolian Cavalry Divisions) attacked Japanese troops in Manchuria.[4]

Maria Theresa and *Florian Geyer* were next deployed to defend Budapest's suburbs. The units left their mounts in the city center; this was an ignominious end for their warhorses but a welcomed happenstance for Hungarians: "more than 30,000 horses were left wandering around Budapest, and many ended up providing essential nourishment for the inhabitants and the army."[5] Soviet attacks reached Budapest itself by the end of December, led, appropriately enough, by Cossack Cavalry and tanks. The campaign was the final battleground for both cavalry armies.

The Wehrmacht's remaining horsed formation, the 1st Cavalry Corps, surrendered to the British army on May 8, 1945, and were ordered to slaughter the horses for prisoner rations. The cavaliers organized polo tournaments and won over their English captors, traditionally sympathetic to the horse. The British divisional commander arranged to transfer the steeds to the American zone where benevolent Yanks agreed to release the cavalry mounts for farming and transport duties.

Left to its own devices the cavalry of the eastern front was more operational gadfly than strategic nuisance. In opposition to the case made for cavalry before the war, the Second World War relegated cavalry to a force of tactical opportunity. Nevertheless, even the most romantic had to accept that the warhorses' days as a professional arm were finally at an end. This was ratified by no less a successful operative than the Red Army itself, which disbanded the Soviet cavalry in 1957. Still, the Soviets could not bear to completely terminate their connection with the warhorse. Independent cavalry squadrons continued to serve the Red Army as late as 1989; the last squadron was based along with a Mountain Mechanized Rifle Brigade at Osh in Kirghizia, in the Vakish river valley, a link from Afghanistan to the Chinese border. By the new millennium the Afghan border would see more cavalry comprised of Afghan irregulars and American Special Forces cadres.

The turreted fellow:
"Of course we're Cavalry. Don't we look like Cavalry?"

Chapter 16

Cold Warhorse: *Pegasus ex Machina*

Reculer pour mieux sauter.
(Draw back to get a better jump.)

—Cavalry maxim

Cold war cavalry existed in name only. Despite the Red Army's equestrian heroics, the warhorse was passé in the space age. Although some third-world countries conducted mounted border patrols, the horse was actually too complex and delicate a weapon to be used in modern wars. In juxtaposition to the warhorse's professional demise was the cavalry's determination to be reinstated as a viable arm. This chapter will consider two aspects of cavalry's mercurial fortunes in separate yet related incidents, each of which prophesized cavalry's, indeed armor's, end: the appearance of the helicopter which promised another epiphanic moment, and the deployment of guided missiles designed to kill tanks and aircraft. This resulted in a military watershed creating yet another corps of hi-tech archers to challenge airborne and tracked chivalry. Israeli battle experience is notable not because of a direct use of cavalry but because of a cavalry style and specifically, the first confrontation against sophisticated missile systems that changed war forever.

A half century after the mechanization debate contrived to terminate the warhorse there remained but one effective "cavalry" on the planet. While armored cavalry existed as swank regiments in the Commonwealth, particularly British armies, only the United States actually maintained a bona fide cavalry branch. Republican Americans, least expected to harbor old world longings for aristocratic eras, maintained a credible and distinct cavalry arm that boasted both modern equipments and doctrine. Its determination to survive, indeed prosper within the Space Age, succeeded despite the challenge of the Asian wars and the cybernetic modernization. This *Pilgrim's Progress* included the acquisition of a new maneuver doctrine, *AirLand Battle* and finally participation in its trial by fire via Middle East war.

APOCALYPSE THEN: CAVALRY IN VIETNAM

> Cautions against piecemeal use of armored units ... came after a long and bitter struggle between a handful of American cavalrymen who saw in armored forces something more than support for dismounted infantry and American infantrymen who clung tenaciously to the idea that armored forces were merely for support.
>
> —Gen. Donn A. Starry, *Armored Combat in Vietnam*

The helicopter suggested an ideal anthropomorphic successor to the warhorse: a *Pegasus ex machina.* The helicopter's promised mobility inspired doctrinal optimism. Cavalry, keen to restore its past clout, went to war in jungles as infantry support tanks and airborne dragoons twinned to an ultra modern arm. Soaring charges introduced a fourth dimension into the trinity of maneuver, *vertical envelopment,* which resulted in far more dramatic Cannaes than Hannibal could have imagined. Ironically, *vertical envelopment* doctrine was assigned to the infantry and only later awarded to *armor,* which was finally requested to develop "a cavalry role"[1] for helicopters.

Vietnam was a helicopter war or remembered as such. The actual ground slogging which accounted for the majority of the dirty work pales beside the quixotic aerial charges by cavaliers as brave and brazen as Murat or Custer. The surreal film, *Apocalypse Now* (1979), presents the helicopter as a *retro cavalry* comprised of macabre romantics. The attack led by Major Kilgore (Robert Duval in blue Stetson and yellow scarf) is accompanied by trumpet calls as well as Wagner's *Ride of the Valkyries.* The cruel burlesque catches the essence of cavalry's desperate attempt to resurrect its raison d'être via the machine.

"Air cavalry" restored the dragoon into a new prominence with measureless mobility and maneuver. The Air Cav fought on foot; the cavalry part of the enterprise was left to the skill and derring-do of the pilots, a martial sect akin to feudal knights. As aerial steed, the helicopter restored a certain lost style; conversely, it did not restore the congregational élan that the cavalry so missed. Any outfit could and did use the magic machines; the difference between *troopers* and *grunts* became moot. The helicopter restored some of cavalry's missed status but, in an egalitarian style, raised the infantry to equal footing. More practically, in bad weather ground elements could move to a fight when air cavalry could not.

Air cavalry enhanced two traditional mounted missions: reconnaissance and surveillance, as well as the specter of mounted paladins. It was a short-lived Camelot for electronic surveillance and loitering aircraft soon shared, then dominated, the stage. Lt. Gen. L. D. Holder pointed out: "Air cavalry flew in and out of secure bases and their gun and scout pilots lived a lot like the aircrews of the air force. Like those other fliers, they went straight to the hottest fights and saw more action than their compadres in infantry and heavy cavalry."[2] The ground-to-air rocket sobered the marauder tendency of helicopter templars; it became obvious that the helicopter, like the medieval knight, was too valuable a commodity to risk against peasant archers armed with *SAM 7s*. The future of the airborne gunship lay in Europe where antitank missiles, launched thousands of yards distance, would stop the *Red Menace* and save Europe.

The Vietnam People's Army was a light infantry force and expert in asymmetrical warfare. It seldom fought in larger than battalion sized groups unless surprised by helicopter mobility. Its unpredictable strike tactics forced a surfeit of search and destroy missions or operations designed to dominate selected areas. Vietnam finally did include armored cavalry, which used tanks not armored cars and strived to succeed where the French had failed. As noted by Gen. Donn A. Starry, "The great 1–9 Cavalry [Air] of the 1st Cav Div [AASLT] claimed to have made as many kills as the remainder of the division in the bad old days of body counts. Their mission was to find, fix and strike moving enemy forces all over the large division area and they enjoyed considerable success."[3] Mechanized and air cavalry units performed missions similar to mounted forces on the western American frontier or in the Philippines. They only rarely fought squadron or regimental-sized engagements and their actions were only occasionally part of divisional operations. Rather, they patrolled, provided area and unit security, performed area reconnaissance and acted as mobile reserves or pursuit forces. Cavalrymen, air and ground were idiosyncratic and somewhat different from the infantry; they worked as troops and platoons and stayed in the field more or less permanently. Vietnam veteran and troop leader, Holder, recalled:

> The cavalrymen lived on their equipment and carried not only very heavy weapons but also luxuries like ice, 5-gallon cans of water and Australian showers. The working infantrymen envied all this and lived much rougher lives in the field. However, the field duty for infantry companies usually ran in one or two week segments. The division leadership kept the cavalry troops permanently employed. While infantry units rotated back to the fire bases frequently, the cavalry troops only came in for quarterly maintenance.[4]

The armored cavalry presence in the Vietnamese War was most vigorously maintained by the 11th Cavalry Regiment ("the Black Horse") which was a multifaceted organization, indeed, a miniature high tech army on its own. An aggregate of tanks, helicopters, airborne dragoons, artillery and a surfeit of supporting and logistical addendum, it was never permitted cavalry maneuver in the traditional sense. The nature of the war and a certain resistance to let the cavalry loose limited armored operations to fire support and convoy escort. There was no armored opposition until the last months of the war. The Black Horse got a lot of credit but tended to overshadow the other cavalry outfits because of its size.[5]

Tracked cavalry outposted roads, escorted convoys and were expected to react particularly quickly to any sudden threat but the air cavalry was most effective in getting to fights in progress. However ground cavalry (armored) could stay in an area for weeks and suppress enemy activities by sweeps, ambushes and local attacks. Armor seldom surprised the indigenous enemy or the NVA who generally chose when, where and if to fight. Instead, they disrupted the enemy's actions by moving unpredictably through contested areas and by getting into actions that the enemy had initiated relatively quickly. The Vietnamese were methodical and the presence of mounted units upset their routines, mainly by unpredictable movement.

Finally, there were seasonal differences in cavalry employment. During monsoons tanks and ACAVs were less capable of moving cross country and stayed closer to the roads; concurrently, their value as mobile reaction forces increased because heliborne infantry and gunship reinforcement couldn't be done as reliably. Mobile operations simply permitted the Vietnamese guenillas to reoccupy terrain. Viet Cong terror warfare against civilians and the military resulted in frustrated anger and command paralysis within a conflict of ambushes, booby traps and mines. The style was similar to Algeria, Somalia or the prolonged occupations of Iraq and Afghanistan in the twenty-first century.

Vietnam armored operations were not the stuff of Patton, Wood, or Abrams. Tanks in intimate support were "combat multipliers" and helped reduce infantry casualties; "however, only the minimum number of tanks required to accomplish the mission would be used."[6] The American ground commander, General Westmoreland, saw little use for armor or armored cavalry in a guerilla war. Finally, Gen. Harold Johnson, Army Chief of Staff, imposed a rational compromise for the force in Vietnam: the divisional cavalry squadron (4th Cavalry) would keep its medium tanks (M48 A3s) to test the effectiveness of armor in Asian operations. If the cavalry proved it could do the work, the Pentagon would dispatch a complete tank battalion. Westmoreland grumbled: "Vietnam is no place for either tank or mechanized infantry units."[7] He promptly withdrew M48s from cavalry troops and parked them at Phu Loi. But perseverance finally paid off: "It took six months . . . to convince General Westmoreland that tanks could be properly employed on combat operations."[8] Westmoreland may have relented but never completely abandoned his "no tanks in the jungle" attitude despite an impressive dossier of accomplishments.

Australian forces were even more infantry-centered, but they did deploy a heavy tank into Vietnam (the British Centurion Mk III, modified to Mk. s/i Australian). Aussie armor was strictly handmaiden to the infantry even though the Centurion was Britain's first attempt to produce a universal tank and do away with divisions between infantry and cruiser tanks. Operating much like American armor, Australian tanks proved their worth on many occasions.[9]

The appearance of enemy armor was rare until the last years of the war. Formal battles were waged late in the war, when western withdrawal was imminent. During the battle of An Loc (April 1972) North Vietnamese and Viet Cong units were supported by Soviet-made T54 and PT76, including captured American-M41s (the Walker Bulldog). The Russian trained crews aggressively spearheaded their infantry into An Loc. They were stopped with standard Second World War tactics. When their accompanying infantry had been pinned down by small arms fire, the tanks were soon knocked out by M72 LAW (light anti tank weapon) rocket launchers, the space age *panzerfaust*. U.S. Army tanks only encountered North Vietnam's armor on one occasion; PT76 light tanks, supported by BTR50 APC's, attacked a Special Forces camp at Ben Het in 1969. They were welcomed by the 1st Battalion, 69th Armor; the battle occurred at night and demonstrated that Euro obsolete tanks like the M48 could knock out Warsaw Pact armor. Despite the total battlefield dominance of tactical air, a few tanks on the battlefield could quickly play the fox in the henhouse.

The helicopter gave Air Cavalry a distinct tactical characteristic but the Vietnam War mainly featured fire support for foot soldiers in difficult terrain; infantry tanks dominated. Beyond the romantic nomenclature, cavalry action in Southeast Asia was a greater harbinger of future war than appreciated at the time. Regarded as a sideshow to the real business of the cold war, fighting the Warsaw Pact, Vietnam was the precursor of asymmetrical warfare in the new millennium.

YOM KIPPUR: CHUTZPAH AS *FINGERSPITZENGEFÜHL*

> Am I surrounded or surrounding? Danny Matt is encircling the Egyptians but according to you, they're encircling him. Amnon [Reshef] is surrounding the enemy- but as you put it, the enemy is surrounding him ... when will you finally understand that in mobile desert war, at one stage you encircle, and at another you are encircled?
>
> —Gen. Ariel Sharon, Tank Division Commander, *Chinese Farm*, 1973

The Israeli Armored Corps did not have a cavalry tradition and if anything it associated with the David versus Goliath myth or at best, war chariots. The kibbutz mentality preferred an egalitarian approach to war; the regimented, mechanical requirements of tanks (specific drills, prescribed maintenance, controlled procedures) seemed almost Fascist. But the predominating survival ethic did away with the almost casual approach to armored combat demonstrated in the 1947 and 1956 campaigns. The Israeli Defence Force (IDF) of the sixties emphasized discipline and mechanical precision and was equipped with a compendium of French, British and American tanks.

The 1967 "Six Day War" concluded with Israeli occupation of vast Egyptian territory and a blockade of the Suez Canal, pretty much ensuring another Middle East War. By 1973, the Soviet Union had rebuilt, retrained and reequipped the Egyptian forces. One legacy of the Vietnamese War was a Soviet sophistication in anti aircraft missiles (SAM: surface-to-air guided missile); a second cold war expertise was imposed by NATO's armored capability, the antitank guided missile (ATGM). The Red Army's Sagger (Soviet *Matlyutka* ATGM) missile was simple, portable and accurate. Both weapons were known but caused little concern in the Israeli cabinet for it was assumed the air force would quickly dispose of SAM sites and the Sagger threat was considered inconsequential in the hands of bucolic, poorly trained Egyptians. The technical success of the surprise offensive on October 6, 1973 (the Yom Kippur War) shook Israel and its Western allies as much as it astonished the Soviets. The subsequent campaign featured both bull headed attacks and dramatic reversal of fortunes. By October 10 the Egyptians were in a dominant victorious position; a week later the Israelis were deep in the West Bank, the capital, Cairo threatened and two Arab armies surrounded.

Egypt's army breached the canal defenses en masse, which was a difficult military-engineering enterprise; initial success was followed up by the deployment of a thick screen of Sagger missiles on the east bank to protect the canal bridgeheads. One in every three Egyptian soldiers had an antitank weapon. The results prompted inflated accounts: "Never before had such intensive anti-tank fire been brought to bear on the battlefield."[10] It was nevertheless, an unprecedented mass of missile weapons; every other infantryman carried a Soviet RPG in addition to hundreds of Sagger kits. The IDF launched a hasty counterattack on October 8. Preliminary reconnaissance should have reported the missile screen but that required time. Air recce proved extremely difficult because the second hi-tech shocker, a SAM umbrella, protected the Egyptian crossings.[11] The surface-to-air missile launchers created a "no-fly" zone that extended into Sinai; for the first time the Israeli air force did not achieve air supremacy over a designated battlefield. The coterie of new weapons required determined set piece attacks (slogging matches) that favored the Egyptians; Israel could not survive a war of attrition.

On October 14, Sadat ordered a new offensive to expand the conquered bridgehead. The armored attack was "a total failure, the first major Egyptian reversal of the war. Instead of concentrating forces of maneuvering . . . they had expended them in head-on attack against the waiting Israeli brigades."[12] Too confident in its advantage of over 1,000 tanks to 750 Israeli, the Egyptian army abandoned its trump card of positional antitank defense beneath SAM protection. The attack achieved nothing and cost 264 Egyptian tanks, compared to 40 Israeli tanks lost. October 14 became the turning point of the war.

Seizing the initiative, the Israelis followed up with a bold counter stroke. Inspired maneuver warfare repeated the Egyptian gambit and secured a *western* crossing of the Canal. This was directly to be followed by tanks overrunning the SAM sites devastating rear areas and cutting off the Egyptian army from its base of operations. Operation Gazelle was based on an entire armored corps of three tank divisions. Maj. Gen. Ariel "Arik" Sharon's division, "Ugda Arik" (three brigades of 240 tanks reinforced by an airborne brigade) was the first echelon, tasked to open a corridor to the canal and secure the initial bridgehead. This included recapturing sections of the Bar-Lev Line and a Japanese agricultural station, known as "Chinese Farm," which dominated the selected crossing site just south of the Great Bitter Lake.

Sharon made an intrepid crossing and brazenly sent SAM-killing teams into the west bank to cause havoc. This initiative met with disapproval. Sharon appeared to be playing *le cavalier seul* while ignoring the less stimulating task of clearing the east bank. IDF Command forbade further western sorties until the second echelon division had crossed. When bridging was complete, General Adan's tank division was sent across. Sharon, to his frustration, remained on the east bank. The mass of Egyptian armor north and south of the bridgehead posed a threat that was bagatelle to Sharon. His constraints were what another desert warrior, Rommel, might have faced if he had to clear his gambits with Berlin. Distance played into Rommel's favor whereas Sharon was just down the highway from Tel Aviv.

This battle demonstrated both the complexities and dangers of daring maneuver. It was a "cavalry" operation in that it rejected the center of gravity to the north and solved a strategic problem with tactical creativity. In the end, the Israeli army is not cavalry by culture nor perhaps by temperament. It was not surprising that when the IDF did produce a homegrown tank it clearly delineated between the cavalry psychology and its own history and tradition. Its new tank was called the *Merkava*—"the Chariot." It was initially dismissed but is now regarded as "the future in the millennium tank and fire team/ scout team."[13]

FOMENTING A CAVALRY DOCTRINE—AIRLAND BATTLE

New weapons require new tactics. Never put new wine into old bottles.
—Heinz Guderian

Cavalry emerged from Vietnam as an integral part of the modern army; more specifically, air cavalry had immediately established itself as part of the cavalry-maneuver force. Its reputation rested on airborne/air assault operations rather than bracing mounted attack. The sobering question for armored cavalry's collective future was how this new characteristic would play itself out on the North German Plain facing a surfeit of successive Warsaw Pact Armies led by elite Red Guards Tank Corps. The Soviet army of the seventies and eighties was a real bogeyman for the West. Taking advantage of American involvement in Southeast Asia, Moscow had built up a formidable mechanized force that groaned with new armor. Soviet tanks were not only respected, they were admired. Western kit appeared bland by comparison. The M60, backbone of the NATO force, was a worthy tank but oozed Second World War design and traits; the British Chieftain was aging and, despite fine lines, a dog's breakfast to maintain. The Soviet larder was crammed with impressive new items that featured tanks (new 125 mm armed T 72 and T-64) as well as trend setting infantry fighting vehicles like the Sagger toting BMP (*Voyevnaya Mashina Pechotna*—"infantry fighting vehicle") mounting with an imposing 30 mm gun. NATO became demonstrably nervous; the U.S. Army's morale was insipid, equipment dated, and the war record debated. The election of President Reagan infused new life into the American military and, by intimate association, NATO itself. A flood of new equipment arrived in Europe—tank killing gunships, tank killing infantry carriers (the M2 Bradley Fighting Vehicle with a 25 mm Bushmaster chain gun supplemented with TOW antitank missile launchers) and, la crème de la crème of western armor, the 120 mm M1 Abrams main battle tank. NATO finally boasted a tank that not only dominated the battlefield technically, but also drew obsequious endorsement. The Abrams-Bradley dynamic duo was as maneuverable as it was deadly. Buttressed by new age British armor, the impressive Challenger and the Abram's most serious competitor for "tank of the decade" laurels, the German Leopard II, it almost seemed a shame to just *wait* for the Bolshies and shoot from hull down positions. NATO needed a bracing new doctrine that would address the enemy's latest version of deep battle.

Any doctrinal quest was complicated and any new system adopted by the American army would have to be understood and practiced by all NATO members. Global realities had reduced the Western allies to auxiliaries of the new Rome. If one expected to be accommodated in the empire and serve with the legions on the barbarian frontiers, one had to *learn Latin,* that is, American doctrine, and be au courant with nouveau *armyspeak* containing avant-garde terms like *warfighting* that defied grammatical interpretation. Any dogma that emerged from the templar monasteries of Fort Monroe or Leavenworth would have to be implicitly grasped at the risk of operational excommunication on the modern battlefield.

The American army experimented first with *active defence* advocated by General William DePuy, the first Commander of the Training and Doctrine Command (TRADOC)—the Vatican for doctrinal thought. DePuy was a keen student of German technique and motivated by analysis from the Arab-Israeli

War. He decided to rewrite the army tactical bible.[14] The new manual was unlike any other FM100; it appeared in a camouflaged jacket, slick and hard to miss; it imposed the new catechism, *active defense*. Within a month of publication, it came under strong attack.[15] DePuy's doctrine insisted on the primacy of *defence*: "Operational art wasn't mentioned and neither were large unit operations: FM 100–5 contained a bromide that held that 'captains fight the battle, colonels position the forces'—everything significant happened at company level. Most officers knew that that couldn't be right."[16] DePuy, "likely the most important figure in the recovery of the United States Army from its collapse after the defeat in Vietnam," was replaced in 1977.[17]

The new TRADOC commander was Gen. Donn A. Starry, an alumnus of DePuy's team and a veteran cavalier who had commanded the Black Horse Regiment in Vietnam. Starry arrived convinced "we needed an operational level doctrine—a von Seeckt Truppenführung."[18] As Commander of V Corps in Germany, he walked the ground with his brigade and division commanders discussing how they intended to employ the active defense doctrine. "They convinced themselves they could likely win the battle against the first echelon GSFG [Soviet] force. But the three follow-on echelons were another problem."[19] General Starry concluded NATO defenders would have to deal with fresh echelon attackers via *deep battle*. He decided to create a space age *Glubokii Boi*.

THE JEDI KNIGHTS—A NEW HOPE

> Doctrine is the engine of change.
>
> —Gen. Donn A. Starry

AirLand Battle (ALB) appeared during the first series of *Star Wars* space fantasies; the writers who produced the 1982 version, and particularly their students, became known as the "Jedi Knights."[20] This collection of brains and operational experience well served Starry who emerged as an American Sir John Burnett-Stuart, the general who mechanized the British army in time for blitzkrieg. Starry launched a doctrine that would govern American thinking into the next millennium and influence victory in two Middle East wars.

AirLand Battle restored the balance between maneuver and firepower. ALB doctrine aimed to thwart follow-on echelon attacks via air interdiction, maneuver and attacks at geographic "choke points." AirLand Battle elevated Army tactics beyond the operational and into strategic strata. Generals now required resources and weapons to look deep and strike deep—a *Glubokii Boi* evolution that Tukhachevsky would have applauded. It also introduced the heretofore rather Russian concept of the *operational art* into Yankee terminology as legitimate doctrine. AirLand Battle was both the final evolution of deep battle and a progressive cavalry doctrine. One of the Jedis, Don Holder, went to war fighting his own doctrine commanding the 2nd Armored Cavalry Regiment, a brigade sized recce unit that was the armored corps' vanguard in Desert Storm.

THE PERSIAN GULF WAR

The best armored attack is one which is barely under the control of the commander.

—Gen. Frederick M. Franks, 1999

The warhorse saga was finally corralled by Middle East machinations. A mighty host[21] appeared in the Arabian Desert, perhaps the last great marshalling of the armored cavalry, a collective of militaria on the cusp of cybernetic transmutation. The arsenal included the latest military technology accented by precision weapons—truly the stuff of *Star Wars*. The enemy force featured a *Schutzstaffel* alter ego, *The Republican Guard,* a corps sized bund of selected Iraqi formations equipped with armor mostly acquired from the Soviet Union. Coalition armor (2,042 tanks: 1,905 Abrams, 157 Challengers, 140 M 60 and French AMX 30 B2[22]) faced over 2,500 Iraqi main battle tanks, including 500 T-72s. The numeric designation betrayed the status of the T-72; it was twenty years old and despite a few new bells and whistles, totally outclassed by the steel behemoths of the allied host, particularly the Abrams and British Challenger tanks, both sporting space age variations of *Chobham* armor that gave them the same ascendancy medieval chivalry enjoyed over footmen and light cavalry.

The Gulf War offered a good look at the final evolution of the twentieth century tank. The *marriage de raison* with the cavalry had produced a machine that was a marvel of technical and cybernetic achievements; there was little left to do save simply replace the human element altogether and create cyborg armor. Western tanks echoed their democratic bourgeois roots in that they were imposing, spacious, and expensive. They respected the citizen's right to choose and accommodated all types, from football players to diminutive clerks. Soviet tanks reflected the practical solutions of the totalitarian state. Despite the proletarian to horse image of the classless army, they were built for Napoleonic warriors. A tanker taller than five foot five inches found his already Spartan quarters cramped, with little headroom. The logic was simple, build smaller tanks with low silhouettes since smaller targets are harder to hit. But even size became moot in the 1990s as western tanks were fitted with superb optics: "vision devices that proved effective not only at night, but also in the dust and smoke of Kuwaiti daytime. On average, an Abrams outranged an Iraqi tank by about 1,000 meters."[23]

Even better, they trained via computer simulators and in Californian military Disneylands[24] where a doppelgänger Bolshi force lay waiting to tutor the unacquainted. OPFOR (opposing force) units were created as ultrarealistic opponents that resembled and fought like potential adversaries. They even dressed like Russians or Iraqis. The system permitted a level of training and expertise that dwarfed anything the Russians could hope to achieve, let alone the off-the-shelf Iraqi army. Although the Republican Guard units were no slouches, the gap in professional ability was immense. In the final tally, the Allies lost no tanks to enemy fire.

THE MOTHER OF ALL BATTLES

> Desert Storm reflected more Montgomery-like concern for tidy battlefield and balanced attack than pursuit of the "unforgiving minute."
>
> —Richard M. Swain, *Lucky War*

The ground war was dubbed *Operation Desert Storm* (February 24–27, 1991) and featured an allied armored force the likes of which had not been seen since the great breakout from Normandy. The maneuver element comprised the Third Army whose units were a who's who of American and British military history and included the 1st Cavalry Division, poised to maneuver as *the arm of decision.*

The British resurrected the much missed "Desert Rats" as the 1st UK Armoured Division and deployed pedigreed cavalry regiments like the Queens Royal Irish Hussars, the 17/21st Lancers and Royal Scots Dragoon Guards (the former Scots Grey of Waterloo); French army armor included the *4e Régiment de Dragons* and *1e Régiment de Spahis* as well as some exotic and bizarre recce, *1er Régiment Etranger de Cavalerie* (Foreign Legion Cavalry), and *1er Régiment de Hussards Parachutistes* (the First Hussar Para Regiment)!

The American cavalry congregated the 2nd and 3rd Armored Cavalry Regiments (ACR) and units from five historic regiments. The final communion of military equestrians were mounted in Abrams, Challengers, and various recce vehicles. The 1st Cavalry Division's "Cavalry Brigade" which contained a squadron of the 7th Cavalry, was an "aviation" assault force teeming with attack helicopters.[25] The cavalry brigade behaved in the grand old style featuring heavy *cuirassier* like advances and audacious reconnaissance.

The strata between recce and the *armored-fist* was occupied by the ACRs. By the time it had crossed the berm, Holder's 2nd Armored Cavalry Regiment was a force that would have made an SS panzer corps blanch. The regiment comprised Abrams tanks, Bradley infantry fighting vehicles (both capable of destroying any Iraqi armor), its own panzer grenadiers plus scouts, artillery, attack helicopters and generous augmentations of military kit from its parent corps, including MRLS—the final word in the evolution of the *Katyusha.* As General Fred Franks' VII Armored Corps vanguard, within hours 2 ACR had advanced more than forty kilometers. It was delayed mainly by inclement weather and stopped only by corporate conservatism. The greatest threat turned out to be running out of fuel and ammunition.[26]

FIGHTING THE DOCTRINE — CAVALRY À LA GRANT

> "Fred" I interrupted, "for chrissakes don't turn south! Turn east. Go after 'em!"
> —General H. Norman Schwarzkopf

Desert Storm was a test of AirLand Battle doctrine.[27] There was some post factum debate about the applied tactics. The commander of the main strike force, Lieutenant General Frederick M. Franks, was a veteran cavalry officer, refined and much liked. His ultimate boss, General H. Norman Schwarzkopf, was a tough paratrooper, another Arik Sharon, direct and often abrasive (dubbed "Stormin' Norman" by his weary staff). Schwarzkopf was appalled at what he considered Frank's noncavalry style. After a half decade of maneuver warfare debate and AirLand Battle dogma, he expected dynamic maneuver and breathtaking attack. He was livid when he discovered his cavalry commander, after successfully and uneventfully crossing the frontier obstacle, had ordered an "operational pause" to sort out logistics and carefully arrange his armored juggernaut to form a great armored fist for the Hail Mary maneuver against fourteen Iraqi divisions, a number of whom were Republican Guard units.

Schwarzkopf may have expected a Murat like advance by the *arme blanche* but was presented with a careful, patient ployment that got all the ducks in a row and ensured the petrol trucks were forward. It was professional but not the sort of cavalry style that Schwarzkopf anticipated: "All very impressive, I thought, except Franks, whose plan was still too deliberate."[28] As the operational pause continued, the commander in chief became irate.[29] In Franks' defense, the weather was erratic; rainstorms and sand storms (*Shamal,* a perverse mix of rain and blowing sand that can reduce visibility to next to nothing[30]) appeared with suddenness, shut down air operations, and stymied any determined advance. Communications proved erratic and Franks decided to move forward to "talk face to face with my commanders"; he opined: "What I lost in comms, I gained in Fingerspitzengefühl."[31] Oddly enough, Franks later said: "The best armored attack is one which is barely under the control of the commander."[32]

Schwarzkopf, in turn, has been cited as "unable by temperament to leave execution entirely to his senior subordinates."[33] It was an interesting test of *Auftragstaktik.* Franks, the tactical commander, dealt with the battle as *he* saw it; Schwarzkopf, as a modern Eisenhower, dealt with a complex coalition while juggling the Pentagon or White House on his ringing phones. As mikado to a pride of operational commanders Schwarzkopf was absorbed by the big picture as he watched "hundreds of enemy vehicles fleeing north in real time, as though on a TV screen."[34] In the end, the Corps commander was allowed to have his way. Subsequent events suggest that Franks over estimated the opposition. 2 ACR is a good example. Holder's regiment, after struggling through storms and conferences finally bumped the first of the Republican Guard outfits—the *Tawakalna* Division, which derived its name from the phrase *Tawakalna Ala Allah* (roughly, "God help us") and proved prophetic.

In one of the classic actions of Desert Storm, 2 ACR defeated Iraqi formations in the "Battle of 73 Easting." The Iraqi-Soviet armor proved no match for the Abrams-Bradley team. The regiment was a chainsaw—its tank companies the teeth which chewed through opposition within minutes. Engagements were concluded in less than an hour; "enemy tank turrets were hurled skyward as 120 mm SABOT rounds ripped through T-55s and T-72s. The fire balls that followed hurled debris one hundred feet into the air."[35] Holder had been ordered by Franks not to get decisively engaged; by February 26, 2 ACR had fought a series of gun duels, defeated a counter attack, captured an Iraqi battalion strong point, destroyed the Iraqi 50th Armored Brigade, and had pretty much chewed up the *Tawakalna*.[36] Low on fuel, 2 ACR was ordered to halt and conducted a passage of lines; the advance was taken up by the 1st Infantry Division. Holder's stablemate, 3 ACR, served as a screen on far right of the XVIII Corps and assisted the 24th Mechanized division in its lightning dash to the Euphrates river.[37]

Medina Ridge is often cited as the equal to *73 Easting.* The decisive tank battle was fought on the fourth day of the attack (February 27); Col. Montgomery Meig's "Iron Brigade" (1st AD) destroyed the 2nd Brigade of the Republican Guards *Al Madina Al Munawara* (Medina the Luminous) outside Basra. It demolished 186 Iraqi tanks (T-72s and T-55s) and 127 armored vehicles in about two hours. Not a single tank was lost in the action. Perhaps the most cavalier thrust was by the 24th Mechanized *Infantry* Division led by Maj. Gen. Barry McCaffery. It dashed to the Euphrates River paralleling the bold vertical envelopment executed by the 101st Airborne Division, which leapfrogged deep into Iraq via helicopter augmented by 3 ACR's aggressive reconnaissance. General Binford "Binnie" Peay would suggest that his 101st Air Assault's closing of the Highway 8 escape route from Kuwait was the classic deep operation.[38]

As a grand offensive Desert Storm was more Grant, less Custer. It was no Cannae; an imposed, arguably premature, cease-fire ensured that most of the Republican Guard divisions managed to escape. The greatest threat to coalition armies proved to be "friendly fire"; *fratricide* accounted for nearly 30 percent of the allied casualties. Despite modern communications, optics and night vision devices, the battlefield remained a confused jumble. Maj. Gen. Rupert Smith, whose 1st UK Armoured Division had displayed elegant demonstrations of maneuver warfare, decided to issue "written, rather than oral orders to avoid confusion on the part of sender and receiver."[39]

Desert Storm demonstrated the capabilities of Star Wars tech and was the last grand cavalry romp. The 1st Cavalry Division, husbanded for the *coup de grace* in the Mother of All Battles, was a victim of conservative prudence and rapid Iraqi collapse. It remained on the shelf, never used.[40]

The outside pony: "Buzkashi?"
The inside pony: "No, a *Blackwater* Condottieri threw out a bag of money."

Chapter 17

The Warhorse in the New Millennium: Hoofed and Tracked

Cavalry brings the great élan that our history of war has reflected. I hope we don't throw it away. The Cavalry soldier had a special quality that made the other maneuver arms much better.

—Gen. William R. Richardson[1]

The new millennium arrived with an electronic purr rather than a roar. When it looked back, the cavalry realized it had been a decade since Desert Storm with nothing much to show save for the appearance of eight wheeled armored cars, computer besotted senior officers, and the prospects of yet another campaign in Iraq, this time with a surfeit of digitized units. Pessimists foresaw a bleak future. Battle labs and virtual-reality training enclaves all preached the importance of the human factor even as they inexorably sought to make it redundant.

This time the threat was more sinister than the one General Herr faced with cyborg robots intent on replacing both cavalry *and* cavalier. It was shrugged off in the best *arme blanche* tradition which has always considered itself simply irreplaceable. This chapter will recount the designation of the warhorse to an adornment and tourist attraction in consort with the armored cavalry's attempt to become ultra modern and share battle space with the computer. Operation Cobra II (2003), the premier millennium cavalry campaign (better described as the *latest* rather than the *last chevauchée*) will be considered. It was a very Attila-like takeover of ancient Parthian river valleys that eventually became an altogether unexpected type of conflict and perhaps the precursor of future war. Finally, through the electronic mists of satellite imagery, the warhorse returned to the battlefield, in of all places, the Hindu Kush.

FAREWELL OLD DOBBIN

Cavalry converted to syncretic tactics when it adopted the tank and cloaked its equestrian passion with the pseudonym *armored cavalry*. The symbiotic melding of man and horse morphed through unanticipated stages: the union of horseman and tank, the creation of "tankmen" and finally, the morphing of cavalier tankmen with the robot. The last stage of cavalry evolution threatens to be cybernetic mutation of organic process, mechanical and electronic systems. Armored cavalry has achieved retronym status. Its future will likely include applying a *guidon* logo on the hard drive; the servicing technicians may even wear spurs.

The post war retirement of the Western warhorse was quietly done, made mute by rattling Bolshevik sabers and nuclear tests. Except for the cavalry units in the U.S. Constabulary and those in the 1st Cavalry Division, there were no other active horsed regiments in the regular army until the 3rd Armored Cavalry was organized in 1948.[2] The U.S. Quartermaster Corps continued to provide cavalry mounts and pack animals until the Korean War. Finally, the Remount Purchasing and Breeding Headquarters Offices were ordered closed and the Army Horse Breeding Program reassigned to the Department of Agriculture in l948. All mounted programs were terminated the next year; what remained of cavalry stock was sold at public auction. A troop of horses were stabled at Fort Carson, Colorado, for training purposes in case of emergency; finally these too were inactivated in February l957. The last horses were sold or reassigned to other government agencies.

Two mounted organizations, the 35th QM Pack Company and the 4th Field Artillery Battalion, were active as late as 1952. Both were reequipped with helicopters and the last serving army mules were given a final parade:

> In ceremonies befitting and honoring the long service of this patient but sometimes cantankerous Army animal, the mules were publicly mustered out of the Army, to be replaced by the helicopter. Upon retirement of the colors and guidons, "Trotter" and "Hambone" . . . were brought before the commanding general, and each was given a citation.[3]

Chief, the last cavalry remount, was carried on government rolls until his death in 1968 at age 36. The only serving horses in the United States are used exclusively for ceremonial purposes and in military funerals at Arlington National Cemetery. The U.S. Military Academy at West Point, New York, has a mule as its mascot.

The warhorse survives in three main areas: ceremonial, operational and mounted police. As a ceremonial show piece, it is featured in crowd pleasing demonstrations of technique and grandeur from various regimental "musical rides." Its martial duties were relegated to frontier struggles, particularly in Africa. The French Army deployed Spahis squadrons in concert with the Foreign Legions (*1ère Régiment étranger de cavalerie*) for patrol missions in the rough terrain of Algeria circa 1954–62. The Chinese cavalry was reported to have operated along the Vietnamese frontier and engaging Vietnamese troops in skirmishes. South American armies continued to employ cavalry well after Europe mechanized; the Mexican army included horse cavalry regiments into the 1980s while the Chilean army operated five regular cavalry regiments in 1983 as "mountain cavalry." The frugal Swiss army used mounted dragoons for mountain patrolling.

Global cavalry was not left to rusticate in tranquil camps. Many units enjoy a professional equestrian status. Mounted gendarmerie and ceremonial cavalry squadrons exist in England, France, Italy, Denmark, Sweden, Holland, Chile, Portugal, Morocco, Venezuela, Brazil, Argentina, and Spain. A number of armored regiments in the Commonwealth continue the historic designations of hussars, dragoons, or lancers. The British army still maintains a Mounted Military Police unit. The Household Cavalry divides its duties between ceremony and combat, maintaining complete horse squadrons for ceremonial duties in London's Knightsbridge Barracks as well as squadrons of tanks and recce vehicles in rural bases. Operational employments included the Gulf, Kosovo, and "Operation Iraqi Freedom." Both royal princes, Henry and William, were gazetted into the Blues and Royals as subalterns; Harry was scheduled for duty in Iraq circa the summer of 2007. The mounted unit of the Household Cavalry performs daily parades and conducts ceremonial duties on state and royal occasions.

The King's Troop, Royal Horse Artillery, is a regular army unit and based at St. John's Wood Barracks, just north of Regent's Park. When on parade with its guns the King's Troop takes precedence over all other regiments and has the honor of parading on the right of the line. Resplendent in Busby and Waterloo era dress, the Troop's establishment is seven officers, including the veterinarian and 164 other ranks who work as gun numbers, saddlers, farriers, tailors, and drivers. The guns, as in all artillery regiments, are "the colors."[4]

The mounted regiment of France's *Garde Républicain* is equally resplendent. The *Garde,* part of the Gendarmerie Nationale, is comprised of two infantry regiments and the cavalry regiment, uniformed as nineteenth-century cuirassiers. Its missions include protecting key buildings, mounted escorts and security for visiting heads of state. Not as popular, but eminently more skilled, is the French army's equestrian display team, *le Cadre Noir.* France continues its cavalry traditions and fields modern armored cavalry regiments whose titles continue historic antecedents: cuirassier, hussard, chasseur and spahis. Poland has a squadron of Ulans in traditional costume. The Russian Federation has organized a ceremonial mounted squadron in Czarist dress. Australia and

New Zealand armored corps maintain their splendid traditions of light horse and mounted rifles via their reserve forces. The Indian Army's 61st Cavalry is a working, nonceremonial horse regiment amidst dozens of armor units that trace their lineage to nineteenth-century cavalry.

The U.S. 1st Cavalry Division stables a volunteer cavalry troop based at Fort Hood, Texas. The "Horse Cavalry Detachment" is the last horse mounted cavalry unit in the U.S. Army and organized as an 1870 era "horse soldier" troop— its mounted drills are from the 1883 *Manual of Cavalry Tactics*.[5] There is a ceremonial horse troop in Washington, which is used mainly for state burials.

The Canadian Army includes quasi equestrian units: the Governor General's Horse Guards, The Royal Canadian Hussars and The Strathcona's Horse— all armoured cavalry regiments. The hardest working professional equestrian unit may well be the Mounted Troop of the Royal Canadian Mounted Police, which employs regular constables, posted to a three-year "tour" with the horses. The RCMP is unique in the world as it is a municipal, provincial and federal policing body; in its national and international duties it is equivalent to the FBI or MI5. The Mounties first performed their renowned "Musical Ride" in 1887. The modern Troop parades 36 riders, 36 horses, and a farrier. Training is year long and features equestrian skill at arms including "tent pegging," an activity that involves skewering targets with sword or lance at a decent canter. The Mounties demonstrate the same tactics used by uhlans and British lancers in the Great War.[6]

The international warhorse is regularly feted and tested via competitions. World Military Equestrian Championships were dominated by South American teams in the early millennium.[7] The U.S. Cavalry Association holds an annual National Cavalry Competition incorporating skill at arms events including "Mounted Saber, Pistol, Military Horsemanship, and Military Field Jumping."[8] The 2007 International Tent Pegging Championships and world equestrian skill at arms games were held in the Sultanate of Oman. The Canadian entry, from the Governor General's Horse Guards, chronicled the competitive nature of the military horse—little changed from Baron Marbot's charger Lisette at Eylau. Guardsman Maharaja was forced to: "restrain my horse *Shomool* from savaging the neighboring rider . . . had just attempted to deliver a slaying kick . . . [and] seemed dejected that I insisted on coming between him and his wrath."[9]

REPASSAGE—POLO AND CAVALRY IN AFGHANISTAN

> Let other people play at other things.
> The King of Games is still the Game of Kings.
> —Attributed to Guy u Chawgan

The origins of polo ("the game of kings") are vague and believed to have originated among Iranian tribes then spread throughout the Persian plateau as an addendum to training light cavalry. When Alexander assumed the throne of Greece, the Persian emperor Darius allegedly sent him a polo ball and mallet with the message that he should stick to the sport, and leave the business of war to those better suited. In 1869, Captain Edward "Chicken" Hartopp, of the 10th Hussars, organized the first European match at Aldershot Camp. The Tenth Royal Hussars (known as the "Chainy Tenth" because of their elaborate cross belts, eventually, the *Shiny Tenth* or *Shiners*) played a competitive game against the 9th Lancers. The Hussars won by three goals to two—the game became instantly popular and all fashionable London made a point of attending matches.

Polo is an active sport in eighty countries and played professionally in six.[10] It has mushroomed in popularity and is unique among team sports in that amateur players play alongside top professionals.[11] It is encouraged by most cavalries. A good polo player will make a good officer it is argued, because polo teaches physical and mental agility and requires aggressive courage. While the infantry likes its officers to play rugby or football, many mounted regiments strive to maintain polo teams. It is encouraged as is hunting, which is an authorized military activity in the British Army to develop an eye for country (i.e., ground), and mental agility (i.e., a quick response to rapidly changing events). As long as governments provided the horses, polo was a popular pastime; even in the republican United States most cavalry officers had played polo. This pleasant interlude was ended by the tank. Mechanization not only killed off the cavalry, it terminated *proletarian polo.* Although the martial benefits of the game are considerable, supporting arguments became moot. As the Soviets were quick to point out, it was a particularly bourgeois sport—western governments were loath to risk criticism and "subsidize decadence." Polo, as a bona fide training system, reflected antiquated epochs. However, in countries where a horse is still de rigueur, versions of polo thrive, particularly in Afghanistan where it is the national sport and is called *Buzkashi.*

YANKEE CHAPANDAZ

> The heavily robed Afghans appeared to one American like the "Sand People" from the movie "Star Wars."
> —Report, U.S. Army Special Operations Forces in Afghanistan[12]

One of the more intriguing spectacles of new millennium warfare is American Special Forces playing *Buzkashi* with Afghan tribesmen in the more inaccessible valleys of the Himalayan Kush. Midst robotic sensors, gun ships and stealth bombers, Afghan cavalry endures in the complex tribal and international struggles that continue to be waged in Afghanistan.

Buzkashi, which literally translated means "goat grabbing," features a headless carcass placed in the center of a circle and surrounded by the players of two opposing teams. *Buzkashi* (from Persian *boz* "goat" and *koshi* "killing") is played in the northern Afghan provinces where games can last for several days—a particularly violent version of polo.

Deaths are common, mostly ridden-over spectators, as the goat carrying rider is followed by a host of fanatic master *Chapandaz* (from the *chapan* or cloak); players generally receive face cuts from whips, broken noses and broken bones. Wrestling is permitted but biting is considered very bad form—for the riders. Horses are trained to "attack, bite, kick, push other attackers out of the way and, above all, to stop for nothing."[13] During Taliban rule, many of the best Buzkashi players left their villages to participate in the fighting. After the NATO incursion, the sport resumed as top players returned. Certain matches included strange would be *Chapandaz*—American Green Berets.

American action in Afghanistan augmented cybernetic weaponry with traditional patrols and isolated commando work in isolated quadrants like the Panjshir Valley where, in the fall of 2001, Special Forces teams were landed to assist the "Northern Alliance." Army Special Forces, who prefer to be called simply "operators," were organized into 12-man operational detachments (ODA), each led by a young captain. The Panjshir detachment was sent to assist the controversial and flamboyant guerilla fighter, General Dostum. They were surprised when twenty horsemen "armed to the teeth . . . looking pretty rough" galloped into camp. "Thirty more cavalrymen [were] escorting General Abdul Rashid Dostum."[14] Dostum, a millennium version of Count de La-Salle "a burly figure with short, spiky salt-and-pepper hair that comes down low above his brow, giving him the appearance of an irritable bear,"[15] was an Uzbek warlord who had been fighting for various sides during the extended Afghanistan war.

The Americans were made to quickly master horse-handling skills in order to tackle treacherous mountain paths. A Special Forces sergeant recalled:

> It was pretty painful . . . they use simple wooden saddles covered with a piece of carpet, and short stirrups that put our knees up by our heads. The first words I wanted to learn in Dari were, "How do you make him stop?" . . . [Afghan War-horses were] tough little mountain ponies . . . like American mustangs . . . all stallions that pushed, bumped, and bit each other if they got close.[16]

Transition was difficult and uncomfortable, even for experienced riders since the primitive saddles were too small and the stirrups short and not adjustable. The detachment leader attempted to have McClellan saddles parachuted in. ODA 595 conducted its mounted operations mostly using Afghan horse furniture, like the rest of Dostum's *mujahideen* bund. Riders endured bent knees and discomfort; worse, American combat boots got stuck in the stirrups. The most sobering threat was a fall. "Horse SOPS" (standard operating procedures) were developed: "Keep your feet light in the stirrups . . .

If anyone is thrown by his mount and has a foot caught in the stirrup and the horse doesn't stop immediately, the nearest man has to shoot the horse dead . . . You'll be killed if you're dragged on this rocky ground."[17]

Much like Stirling's SAS in the Western Desert the American commandos grew beards and sported eclectic outfits combining elements of U.S. Army uniforms with articles of Afghan clothing. Skirmishes with the Taliban soon followed. On several occasions, the Green Beret detachments were in dire peril only to be saved by timely air attacks: "[We are] surprised that we have not been slaughtered."[18] The teams attacked using conventional arms supplemented by radio controlled precision air strikes from silent, high altitude bombers. A decidedly cavalry attack occurred at Bai Beche:

> A Green Beret told one of Dostum's lieutenants to get his horses ready for action while they got aircraft into position. This was misinterpreted as a signal to charge. The men of ODA 595 watched in disbelief as 250 horsemen galloped straight at a Taliban position a mile away that was about to be bombed . . . No one would ever have intentionally ordered a cavalry charge in such close proximity with an air strike. But it worked out better than anyone could have expected . . . "Three or four bombs hit right in the middle of the enemy position. Almost immediately after the bombs exploded, the horses swept across the objective—the enemy was so shell-shocked. I could see the horses blasting out the other side. It was the finest sight I ever saw."[19]

Omdurman and Beersheba are too often presented as "the last cavalry charge"—they properly represent select eras. Little known actions in the Himalayas may well constitute the last cavalry battles for the warhorse but given the convulsions and vicissitudes of history, it would be dangerous to speculate. Cavalry now conducts the business of war conversing on cell phones, supported by Stealth bombers, cruise missiles, and satellite intelligence. The warhorse soldiers on into the millennium.

OPERATION COBRA II—CAVALRY MANEUVER

> Rapid attempts to affect the will, perception, and understanding of the adversary to fit or respond to our strategic policy ends through imposing a regime of Shock and Awe.
> —Harlan K. Ullman and James P. Wade

Despite battlefield success, the Gulf War simply sowed the seeds of yet another desert adventure. Twelve years later, another, albeit reduced coalition host, returned to the sands around Iraq. Operation Iraqi Freedom (Operation Telic for the British) carried a Byzantine collection of objectives but its basic goal was to overthrow the President of Iraq, Saddam Hussein. Participation included two major combatants, the United States and Britain plus a corporal's guard of smaller contingents of seven states, including Australia and Poland, all wryly referred to as "the Coalition of the Willing." There was no air campaign as such, for the Iraqi Air Force had not recovered from the initial Gulf War. Again, the operation served to demonstrate the evolution of military technology and doctrine. While the tanks looked pretty much the same, the computer hardware and a myriad of clever addendums set both wars well apart—in fact, by a complete millennium. Doctrine had evolved; while aspects of AirLand Battle prevailed, there was greater emphasis on strategic and operational maneuver. The sheer ascendancy of the western force allowed them to do more with less, and move with the audacity that total air supremacy and cybernetic godliness bring.

The invasion of Iraq was christened "Cobra II," a nostalgic tribute to the armored breakout by Bradley-Patton that ended the Normandy campaign. Commander in Chief General Tommy Ray Franks (no relation to General Fred Franks of Desert Storm), expecting a double envelopment from Turkey in the north and his main force from the south, had reason for optimism. In fact, it was to be the mother of maneuver battles and feature a triple envelopment as Franks' impressive array of airborne and airmobile divisions prepared to descend on southern and northern objectives. The master plan encouraged equestrian parishioners to shout "Cavalry!" It was indeed bold, wide ranging, exhibiting a certain horsy cheek and galloping élan. The force show-cased *elitist cadres;* the more spectacular maneuver formations were airborne and air assault (82nd and 101st) augmented with battle groups from the 1st Armored Division (1 AD).

The 1st Marine Division included an armored task force from 1 AD. The second "leg" unit was the 3rd Infantry Division, a state of the art mechanized formation with its own tank and armored cavalry assets. The British force was based again on the "Desert Rats," the 1st UK Armd Div. The attackers were elites from a collective of elites.

The intent was to invoke simultaneous air and ground assaults to decapitate the Iraqi forces as fast as possible. Emphasis was on "shock and awe" with a new sobriquet, *rapid dominance.*[20] The doctrine, a chip off the Douhet Air Power philosophy, would paralyze command, cloud battlefield perception and destroy the will to fight. Subsequent results and the incredible disparity between attacker and opponent suggested that was exactly the result.

Maneuver alternated cavalry assaults by mechanized units with Waterloo charges by attack helicopters. It was perhaps a cybernetic version of the medieval *chevauchée,* with Franks playing the role of King Edward. Cobra II emphasized strategic deployment followed by quick attack with a small force of high tech units. Desert Storm veterans grumbled about not enough troops but they were to be proven wrong, initially.

The Iraqi army collapsed like the deck of cards portraying key enemy persona issued to soldiers. The main ground offensive was launched from Kuwait (March 19, 2003); Baghdad fell 21 days later. Comparisons between the two campaigns are interesting: "Schwarzkopf ran a long air operation, then launched well over 15 divisions (Arab, UK, U.S., French) at puny little Kuwait. Franks and his crew took apart a rather large country with 5 divs and a concurrent air op."[21] The most serious opposition was logistics and weather. Like Desert Storm, the campaign accepted an "operational pause" to sort out its lines of supply. The air cavalry attack was disappointing, losses from even primitive ground fire prevented melee behind the lines; indeed, the gunships behaved more like cautious cuirassiers than brash hussars. "You had never seen helicopters so muddy, so many canopies with holes in them. Stunned pilots sat slumped in their cockpits . . . On average, each helicopter had fifteen to twenty bullet holes."[22] Cobra II's sweeping deep battle was better understood via laptops and satellite feeds: "Soldiers see what is in front of them, not the big picture."[23]

The tank-cavalry combat teams dominated all before them. Using a bit of ALB script the coalition dealt with a choke point (the Karbala Gap) then quickly raced toward Baghdad. To demonstrate total control and a disdain for the foe, a "Thunder Run" cavalierly galloped into Baghdad airport; two days later another *thunder run* was launched into Baghdad itself. Its opposition consisted of local ambushes and scattered fanatical resistance. The Iraqi army virtually disappeared and the west had entered the combat of the new millennium—asymmetric warfare. The best defence is not to defend but to terrorize from within. The new enemy was the unattended road bomb or quick ambush. Cavalry activity now consisted of guarding convoys or patrols along vast frontiers and closed suburbs.

The conventional war stressed cyber precision, maneuver and fire power: "By applying military mass simultaneously at key points, rather than trying to push a broad slow conventional advance, we throw the enemy off balance. We saw this in Afghanistan—fast, rapid maneuver. This creates momentum."[24] The difference between cavalry and infantry became hazy as both maneuvered, fought close quarter battles and both eventually conducted police duties in a hostile environment.[25] There were some "proper" armored cavalry set-tos though not particularly demanding contests. The British dash into the southern city of Basra (March 27) was achieved after two weeks of battle and included the biggest tank battle by British forces since the Second World War. The Royal Scots Dragoon Guards battle group (the venerable Scots Grey teamed with their Waterloo chums, The Black Watch), bumped an Iraqi rearguard. A squadron of fourteen Challenger tanks engaged and destroyed fourteen aging Iraqi tanks, prompting wags to dub the battle "the 14 Zero Engagement." A regimental officer described the contest between the T55 and Challenger 2 as "like the bicycle against the motor car."[26] The deadliest tank killers were not tanks but hand held RPG rockets and, as in Storm, "fratricide" was a constant danger. Few coalition tanks were lost, none to enemy tank fire but a Challenger from the Queens Royal Lancers was hit by another Challenger, killing two crewmen.

Cobra II appears the perfect military exercise, but after the spectacular victories western arms bogged down completely both in Iraq as well as Afghanistan.[27] Battlefield intuition was blunted by control and technology; Lt. Gen. William Wallace, veteran of both desert campaigns, referred to it as "Gizmology."[28] The great burden of Iraq occurred as maneuver warfare was succeeded by occupation warfare. Like a field force from The Lace Wars, the millennium army arrived encumbered by an extended train of camp followers, cyber sutlers and service providers—Gen. Franks' army was attended by the largest contingent of private contractors ever deployed in a war.

Modern opportunity for cavalry commanders requires creative definition. Vintage cavaliers arguably understood maneuver because of stints in horsed regiments, chasing Pancho Villa or sabering across the steppes with the *Konarmiya,* but that is often wishful thinking by the cavalry. The larger part of successful tank commanders were from noncavalry backgrounds and simply intuitively understood maneuver. They all of course shared that trait best demonstrated by LaSalle—a touch of madness and a love of risk. Cybernetic communication sterilizes bravado and tactical gambling at all but the very highest or lowest levels. Commanders of armored hosts are closely watched by their patrician bosses lest they demonstrate apolitical cavalry chutzpah. The great gambles of the operational art are now the exclusive purview of the least qualified. That perhaps is the great frustration of modern cavalry. The great advantage that traditional cavalry commanders enjoyed in the past centuries was that they were out of sight, generally out of communications, and too far forward for a political or military mikado to visit. Rommel and Patton got away with stuff that new millennium generals could only imagine.

The stabled Warhorse: "Who is your tailor?"

Chapter 18

The Deliquescence of the Cavalry

For he doth nothing but talk of his horse.
> —Shakespeare, *The Merchant of Venice*, Act 1, Scene 2

No philosophers so thoroughly comprehend us as dogs and horses. They see through us at a glance. And after all, what is a horse but a species of four-footed dumb man, in a leathern overall, who happens to live upon oats, and toils for his masters, half-requited or abused, like the biped hewers of wood and drawers of water? But there is a touch of divinity even in brutes, and a special halo about a horse, that should forever exempt him from indignities.
> —Herman Melville, *Redburn: His First Voyage*, 1849

The cavalry resisted mechanization until it was forced to attend its own requiem mass. It then surprisingly acquired a born-again fervor and embraced the *tank* as savior, content to philosophically explain its complete reversal via agreeable sophistry. The most elegant was General Grow's "Cavalry is a state of mind" and served to excuse a prolongation of idiosyncrasies. This worked best where cavalry had horses stabled behind the officers' mess, played polo, or perhaps had a duty squadron parading regularly up the Mall.

Elsewhere, the *arme blanche* accepted whatever technical accoutrements were offered, from armored cars to tanks to helicopters; its psychological struggle with the past drew varied reaction. There were convoluted themes within themes. On the eve of Operation Desert Storm, minutes before H Hour, the radios of the Scots Grey armored regiment skirled with a rousing version of "Cock o' the North" as highland pipes echoed through each tank and recce vehicle.[1] That, or the regimental band playing "God Bless the Czar" at dinner, is far too complicated to explain to mere mortals.[2] This chapter will examine the ostensible final challenge to the cavalry as well as its current status via dress and doctrine. The last great cavalry battle takes place in the U.S. Army and will likely take some time to fully resolve. The coming Apocalypse, in the form of cybernetic machines, as well as the cavalry's rebuttal, will be considered.

Horsy distinctions have been inundated by technological appurtenances and capricious military fashion. With perfunctory resignation cavalry were forced into a tanker's *beret* which became as popular at the turn of the twenty-first century as the French *Kepi* during the Civil War or the spiked helmet after 1870.[3] The black beret continues to be sniffed at by pedigreed cavalry regiments, many of whom prefer to sport headgear of different colors or wear wedgies and garrison caps, rather than mimic the rude mechanicals.[4] Cavalry mode loitered in most armies. The regimental *stable belt* is a particularly horsy bit of kit, comfortably resilient and secured by a smart pair of leather straps and brass buckles. Modern versions are worn in cavalry style, clasped at the side to avoid rasping the trooper's stomach as he toiled.[5] Riding or "shooting sweaters" with cloth shoulder and elbow pads remained popular in varied modes. The Light Dragoons continue to have their officers' sweaters custom made in muted Scottish yarns that display the regiment's blue, silver-grey and green colors. Unfortunately, comely style is reserved to garrison life. The millennium armies, in determination to appear constantly *battle ready,* whether in offices or an actual front line, prefer to wear a "combat" uniform. The cavalry obediently succumbed as their headquarters ordered couturiers to produce warlike costumes. From 1980 to 2007 "warlike" became synonymous with "camouflage."

Modern camouflage moved from Impressionism to embrace a cybernetic Pointillism, very different from "traditional" camouflage, which featured multicolored swirls in Marc Chagall confusion. The Canadian "digital pixilated pattern"[6] was first used in the late 1990s and like most military haute couture, was copied "first slavishly and then with increasing fantastication."[7] With the zeal of Armani, military *ateliers* designed climatic versions from jungle verdant to urban warfare grays and blues, ensuring Western armies arrive stylishly tailored for asymmetrical warfare. Camouflage—the French army used to mockingly refer to it as *Zebratage* before 1940—acquired an environment friendly electronic style and military fashion included a smorgasbord of accessories: name tags, unit patches, rank badges, armored vests, ammo pouches, harnesses, holsters, mini radios, and Kevlar helmet, all accented by delightful miniature national flags on the shoulder. Most of this was attached by the only real modern revolution in military costume: *Velcro.*

This could be mere military anthropology and bagatelle except that by 2007 the vast majority of cavalry units were patrolling and fighting *on foot* in urban and rural environs—less *dragoons* and more *grunts*. The cavalry's quest for individuality is reduced to the odd regimental ascot and the beret which is no longer worn in fighting vehicles. The only way to distinguish troopers from infantry is to wait to see what they wear *after* they remove their combat gear. Laver's prediction is proven correct: "uniforms will continue to exist, paradoxically, as the costume of a soldier *when he is not fighting.*"[8]

A SECOND HORSY GARROTING

> The cavalry is anachronistic, incompatible with modern mores, and alien to the contemporary spirit of mechanised instant gratification.
> —Akaash Maharaj, the Governor General's Horse Guards, May 2007

The U.S. Cavalry's impending demise began shortly after Desert Storm. With the return to normalcy the new TRADOC chief, Desert warrior General Frederick Franks, was directed by the Army's Chief of Staff, Gen. Gordon Sullivan, to "make Doctrine the engine of change."[9] Franks eventually produced the "Battle Laboratory process"—an electronic method of andragogy that extended the Louisiana Maneuvers tradition.[10] Part of the drive for change was initiated after the 1995 "middle weight unit" debates which influenced Gen. Erik Shinseki,[11] the Chief of Staff, to launch the U.S. Army's "transformation plan." This scheme permitted strategic operational maneuver via C130 transports and led to a brigade based army. Gen. Peter J. Schoomaker, a Special Forces philosophe committed to elite units, completed the program that created the Stryker brigades and the "modular force" that garroted the cavalry regiments and divisional squadrons.

The new-look army rode on eight wheeled armored cars. The Canadian designed LAV III was adopted by the American army as the "Stryker" and deployed throughout global battlefields. The decision to accumulate air mobile light armor was calculated to save monies and encouraged strategic operational maneuver. Brigadier Huba Wass de Czege warned that the new cybernetic army would be threatened by "bureaucrats cultivating managerial skills over leadership."[12] Nevertheless, change would occur. If an Airborne Brigade could capture all of northern Iraq, why not the rest of the world? Air deliverable, ubiquitous, multifaceted units, preferably elite, became the martial *plat du jour*. New formations were created and traditional roles reconsidered: "We have transferred some of the responsibility for doing those missions to the brigade combat teams that used to reside in cavalry organizations, per se, armored cavalry."[13]

THE FANFARONADE OF CYBERNETIC CAVALRY

Evolution quickly passed beyond the theoretical. Tests using unmanned robot controlled Strykers to escort convoys were conducted at Fort Gordon in the fall of 2006. The system passed "electronic bread crumbs from the manned lead vehicle back to the autonomous follower vehicle" and required only a "minimum of human intervention and control from the lead vehicle."[14] From Strykers to motorcycle-sized machines, robots were soon baptized with the brisk techno titles: autonomous robot for military systems (ARMS), the anticipated unmanned ground combat vehicle (UGCV), and the Special Weapons Observation Reconnaissance Detection system (SWORD). These are popular evolutions; robots reduced human casualties in both combat and non-combat roles which included bomb disposal and reconnaissance. The U.S. Army used surveillance robots in Afghanistan to explore caves used by the Taliban; the "robot soldiers" that appeared in Iraq and the Kush in 2006 resembled miniature tanks rather than androids. "We call them tactical *autonomous combatants* because they'll operate largely autonomously with some limited human supervision."[15]

"Molti roboti"[16] became a reasonable military neologism to describe the new battlefield. Environment dictated the style of war. By February 2007 American, British, and Canadian armored casualties were about equally divided between ground combat and road mines. Dubbed "IED" (improvised explosive device) the hidden bombs were nothing of the sort but rather sophisticated apparatuses that blew apart armored vehicles. Cavalry patrols became a lotto ticket with optimists betting that the assigned route would not include a hidden trap. Asymmetrical warfare was galling and western War Colleges were chastised for being unprepared for the realities of millennium warfare: "The Army still tilts toward conventional threats. I keep telling them, 'There's no tank army out there for you guys to fight.'"[17] But in fact little had changed. The exasperation of the modern mounted regiments echoed von Poseck's Great War rage: "Many a good cavalryman had become victim of the bullet of a cowardly assassin in ambush."[18] This was preceded by Kipling's *Arithmetic on the Frontier* a nineteenth-century forecast of *asymmetrical* operations:

A scrimmage in a Border Station;
A canter down some dark defile;
Two thousand pounds of education
Drops to a ten-rupee jezail
The Crammer's boast, the Squadron's pride,
Shot like a rabbit in a ride![19]

The desire for greater strategic and operational mobility relegated a large cavalry force to a mere seasoning—a dash of horse. Middle-weight mounted units didn't directly challenge the cavalry *idea* but they did undermine armored cavalry-tanks *ensemble.* Change wafted the drift toward elimination of cavalry since, after all, the new brigades could presumably do their own scouting. The theory proposed that nouveaux sensors will gather intelligence and paint the situation with less risk. Veterans argued this ignored the cardinal aspects of combat which determine the ployment of recce: ground and the enemy.

Armored cavalry regiments and their kin were morphed into RSTA (recon, surveillance, target acquisition); scouts were rounded up and formed into pathetic little modular brigade RSTA squadrons.[20] In the new tactical Jerusalem, reconnaissance is supplemented by a cornucopia of electronic devices. Corps and divisional commanders can acquire information without the assistance of working cavalry via sensors, including direct access to theater-level sources. With satellites, aerostats, electronic intercepts, and airborne sensors of various kinds available at the touch of the millennium commander's *mouse,* why would he need cavalry?

Like most exacting millennium jobs, traditional cavalry missions were *outsourced.* The arme blanche was gently but firmly eased to pasture as armored cavalry regiments were excised or reconstituted with a potpourri of noncavalry outfits. "It's not the same old cavalry any more," groan die hard cavaliers.[21] They have a point: "You may see more recce units and less pure cavalry units in the future."[22] Yankee cavaliers argued against robots and homogeneous blending of recce and presented a patrician defense of the semiotic rituals of the recce trooper:

> Human scouts can also pick up details and dimensions that sensors can't. They can identify dummies and decoys, tell you about enemy morale and fervor capture material and talk to locals and prisoners and look at the ground in detail. The sensor that can evaluate the going isn't here yet, nor is the one that finds minefields, looks under bridges and culverts or brings you a captured map or enemy colonel.[23]

The Armored Cavalry Regiment used to be the most flexible and hardhitting outfit in the U.S. Army; schooled in reconnaissance operations at the tactical and operational level, armed with a combination of mighty weapons, it was not to be trifled with. The new organization was lighter, proletarian, and, diehards argue, less specialized—the *Casper Milquetoast* versions of ACR counterparts: no integral tanks, artillery, or helicopters.[24] By 2007 only a single "proper" Armored Cavalry Regiment (3 ACR, *Brave Rifles*) had escaped the scalpel. The apocalypse had been forecast by an alarmed Col. John D. Rosenberger who warned of "the demise of Cavalry within the conventional forces of the United States Army, assuring its placement on the ash heap of history along with coastal artillery."[25] The former Chief of Armor, Desert Storm veteran Gen. Terry L. Tucker, noted:

[we] are moving from uniquely trained and organized ground reconnaissance units . . . to one made up almost exclusively of sensors, unmanned aerial vehicles, and helicopters . . . the idea that the future of tanks, cavalry, and reconnaissance is obsolete, no longer needed, and not designed for the current operating environment is hogwash![26]

The paths of history are paradoxical. Desert Storm signaled a cavalry renaissance. By the mid-90s, senior headquarters, including the Pentagon were chockablock with cavalry officers, perhaps out of proportion to their commissioned numbers.[27] Any post factum decision to garrote the cavalry came from *within* the cavalry.

There may be some *Schadenfreude* by armor as it watches the spasms of "its quirky brother," the cavalry, still besotted with bizarre Custeresque apparel (sabers, spurs on combat boots and frontier Stetsons). It is ironic that in 1940 the cavalry rejected modern technology and was terminated trying to save the horse from the tank while millennium cavalry generals fight a rearguard action trying to save the trooper from the robot.

THE LEOPARD IS KING ON THE SOUTHERN AFGHANI PLAIN . . .

> War no longer exists—confrontation, conflicts, and combat certainly do.
> —Gen. Rupert Smith, *The Utility of Force*

> As symmetrical engagements are inherently attritional and costly, we need to seek favourable asymmetries in order to exploit the enemy's weaknesses.
> —Maj. Trevor Cadieu, Squadron Commander,
> Lord Strathcona's Horse, Afghanistan

It would be presumptuous to hasten the end of armored cavalry's rococo saga. Midst the brooding last act there are flashes of optimism that offer solace—bitter realists will call it false hope. Modern cavalry appears to spend as much time patrolling on foot as it does swanning around but there are stalwart contributions; Abrams and Challengers lead patrols and reaction teams in Baghdad and Basra, and Canadian army headquarters ate humble pie and resurrected tanks it had previously buried in western retirement homes. In the late fall of 2006 a refurbished squadron of Leopards quietly appeared in Afghanistan. The troopers were from The Lord Strathcona's Horse (Royal Canadians), a cavalry regiment raised for the Boer War.[28] Armored grognards said *we told you so;* an infantry officer observed: "The Leopard is king on the Southern Afghani plain. It can move almost anywhere on the plains with infantry support, and attack any opponent with impunity, by day or by night."[29] The saga excited the armored cavalry soul and gave sympathetic encouragement to the pedestrian infantry: "The Taliban choose not to fight us in the open desert."[30]

Armored cavalry continues to patrol Mesopotamian and Himalayan valleys as its plough equipped tanks smooth the way for LAVs and Strykers across the washboard terrain of the grape fields.[31] This is perhaps more a triumph of technology than the cavalry esprit de corps. The Canadian panoply resulted in a temporary reunion of light cavalry and the heavies in traditional roles. The recce piquettes of Coyotes sniffed out the foe as the Leopards rumbled forward and knocked them out. The achievements of its armored cavalry prompted the Canadians to visit "the great *DeutschePanzerSchlussverkauf* (German Panzer fire sale)" and modernize its tank fleet.[32] The theater commander, an infantry general, detected a "flexibility of mind one associates with cavalry—comfortably making decisions with less than full situational awareness. Where other officers seek the complete picture, armor officers are at ease proceeding with the information at hand."[33] A sober adjudication will admit that while there are guidons aflutter, these are in fact "infantry tanks" in the traditional sense and the cavalry is more likely to perform police work against Iraqi urban guerrillas or "Timmie Taliban" than killing enemy tanks.[34] Worse, the effectiveness of armored cavalry simply forced the enemy to adopt tactics that avoided combat yet killed men and had political repercussion: ambush via improvised explosive devices (IED).

CAVALRY'S AVE ATQUE VALE

> The best thing for the inside of a man—Is the outside of a horse.
>
> —Cavalry maxim

The age of "cavalry" appears to be over. The plutocratic have replaced the aristocratic. Insouciant style has been suffocated by doctrinal accountants and political scientists. The question whether warfare is an *art* or a *science* remains unresolved. The parochial insistence of the U.S. Cavalry that it alone maintained a distinct specialized role, of robust recce, became moot by 1940, redundant by 1945, and archaic by 2007. Horsed regiments and their tracked antecedents have either disappeared or attempt Phoenix resurrection as tank and reconnaissance battalions. For millennium armor, the globe has become *good tank country* within the revered caveat that *good tank country is where there are no good antitank guns* (or missiles).[35] Tanks are welcomed with the same enthusiasm that footmen gave a supporting pride of knights. Afghanistan, as feudal a fiefdom as any left on the planet, appears to be a grand finale for the horse-tank team. The reconnaissance patrols conducted by *Bozkashi* playing Afghan tribes is a humble but nonetheless legitimate equestrian sidebar to this Kafkaesque struggle.

There will always be some type of armored force or cavalry—but it will be simply *seasoning*: a soupçon of piquette, a *Magnum* of recce or a *Balthazar* of armor, mother-henning infantry beyond a threatening spot. Although wide-ranging armored operations *appear* to be over, this is best said with caution. The tank will gradually morph into a branch of the infantry (as it was predicted in 1918) much the same way that the United States Marine Corps has its own tank assets yet thoroughly adamant of podiatric status. This will take a while, particularly in the Third World where it is still common to see companies of T-55 tanks. The Sherman tank, a most respected Second World War warhorse, served the Israeli army well into the 1980s; the last batch was sold to Chile where they soldiered on almost into the millennium. The invulnerable Abrams should easily endure to the twenty-second century, somewhere on the globe.

The drift to robotics and über-tech invariably evokes a Cassandra reaction from philosophes who urge the military to: "Denounce the orthodoxy of near certainty in future war and make an explicit statement that future war will remain in the realm of uncertainty."[36] Surviving cavalry regiments will likely be hybrid units, cavalry in the sense of dragoons, and occupy a niche between the light infantry and mechanized heavy infantry. Nuances aside, ersatz cavalry and robotic sensors will dominate the future as surely as panzers rode down the warhorse. The challenge of maintaining romantic traditions and corresponding élan while keeping pace with technology and doctrine is ultimately lethal to the warhorse. Millennium observers casually note: "This manifests itself for all members of the Regiment in the bond between man and machine. One is useless without the other."[37] The modern union reflects the psychology of the cyber soldier, understandable yet repugnant to diehard cavaliers.

Doctrine ex machina forced the cavalry to abandon its numinous status and symbiotic relationship with the horse to become scientific, which was as unacceptable in the 1930s as it is today. It corresponds to asking the Theology Department to meld with the Science Faculty. It makes the Vatican a subsidiary of General Motors. Marriage with the rude mechanicals was in the end, a practical solution but anathema to the *essence* of the cavalry: passion and the triumph of flesh and will.

The unpredictability of cavalry and the natural capriciousness of this complex arm requires the most carefully balanced program of equipments, tactical training and delicate handling. Cavalry's perceived schizophrenia resulted from its outward façade. Its rococo splendor endured in bits and pieces into the twentieth century where despite cuirasses and lances, cavalry adopted progressive tactics, at the operational as well as strategic strata. Doctrinal philosophe Lt. Gen. Don Holder offered a review of the status quo in the fall of 2006:

> Analysts now question the future need for large mounted formations, ground attack by large units and for reconnaissance units at division and corps levels. Those questions are worth asking. But the size and shape of the earth, the political organizations of the states and the technical qualities of armies and air

forces suggest that all these things will have future value. If they are not the most common form of combat, they will still be invaluable in some cases. . . . In such operations the cavalry functions will still matter. . . . In future conflicts where opposing forces can conceal themselves from remote detection and mask their intentions by deception, ambivalent dispositions or speed of movement, air and ground scouts may still make the difference in understanding early or late. Whether the troops that perform those missions in the future fly cavalry guidons or not is an unsettled issue.[38]

Cavalry doctrine may be a pastiche of mounted shock, prowling dragoon, and melancholy longing. But it should be remembered, the first enemy troops in Paris in 1815, 1870, 1940, and 1944 were the cavalry, mounted or mechanized. The enveloping of both Kuwait and Baghdad was conducted by cavalry squadrons. Cavalry regiments conduct counter insurgency patrols in the alleys of Basra and the boulevards of Baghdad, from rugged trails in the Kush to the grape fields of Kandahar, much as they did for the past three millennia.

Better to assume that there will always be some type of cavalry—it's élan appreciated, but the panache much reduced. Flying drones or stalking robots will be preferred since they are cheaper, life saving but of course, soulless. Bereft of horse, tank or gunship, but permitted lingering arm-patch heraldry and the odd *collar dog,* it will be increasingly difficult to spot a cavalier. In the end, the Horse will triumph over technology because as a beast of leisure and sport, it will be cared for by those that love it and can afford to treat it well. Being prettier than tanks and far more acceptable in a society intent on worshiping things natural, the horse will persevere in a state of sublime esteem. The warhorse will continue as ceremonial accoutrement to the delight of admiring aficionados who enjoy equestrian martial splendor. In the end, Grow's observation will be correct for, even if denied mounts and a doctrine that is materially or operationally discernable, cavalry will continue to exist, if only as a state of mind.

Make much of your horses.[39]

The Hussaria charger: "I quite like it. It gives me a kind of *Pegasus* je ne sais quoi."

Notes

FOREWORD

1.   Baron Henri Jomini, *The Art of War,* Roots of Strategy, Book 2 (Harrisburg, PA: Stackpole Books, 1987), 547.

2.   Ibid., 547.

3.   John Ellis, *Cavalry, The History of Mounted Warfare* (North Vancouver, BC: Douglas David and Charles Ltd., 1978), 139.

4.   2 Tim. 4:1–4.

PREFACE

1.   Peter Gray, *The Organic Horse,* (Newton Abbot, UK: David and Charles, 2001), 46.

CHAPTER 1

1.   Col. John D. Rosenberger, "Breaking the Saber: The Subtle Demise of Cavalry in the Future Force" (Landpower Essay, AUSA, Institute of Land Warfare, Arlington, VA, June 2004).

2.   Barbaro's struggle against multiple complications ended with his being euthanized on January 29, 2007.

3.   After jockey Calvin Borel won the 2007 Kentucky Derby in the presence of Queen Elizabeth II, he was invited by President Bush to join him and the British monarch for a white-tie state dinner in Washington, D.C.

4.   John T. Nelsen, "Auftragstaktik: A Case for Decentralized Battle," *Parameters* (September 1987): 21.

5. Maj. Gen. Werner Widder (German army), "Auftragstaktik and Innere Führung: Trademarks of German Leadership," *Military Review* (September–October 2002): 6.

6. *Schwerpunkt:* refers to the focal point of an attack; the point of maximum effort, the center of gravity.

7. Erich von Manstein, *Verlorene Siege* (Bonn: Athenaeum-Verlag, 1955).

8. A. A. Svechin, s.v. *Strategiya* ["strategy"], *Sovetskaya Voyennaya Entsiklopediya* [Soviet military encyclopedia], vol. 7 (Moscow: Voyenizdat, 1979).

CHAPTER 2

1. Jean-Baptiste-Antoine-Marcelin, Baron de Marbot, *The Memoirs of Baron de Marbot,* trans. Arthur John Butler (London: Longmans, Green and Co., 1892; New York: Longmans, Green, 1913).

2. Gaius Julius Caesar, *The Gallic Wars*—Book IV, 4.33.

3. Tacitus, *Annals* 14.29–37.

4. Ibid.

5. Lieutenant G. S. Patton Jr., *Mounted Swordsmanship*, http://www.pattonhq.com/textfiles/mounted.html.

6. In Alexander's time, a good warhorse could cost as much as 500 *drachmae* (nearly $50,000).

7. S. Bökönyi, *Data on Iron Age Horses of Central and Eastern Europe* (Meklenberg Collection American School of Prehistoric Research, Harvard University, Cambridge, MA, 1968).

8. Plutarch, *Alexander 356–323 BC,* trans. John Dryden (The Internet Classics Archive, 2006), http://classics.mit.edu/Plutarch/alexandr.html.

9. Ibid.

10. Ibid.

11. Ibid.

12. Andrew Felando, *The Legend of Bucephalus* (2006), http://www.pothos.org/alexander.asp.

13. Plutarch, *Alexander 356–328 BC.*

14. See Col. George T. Denison, *A History of Cavalry* (London: Macmillan, 1913) and Nick Sekunda, *The Army of Alexander the Great* (London: Osprey, 1984).

15. E. S. Creasy, *The Fifteen Decisive Battles of the World* (New York: A. L. Burt, 1937) and Peter Connolly, *The Greek Armies* (London: Macdonald, 1977).

16. Virgil, *The Georgics,* trans. Cecil Day-Lewis (London: Cape, 1941).

17. Ibid.

18. Denison, *A History of Cavalry,* 55.

19. Alfred von Schlieffen, *Military Writings,* trans. R. T. Foley (London: Frank Cass, 2003).

20. Will Durant, *The Story of Civilization, Caesar and Christ,* vol. 3, bk. 1 (New York: Simon and Schuster, 1944), 51.

21. Vegetius, *De Re Militari,* trans. Joe Clark (1767), http://www.pvv.ntnu.no/~madsb/home/war/vegetius/dere07.php#21. See also, Peter Connolly, *Greece and Rome at War* (London: Macdonald, 1977).

22. Plutarch, *Alexander 356–323 BC.*

CHAPTER 3

1.   Ammianus Marcellinus, *History of Rome*, cited in Arthur Ferrill, *The Fall of the Roman Empire, The Military Explanation* (London: Thames & Hudson, 1986).

2.   The Gaetish king Gizur, in the Scandinavian *Hervarar* saga. See *The Saga of King Heidrek the Wise*, ed. and trans. Christopher Tolkien (London: Thomas Nelson, 1960).

3.   Col. George T. Denison, *A History of Cavalry* (London: Macmillan, 1913), 58–59.

4.   Lieutenant G. S. Patton Jr., *The Rasp*, 1914, http://www.pattonhq.com/textfiles/mounted.html.

5.   Priscus, cited in *Priscus at the Court of Attila*, trans. J. B. Bury (Priscus, fragment 8 in *Fragmenta Historicorum Graecorum*). *Attila* means "little father" in Gothic.

6.   Ibid.

7.   Edward Gibbon, *The History of Rome*, vol. IV (New York: Fred DeFau, 1906).

8.   Cassiodorus, cited in Jordanes *Getica*, an abridgement of Cassiodorus' *Gothic History*, trans. Charles Mierow; see also, William Stearns Davis, ed., *Readings in Ancient History*, vol. II (Boston: Allyn and Bacon, 1912–13).

9.   Edward Gibbon, *Decline and Fall of the Roman Empire*, vol. II (New York: The Modern Library, 1932), 1089.

10.   More popular via its paraphrased version in *Conan the Barbarian, 1982*: "Crush your enemies, see them driven before you, and hear the lamentations of their women!"

11.   "Warrior poet of the Grand Duchy of Muscovy," cited in Pól-Michel Seachra and Ann Daingean, *The Golden Horde* (The Golden Horde Origin Systems, October 2006), http://www.ecomouse.u-net.com/.

12.   Jack Weatherford, *Genghis Khan and the Making of the Modern World* (New York: Random House, 2004).

13.   Ann Hyland, *The Medieval Warhorse from Byzantium to the Crusades* (Conshohocken, PA: Combined Books, 1996).

14.   The Avars, a nomadic equestrian tribe, may have also introduced the stirrup to Europe. See John Sloan, posted at the online discussion "The Stirrup Controversy," October 5, 1994, mediev-l@ukanvm.cc.ukans.edu; Oliver Lyman Spaulding, Hoffman Nickerson, and John W. Wright, *Warfare: A Study of Military Methods From the Earliest Times* (Cranbury, NJ: Scholar's Bookshelf, 2006); and Lynn White Jr., *Medieval Technology and Social Change* (New York: Oxford University Press, 1966).

15.   Per Inge Oestmoen, University of Oslo, correspondence, January 2007; See also, Oestmoen "The Mongolian Bow," December 27, 2002, http://www.coldsiberia.org/monbow.htm.

16.   See George Vernadsky, "The Scope and Contents of Chingis Khan's Yasa," *Harvard Journal of Asiatic Studies* 3, no. 3/4 (December 1938), 337–60.

17.   Oestmoen, correspondence, January 2007.

18.   George Vernadsky, *The Mongols and Russia: History of Russia*, vol. 3 (New Haven: 1953), 105.

19.   See Oestmoen, "Women in Mongol Society, The Characteristics of Females among the Mongols," January 23, 2001, http://www.coldsiberia.org/monwomen.htm; and Morris Rossabi, "Women of the Mongol Court", http://www.woodrow.org/teachers/world-history/teaching/mongol/women.html.

20. Oestmoen, "The Mongolian Bow," January 18, 2002.

21. Cited in Stephen Tanner, *Afghhanistan: A Military History* (Da Cappo: 2002), 85.

22. Marco Polo, *The Travels of Marco Polo the Venetian,* trans. William Marsden.

23. Description of *Cosmos* or *Araka* by William of Rubruck, see *The Journey of William of Rubruck to the Eastern Parts of the World, 1253–55,* trans. William Rockhill (London: Hakluyt Society, 1900).

24. Ammianus Marcellinus (ca. A.D. 330–95), cited in ed. William Stearns Davis, *Readings in Ancient History: Illustrative Extracts from the Sources,* 2 vols. (Boston: Allyn and Bacon, 1912–1913).

25. Ronald Latham (trans. and ed.), *Travels of Marco Polo* (London: Penguin Books, 1958).

CHAPTER 4

1. Maj. Dan Acre, The Royal Canadian Hussars, correspondence, January 17, 2007.

2. Jean Froissart, *Chronicles,* bk. II, chap. 92, "A French Knight and an English Squire Joust," cited in "Tales from Froissart," ed. Steven Muhlberger, http://www.nipissingu.ca/department/history/muhlberger/froissart/tales.htm.

3. Christopher Hibbert, *Agincourt* (London: Batsford, 1964), 129.

4. François Rabelais, *The Histories of Gargantua and Pantagruel,* trans. J. M. Cohen (Harmondsworth: Penguin, 1955), chap. 3, VII: "How Panurge had a flea in his ear, and forbore to wear any longer his magnificent codpiece."

5. Hibbert, *Agincourt,* 111.

6. Lynn White Jr., *Medieval Technology and Social Change* (New York: Oxford University Press, 1966).

7. Ann Hyland, *The Medieval Warhorse from Byzantium to the Crusades* (Conshohocken, PA: Combined Books, 1996).

8. Feudal equestrian, Richard P. Alvarez, correspondence, January 4, 2007. See also Alvarez, "Saddle Lance and Stirrup, An Examination of the Mechanics of Shock Combat and the Development of Shock Tactics," *Hammerterz Forum* 5, no. 3, 4 (July 1998); Richard Barber and Juliet Barker, *Tournaments.* (London: Weidenfield and Nicholson, 1989); Philippe Contamine, *War in the Middle Ages* (Malden, MA: Blackwell Publishing, 1984); R.H.C. Davis, *The Medieval Warhorse* (London: Thames and Hudson, 1989); Edge and Paddock, *Arms and Armor of the Medieval Knight* (New York: Crescent Book, 1988); Kelly R. DeVries, *Fighting Techniques of the Medieval World* (New York: St. Martin's Press, 2005) and *Infantry Warfare in the Early Fourteenth Century* (Woodbridge, UK: Boydell Press, 2000); King Dom Duarte, *The Royal Book of Jousting, Horsemanship and Knightly Combat* (1438), trans. Franco Preto (Highland Village, TX: The Chivalry Bookshelf, 2005).

9. Alvarez, correspondence, January 7, 2007.

10. Ibid.

11. Roy William Cox, Master of Horse, director, Free Lancers, September 18, 2006. Equestrian medievalist Dianne Karp's experiments showed a warhorse can manage a football field comfortably within 15 seconds, correspondence, October 17, 2006. See also Eduard Wagner, *European Weapons and Warfare* (London: Octopus Books, 1979).

12. Alvarez, "The Horse: Selection and Training 2000," http://www.classicalfencing.com/horsetraining.php, 2006–2007.

13. Malcolm Vale, *War and Chivalry* (London: 1981), 114.

14. Roger Ascham, *Toxophilus, The Second Book of the School of Shooting*, 1545. Extracts from 1864 ed. Rev. Dr. Giles Edition and 1895 ed. Edward Arber. Cited in http://www.archerylibrary.com.

15. Hugh David Hewitt Soar, *The Crooked Stick: A History of the Longbow*, Weapons in History (Yardley, PA: Westholme Publishing, 2004).

16. "20 sous [20 shillings] was approximately one day's pay of one knight, or four archers." *Medieval Sourcebook:* Kenneth Hodges, "Medieval Prices"; http://www.fordham.edu.

17. Correspondence with Alvarez, Hector Cole, David Kuijt, Cox and Karp, Aug 2006–January 2007. See David Kuijt, *Tactics, The Long and Short of Bows*, 1998. Medieval Armies, http://www.umiacs.umd.edu, 2007.

18. Arrow length was a "cloth yard," the distance from nose to the middle finger. The Royal Antiquaries Society describes longbow of five or six feet in length of yew [or ash etc.], with a three foot arrow. Geoffrey Trease, *The Condottieri: Soldiers of Fortune* (New York: Holt, Rinehart and Winston, 1971).

19. Hector Cole ("Britain's top arrow smith"), correspondence, January 8, 2007.

20. Terrence Wise, *Medieval Warfare* (New York: Hastings House, 1976), 114.

21. Robert E. Kaiser, "The Medieval English Longbow," *Journal of the Society of Archer-Antiquaries*, Vol. 23, 1980.

22. "[there is] residual evidence of glue on the *Mary Rose* shafts. Henry V at the battle of Shrewsbury was hit in the face by a glancing arrow and when it was pulled out the arrowhead remained stuck in the back of his scull." Hector Cole 8 Jan 07. The *Mary Rose* (1545) raised in 1982 contained more than 3,500 arrows and 137 whole longbows.

23. Hector Cole, "Medieval Arrowheads," December 2001.

24. Cited in Wise, 91.

25. Cole, correspondence, January 4, 2007. Shrivenham tests conducted August 2005 to August 2006.

26. Cited in The Fraternity of St. George 1509, British Longbow Society, http://www.longbow-archers.com, October 2006; "The method of re-supply was well rehearsed with archers going a short distance for supplies, while others took their place." See also, Anne Curry, *Agincourt: A New History* (Stroud, UK: Tempus, 2005).

27. Correspondence Kuijt, et al.; see also Anne Curry, *Agincourt, A New History*.

28. Abbie Thomas Medieval Weapons of Mass Destruction September 11, 2003; http://www.abc.net.au/science/news, 2007.

29. High as a three-story building but broken down into transportable parts; not superseded until the seventeenth century—one Trebuchet constructed as late as 1779 by the British at the siege of Gibraltar.

30. Jean Froissart: *Chroniques—The Chronicles of Froissart*, translated by Lord Berners, ed. G. C. Macaulay, "The Hundred Years' War" (Harvard Classics New York, 1910), 22–24; cited in Froissart electronic, J. Boss, converter: University of Virginia Library Electronic Text Center, http://www.fordham.edu, 26.

31. Cited by James Burke, *Connections*, BBC Television, Longbow Web page, http://www.liquidnarrative.csc.ncsu.edu.

32. Froissart, *The Chronicles*, 27.

33. The left wing included the Count of Northampton and Count Arundel, 1,000 knights/men at arms and 3,000 archers; the right wing was led by The Black Prince

with 1,000 knights/men at arms, 1,000 Welsh spearmen and 3,000 archers; in reserve, with Edward was the last battle, 700 knights and 2,000 archers.

34. A nineteenth-century map by F. S. Wellen has them deployed as an intermediate line, almost as *volitgeurs* between the first and second English lines.

35. Tactics on both sides featured divisions or "battles" of dismounted knights and men at arms. For convenience, unless specified, references to "knights" or "men at arms" refers to both.

36. Froissart, *The Chronicles*, 22–24.

37. "an archer carried twelve Scots' lives in his girdle." Oman, 122; Extra bundles of arrows were in barrels in the laager; troops used a replacement drill: alternate archers running back for sheaves.

38. Froissart, See also: C.W.C. Oman, *The Art of War in the Middle Ages, AD 378–1515* (New York: Cornell University Press, 1960).

39. Froissart, *The Chronicles*, 27.

40. Ascham, *Toxophilus*, 6–7.

41. Froissart, *The Chronicles*, 27.

42. Ibid.

43. Froissart, *The Chronicles*, 28.

44. Froissart, *The Chronicles*, 27.

45. Froissart, *The Chronicles*, 27–28.

46. *Henry V*, ed. William George Clarke and William Aldis Wright, *The Plays and Sonnets of William Shakespeare*, vol. 1 (Chicago: Encyclopedia Britannica, Inc., 1952), 3.1. 1–2.

47. Cited in, Matthew Bennett, *Agincourt 1415*, Osprey Books, 1991; see also Hibbert, *Agincourt*, 103.

48. "[the] position adopted by the French seems to have been taken less from a desire to provide a battle-ground free from unfair advantages to either side as from lack of foresight." Hibbert, 106.

49. Shakespeare, *Henry V*, 4.3. 60–62.

50. Anne Curry, *Agincourt: A New History*, cited in Curry, http://www.history.soton.ac.uk/curry.htm. See also, Curry, *The Battle of Agincourt: Sources and Interpretations* (2000).

51. Hibbert, *Agincourt*, 114.

52. Hibbert, *Agincourt*, 117.

53. Hibbert, *Agincourt*, 114.

54. It remains a defiant gesture (the "Archer's Salute"). "[Henry] reminded them that the French had boasted they would cut off three fingers from the right hand of every archer." Hibbert, 110.

55. Cole, January 11, 2007.

56. Enguerrand de Monstrelet, *The Chronicles of Enguerrand de Monstrelet*, Vol. 1, "The Battle of Agincourt, 1415," trans. Thomas Jhones, Esq, cited http://www.maisonstclaire.org.

57. Royal Newfoundland Regiment, Battle of Beaumont-Hamel, Veteran Affairs Canada, http://www.vac-acc.gc.ca.

58. Medieval historian and archery expert Robert Hardy interviewed by BBC radio, July 2003, http://www.bbc.co.uk.

59. Henry was never crowned, dying of dysentery in 1422, two months before Charles VI's death. He was 34 years old.

60. Oman, *The Art of War,* 137.

61. David Grummitt review: "Agincourt 1415: Henry V, Sir Thomas Erpingham and the triumph of the English archers" ed. Anne Curry, http://www.deremilitari.org.

CHAPTER 5

1. Jay Luvaas ed. and trans., *Frederick the Great on the Art of War* (London: Collier-Macmillan, 1966), 150.

2. Col. George T. Denison, *A History of Cavalry* (London: Macmillan, 1913), 179.

3. Machiavelli, *The Art of War,* Vol. IV (London: 1775), 55–56.

4. Machiavelli, *Dell'arte della guerra Discourses,* chap. 18, http://www.etext.library. adelaide.edu.au.

5. C.W.C. Oman, *The Art of War in the Middle Ages, AD 378–1515* (New York: Cornell University Press, 1960), 164; Artillery quip from: C. T. Iannuzzo, "The Art of Warfare," http://www.lepg.org/warfare.

6. Cited in Denison, *A History of Calvary,* 190.

7. Meaning *corsair* or perhaps a levy (*one in twenty*) extracted from Magyars and Serbians to patrol against Ottomans.

8. Jean-Martin De La Colonie, *The Chronicles of an Old Campaigner, 1692–1717,* trans. W. C. Horley (London: 1904), 159.

9. Cited Govt of Poland Historical publication, *The Polish Army (1550–1683),* http://www.kasprzyk.demon.co.uk.

10. *The Polish Army (1550–1683),* http://www.kasprzyk.demon.co.uk/www/ history/Army.html.

11. Radoslaw Sikora, *How the Hussars Fought,* from "Polish-Lithuanian Commonwealth, XVII C," trans. Rick Orli; http://www.kismeta.com/diGrasse/Koncerz; and, Zdzisław Żygulski, *Broń w dawnej Polsce,* Warsaw: 19750; Zofia Stefańska, *Muzeum Wojska Polskiego w Warszawie,* Katalog zbiorów wiek XVII, Warszawa 1968; Marek Wagner, *Kadra oficerska armii koronnej w drugiej połowie XVII wieku,* (Toruń: 1995).

12. Sikora, *How the Hussars Fought.*

13. Frederick cited in Robert B. Asprey, *Frederick the Great, The Magnificent Enigma* (New York: Ticknor & Fields, 1986), 584.

14. Robert Ergang, *The Potsdam Führer: Frederick William I, Father of Prussian Militarism* (New York: Columbia, 1941), cited in Asprey, 92.

15. Lt. Col. Ian McCulloch, correspondence, March 3, 2006. See McCulloch, *Sons of the Mountains: The Highland Regiments in the French and Indian War, 1756–1767,* 2 vols. (Toronto, ON: Robin Brass, 2006).

16. Latin: *faber,* craftsman; *ferrarius* metal, *blacksmith.* Veterinarians note Henry de Farrariis, Norman nobleman and horse doctor, with William in 1066.

17. *Adjutant General's Report to the Duke of York* (London: 1796) cited by Tom Ryan in *The Farrier and Hoofcare Resource Center,* http://www.horseshoes.com.

18. Fortescue, *History of the British Army* II, 116, cited in Jon Manchip White, *Marshal of France* (McNally: New York, 1962), 159–160.

19. D'Authville, *Essai sur la cavalerie tant ancienne que moderne* (Paris: 1756), 309.

20. Frederick, c 1755, cited in Alvarez, "Mounted Combat: Weapons," http://www.classicalfencing.com/mcweapons.php.

21. Frederick, *Die Politischen Testamente Friedrichs des Grossen,* cited in Christopher Duffy, *The Military Life of Frederick the Great* (New York: Athenaeum, 1986), 106.

22. Frederik II, *Oeuvres posthumes de Frédéric II, roi de Prusse:* Tome 10. (Berlin: Voss, 1788) iv, 167. Cited in Thomas Carlyle, *History of Friedrich II of Prussia* (London: Chapman and Hall, 1894); cited in *History of Friedrich II of Prussia.* http://www.gutenberg.org.

23. Robert Citino, *The German Way of War: From the Thirty Years' War to the Third Reich* (Lawrence: University Press of Kansas, 2005), 1.

24. Jacques Antoine Hippolyte de Guibert, *Essai général de tactique.* 2 Vols. (Liege: 1775), 223.

25. Frederick, *Die Werke Friedrichs des Grossen* (Berlin: 1913), VI, 301–303, and Luvaas, 152–153. See also John Ellis, *Cavalry* (Vancouver: Douglas, David & Charles, 1978), 92.

26. "Prussia is not a state that owns an army; it is an Army that owns a state." Honoré Mirabeau, quoted in Jacques Benoist-Mechin, *Histoire de L'Armée Allemande,* vol. 1 (Paris: Albin Michel, 1938), 13.

27. Frederick called the wolfhound who slept in his bed "his *Pompadour.*"

28. Johann Wilhelm Archenholtz, *Histoire de la guerre de sept ans en Allemagne de 1756 à 1763.* Trans M. d'Arnex, I, 109; cited in Thomas Carlyle Leuthen, chap. 10; "The Old Dessauer" was Leopold I, Prince of Anhalt-Dessau, one of the "sternest disciplinarians in an age of stern discipline." Johann Archenholtz, *Histoire de la guerre de sept ans en Allemagne de 1756 à 1763.* Trans. M. d'Arnex.

29. Ibid.

30. The "Parchwitz address" is found in varied versions see: Carlyle, Leuthen, chap. 10, and, Jay Luvaas 234–235; also: Grossen Generalstabe, Der Siebenjährige Krieg, 1756–1763, VI. Leuthen (Berlin: 1904), 138–139; also quoted in Krugler, Francis, *Life of Frederick the Great: Comprehending a Complete History of the Silesian Campaigns and the Seven Years War* (London: Routledge, 1877), 254–256.

31. Carlyle, *Leuthen,* chap. 10.

32. Military historian Robert Citino, correspondence, January 20, 2007; see: Hugo von Freytag-Loringhoven, *Feldherrngrösse: Von Denken und Handeln hervorragender Heerführer* (Berlin: Mittler, 1922), 56. Also Pelet Narbonne, *Der grosse Kurfürst* (Berlin: 1905).

33. C. F. Barsewisch, *Meine Kriegs-Erlebnisse wahrend des Siebenjährigen Krieges 1757–1763* (Berlin: 1863) cited in Duffy, 177.

34. Carlyle, *Leuthen* chap. 10; Frederick brought ten 12-pounders from Glogau fortress and used his cavalry to help crew them; they were known as *Die Brummer (Bellowers)* after a gibe made by the King. Their range and effect tormented the Austrians who later suggested their use was against international law.

35. Carlyle, *Leuthen,* chap. 10.

36. Total Austrian cavalry: 13 brigades (5 cuirassiers, 5 dragoons, and 3 brigades of hussars *Chevauleger.*

37. Duffy, *The Military Life,* 178.

38. Patton, cited in Carlo D'Este, *Patton, A Genius for War,* 306; Patton is also credited with saying: "A good plan, violently executed now, is better than a perfect plan next week."

39. Cited in Denison, *A History of Calvary,* 321.

40. T. A. Heathcote, "The Age of Frederick the Great," in James Lawford (ed.), *The Cavalry* (New York: Bobbs-Merrill, 1076), 112.

41. Cited in Walter Goerlitz, *History of the German General Staff 1657–1945,* trans. Brian Battershaw (New York: Praeger, 1964), 4.

42. Cited in, Robert Asprey, *Frederick the Great, The Magnificent Enigma* (London: Ticknor & Fields, 1986), 471.

43. Varnhagen V. Ense, *Leben des Generals Freiherrn v. Seydlitz* (Berlin: 1854), 70; The same thing occurred after the battle of Kundersdorf.

44. Cited in Denison, *A History of Calvary,* 320–321.

45. Ibid.

46. Famous as the *Blue Max;* personally awarded by Frederick. The highest award was *The Black Eagle;* upon its receipt, it was customary to hand back the *Pour le Mérite.*

47. W. Unger, *Wie ritt Seydlitz?* (Berlin: 1906), 69; Duffy, 93.

48. From Nolan's *History and Tactics of Cavalry,* 33, cited in Denison, 323.

49. "by his drinking and whoring he . . . put himself out of action for weeks at a time." Duffy: 174, 190. When Frederick visited his deathbed "Seydlitz turned his face into the pillow to hide his nose, ravaged by the disease." Frederick was anguished: "I cannot spare you!" Varnhagen, 225.

CHAPTER 6

1. Napoleon, cited in *Military Maxims of Napoleon,* http://www.napoleonguide.com.

2. Two regiments of carabiniers, 20 dragoon regiments, 18 regiments of chasseurs à cheval and 10 hussar regiments.

3. Christopher Duffy, *The Military Life of Frederick the Great* (New York: Athenaeum, 1986), 95.

4. Sir Charles Oman, *History of the Peninsular War,* I (Oxford: 1902), 628.

5. Wellington to Hill, 18 June, 1812, Dispatches, IX; 238; cited in Ian Fletcher, *Galloping at Everything—The British Cavalry in the Peninsular War and at Waterloo 1808–15, A Reappraisal* (Mechanicsburg: Stackpole, 1999), 173–174.

6. Fletcher, *Galloping at Everything,* 174.

7. Sir Herbert Maxwell, *The Life of Wellington,* II (London: 1899), 138–139.

8. Fletcher, *Galloping at Everything,* 280.

9. *United Service Journal,* in March 1831. "written by an officer who served in the 1st Royal Dragoons"; cited in "The British Cavalry on the Peninsula," December, 2002.

10. Cited in Fletcher, *Galloping at Everything,* ff 142.

11. General Sir Charles Stewart, in Col. George T. Denison, *A History of Cavalry* (London: Macmillan, 1913).

12. Denison, *A History of Calvary,* 388.

13. Denison, *A History of Calvary,* 388.

14. Lt. Gen. Count Morand, cited in Denison, *A History of Calvary,* 407–408.

15. General de Gaulaincourt, *With Napoleon in Russia—The Memoirs of General de Gaulaincourt Duke of Vicenza* (New York: Grosset & Dunlap, 1935), 90–91.

16. The Russians also imported Bashkirs from the Urals; small and bony, but hard workers with great endurance; cross bred with draft horses, Kazakh studs from the Kazakhstan and Yakuts from Siberia.

17. *The Diary of Lieutenant Charles Dudley Madden,* cited in Fletcher, 518.

18. Emile Marco de Saint-Hilaire, *History Anecdotal, Political and Military of the Imperial Guard* (London: 1845) and de Saint-Hilaire, *Personal Recollections of the Empire,* trans. Constance de La Warr (London: Simpkin, Marshall, Hamilton, Kent, 1916).

19. Ugo Pericoli, with Michael Glover, *1815: The Armies at Waterloo* (New York: Charles Scribner's Sons, 1973), 78–79.

20. James Laver, *British Military Uniforms,* (London: Penguin, 1948), 26.

21. Ibid.

22. De Saint-Hilaire, *History Anecdotal.*

23. Ibid.

24. Glover, *1815,* 9.

25. Wellington's friend Mrs. Arbuthnot, cited by Michael Glover in, Ugo Pericoli, with Michael Glover, *1815,* 9.

CHAPTER 7

1.   Gunther E. Rothenberg, *The Art of Warfare in the Age of Napoleon* (Bloomington: Indiana University Press, 1978), 72.

2.   Steven T. Ross, "Napoleon and Maneuver Warfare", US Air Force Academy Harmon Memorial Lecture #28, 1985, http://www.au.af.mil/au/awc/awcgate/usafa/harmon28.doc.

3.   Corps comprised at least two, sometimes as many as five, infantry divisions augmented by a division of Cavalry (with its own horse artillery) and Corps artillery (five or more batteries). In addition, the corps commander had access to engineers, logistic units and medical services.

4.   Napoleon and Maneuver Warfare, cited in Ross.

5.   Jean-Baptiste-Antoine-Marcelin, Baron de Marbot, *The Memoirs of Baron de Marbot,* trans. Arthur John Butler (London: Longmans, Green, 1892), vol. 2, 250. See also, Francis Newton Thorpe, "Two Diaries of Waterloo," *The English Historical Review,* vol. 3, no. 11 (July 1888), 539–552.

6.   Captain C. Parquin, *Napoleon's Victories From the Personal Memoirs of Capt. C. Parquin of the Imperial Guard* (Chicago: Werner Company, 1893), 70.

7.   Marbot, vol. 2, 226.

8.   David Chandler, *The Campaigns of Napoleon* (New York: MacMillan Publishing Company, 1966), 356.

9.   130,000 in the French coalition against 154,000 Russians with 624 cannon. Napoleon's artillery was 600 guns. The opposing cavalry forces were prodigious: four full corps of Russian cavalry with two corps of Cossacks. The Coalition fielded four corps of cavalry plus another four cavalry divisions attached to the forward infantry corps.

10. Correspondence, Dr. Scott Delaney, Royal Victoria hospital, Montreal and Dr. Lawrence Hoffman, Alan Institute, McGill University, March 2006; Feb 2007.

11. "They kissed their cannons while their bodies were cut to pieces by our sabers, but still they would not retreat." Konstam, Angus. *Russian Army of the Seven Years' War,* 2 vols. (Oxford: Osprey, 1996), I, 6.

12. Marbot, vol. I; Philip Haythornthwaite and Paul Hannon, *The Russian Army of the Napoleonic Wars,* vol. 1 (Oxford: Osprey, 1987), 5.

13. Brig. Gen. V. J. Esposito and Col. J. R. Elting, *A Military History and Atlas of the Napoleonic Wars* (New York: Praeger, 1963), text to Map 118.

14. Grouchy's "Right Wing" pursuing Blücher comprised four Corps: IIIrd, IVth Inf, Ist and IInd Cavalry Corps (30,600 Infantry, 5,500 Cavalry and 104 guns) versus Ney's "Left Wing" opposing Wellington at Waterloo comprised of six Corps: Ist, IInd, VIth Infantry, IIIrd and IVth Cavalry Corps and The Guard (52,700 Infantry, 15,500 Cavalry, 266 guns). Grouchy controlled 40 percent of Napoleon's infantry, 26 percent of the cavalry, and 28 percent of the artillery.

15. Sir, Archibald Allison, The History of Europe, Vol. 12 (London: 1855), 246.

16. Glover, "Orders of Battle of the Armies," 99–109; Napoleon owned 2 Brigades of Guard Cavalry and 15 Brigades of line Cavalry: 17 versus Uxbridge's 11 Brigades. The British had more horses; the French had more "heavies"—fourteen regiments of *cuirassiers* and eight regiments of Lancers.

17. David Chandler, *Waterloo The Hundred Days* (New York: Macmillan, 1980), 148.

18. Chandler, *Waterloo The Hundred Days*, 148.

19. Victor Hugo, *Les Miserables*, (Paris: 1862), Chapter ix, http://www.online-literature.com/victor_hugo/les_miserables/79/.

20. David Chandler: "Popular Myth versus Historical fact. One short portion of the Chemin d'Ohain to the west of the cross-roads was in 1815 a sunken lane. This fact was seized upon by the great French novelist, Victor Hugo." See: Chandler, *Waterloo The Hundred Days*, 150.

21. Marbot, vol. 1, xxx.

22. Capt Rees H. Gronow, *The Reminiscences and Recollections of Captain Gronow, being Anecdotes of the Camp, the Court, and the Clubs, and Society to the Close of the Last Wwar with France.* rev. ed. (London: 1900), Vol. 1, 195.

23. David Johnson, *Napoleon's Cavalry and Its Leaders* (New York: Holmes and Meier Publishers, 1978), 52. The French cavalry claimed six colors captured at Waterloo versus three taken by the British. See: John Cook "British Colours captured at Waterloo," January 11, 2007.

24. Duke of Wellington to Marshal Lord Beresford, July 2, 1815, cited by Glover in Pericoli/Glover, 70; there are variations of this letter published elsewhere; see: Jacques Garnier, Director of the Napoleonic Institute, "Perspectives on the Battle"; http://www.culturespaces.com.

25. Louis Antoine Fauvelet de Bourrienne, Ed R. W. Phipps, *Memoires of Napoleon Bonaparte* (Paris: 1836), 16.

26. Ernst Otto Odeleben, *Sachsen und seine Kriegen in den Jahren 1812 und 1813* (Leipzig: 1829). See also Jill Hamilton, *Marengo: The Myth of Napoleon's Horse* (London: Fourth Estate, 2000).

27. Sir Archibald Alison, *Some Account of My Life and Writings,* ed. Lady Alison, (Edinburgh: 1883), 101. See also Col. George T. Denison, *A History of Cavalry* (London: Macmillan, 1913), 385.

28. The definitive portrayal of the LaSalle persona is by actor Harvey Keitel who played Captain Feraud in Sir Ridley Scott's brilliant film about Napoleonic cavalry, *The Duelists* (1977).

29. Count Roederer, economist and politician, who met LaSalle twice. Cited in James Lawford (Ed), *Cavalry* (New York: Bobbs-Merrill, 1976), Peter Young, "The Napoleonic Wars," 132.

CHAPTER 8

1. Patton preceded the AEF into France in 1913 when he attended the French Cavalry School at Saumur. He studied French sword drill and became the U.S. Army's first "Master of the Sword."

2. Denison, *A History of Cavalry*, 426.

3. Cecil Woodham-Smith, *The Reason Why* (New York: McGraw-Hill, 1953), 221.

4. W. Baring Pemberton, *Battles of the Crimean War* (London: Batsford, 1962), 85–86.

5. Sergeant Mitchell, *Reminiscences* quoted in C.R.B. Barrett, *History of the XIII Hussars* (London: William Blackwood and Sons, 1911).

6. Woodham-Smith, *The Reason Why*, 235.

7. Col. J. H. Tremayne, a captain in 13th Light Dragoons—eventually 13th Hussars, quoted in Barrett, 365.

8. Barrett, *History of the XIII Hussars*, 361, and Woodham-Smith, *The Reason Why*, 241.

9. Bosquet's now famous quote is cited in Woodham Smith, *The Reason Why*, 238 and Christopher Hibbert, *The Destruction of Lord Raglan* (Toronto: Little, Brown and Co., 1961), 147; Barrett, Denison and Baring Pemberton do not mention it.

10. Hibbert, *The Destruction of Lord Raglan*, 149.

11. Pemberton, *Battles of the Crimean War*, 99.

12. J.F.C. Fuller, *War and Western Civilization 1832–1932: A Study of War as a Political Instrument and the Expression of Mass Democracy* (Andover, England: Chapel River Press, 1932), 99.

13. The first American cavalry units were Light Dragoons, organized in British fashion. General George Washington incorporated the Continental Light Dragoons into his army (1776) and used them as classic dragoon, that is, mounted infantry.

14. The Memoirs of Colonel John S. Mosby edited by Charles Wells Boston, Little Brown, 1917.

15. David Keough contends that the Army of Northern Virginia had a limited number of horse batteries "6–8 batteries of 4–6 guns each and some light artillery as a supplement ... shorter bronze 12 pounders with modern slimmed down carriages, drawn by 4 horses (as opposed to 6 for horse artillery) with a similar number for ammunition wagons." Correspondence, February 23, 2007.

16. Henry C. Whelan to Charles C. Cadwalader, June 11, 1863, Cadwalader Family Collection, Historical Society of Pennsylvania, Philadelphia.

17. Custer graduated (bottom of his class) from USMA in 1861; he was promoted to Brigadier General, June 29, 1863. See Cullum, *Biographical Register of the Officers and Graduates of the United States Military Academy.*

18. A trooper from a Pennsylvania regiment; Stephen W. Sears, *Gettysburg* (Boston: Houghton Mifflin, 2003), 462. See also Stephen Z. Starr, *The Union Cavalry in the Civil War*, 3 vols. (Baton Rouge: Louisiana State Press, 1979), III, 436–438.

19. Lieutenant (Colonel) William Harrison, 2nd US Cavalry; cited in *Civil War Cavalry Battles and Charges*, http://www.civilwarhome.com.

20. Brig. Gen. G. A. Custer, cited in *Civil War Cavalry Battles and Charges*, http://www.civilwarhome.com

21. 2556 prisoners, 71 guns, 50 caissons, 100 wagons. 2550 horses and 7000 head of cattle. He had burned nearly a thousand barns and half a million bushels of wheat.

22. Starr, vol. III, 592.

23. Cited in "William Tecumseh Sherman", htpp://www.ngeorgia.com.

24. Emir Bukhari, *Napoleon's Cuirassiers and Carabiniers* (London: Osprey, 1977); Emir Bukhari, *Napoleon's Hussars* and, *Napoleon's Line Chasseurs* (London: Osprey, 1978 and 1977); Bryan Fosten, *Wellington's Heavy Cavalry* (London: Osprey, 1982); Philip Fosten, *Austrian Army of the Napoleonic Wars (2): Cavalry* (London: Osprey, 1986); Philip Haythornthwaite, *The Russian Army of the Napoleonic Wars (2): Cavalry 1799–1814* (London: Osprey, 1987); Peter Hofschröer, *Prussian Cavalry of the Napoleonic Wars Vols I, II: 1792–1807* (London: Osprey, 1985, 1986); Rodolfo Puletti, *Caricat! Tre secoli di storia dell'Arma di Cavalleria* (Bologna: Edizioni Capitol, 1973).

25. "Exactly the same evolutions were applicable for horseback or for foot fighting, but the latter method was much oftener practiced—we were in fact, not infantry, but mounted riflemen." General Basil W. Duke, CSA. *History of Morgan's Cavalry* (New York: Neal Publishing, 1906), 150.

26. Starr, vol. III, 593. "The cavalry in our late war always felt shy, naturally, of fighting the rifle with the sabre—it was like the contest of wooden ships with iron, an unfair advantage"; General S. D. Lee: "[saber] little used in the late war . . . in every instance under my observation, the revolver replaced the sabre." "Rifle and Sabre" *Army Navy Journal*, Vol. VI, No. 11, New York, October 1868.

27. Starr, vol I, 46.

28. J. H. Wilson, *Under the Old Flag* (New York: 1912), vol. II, 180–181; Starr, vol. I, 21.

29. Wilson, vol. II, 181.

30. Denison, *A History of Calvary*, 470–471; see also Griffith, *Battle Tactics of the American Civil War*, 181–184.

31. Colonel William G. Rambo "The Selma Campaign" cited in 11th Annual Re-enactment of The Battle of Selma, Alabama; http://members.aol.com.

32. Wilson, vol, II, 217 and Starr, vol. I, 36.

33. Starr, vol. I, 36, see: J. H. Wilson and James Pickett Jones, *Yankee Blitzkrieg: Wilson's Raid through Alabama and Georgia* (Athens: University of Georgia Press, 1976). Also: Donald J. Haynes "Wilson's Cavalry Raid," cited in *The Cincinnati Civil War Round Table,* http://www. users.aol.com/wilson; Jerry Keenan, *Wilson's Cavalry Corps: Union Campaigns in the Western Theatre, October 1864 through Spring 1865* (Jefferson, NC: McFarland & Co., 1998).

34. Maj. Gen. G. H. Thomas; "Reports for Wilson's raid to Selma 22 March–22 April 65"; "Wilson's Raid from Chickasaw to Selma, Ala., and Macon, Ga." Cited in "Army of the Cumberland," http://www.aotc.net.

35. Denison, *A History of Calvary*, 474.

CHAPTER 9

1. Trevor Dupuy, *A Genius for War: The German Army and General Staff, 1807–1945* (Fairfax, VA: Hero Books, 1984), 18.

2. Moltke, *Militärische Werke,* Vol. II, Part 2, pp. 33–40.

3.   Cited, Canadian Forces War College, http://www.cfc.forces.gc.ca; see also Kenneth Macksey, *From Triumph to Disaster: The Fatal Flaws of German Generalship from Moltke to Guderian* (Mechanicsburg: Stackpole, 1996).

4.   Henry Montague Hozier, *The Franco-Prussian War: Its Causes, Incidents, and Consequences* (London: Mackenzie, 1872), 374–375.

5.   The regiment adopted the name of its colonel in chief, Prince Ludwig Graf von Trani.

6.   John Pocock *Bitter Victory—The Campaign in Venezia and the South Tyrol and the Battle of Custoza, June–July 1866* (London: Barbarossa, 2002); see also M. Bennighof, "Second Custoza: Charge to Glory," http://www.avalanchepress.com; and Maximilian Ritter von Rodakowski, http://www.austro-hungarian-army.co.uk.

7.   J.F.C. Fuller, *The Conduct of War, 1789–1961: A Study of the French, Industrial, and Russian Revolutions on War and Its Conduct* (London: Eyre and Spottiswoode, 1961), 113–114.

8.   French Imperial Cavalry comprised 11 regiments of cuirassiers; 1 of carbineers; 13 regiments of dragoons and 9x lancer regiments. Light cavalry included 17x chasseurs, 9x hussars and 3x spahis (native North Africans). The two guard units included light and heavy regiments, six squadrons each; each corps d'armée had a division of cavalry. The North German cavalry consisted of 10x cuirassier, 21x uhlan, 21x dragoons, 18 hussars and six Cheveaux-Légers Regiments. See Denison, 492–493.

9.   Denison, *A History of Calvary,* 497.

10.   General Philip H. Sheridan, *An American Account of the Franco-Prussian War:* "From Gravelotte to Sedan." *Scribner's Magazine,* vol. IV, no. 5, November 1888.

11.   Canonne, cited in "Mars la Tour," http://mlt1870.chez-alice.fr/combats.htm.

12.   Aftred Borbstaedt, *The Franco-German War,* trans F. Dwyer (London: 1873), 405–406.

13.   Denison, *A History of Calvary,* 499–500.

14.   R. Morris, *Sheridan: The Life and Wars of General Phil Sheridan* (New York: Crown, 1992), 329–330.

15.   1st Lt. Eben Swift, Fifth Cavalry, "*History of the 5th U.S. Cavalry,*" chap. 226 cited by *US Army Center of Military History:* http://www.army.mil; see also http://www.usregulars.com.

16.   Orland Ned Eddins, "Mountain Men Plains Indian Fur Trade History" and, "Spanish Colonial Horse and the Plains Indian Culture": http://www.mountainsofstone.com; see also http://www.spanishmustang.

17.   Orland Ned Eddins, "Spanish Colonial Horse and the Plains Indian Culture": http://www.thefurtrapper.com.

18.   "Indian symbols used on the war horse", http://www.aaanativearts.com.

19.   George J. Vogler, "Counting Coup in Ancient Ways and Courtroom Days," 1991, http://www.aepronet.org.

20.   Swift, *History of the 5th U.S. Calvary,* 223–224.

21.   Ibid.

22.   Ibid.

23.   *Bulletin of the Texas Archeological and Paleontological Society,* Vol. 1 No. 1, September 1929 38–39; Rupert Richardson "Culture of the Comanche Indians."; also, Laurie Moseley, *Comanche Indians,* Texas Archaeological Society, http://www.txarch.org/arch.

24. George Herendon, scout for the 7th Cavalry; reported in the *New York Herald* July 1876; cited in "The Battle of the Little Bighorn, 1876": http://www.eyewitnesstohistory.com; see also: http://www.axel-jacob.de/little_bighorn.

25. Benteen added later: "I'm only too proud to say that I despised him."

26. George Herendon, cited in *The Battle of the Little Bighorn*, 1876; Evan S. Connell, *Son of the Morning Star: Custer and The Little Bighorn* (San Francisco: North Point Press, 1984); *New York Herald* (July 1876).

27. White Man Runs Him (Miastashedekaroos) was also known as *Crow-Who-Talks-Gros-Ventre* and *White-Buffalo-That-Turns-Around,* was the last surviving of the Crow Scouts. He died in 1928; cited in "Little Bighorn", http://www.wyomingtalesandtrails.com/custer4a.html.

28. Low Dog (*Xunka Kuciyedano*), 1881; cited in "Little Bighorn," http://www.wyomingtalesandtrails.com/custer4a.html.

29. Mark Gallear, *Guns at the Little Bighorn,* http://www.westernerspublications.ltd.uk/htm. See also: R. G. Hardorff (1991) *Lakota Recollections of the Custer Fight* (Lincoln: University of Nebraska Press, 1997); Martin Pegler, *US Cavalryman 1865–1890* (London: Osprey, 1993); John Walter, *The Guns That Won the West—Firearms on the American Frontier, 1848–1898* (London: Greenhill Books, 1999).

30. The term "Buffalo Soldiers" eventually encompassed the following units: U.S. 9th, 10th, 24th and 25th Regiments. The "Buffalo Soldiers" were confirmed by the American Congress as the first black regiments in the regular Army. The Mexicans dubbed them "Smoked Yankees."

31. Winston Spencer Churchill, *The River War: An Historical Account of the Reconquest of the Sudan,* 2 Vols., ed. Col. F. Rhodes, illus. Angus McNeill (London: Longmans, Green, 1899), 82–164.

32. Churchill, *The River War,* XV.

33. Ibid.

34. Ibid.

35. Ibid.

36. Ibid.

37. Edwin Gerard, "The Horse that Died for Me," cited in: http://www.lighthorse.org.

38. The second Canadian contingent for South Africa initiated "cavalry" reorganization.: 1 CMR (mostly easterners) was renamed The Royal Canadian Dragoons (RCD); 2 CMR, mainly from the west and included many North West Mounted Police (NWMP) became simply, "the CMR." The Lord Strathcona's Horse (LdSH), though technically a Montreal outfit, actually incorporated many westerners and Mounties via the efforts of Colonel (NWMP Superintendent) Sam Benfield Steele.

39. The British first adopted *khaki* during the Zulu Wars and the Indian Mutiny.

40. From an article written in the early 1900s; cited by Gibby Bauld, Victoria and Robert Cooke, "21st Light Horse," The Australian Light Horse Association, Wagga Wagga, NSW 2006.

41. "21st Light Horse," The Australian Light Horse Association.

42. K. R. Gibbs, "Bars and Medals," *Die Suid-Afrikaanse Krygshistoriese Vereniging Military History Journal*—Vol. 2, No. 3, 2006; http://rapidttp.com/milhist/vol023kg.html.

43. Captain Engelhardt, of the Nerchinski Cossacks, quoted in *Le Journal des Sciences Militaires,* Aug 1905, Capt Serge Nidvine, *La Cavalerie Russe pendant la Guerre*

Russo-Japonaise, "The Russian Cavalry during the Russo-Japanese War"; trans. Capt. H. Tupes; cited in http://www.russojapanesewar.com.

44. Nidvine, *La Cavalerie.*
45. Nidvine, *La Cavalerie.*
46. Nidvine, *La Cavalerie.*

CHAPTER 10

1. British Army Council, *Cavalry Tactics* (London: 1907) also cited in Dr. Gavin Hughes "The British Army," *British Cavalry Units 1914–1918;* http://renegade miniatures.com.

2. *German Cavalry Drill Instruction* (paragraph 417), cited in Hughes "German Cavalry Units 1914–1918"; http://renegademiniatures.com.

3. The entire German Army was to be sent west leaving three active corps, one reserve corps and one cavalry division to deal with invasion by Russian armies.

4. Maj. Gen Sir Edward Spears, *Liaison 1914, A Narrative of the Great Retreat* (Eyre & Spottiswoode: 1930), 36.

5. Benjamin Haydon, cited in Kiley, *The Napoleon Series.*

6. Copied as "Prussian Rose" by the Germans: Schnurr, Feb 07.

7. The 1882 model sword was a straight thrusting sword; the Cavalry used the Carabine modèle 1890, 9.52mm; *Les Cuirassiers 1845–1918,* Ed Louis Delpérier, *Uniformes* No. 5 (Paris: L'Emancipatrice, 1981) 59. See also Liliane et Fred Funcken, *L'Uniforme et les Armes des Soldats du XIXe Siècle,* (Casterman: 1982); and Liliane and Fred Funcken, *Arms and Uniforms. Volume 2. 18th Century to the Present Day.* See also: Ian Sumner, *The French Army 1914–1918* (Osprey: 1995).

8. Sumner, *The French Army,* 43.

9. There were 59 cavalry regiments in metropolitan France before the war, upon mobilization a further 30 regiments became available: 12 regiments of Cuirassiers, 32 regiments of Dragoons, and 35 regiments of light cavalry (21x Chasseurs a Cheval, 14x Hussars and, from North Africa, 6x *Chasseurs d'Afrique* and 4x spahis). Supporting horse artillery was divided into Artillery Groups (groupes d'artillerie); each *Groupe* comprised 3x cannon batteries (12x75 mm guns).

10. Each infantry division received a divisional cavalry squadron, (150 sabers) for reconnaissance and screening tasks. Each *division de cavalerie* comprised three brigades, each with two regiments; plus *une Groupe d'artillerie à cheval:* 3 batteries of 12 (36x75mm guns).

11. *Fr Cavalry Division deployment:* 6th and 8th with the First Army, 2nd and 10th with the Second. The 3rd, 4th and 5th Armies: 7th, 9th and 10th Cavalry. GHQ Reserve ("Corps de cavalerie Sordet"): 1st, 3rd and 5th Cavalry Divisions (hereafter CD). See: "Opérations du corps de cavalerie Sordet" from: "Les opérations des 3ème et 4ème armées françaises, 6 au 25 août 1914", *généalogie et aux parcours de régiments en 1914–18, Historique de Régiments:* www.chtimiste.com; and, Ian Sumner, *The French Army 1914–1918,* (Osprey: 1995) 4–6; and, Graham Watson, *France Army August 1914;* Deployment: GHQ Reserve: 1st CD, Paris, 2nd CD, Meaux, 3rd CD, Melun, 8th CD, Dohl—det Alsace Army, 10th CD—Army command: 2nd CD, Luneville, 6th CD, Lyons, 7th CD, Rheims and, 9th CD, forming.

12. *Le Corps du général Sordet:* 1e, 3e and 5e DC (*division de cavalerie*); *Le Corps de cavalerie de général Conneau* (created August 14, 1914).

13. Capt. L.A.E. Price Davies to Mrs. Price Davies, October 17, 1914. Cited in Nikolas Gardner, "Command and Control in the 'Great Retreat' of 1914: The Disintegration of the British Cavalry Division"; *The Journal of Military History,* Vol. 63, No. 1 (January, 1999), 32.

14. Reginald Cleaver, "Military Education," *Punch, or the London Charivari,* (December 10, 1892), 274.

15. Mike Chappell, *British Cavalry Equipments 1800–1941* (London: Osprey, 1983), 19.

16. Chappell, *British Cavalry Equipments,* 19–20.

17. Chappell, *British Cavalry Equipments,* 19; See also: A. W. Andrew, *Cavalry Tactics of Today* (London: 1903).

18. Richard Holmes, *Riding the Retreat—Mons to the Marne 1914 Revisited* (London: Jonathan Cape, 1995), 64–65.

19. Cited by Edmonds, to Archibald Wavell, June 17, 1938. Allenby Papers VI/I, LHCMA; Haig also noted: "The ideal cavalry is one that can fight on foot and attack on horseback." Douglas Haig, *Cavalry Studies Strategic and Tactical* (London: Hugh Rees, 1906).

20. 6x heavy regiments, 5x Hussar regiments (with squadrons from two other Hussar regiments) and 4x Lancer Regiments.

21. Dale Clarke, *British Artillery 1914–18: Field Artillery* (Oxford: Osprey, 2004), 3–4.

22. British Cavalry Divisions: 1st, 2nd, 3rd, 4th Mounted, 1st Indian, and 2nd Indian Cavalry Divisions. The Australian and New Zealand Mounted Division (ANZAC), 1st and 2nd Mounted Divisions, the Yeomanry Division and the 74th (Yeomanry) Division.

23. Army Order Issued by Emperor William II, August 19, 1914; "Source Records of the Great War, Vol. II, ed. Charles F. Horne, (London: National Alumni 1923); The BEF subsequently referred to itself as the "Old Contemptibles."

24. Friedrich's father, Frederick I, instituted The Order of the Black Eagle in 1701 with the motto *Suum Cuique* ("to each his own"); *Chacun à son gout* ("each to his own taste"); The *Gardes du Corps* was unique. German 1914 heavy cavalry comprised 14 regiments: the Gardes du Corps, Garde-Kürassier, and Line regiments 1 to 8. (2x regiments of Saxon heavy cavalry; 2x regiments of Bavarian Schweres Riter.) Costume authority Captain Anthony Schnurr, correspondence Jan-Mar 07; detailed photographs: http://www.kaisersbunker.com/.

25. Schnurr, correspondence, February 2007. See also: German Cavalry 1914. The Imperial German Army: Dr. Gavin Hughes http://renegademiniatures.com.

26. Except for the Uhlanen from Saxony who carried the M1896 pine shaft lance. Schnurr, February 2007.

27. The German Cavalry comprised: 10 Kurassier' regiments (and two Saxon Heavy Cavalry regiments) 13 *Jager zu Pferd* (Mounted Rifles) regiments, 28 dragoon regiments, 21 hussar regiments (including 1x Life Guard), 24 uhlan regiments; 2 Bavarian (1st & 2nd) uhlans, plus 12 Bavarian *Cheveauxlegers* and heavy cavalry regts; each division comprised 5590 warhorses. A cavalry corps was two or three divisions, each three brigades of two cavalry regiments apiece. Cavalry divisions attached to in-

fantry corps were often converted to permanent infantry status "Kavallerie Schutzen" and given machine guns.

28. Marshal Foch, *The Principles of War,* trans Hilaire Belloc (Chapman & Hall: 1918), 284.

29. A. F. Pollard, *A Short History of the Great War*, page 13, online book found at http://www.gutenberg.org.

30. The French attached squadrons to Army HQs; the BEF arrived with The Royal Flying Corps' 2nd, 3rd, 4th and 5th Aeroplane Squadrons (63 aircraft). See: Hugh Gibson, *A Journal from our Legation in Belgium* (Doubleday: 1917).

31. The *Taube* was created by Austrian engineer Dr. Josef Etrich and supposedly modeled after Zanonia macrocarpa seeds, which glide to the ground in a slow spin— but this was not the case.

32. Spears, *Liaison 1914,* 72.

33. General Alexander von Kluck, *The March on Paris and the Battle of the Marne in 1920* "Source Records of the Great War", Vol. II, ed. Charles F. Horne, (London: National Alumni, 1923).

34. "les Allemands avaient jeté en avant pour couvrir la marche de leurs Corps d'Armée, dont nous ne soupçonnions pas le dédoublement"; "Opérations du corps de cavalerie Sordet" ("dédoublement": "a collectivity which explodes").

35. Sir J. A. Hammerton, H. W. Wilson (eds.), "The Battle of Haelen, August 12– 13, 1914", *The Great War* 6 Vols. (London: 1914), I, 213.

36. German officer's letter, *History of the Great War,* ed. N. Flower (London: Waverley Press, 1917), III, 146.

37. Gibson, "A Trip to the Haelen Battlefield."

38. Maximilian von Poseck, *The German Cavalry 1914 in Belgium and France,* Edited Jerome W. Howe (Berlin: Mittler 1923); see also Poseck, *Der Aufklärungsdienst der Kavallerie, nach den Erfahrungen des Weltkrieges* (Berlin: Mittler, 1927). Poseck was Inspector General of Cavalry in 1914.

39. Von Moltke, 5 August 1914: ". . . Our advance in Belgium is certainly brutal, but we are fighting for our lives and all who get in the way must take the consequences." Cited in "*Schrecklichkeit*" War in Europe, 1914; also see S.L.A. Marshal, *World War 1* (New York: Mariner, 2001), 61.

40. German Cavalry Aug 1914: I. Kavallerie-Korps: Gen. Lt. von Richthofen (Garde-Kav-Division; 5.Kav-Division—hereafter KD); II. K-Korps: Gen. von der Marwitz (2.KD; 4.KD; 9.KD); III. K-Korps: Gen. Ritter von Frommel (7.KD; 8.KD; Bayr. KD); IV. K-Korps Gen. Lt. von Hollen (3.KD; 6.KD).

41. *Corps de cavalerie Sordet:* 1st, 3rd and 5th Cavalry Divisions. 1e division: with 2e Heavy Cavalry Brigade (Cuirassiers), the 5th and 11th Cavalry Brigades (Dragoons); 3e division: 4th Cavalry Brigade (Cuirassiers); 13th Cavalry Brigade (Dragoons) and the 3rd Light Brigade; 5e division: 3rd and 7th Cavalry Brigades (Dragoons) and the 5th Light Brigade; Each division: 2 Horse Artillery batteries and a cyclist squadron. Terraine, *Mons the Retreat,* 47.

42. *Opérations du corps de cavalerie Sordet.*

43. *Opérations du corps de cavalerie Sordet;* See Colonel Marcel Boucherie, *Historique du Corps de Cavalerie Sordet* (Paris : Lavauzelle, 1924) and Eric Labayle, "L'odyssée du corps de cavalerie Sordet (août-septembre 1914)," *14–18 le Magazine de la Grande Guerre,* no.15, Août-septembre 2003.

44. General Maximillian von Poseck, *The German Cavalry, 1914 in France and Belgium,* translated for the U.S. Cavalry by E. S. Mittler & Sohn (Mittler, 1923), 54.

45. Spears, *Liason 1914,* 74–76; Terraine, *Mons the Retreat,* 53–56; Lanrezac was more generous, and wrote in his own history: ". . . our military relations with the British would be anything but easy, in spite of undeniable good will on both sides. We did not speak the same language, and more over had very different ideas on the conduct of the war." Spears, *Liason 1914,* 76, 77–78.

46. Sir James E. Edmonds, *Military Operations France and Belgium 1914* (London: Macmillan, 1933).

47. De Lisle, "My Narrative," 22 August 1914.

48. Terraine, *Mons the Retreat,* 115.

49. Gardner, "Command and Control," 37 and James, *Imperial Warrior,* 46.

50. De Lisle, "My Narrative," August 24, 1914; see also Gardner, "Command and Control," 43–44 and Terraine, *Mons the Retreat,* 115–117.

51. Terraine, *Mons the Retreat,* 116.

52. Gardner, Command and Control," 44 and, Sir Hubert de la Poer Gough, *The Fifth Army* (London: Hodder, Stoughton, 1931), 17.

53. Lawrence James, *Imperial Warrior: The Life and Times of Field Marshal Viscount Allenby, 1861–1936* (London: Weidenfeld and Nicholson, 1993), 59.

54. Cited in Gardner, "Command and Control," 49.

55. Spears, *Liason 1914,* 316.

56. Sir John French's First Despatch, the Third Supplement to the *London Gazette,* September 8, 1914.

57. General Sir Horace Smith-Dorrien, *Memories of Forty-Eight Years Service,* Chapt 24d – "The Retreat from Mons: Le Cateau" cited, Sir Horace Smith-Dorrien: www.richthofen.com/smith-dorrien. Smith-Dorrien added: "From the British Cavalry point of view I consider that the Huns gave us no trouble at all after Le Cateau, as we were always able to fight delaying actions and retire at our leisure, once the German outflanking movement had petered out."

58. Sir James Edmond's Official British history; cited in http://batmarn1.club.fr/bef_1914.htm; Chapt VII.

59. Paul Greenwood, "The British Expeditionary Force—August/September 1914; cited in http://batmarn1.club.fr/bef_1914.htm and, Esposito, Map 8.

60. Spears, *Liason 1914,* 101; see also Holmes, 162–163.

61. Correspondence, Stephane Commans, Chatenay-Malabry, March 2007. See also: Général Sordet and, Colonel Boucherie, *Historique du Corps de Cavalerie Sordet* (Paris: Charles-Lavauzelle, 1925).

62. Spears, *Liason 1914,* 244; see also: Gardner, "Command and Control," 49; General Edmonds, then chief staff officer of 4th division, visited II Corps Chief of Staff, Brigadier-General Forestier-Walker and inquired as to the whereabouts of the cavalry. Forestier-Walker could only reply, 'I wish to God we knew.' Edmonds to Wavell, June 18, 1938, cited in Gardner, "Command and Control," 49.

63. Général Jacques de Mas Latrie, *Mémoires,* cited in *Mas Latrie Site Généalogique et historique* , http://www.mas-latrie.com/.

64. Von Kluck: "General von Kluck's Account of the First Battle of the Marne, September 1914" *Source Records of the Great War, Vol. II,* ed. Charles F. Horne (London: National Alumni, 1923).

65. "we are f—ked!", cited in John Terraine, *Mons the Retreat to Victory* (London: Batsford, 1960), 81, 194, 199.

66. "Well, Monsieur War College Professor, what do you think of these tactics?" cited in Terraine, *Mons the Retreat*, 176 and Spears, who acknowledges "I do not know whether this is true . . . [but] it is so typical of the man." Spears, *Liason 1914*, 272.

67. von Kluck, II,2.

68. Cited in Terraine, *Mons the Retreat*, 196.

69. Spears, *Liason 1914*, 319.

70. Ibid., 325.

71. Ibid.

72. Ibid., 324.

73. Ibid., 307.

74. Ibid., 301.

75. Esposito, Map 10: World War 1.

76. See: Spears, *Liason 1914*, 319–324 and, Nikolas Gardner, "Command and Control," 29–54.

77. Edmonds, "Race to the Sea".

78. I. Cavalry Corps : Guard and 4th Cavalry Divisions; II. Cavalry Corps : 2nd, 7th and 9th Cavalry Divisions; IV. Cavalry Corps : 3rd, 6th and Bavarian Cavalry Divisions. Edmonds, "The Race to the Sea" xxii.

79. Edmonds, "Last Days on the Aisne" xxi, 6.

80. Conneau's Corps had three Cavalry Divisions (2e,6e,10e) August 1–21; reduced to two Cavalry Divisions (2e,10e) till August 22—September 1; reinforced to three Cavalry Divisions (4e,8e,10e) September 2—September 18; reduced to two Cavalry Divisions (3e,10e) September 19–25; See: General Louis Conneau, *Historique des Corps de Cavalerie commandés par le Général Conneau du 14 Août 1914 au 2 Mars 1917* (Paris: Lavauzelle, 1924).

81. See: Edmonds, Spears and Maj. A. Peteau, *Aperçu historique sur les Mouvements et Opérations des Corps et Divisions de Cavalerie en Liaison avec les Armées, 1914–1918* (Liège: Vaillant-Carmanne, 1924).

82. Edmonds, "Last Days on the Aisne," xxi, 6; "Generalmajor von Gleich in *Die alte Armee* wrote: 'as regards concealment from aeroplanes, we had learnt as good as nothing . . . 'Camouflage' we actually only learnt from the English after our losses had made us wise."

83. Spears, *Liason 1914*, 44.

84. Spears, *Liason 1914*, 102.

85. Phillip-Howell to Wavell, July 20, 1938, Allenby Papers VI/I.

CHAPTER 11

1. Quote originated with Canadian cavalry during the Boer War when units received maps with no grid lines and vague directions; attributed to CO, Fort Garry Horse. See Brig. Gen. J. E. B. Seely, *Adventure* (London: Hinneman, 1930). Also cited in John Ellis, *Cavalry* (Vancouver: Douglas, David & Charles, 1978), 174.

2. Ellis, *Calvary*, 114.

3. Schlieffen, quoted in K. Krafft von Dellmensingen, *Der Durchbruch* (Hamburg: 1937), 405.

4. The selected March Past of the Royal Armoured Corps and the Royal Canadian Armoured Corps is appropriately, the merry English folk song, "My Boy Willie."

5. Ernest D, Swinton, *Eyewitness: Being Personal Reminiscences of Certain Phases of the Great War, including the Genesis of the Tank* (London: Hodder & Stoughton, 1932).

6. Lt. Col. G. Le Q. Martel, *In the Wake of the Tank* (London: Sifton Praed and Company, 1931), 12.

7. Cited in Mark Urban, *Generals* (London: Faber, 2005), 250.

8. "Gentlemen, victory belongs to the side that first succeeds in placing a 75mm gun into a vehicle capable of moving across any terrain. . ."; Gen. J. B. Estienne: *Conférence faite le 15 février 1920;* See: J. J. Clarke, "Military Technology in Republican France: The Evolution of the French Armored Force, 1917–1940," thesis, Duke University, 1969.

9. Kenneth Macksey, John H. Batchelor, *Tank, A History of the Armoured Fighting Vehicle* (London: Macdonald, 1970), 33.

10. "A novel feature of the plan was the use of tanks to carry men and supplies. The most crucial aspect of this was the ability of supply tanks to eliminate the necessity for the fatiguing infantry carrying parties." W. F. Stewart, "Attack Doctrine in the Canadian Corps, 1916–1918," Unpublished thesis, University of Alberta, 1980. See also: "The Offensive and the Problem of Innovation in British Military Thought 1870–1915," T. H. E. Travers, *Journal of Contemporary History,* Vol. 13, No. 3 (July, 1978), 531–553.

11. Stewart, "Attack Doctrine," 199.

12. "Through the mud, the blood to the green fields beyond."

13. J. F. C. Fuller, *The Conduct of War, 1789–1961: A Study of the French, Industrial, and Russian Revolutions on War and Its Conduct* (London: Eyre and Spottiswoode, 1961), 243.

14. Travers/Archer, editors: *The Captain Who Teaches Generals. Men at War.* 380. See also: B. H. Liddell Hart, *Paris: or the Future of War* (EP Dutton: 1925). —. *The British Way in Warfare* (London: Faber & Faber,1932). —. *The Future of Infantry.* (London: Faber & Faber, 1933).

15. Virtually all American artillery manuals and many tank manuals were translations of French manuals. The AEH modified the doctrine as they acquired experience. Robert Doughty, *The Seeds of Disaster: The Development of French Army Doctrine 1919–1939* (Hamden: Archon, 1986), 100–101.

16. Only the 2nd US Cavalry Regiment was sent to France in 1917. See: Merrill, James M. *Spurs to Glory The Story of the United States Cavalry.* (New York: Rand McNally, 1966).

17. Capt D. E. Wilson, *Treat 'Em Rough! The Birth of American Armour, 1917–20* (Navato: Presidio, 1990), 112.

18. Capt D. D. Eisenhower, "A Tank Discussion." *Infantry Journal* Vol. 17 No. 5; November 1920.

19. General Sir John Hackett, *The Profession of Arms* (London: Sidgwick & Jackson, 1983). Also cited by General Anthony C. Zinni, Interview, "Conversations with History", Institute of International Studies, UC Berkeley, March 2001, http://www.berkeley.edu/conversations/zinni.

20. Trevor Jones, cited in *1918, Australians in France;* http://www.awm.gov.au/1918//memories.

21. H. S. Gullett, *Official History of Australia in the War of 1914–18: "Vol. VII: Sinai and Palestine* (Sydney: Angus & Robertson, 1938); Patrick Hamilton, *Riders of Destiny: The 4th Australian Light Horse Field Ambulance 1917–1918: An Autobiography and History* (Melbourne: MUMHR Publications, 1985).

22. D. Haig, WW1 Diaries, cited in "Remember the Somme"; http://www.telegraph.co.uk/; see also: *Douglas Haig: War Diaries and Letters, 1914–1918.* Ed. Gary Sheffield and John Bourne. (London: Weidenfeld & Nicolson, 2005).

23. Timmis, cited in John R. Grodzinski "The Battle of Moreuil Wood"; LdSH site: http://www.strathconas.ca; also, Capt S. H. Williams, *Stand to Your Horses* (Winnipeg: Friesen, 1961), 202–214.

24. Williams, *Stand to Your Horses,* 205; "So rarely used, [the] command 'attacking cavalry to right'. *Feldartillerie-Regiment 238* History, cited in John Grodzinski, M. Mc-Norgan, "Cavalry Action at Moreuil Wood," *Fighting for Canada Seven Battle* Ed. D. Graves (Robin Brass: 2000), 260.

25. Williams, *Stand to Your Horses,* 206.

26. Ibid., 207.

27. Sir Alfred Munnings painting, "Charge of Flowerdew's Squadron," reproduced in the Cdn War Museum site: http://www.civilization.ca/cwm/munnings.

28. Trooper Alan Dale, cited in Williams, *Stand to Your Horses,* 208; Dale continued "When I woke up I was pinned under my horse, which was mercifully dead."

29. German accounts say: "the last horses collapsed 200 meters in front of the Company. Only one horse and two wounded troopers reached our lines." Grodzinski/McNorgan, 265.

30. Moreuil Wood was briefly recaptured: "1 April dismounted units of the 2nd Cavalry Division attacked. It was the third wave, consisting of 488 all ranks of the Canadian Cavalry Brigade, which entered and cleared the wood." Col. G. W. L. Nicholson, *Canadian Expeditionary Force 1914–1919* (Ottawa: Queen's Printer, 1962), 370–373.

31. Marshal Ferdinand Foch, New York, 29 October, 1921; cited in Williams, *Stand to Your Horses,* iv.

32. Vladimir Litauer, *Russian Hussar: A Story of the Imperial Cavalry, 1911–1920* (London: 1933).

33. Maximillian von Poseck, *The German Cavalry, 1914 in France and Belgium* Translated for the US Cavalry by E. S. Mittler & Sohn, (Mittler: 1923); see also: *Der Aufklärungsdienst der Kavallerie, nach den Erfahrungen des Weltkrieges* (Berlin: Mittler, 1927), 236.

CHAPTER 12

1. Lt. Col. C. E. Morgan: *Trooper Jones of Swank's Horse Laments Transfer to the Tank Corps.*

2. J. F. C. Fuller, *Memoirs of an Unconventional Soldier* (London: Ivor Nicholson and Watson, 1936): 361, 363.

3. Tim Taylor, "Red Star—White Eagle The Soviet Counter-Offensive in the Russo-Polish War. Summer 1920" cited in *Red Star—White Eagle,* http://www.columbiagames.com.

4.　See Janusz Szczepański "Kontrowersje Wokol Bitwy Warszawskiej 1920 Rok"; *Przejdz do Historii,* http://www.mowiawieki.pl/artykul.

5.　Isaac Babel, *Red Cavalry* (New York: R.W. Norton, 2003), 210, 284.

6.　It was a Russian combination of English thoroughbred, Don mares including the best of the Cossack and Asian–Mongol ponies: the Cherkassky, Nogai, Persian and Karabakh. Army breeding farms were reorganized after the Revolutionary wars. Controlled development of the breed began only during the 1920's. The S. M. Budyonny and Yulovsky Farms, near Rostov produced warhorses for the Red Army before 1941, retreated east, then continued to provide quality remount stock.

7.　Cited in *The Magistral Grand Priory of The Holy Lands,* The Most Revd. Gary Beaver KGCTJ, http://www.ordotempli.org.

8.　V. K. Triandafilov was head of the Operational Directorate; often touted as more deserving of credit for Deep Operations than Tukhachevsky. Triandafilov was killed in an air crash in 1931.

9.　"The Red Army came about as a result of a political bargain struck between Tukhachevskii and Stalin." Christopher Duffy, *Red Storm on the Reich* (New York: Da Capo, 1993), 314, 356.

10.　Three out of five marshals, thirteen of fifteen army commanders, all 16 army political commissars, 21 corps commanders, 37 divisional commanders. There is evidence that Tukhachevsky was framed by the Nazis and set up by Himmler. See: John Erickson, *The Soviet High Command* (London: Macmillan, 1962), 505–506; R. Simpkin, *Deep Battle—The Brainchild of Marshal Tukhachevskii* (London: Brassey's, 1982); W.J. McGranahan, "The Fall and Rise of Marshal Tukhachevsky," *Parameters* (July 1978): 62–72; and, Duffy: 314, 356.

11.　The 1935 'Instructions on Deep Battle' were finally made into fixed doctrine in the 'Provisional Field Regulations' of 1936. Tukhachevskii and Triandafilov were the driving force.

12.　R. J. Jarymowycz, "Jedi Knights in the Kremlin: Soviet Military in the 1930s and the Genesis of Deep Battle." B.J.C. McKercher and R. Legault, eds., *Military Planning and the Origins of the Second World War in Europe* (Westport, CT: Praeger, 2001).

13.　Major George S. Patton, Jr., 'The Cavalryman"; cited in The Patton Society Library, http://www.pattonhq.com.

14.　The Royal Tank Regiment's floppy black beret (to hide the oil and grease stains) was modeled on the Chasseurs Alpine.

15.　Field Marshal Haig in 1926. See: John Ellis, *Cavalry: The History of Mounted Warfare* (Devon: Westbridge, 1978), 182.

16.　J. B. Estienne: Conference faite le 15 fevrier 1920; quoted in J. J. Clarke, "Military Technology in Republican France: The Evolution of the French Armored Force, 1917–1940," thesis, Duke University, 1969, 57.

17.　V. W. Germains, *The Army Quarterly* XVI, 373.

18.　See: Michael Carver, *The Apostles of Mobility: The Theory and Practice of Armoured Warfare* (New York: Holmes & Meier, 1979).

19.　SLA Marshall noted: " . . . notorious that soldiers do not read books. In fact, our own Infantry Journal received but failed to review [Fuller's] FSR III . . . Guderian read Marshall Timoshenko ordered that FSR III [by Fuller] be made a "table book" for the Red Army."

20. Fuller: "Tank warfare, therefore, is likely to reduce, if not altogether to cancel out, an attack directed against civil will." *The Army Quarterly,* London 1933, Vol. XXV Oct 32–Jan 33, Maj. Gen. J. F. C. Fuller, "Military Inventions; Their Antiquity and Influence on War."

21. As late as 1939 an article entitled "Infantry and Tanks in the Spanish Civil War" announced "tanks proved of little military value." *Military Gazette,* 8 Aug 1939, Page 3.

22. By mid 1939, the British Cavalry had been reduced to three mounted regiments—all that were available for the formation of a cavalry division in the Middle East. Mike Chappell, *British Cavalry Equipments 1800–1941* (London: Osprey, 1983), 22.

23. Colonel George T. Denison, *A History of Cavalry* (London: MacMillan, 1913), 419.

24. *CDQ* 1934 "Toronto to Niagara." Compare to a companion article by Maj. C. W. Devey LSH (RC) "A Cavalry Trek Through Alberta", 216 and, a 1924 article (*CDQ* Vol 2) Maj R. S. Timmons "Some Lessons from a Four Days' Cavalry Trek," 10.

25. Jack Coggins, *Arms and Equipment of the Civil War* (New York: Doubleday & Co, 1962), 53. Maj. C. W. Devy, LSH(RC), "A Cavalry Trek Through Alberta" *CDQ* Vol 3 (Ottawa:1934) 216. Devy records a normal hour's pace as "Halt 10 min. (loosen girth); Walk 5; Trot 10; Walk 15 (partly dismount and lead); Trot 10; Walk 10 or less. Hills and rough terrain could affect this . . ."

26. Capt C. D. Rhodes, *CDQ* Vol 3.

27. *CDQ* Vol XV Oct-Nov 1937. Maj R.S. Timmons, RCD, "The March of A Squadron Royal Canadian Dragoons from St. John, Quebec, to Petawawa Military Camp, Ontario, 13 July–25 July 1937." Page 42.

28. Capt D. S. Perry, "Loss of *Commodore* in the Colorado Endurance Ride", *Cavalry Journal* Vol 32 April 1923, Page 447; and subsequent issues.

29. Sung to the tune "Oh My Darling Clementine"; a bronzed oil can was presented to the Officer's Mess of the 17th, it was still there in 1956 when the two regiments were amalgamated to form *The Royal Canadian Hussars (Montreal).*

30. "Christie was a brilliant maverick." Armor Historian, George F. Hofmann, interview MHI Carlisle, August 1991. "Christie had circumvented the Ordnance Department by writing to the chairman of the House Subcommittee for the War Department Committee on Appropriations." See: Hofmann, "Army Doctrine and the Christie tank" in, George F. Hofmann, Donn A. Starry (Eds), *Camp Colt to Desert Storm, History of US Armored Forces* (Lexington: University Press, 1999), 116.

31. The Chief of Infantry, General Stephen Fuqua, had adjusted the 1929 budget to permit the purchase of five to six Christie tanks. Christie adversaries decided that one was sufficient for testing and returned the remaining money to the Treasury, unused. See: Hofmann.

32. See: Chris Ellis, Peter Chamberlain, *Fighting Vehicles: Machines that revolutionized land warfare in the twentieth century* (Hamlyn:1972); John Macksey, John H. Batchelor, *Tank, A History of the Armoured Fighting Vehicle* (Charles Scribner: 1970); Eric Morris, *Tanks—Weaponry and Warfare* (London: Octopus Publishing Group, 1975).

33. Lt. Gen. Sir Giffard Le Q. Martel, *Our Armoured Forces* (London: Faber and Faber, 1945), 45–48. Martel grumbled Christie's machines "invariably proved to be very unreliable" yet they inspired imitation.

34. Based on a combination of mobility, armor, firepower and serviceability. The T34 edged out the technically superior and ubiquitous M4 *Sherman*. See: Ellis, Chamberlain et al. and, Robert Citino, *Armored Forces—History and Sourcebook* (New York: Greenwood, 1994).

35. Crittenberger Papers, MHI.

36. Roman J. Jarymowycz, *Tank Tactics* (Boulder: Lynne Rienner, 2001), 41.

37. Robert Allan Doughty, *The Seeds of Disaster The Development of the French Army Doctrine 1919–1939* (Hamden: Archon, 1985), 180.

38. "The fighting power of an army lies in its organization, which can be destroyed either by wearing it down or by rendering it inoperative . . . a shot through the brain. The brains of an army are its staff." J.F.C. Fuller, *The Conduct of War*, 243. Also see: J. F. C. Fuller, *Lectures on FSR II* (London: Sifton Praed, 1931). Fuller, *Lectures on FSR III (Operations between Mechanized Forces* (London: Sifton Praed, 1932). Fuller, *Towards Armageddon: The Defence Problem and Its Solution* (London: Lovat Dickson, 1937).

39. Marginal note, W.D.C. Papers; US Army officers attended courses at Mailey Le Camp, France's Fort Knox.

40. See: Stéphane Bonnaud (avec François Vauvillier) *Chars B au Combat—Hommes et Materiels du 15e BBC* (Paris: Histoire & Collections, 1999).

41. The Char B required a chronometer like steering because the driver doubled as gunner and fine tuned the lay of the gun by gently nudging the tracks of a 31 ton tank. First French tank to have electric powered traverse and electric starter: expensive complex to build. See: Chamberlain, Ellis, Foss, Jentz et al.

42. Fourteen feet high and thirty four feet long, top road speed, a bracing 9 mph.

43. Eight Char 2Cs moved via special rail cars but discovered by the Luftwaffe—none saw action. One was brought back to Berlin to be gawked at as a war prize.

44. Col. Charles de Gaulle, *Vers l'Armée de métier* (Paris: Berger-Levrault, 1934); de Gaulle planned an elite army of 100,000 professionals on 6-year contract. de Gaulle in 1943: "[Fuller] was the prophet, we only followed him . . . You will find prophesied in his books everything that the Germans did with tanks."

45. British did not raise first Armored Division until 1940. Canada created two armored divisions in 1942.

46. DCRs armor: 4 *demi brigades;* 2xBBC *Char B* (70 tks) and 2x BBC *Hotchkiss* H39 mediums (90 tks).

47. The DCLs horse parks were buttressed by a Light Mech Brigade: armored car regiment, mech infantry regiment, supported by Anti-tank squadrons, artillery, an aviation squadron and the Divisional anti-tank battery.

48. See: Anthony Kemp, *The Maginot Line—Myth and Reality* (New York: Warnes, 1981).

49. Basil Henry Liddell Hart, *Memoirs,* 2 Vols (New York: G. P. Putnam's Sons, 1965) I, 77.

50. "That's what I need! That is what I want!" The tanks were merely machine gun equipped, two man PzMk Is but their impact was colossal. Cited in Heinz Guderian, *Erinnerungen eines Soldaten* (Heidelberg: Kurt Vowinckel, 1951), 24; For discussion re actual date of occurrence, see Len Deighton, *Blitzkrieg* (London: Jonathan Cape, 1979), 141fn.

51. Cited in Mark Urban, *Generals* (London: Faber, 2005), 261.

52. Dr. J. T. Fowler, *Axis Cavalry in World War II* (Oxford: Osprey, 2001), 5.

53. The German army fielded nearly 2500 tanks in six Panzer Divisions supported by a tactical air force with 1200 modern aircraft including *Stuka* dive bombers for ground attack.

54. Burnett-Stuart (an "apostle of mobility") fired Fuller in 1927 but helped Hobart "develop flexibility in the Tank Brigade"; See: Harold Winton, *To Change an Army* (University Press of Kansas, 1988).

55. Martel, *Our Armoured Forces*, 50–51.

56. Robert Stewart Sheriffs, *Salute If You Must, An Essay in Words and Pictures* (London: Herbert Jenkins).

57. The 4RTR was equipped with A11 Matilda I (BR-68) while 7RTR had a mix of A11s and A12 Matilda II (BR-69). The A11 Matilda I equipped with .303 machine guns or heavy machine gun (.50 cal equiv).

58. Polish cavalry mantra, cited in, "The Life and Times of Jan Pirog, a Polish Soldier"; http://www.janpirog; see also: Henryk Smaczny, Ksiega Kawalerii Polskiej 1914–1947 (Warsaw: Tesco, Zpgraniczne, 1989).

59. The Polish Armored Corps began 1919 when the 1er Regiment des Char Blindés Polonais was formed of Franco-Polish, European and American cadres.

60. *Bron Polski* comprised the Vickers 6-ton tank, 7TP tanks (improved Vickers with 37 mm gun) and a collection of light tanks / tankettes, some modified with long caliber 20 mm antitank guns. The one modern mech unit in 1939 was 10th Cavalry (Mech) Brigade commanded by Col (later General) Stanislaw Maczek. His career would include command of Polish tank formations in France 1940, and Normandy 1944.

61. Fowler, *Axis Calvary in World War II, 7*.

62. Lance Corporal Hormes, 1st Reiter Brigade, 1939, cited in Fowler, *Axis Calvary in World War II, 9*.

63. Polish Cavalry Brigade: 616 sabers and 108 lances augmented by 76 medium and heavy machine guns, two batteries of artillery and 18x 37mm anti-tank guns; also 8 armored cars and 13 tankettes or light tanks.

64. Steven J. Zaloga, *Polish Army 1939–1945* (London: Osprey, 1982), 9–10, and Marcin Lewandowski, Szarże we wrześniu 1939, (Warsaw: 2005).

65. Kamil Dziewanowski, *Last Great Charge of the Polish Cavalry* Polish History Page, Internet Issue (4), September 2001, http://www.polishnews.com/fulltext/history/2001/history4.shtml.

66. 2e Armée, Ordre de bataille, 10/05/1940; http://france1940.free.fr/oob/2armee. See: Horne, end paper ORBAT charts. The Grouping of French Cavalry and Armor formations at May 1940: 1e Armee: 1e DCR, 2e, 3e DLM, 2x Tank Brigade; 2e Armee: 2e, 5e DLC, 1x Cavalry Brigade; 3e Armee: 3e DLC, 1x Cavalry Brigade, 4x Tank Brigade; 4e Armee: 2x Tank Brigade; 5e Armee: 3x Tank Brigade; 7e Armee: 1 DLM; 8e Armee: 1x Tank Brigade, 1x Cavalry Brigade; 9e Armee: 1er, 4e DLC, 1x Cavalry Brigade. Tank Strength: DCRs avg 150 tanks; DLMs 174 tanks, German Panzer Divisions avg 218 tanks (6th, 7th, 8th Panzer Divisions) and 276 tanks (1st, 2nd, 10th Panzer Division); 5th Panzer had 324 tanks.

67. The first fully motorized/mechanized French unit, the 1e DLM was created, 1932–35; 2e DLM formed 1937; 3e DLM, February 1940.

68. The Char B averaged 17 mph as compared to 25 mph for the Somua. Armor: Somua 40mm; Char B bis 40–70mm; German heaviest, the PzMk IV, was 25mm thick. The British main battle tank, the Matilda II, proved to be first rate although slow (only 9 mph off road).

69. The 3e DLM formed in 1940 manned by reservists: not fully trained, some failed to show; tanks went to battle with reduced crews.

70. Cavalry in French armies facing the Ardennes: *9e Armée*: 1er and 4e Division Légère de Cavalerie; 3e Brigade de Spahis ; *2e Armée* : 2e and 5e Division Légère de Cavalerie; 1er Brigade de Cavalerie.

71. "[The Luftwaffe] was entirely mistress of the sky . . ."; General René Prioux, *Souvenirs de guerre,* 1939–1943, (Paris: Flammarion, 1947); see also: Gerard Saint-Martin, *L'Arme Blindée Française,* 2 Vols (Paris: Economica, 1998) I, 263–276.

72. The Hotchkiss and Renault R35 were light (avg 12 tons) and slow with 37mm guns in one man turrets. The Hotchkiss were brigaded in DLM and DCR.

73. B. H. Liddell Hart, *Strategy: The Indirect Approach* (London: Faber and Faber, 1945). See also Citino, 69–78.

74. Saint-Martin, *L'Arme Blindée Française,* 275.

75. Baron Ernst von Jungenfeld, *So kampften Panzer!—Erlebnisse eines Panzer-regiments im Westen,* cited in Saint-Martin, 275–276; DLM commanders, Generals Bougrain and Langlois, were ineffective.

76. Saint-Martin, *L'Arme Blindée Française,* 279.

77. Eddy Bauer, *La Guerre des Blindés,* 2 Vols (Paris: Payot, 1962); Saint-Martin, *L'Arme Blindée Française,* 277.

78. See: Guderian, *Panzer Leader* Tran, Constantine Fitzgibbon, (London: Michael Joseph, 1952), 106–108.

79. Both DCRs of 1er Groupement Cuirassé were near Chalons, forming as a strategic reserve.

80. 4 RTR WD, Lt Peter Vaux cited in, Macksey, 212–213.

81. Martel, *Our Armoured Forces,* 68–69.

82. Erwin Rommel, war diary. Cited in B. H. Liddell Hart (Editor) *The Rommel Papers* Trans. Paul Findlay (New York: Harcourt, Brace and Company, 1953), 32.

83. The *Matilda,* or "ruptured duck" had initially been named after a popular British cartoon character, an ungainly duck. Total force of 16 Matilda II, 60 Matilda I and 60 French lights and mediums. Martel, *Our Armoured Forces,* 65–68.

84. The French considered his withdrawal abandonment. Maj L. F. Ellis*, The War in France and Flanders 1939–1940,* Chapter IX "Fighting on Two Fronts" cited in http://www.ibiblio.org/hyperwar/UN/UK.

85. John Erickson, *The Soviet High Command* (London: Macmillan & Co. Ltd., 1962), 788.

CHAPTER 13

1. The overseas cavalry regiment was the 26th Cavalry of the Philippine Scouts (Regular Army officers with Filipino enlisted men). In addition, 18 cavalry regiments were in the National Guard and 24 in the Organized Reserves.

2. The Chief of Infantry Maj. Gen. G. A. Lynch, went on record "the US Infantry did not want any Panzer Divisions." See Maj. Gen. Robert Grow, "Ten Lean Years,"

Armor (August, 1987), 41. "Herr suggested that Cavalry take everything under ten tons and Infantry take everything over ten tons."

3.   MacArthur, Report to Secretary of War, 1931: "there has grown up a very natural conception that cavalry must include the horse . . . the Mechanized Force will be reorganized as a reinforced cavalry regiment." Gillie, *Forging the Thunderbolt A History of the Development of the Armored Force* (Harrisburg: Military Service Publishing, 1947), 48.

4.   The 1920 National Defense Act assigned the tank to the infantry; the restriction on tanks was not formally lifted until the Army Reorganization Act of 1950. See Gillie, *Forging the Thunderbolt,* 48.

5.   "Tanks under five tons could be transported by the Army's heavy trucks, five tons became a weight ceiling. The fifteen-ton weight limitation for the medium tank followed a similar logic"—15 tons was the capacity of the Army's medium pontoon bridge." David E. Johnston, *Fast Tanks and Heavy Bombers—Innovation in the US Army 1917-1945* (Itahca: Cornell, 1998) 74, 75.

6.   See: The Cavalry Journal 1938–1940, a series of articles re *Bantam* and *Peep.* ETHINT After-Action Reports by U.S. Mechanized Cavalry units regularly refer to "Peeps" as late as 1945, MHI; see Donn A. Starry and George F. Hofmann, *Camp Colt to Desert Storm—The History of US Armored Forces* (Lexington, KY: The University Press of Kentucky, 1999).

7.   Address Brig. Gen. A. R. Chaffee "Mech Cavalry" Army War College. September 30, 1929. Chaffee proposed two divisions: a Reconnaissance Echelon and a Combat Echelon (two Mechanized Cavalry Regiments and an Artillery Battalion), MHI.

8.   Chaffee, "Mech Cavalry," 68.

9.   Col. G. T. Denison, *A History of Cavalry* (London: Macmillan, 1913).

10.   The U.S. Army Maneuvers: 1935 First Army Maneuvers (New York State); 1938 Third Army Maneuvers (Texas); 1939 First Army Maneuvers, (Plattsburgh, NY and Manassas, Virginia); Jean R Moenk, *A History of Large-Scale Army Maneuvers in the United States, 1935–1964* (Fort Monroe: Headquarters United States Continental Army Command, 1969).

11.   See: Jean R. Moenk, "Final Report Third Army Maneuvers, 5–25 May 1940," vol III, Anx 21, "Final Critiques"; also, Col H. H. D. Heiberg Papers, "Report on the Alexandria Meeting." MHI.

12.   As late as November 1940 both Herr and Lynch opposed Maj. Gen. F.M. Andrews (Army G3) when he recommended to General Marshall that "the Armored Force be created as a separate combat arm." Their argument was that it "*violated*" the terms of the National Defence Act of 1920 in creating "*non-infantry and non-cavalry armored units.*" CJ. May-June, 1946. P. 38. For Herr's side, see: John K. Herr and Edward S. Wallace, *The History of the US Cavalry 1775–1942* (Boston: Brown, Little, 1953), 248–262.

13.   See General (USAF) Robert Merrill Lee Papers. Patton Museum Library, Fort Knox. Also see: Colonel H.H.D. Heiberg Papers—"Report on the Alexandria Meeting." MHI.

14.   Chaffee, its first chief, was promoted to brigadier general. There was no Congressional authorization for a separate armored branch, it was established technically "for purposes of service test." Stubbs, Connor, Armor Cavalry, 58. Van Voorhis was the

"Grandfather of Armor"; the Armor family tree includes a "Godfather of Armor" (General Rockenbach, Chief of the AEF Tank Corps, 1918).

15. Maj. Gen. R. W. Grow, "The Ten Lean Years: From the Mechanized Force (1930) to the Armored Force (1940)" *Armor.* Jan–Feb, March–April, May–June, July–August 1987. Also, Robert W. Grow Papers. OCMH Collection, MHI.

16. Herr wrote to General Grow: "I confess I was opposed to the destruction of our cavalry by absorption in the mechanized Cavalry, as it was robbing Peter to pay Paul . . . We needed both . . . What happened then? Failing in this *they set up a conspiracy* [emphasis added] participated in by recreant Cavalry officers of the General Staff to set up an independent Arm so that they could get promotion." Letter from Herr to Grow. 7 June 1945. Special Studies, WWII, Grow Papers, MHI.

17. See: David C. Hardison, *Data on WWII Tank Engagements Involving the US Third and Fourth Armored Divisions* BRL 789, MHI; "ETO Battle Experiences Jul 44–Apr 45" Gillem Papers, MHI; and, ORO-T-117 Alvin D. Coox and L. Van Loan Naisawald, *Survey of Allied Tank Casualties in World War II,* Johns Hopkins University, March 31, 1951, Operations Research Office.

18. American tank production reached 25,000 units, doubling both British *and* German tank output for 1942. By 1943, production reached nearly 30,000 units. By 1945 American factories had produced 88,410 tanks.

19. "At a fence too stiff for his strength to leap / With a rotten take-off, unfirm, too steep / Heavily breasted to top of the bank / Pawed, gasped, and struggled, then hopelessly sank / Shocked, hurt and surprised at the toss we took / Rolling back adown the ditch at Tobruk" From *The Desert Rats,* "The Djebel Stakes" were the see-saw campaigns between Hellfaya and Agheila circa 1941–1942. Cited in LtGen Sir F. Tuker, *Approach to Battle—A Commentary, Eight Army, November 1941 to May 1943* (London: Cassell, 1963), 60.

20. Alan Moorehead, *Desert Trilogy* (London: Hamilton, 1948), 20.

21. Letter to British Commanders, that 8th Army was too preoccupied with Rommel's dynamic style. Desmond Young, *Rommel* (London: Collins, 1950), 23.

22. This elite desert gathering included the 7th, 8th, 11th Hussars ("The Cherry Pickers"), and the 1st Royal Tank Regiment (RTR).

23. O'Connor covered nearly a thousand miles, destroyed ten divisions and captured 130,000 prisoners. Correlli Barnett, *The Desert Generals* (New York: Viking, 1961), 56.

24. "The Desert Fox" sobriquet was British but quickly picked up by Hitler's propaganda machine.

25. Tuker, *Approach to Battle,* 197.

26. David Irving, *Rommel: The Trial of the Fox* (1977) cited in BBC "Generalfeldmarschall Erwin Johannes Eugen Rommel: Der Wüstenfuchs" www.bbc.co.uk; See: Ronald Lewin, *Rommel as Military Commander* (Batsford: 1968), B. H. Liddell Hart (ed.), *The Rommel Papers* (London: Harcourt Brace, 1953), F. W. Von Mellenthin, *Panzer Battles* (U. of Oklahoma, 1956); Desmond Young, *Rommel* (London: Collins, 1950).

27. House of Commons, January 1942: Winston Churchill, *The Second World War* "The Grand Alliance," Vol 3 (Scranton: Houghton Mifflin, 1950), 200.

28. The Axis Army comprised Italian Corps (including two first rate though poorly equipped tank divisions); the DAK had three divisions (21st and 15th Panzer and the

90th Light Division), in theory another corps under Mussolini's control. Rommel was de facto tactical commander.

29. Young, *Rommel*, 138.

30. O'Connor to Dorman-Smith after Beda Fomm, cited in Ronald Lewin, *Rommel as Military Commander* (London: Batsford, 1968), 239.

31. Barnett, *The Desert Generals*, 105–106.

32. Moorehead, *Desert Trilogy*, 354.

33. It was initially a *Task Force* then renamed II Corps; Patton was promoted to Lt. Gen. in March 1943; Omar Bradley was his deputy. Within fifteen months, Bradley was Patton's boss in Normandy.

CHAPTER 14

1. US Army Intelligence Bulletin, "German Horsed Cavalry and Transport WW2"; ETHINT, March 1945, MHI.

2. Infantry divisions had circa 5,300 horses, 950 motor vehicles and 430 motorcycles. By 1943, motor transport was reduced 400 vehicles, but the number of horses increased to 6,300. The type 1944 divisions had 600 vehicles, about 100 motorcycles but allotted 4,600 horses and 1,400 horse-drawn wagons.

3. 2nd Cavalry (2ACR), msn.com/2ndUSCav/ww2germancav,: "More About WW2 US & German Mounted Horse Cavalry".

4. John Grodzinski, correspondence, September 15, 2006.

5. Maj. Matthew Guymer MBE, "The Falaise Gap" Army Article A4887994, 09 August 2005, Recollections, BBC UK, WMCSV Action Desk.

6. The XV SS Cossack Cavalry Corps escaped the Red Army and surrendered to the western Allies in Austria but were promptly turned over to the Soviets and likely soon executed or sent to Siberia.

7. Bayerlein, commander of the Panzer Lehr Division was effusive but not inaccurate in his observation. Lt Gen Fritz Bayerlein, ETHINT 67 "Normandy Critique" ETO August 15, 1945, MHI.

8. Col Chester B. Hansen Chief of Staff, 12th US Army Group, Chester B. Hansen Papers, Hansen Diary, entry week July 16–25, 1944, MHI.

9. James C. Humes, *The Wit and Wisdom of Winston Churchill* (New York: Harper, 1994), 157.

10. Cited by Samuel Huntington in Harry Kreisler, "The Problem of Strategy—Conversations with Samuel P. Huntington, director, Center of international affairs, Harvard." March 9, 1985. http://globetrotter.berkeley.edu.

11. General Günther Blumentritt, Chief of Staff in the West, recalled: "As the American armor suddenly appeared in front of Vitre, Mayenne, Laval and Le Mans, the greatest astonishment and consternation reigned." ETHINT 67 "Normandy Critique" ETO, August 15, 1945, MHI.

12. Rennes was von Kluge's HQ, 80 miles south west of St-Lô. Von Kluge, ETHINT 67, page 3, MHI.

13. National Guard Cavalry comprised 4 divisions but were soon broken up.

14. Lt. Gen. L. K. Truscott, Jr.: "I am firmly convinced that if one squadron of horse cavalry and one pack troop of 200 mules. . . would have enabled me to cut off and

capture the entire German force opposing me along the north coast road and would have permitted my entry into Messina at least 48 hours earlier." *Cavalry Journal,* 1945.

15. Lt. Col. W. D. Smart, "Combat Commands of the Armored Division," *Military Review* XXV, 11 (Feb 1946), 7.

16. There were 13 Mechanized Cavalry Groups attached to Corps or Army HQs but their function was mainly liaison, communication, and proving roads.

17. See Hofmann and Starry, *Through Mobility We Conquer,* 343–344.

18. Correspondence military vehicle restorer Douglas Greville, Broken Hill, Australia, March 2007; The *Staghound* family were large, well armored 4x4 vehicles with a 37 mm gun in a rotating turret. Followed by *Deerhound* and *Boarhound* (six wheels) with 57mm to 75mm guns.

19. Staghound shortfalls; "1) no head out facility for the driver—common fault of its era. 2) thus driver and co-driver had to exit past turret basket—a death trap if vehicle is on fire. 3) 37mm pop gun" Greville, April 2007; see Greville site: http://www.trackpads.net/sites/heavymetal/.

20. Maj "Moe" Shackleton, Interview, Cdn Forces Staff College, Kingston, July, 1989. Shackleton co-authored the excellent "Analysis of Firepower in Normandy Operations of 1944," DND, Ottawa, 1950.

21. Greville, April 2007.

22. By June 1945 8,634 M8s units had been built; they served in the military or police forces of 40 countries and continue to be used as special law enforcement vehicles circa 2007.

23. "Single tanks—assault guns or Mark IVs, rarely Tigers or Panthers—they'd allow the lead cars to go by, then engage the troop leader or main body. We always sent the heavy car first in case of mines—they could withstand the explosion." Interview with Lt. Col. W. C. Bowen, Elgin Quebec, 1990.

24. 87th Cavalry Reconnaissance Squadron, Report, September 7, 1944, MHI.

CHAPTER 15

1.   The Christie first model arrived in Kubinka in 1931; mass production of the BT tank began in 1932; The T34 was contrived by Mikhail Koshkin at the Komintern Factory in Kharkov in 1940.

2.   See P. A. Rotmistrov, *Vremya I Tanki* (Moscow: Voenizdat, 1972); A. Kh. Babadzhanyan, *Tanki I Tankovye* (Moscow: Voenizdat, 1980); and Christopher Bellamy, *Red God of War* (London: Brassey's, 1987).

3.   Interview SS Colonel Hans Siegel, Bad Teinbach, April 1991.

4.   Pliyev's Cavalry Corps comprised two tank brigades, a tank destroyer brigade, an artillery brigade, mortar, artillery and Katyushas regiments, two antiaircraft regiments, two infantry brigades (mechanized and motorized), and five divisions of Cavalry (5th, 6th, 7th, 8th Mongolian and 59th Cavalry).

5.   Nino Oktorino, correspondence, November 2006; see also: Oktorino, "Waffen-SS im Einsatz—Disaster in Budapest"; http://stosstruppen, 39–45.

CHAPTER 16

1.   See: John J. Tolson, *Vietnam Studies Air Mobility 1961–1971* (Washington: U.S. Government Printing Office, 1973), 5; also, LTC Kenneth A. Steadman, "The Evolution of the Tank in the US Army," Study for Combined Arms Center, U.S. Army Command and General Staff College, April 21, 1982.

2.   LTG L. D. Holder, correspondence December 8, 2006.

3.   Holder, correspondence; see also General Donn A. Starry, *Armored Combat in Vietnam* (Salem, NH: Ayer, 1982): 58, 59–60.

4.   Holder, correspondence.

5.   Notable Cavalry in Vietnam: 1–9 Air Cavalry, 3–5 Cavalry, assigned to 9th Inf Div; 1–4 Cavalry of the 1st Inf Div, and 3–4 Cavalry of the 25th Inf Div. See Starry, 227–237.

6.   Brian Ross, "The Use of Armored Vehicles in the Vietnam War" Cited in http://www.faqs/vietnam/armor; see also: Donn A. Starry and George F. Hofmann, *Camp Colt to Desert Storm—The History of US Armored Forces* (Lexington, KY: The University Press of Kentucky, 1999).

7.   Brian Ross, 2.

8.   Brian Ross, 2; See also: Lewis Sorley, "Mounted Combat in Vietnam," Donn A. Starry and George F. Hofmann, *Camp Colt to Desert Storm—The History of US Armored Forces*, 325–326; Starry, *Armored Combat in Vietnam*, 55–58.

9.   Notably, the defense of Fire Support Bases Coral and Balmoral and during the 1968 Tet offensive. See: "The Battle of Coral" and "The Battle of Long Tan" by Lex McAuley.

10.   Abraham Rabinovich, *The Yom Kippur War: The Epic Encounter That Transformed the Middle East* (New York: Schocken Books, 2004), 108.

11.   In addition to the large anti aircraft umbrella (SAM 2, SAM 3, SAM 6, SAM 7, and mobile ZSU23/4 radar controlled quad cannon). Egyptian infantrymen deployed the portable Soviet SA-7 *Strela* (the "Sam 7") a heat-seeking missile that attacked low flying helicopters or fighter-bombers.

12.   Rabinovich, *The Yom Kippur War*, 355.

13.   Huba Wass de Czege, Correspondence, August 2007.

14.   "DePuy wanted a 'how to fight' manual aimed at diminishing the tactical sloppiness he had encountered in WWII and Vietnam." Colonel Richard Sinnreich, correspondence, February 14, 2005. DePuy pulled the 100–5 project out of Leavenworth and into the converted boathouse [in Fort Monroe]. "DePuy took charge got it done at Monroe . . . the *Boathouse Gang* predates the 1982 edition." Starry March 16, 2005.

15.   See Military Review Vol LVII No. March 3, 1977: R W. Lind "Some Doctrinal Questions for the US Army." "[Bill Lind's] MR article was clear, convincing and heartening to soldiers who Lind emboldened to write more forcefully in criticizing Active Defense." Col Rick Sinnreich February 17, 2005.

16.   Holder, correspondence, March 18, 2005. Active Defense became a formulaic "process-driven solution" with slogans about "what can be seen can be hit." Leavenworth issued "calculus of battle" worksheets that required students to count up the systems brought to bear in each terrain compartment and figure out the odds.

17.   "Could the Army that conducted the Gulf War be imagined without the actions of General DePuy?" Colonel R.M. Swain, edited by D. L. Gilmore and C. D. Conway,

Selected Papers of General William E. DePuy, Combat Studies Institute, Kansas 1993. Col Rick Sinnreich: "Bill DePuy was more responsible than any other single individual for the Army's intellectual rebirth after Vietnam." Correspondence, 2005. "ALB was a significant evolution in our thinking . . . but I would not discount the role of the 1978 FM 100–5 (Active Defense) which galvanized Army thinking through its rejection of [dated] ideas." BGen DA Fastabend, correspondence, February 21, 2005.

18. Starry, correspondence, January 2005.

19. Starry, correspondence, May 2003.

20. The writing of FM100–5 was supervised by Generals Donn A. Starry and William R. Richardson with four officers as principal authors—Lieutenant Colonel Huba Wass de Czege, assisted by L. D. Holder (Cavalry), Richmond B. Henriques (Infantry), Richard Hart Sinnreich (Artillery); General Morelli (Artillery) assisted Gen. Starry. Wass de Czege went on to found The School of Advanced Military Studies (SAMS, Leavenworth) succeeded by Sinnreich, then Holder. It is their students who are properly dubbed "The Jedi Knights". Correspondence, Wass de Czege, August 2007.

21. Formations from Egypt, East Senegal, Kuwait, Morocco, North Oman, Pakistan, Qatar, Saudi Arabia, Syria, and the United Arab Emirates; Western forces: Britain, Bahrain, Canada, France, Italy, and the USA.

22. Saudi Arabia and Qatar used AMX-30S tanks in the ground campaign of the Gulf War. The next generation French tank, perhaps the most modern western tank, the *Leclerc,* just missed *Desert Storm,* entering French service in 1992.

23. Norman Friedman, *Desert Victory—The War for Kuwait* (Annapolis: Naval History Press, 1992).

24. OPFOR units often use blank ammunition, coupled with a simulation system such as the MILES. The US Army has three OPFOR training centers. Complimented on coolness in a fire fight a tank officer replied: "Sir, this was not our first battle. This was our tenth battle! We fought three wars at the National Training Center . . . we fought four wars at the Combat Maneuver Training Center, Hohenfels, Germany; and a lot of other simulations . . . This war was just like our training."

25. The western armored host comprised: 1st Armored Division; 1st Cavalry Division; 1st Infantry Division (Mechanized); 2nd Armored Division; 2nd Armored Division (Forward); 2nd Armored Cavalry Regiment; 3rd Armored Cavalry Regiment; 3rd Armored Division; the British 1st Armoured Division, incorporating the 7th Armoured Brigade "The Desert Rats" and the French 6e Division Légère "Dauget."

26. "At the end of the first day, "most of the support squadron's ammunition trucks were stuck in sand that had, during the day's rain, turned to mud. An emergency resupply effort . . . resulted in three CH47 Chinook [heavy helicopters] loads of ammunition being delivered to the regiment." George F. Hofmann, Donn A. Starry, *Camp Holt to Desert Storm—The History of US Armored Forces,* 512.

27. "AirLand Battle, the warfighting doctrine applied by the American Army in Desert Storm, not only survived the initial clash of arms but, in fact, continues as a viable foundation for the development of future warfighting doctrine." *Certain Victory: The US Army in the Gulf War,* the Desert Storm Study Project, Leavenworth, 1993.

28. Schwarzkopf, cited in Richard M. Swain, *Lucky War—Third Army in Desert Storm* (Fort Leavenworth: US Army, 1997), 124.

29. Schwarzkopf's frustration with VII Corps periodically boiled over: "... If Franks can't handle the job, I'll get someone who can." Rick Atkinson, *Crusade—The Untold Story of the Persian Gulf War* (New York: Houghton Mifflin, 1993), 405.

30. Swain, *Lucky War*, 258.

31. Tom Clancy, Fred Franks Jr, *Into the Storm* (New York: Putnam, 1997), 330.

32. Correspondence Gen. F. Franks, LCol David Patterson, Canadian Forces Staff College, June 1999.

33. Swain, *Lucky War*, 331.

34. Swain, *Lucky War*, 337.

35. Michael D. Krause, *The Battle of 73 Easting, 26 February 1991* (Washington: 1991), 20.

36. Hofmann, Starry, *Camp Holt to Desert Storm—The History of US Armored Forces*, 516.

37. 3 ACR captured the first *Storm* prisoners after a skirmish with Iraqi border police. See Swain, *Lucky War*, 180.

38. The 24th's élan and dash annoyed his 82nd Airborne chums on the far left flank screening with the 6e Division Légère: "It was easier to work with the French than it was with Barry McCaffrey."

39. Correspondence, Gen. Rupert Smith, March 2002; Swain, *Lucky War*, 301. 2 ACR also followed all its oral FargOs with written orders as eventually did most units. Holder, December 16, 2006.

40. 1st Cav Div conducted raids (Wadi al-Batin) before the attack—Franks used these demonstrations to distract the Iraqis from the main assault in the west. These operations required some finesse since they involved attacking into contact with the defending divisions, then backing away.

CHAPTER 17

1. Richardson, correspondence, June 2005.

2. Mary Lee Stubbs and Stanley Russell Connor, *Armor-Cavalry Part I: Regular Army and Army Reserve* (Office of the Chief of Military History, US Army, Washington, 1969). Three other *armored cavalry* regiments, the 2d, 6th, and 14th, were organized, from redesignated units of the U.S. Constabulary. From 1951 to 1955 the US Army had two active armored divisions—the 1st and the 2d, the 3d and 4th were added in 1955.

3. *The Quartermaster Remount Service*, US Army Quarter Master Museum, Quartermaster Foundation website, 2006. See also: Anna M. Waller, *Horses and Mulkes in National Defense*, Office of the Quartermaster General, 1958.

4. Its stables hold 13 chargers and 95 horses as mounts and drives for the ten 13-pounder guns and Limbers. Lt. Col. W. A. H. Townend, Secretary, Royal Artillery Historical Society, December 2006.

5. Troop includes workshops and stables. Authentic horse furniture and weapons: 1875 Model 45–70 Springfield Carbine, the 1875 Colt, 45 Caliber Revolver and the 1860 Light Cavalry Saber. Each horse must be no less than 15 hands high, dark, with a minimum of white markings. Cited in 1st U.S. Cav Division website; http://www.first-team.us.

6. "We use lance bucket attached to the right stirrup to hold the lance when it is not being used for the lance drill or the charge. While the average lance only weighs about 4 pounds it would be very tiring and unwieldy trying to hold a lance for ex-

tended periods without the aid of a lance bucket." Correspondence: Sergeant Major William J. Stewart, Riding Master, RCMP Musical Ride Branch, March 15, 2007. In 1874 the NWMP were issued 1868 pattern lances with bamboo staffs. In 2007 the RCMP still use the 1868 pattern with male bamboo staff supplied by the Wilkinson Sword Company of London England.

7.   Although South America dominates, military teams from Italy, Germany, Spain, Belarus, and Turkey have performed well in millennium competitions.

8.   The 2006 (Fort Knox) and 2007 (Fort Riley) included entry from Canadian reserve regiments.

9.   Akaash Maharaj's unit is a Toronto Militia armored regiment; Europe was represented by a team from the Household Cavalry and Royal Horse Artillery. See: GGHG, http://www.maharaj.org/cavalry.shtml.

10.   Argentina, Australia, Britain, India, Pakistan, and the United States.

11.   A full game (six *chukkas* of seven minutes) quickly tires out the horse, a string of *Polo ponies* (about three) is recommended. Master Equestrian Colonel Robert ffrench Blake, correspondence, December, 2006.

12.   Charles H. Briscoe, Richard L. Kiper, James A. Schroder, Kalev L. Sepp, *Weapon of Choice, US Army Special Operations Forces in Afghanistan* (Fort Leavenworth: Combat Studies Institute Press, 2003), 122.

13.   Article by Tom Geraci "It's Buzkashi Fever!" cited by Steve Czaban, http://Czabe.com, October 2006.

14.   Briscoe et al, 123; and, Max Boot, "Special forces and horses" excerpted from "War Made New," *Armed Forces Journal*, October 19, 2001, hereafter cited as Boot.

15.   Special Forces Capt *Mike Nash* (a pseudonym), cited in Briscoe, 123. Nash had been raised on a Kansas ranch and competed in collegiate rodeo while taking his degree at Kansas State University.

16.   Briscoe, *Weapon of Choice,* 124.

17.   Nash: Briscoe, 125. The saddle included a carbine scabbard lined with pure sheepskin for horse comfort; designed by the Australian Stock Saddle Company for Special Forces.

18.   Boot, "War Made New," 2.

19.   Boot, "War Made New," 2.

20.   Harlan Ullman, James Wade, *Shock and Awe: Achieving Rapid Dominance* (National Defense University, 1996); compare to BGen R. H. Scales, *Certain Victory— The US Army in the Gulf War* (New York: Brassey's, 1994).

21.   LTG L.D. Holder, correspondence, July 2004.

22.   Rick Atkinson, *In the Company of Soldiers* (New York: Holt, 2004), 153. "US intelligence detected fifty cell-phone calls made by Iraqi observers as the helicopters pressed north; the same simple but effective early warning system had been used by Somali militiamen in Mogadishu." Atkinson, 149.

23.   Cols Gregory Fontenot, E. J. Degen and David Tohn. *On Point: The US Army in Operation Iraqi Freedom* (Combat Studies Institute Press, 2004).

24.   Gen. Tommy Franks with Malcolm McConnell, *American Soldier* (New York: HarperCollins Publishers, 2004), 395–396.

25.   *The New Republic Archives* December 2006: David Rieff, "What Went Wrong in Iraq?"; see also: M. R. Gordon and General B. E. Trainor *Cobra II: The Inside Story of the Invasion and Occupation of Iraq* (Pantheon: 2006).

26. Dan McDougall, *Desert Rats in Fierce Battle,* cited in the *The Scotsman*—national digital newspaper website, edition: Friday, March 28, 2003.

27. Critics argue the invasion "was based on perhaps the worst war plan in American history." See: Thomas E. Ricks, *Fiasco: The American Military Adventure in Iraq* (New York: Penguin, 2006).

28. W. Wallace, "Network Enabled Battle Command," *Military Review,* May–June 2005, 2; Wallace warns against the "dangerous temptation to shift responsibility of making military decisions from the commanders to the systems themselves."

CHAPTER 18

1. Lt. Colonel Charles Branchaud, formerly *The Royal Canadian Hussars,* seconded to the Scots DG as Battle Captain, *C* Squadron for *Desert Storm.* "Not sure it was Regt net, more Sqn net. . . . one of the boys probably pressed the radio switch with his recorder playing." Interview, Bulford Camp, UK, May 2004.

2. Czar Nicolas II was Colonel-in-Chief of the Scots Greys from 1894 until his death. During formal dinings in, Band plays "The Queen," "God Bless the Prince of Wales," and the Imperial Russian Anthem in his memory. In March 1998, the Commanding Officer led a Regimental party to the refinement of Tsar Nicholas in St. Petersburg.

3. Army Chief of Staff, General Eric Shinseki, a converted cavalryman, ensured the entire American ground force was made to convert to the *black beret* effective June 2001. Cited in "Army Black Beret" www.army.mil; see: Rod Powers, "U.S. Military Beret History" http://www. usmilitary.about.com.

4. Amongst a global diversity: The Queen's Royal Hussars (Queen's Own and Royal Irish), The Royal Scots Dragoon Guards (Carabiniers and Greys) and of course, the American cavalry.

5. See impressive collection of current cavalry stable belts reproduced in "Stable Belt" http://wikipedia.org; See also: *US Army Dress Regulations* 670–1 (Washington: 2005); *Materiel Regulations for The Army,* Vol 3, No.16, *Optional items of dress,* (London: MOD, 1995); A-AD-265–000/AG-001, *Canadian Forces Dress Instructions* (Ottawa: NDHQ, 1999) and M. Dorosh, *Dressed to Kill* (Ottawa: 2001).

6. Dubbed *CADPAT* (Canadian Disruptive Pattern), Canadian Armed Forces. By 2007 most western armies sported their own versions with appropriate CGI graphics in muted tones.

7. James Laver, *British Military Uniforms* (London: Penguin, 1948), 26. See Laver's fourteen conclusions regarding military costumes, 24–26.

8. Laver, 26.

9. Gen. Sullivan letter to Gen. Franks July 1991.

10. Brig. Gen. Huba Wass de Czege "Lessons from the Past Toward Getting The Army's Doctrine *Right Enough* Today"; article; correspondence September 2006.

11. Chief of staff of the United States Army, June 22, 1999–1; called for "emerging strategic challenge . . . and the need for cultural and technological change." June 1, 2003.

12. Wass de Czege; correspondence, September 2006; see also Dr. Antulio J. Echevarria, II, Brigadier General (Ret.) Huba Wass de Czege, "Toward a Strategy of Positive Ends," *National Security Studies Quarterly,* 8:1–26 Winter 2002.

13. Maj. Gen. Robert W. Mixon, director of the Futures Center, Training and Doctrine Command (TRADOC), Jan US Army News, 2005 see also: A. Vick et al *The Stryker Brigade Combat Team Rethinking Strategic Responsiveness and Assessing Deployment.* Rand Project US Air Force, 2003.

14. Cited by Larry Edmond, "Fighting Military Robot," *Fort Gordon Signal Newspaper,* February 23, 2006.

15. US Joint Forces Command, news release, August 4, 2003.

16. *Molti Roboti* is hybrid Latin, coined by Lt. Gen. L. D. Holder circa winter 2004, correspondence.

17. Retired Army officer Andrew Krepinevich, cited in *Time,* April 16, 2007, 24; Paul Yingling, deputy commander of 3 ACR, wrote: "America's generals have failed to prepare our armed forces for war and advise civilian authorities on the application of force to achieve the aims of policy." LtCol Paul Yingling, "A failure in generalship," *Armed Forces Journal,* April 2007; http://www.armedforcesjournal.com/2007.

18. Maximilian von Poseck *The German Cavalry 1914 in Belgium and France,* Edited Jerome W. Howe (Berlin: Mittler, 1923).

19. Rudyard Kipling, *Departmental Ditties and Other Verses* (London: 1886).

20. Conversely, the RSTA squadron of the Stryker Brigade is reasonably large and relatively capable, mounted in LAVs rather than HMMWVs (Mobility Multipurpose Wheeled Vehicle or *Humvee*).

21. The venerable 2 ACR is now called the "Stryker Cavalry Regiment (2 SCR)." Veterans complained: "The nouveau *Stryker Cavalry Regiment* is merely an infantry brigade in costume." Fort Hood TX, April 2007.

22. General William R. Richardson, March 18, 2005.

23. Holder, March 2007.

24. In the winter of 2006, 3 ACR, preparing for a tour in the Middle East was given helicopters. Cavalry diehards continued to argue for complete "ACR restoration."

25. Col. John D. Rosenberger (ret), "Breaking the Saber: The Subtle Demise of Cavalry in the Future Force."

26. Gen. Terry Tucker article.

27. A short list provided by a Cavalry historian includes: "Generals Donn A. Starry, "Butch" Saint, "Monty" Meigs, Fred Franks, Holder, Shinseki, Tilelli, and Sullivan—it also includes cavaliers Tom White, Bob Wagner, John "Doc" Bahnsen, John Kirk, Dave Maddox, Bill Crouch and '06 Tradoc commander, William Wallace . . . Glen Otis, Butch Saint, Donn Starry and other [Cavaliers] were leading the Army well before desert days."

28. Much credit for the decision to introduce tanks to Afghanistan is given to LCol Omer Lavoie, CO of 1 RCR Battle Group in Sept 2006. Correspondence, Pittfield and Cadieu.

29. Colonel David Pittfield, correspondence, Kandahar, January 2007.

30. ". . . they occupy grape drying huts and compounds with concrete-like walls measuring over a meter in thickness. . . One 105 mm High Explosive Squash Head (HESH) round from the Leopard C2 can punch a massive hole . . . allowing us to breech structures with reduced collateral damage and risk to our dismounted soldiers." Major Trevor Cadieu, B Squadron, LdSH, Kandahar, correspondence, April 12, 2007.

31. The Leopard II A6M used by Canadians is "essentially immune to the current range of enemy weapons except perhaps for tilt rod anti-tank mines which could penetrate the hull—if stacked 2 to 4 deep."

32. The initial "Canadian" Leopard C2s were immediately upgraded by 100 ultra modern Leopard II A6M purchased from Germany and "slightly used" Leopard IIA4s from Holland. Low prices featured as Berlin cleared stock to ease its own panzer arm into an armor-light millennium configuration.

33. Brig. Gen. Tim Grant, commander Canadian forces in Afghanistan; Kandahar, correspondence, May 12, 2007.

34. In the fall of 2006 the Canadian infantry sometimes referred to their opponents as "Timmies"—perhaps prompted by a Canadian icon: *Tim Horton's* coffee bar with its miniature donuts, as a field expedient trial in Kandahar. Patrol on horses will always be more romantic, and certainly more comfortable, as tank crews resort to water-filled cooling vests to thwart the searing heat inside tanks.

35. The author first heard it said by Normandy tank ace General Radley Walters, *The Sherbrooke Fusilier Regt,* en passant before Verrières Ridge in May, 1989.

36. See: Lt. Col. H. R. McMaster, "Crack in the Foundation: Defense Transformation and the Underlying Assumption of Dominant Knowledge in Future War," student paper, USAWC, November 2003, 97.

37. Brig. Gen. Grant.

38. "The advantages offered by reconnaissance and security troops are too great to be neglected." L. D. Holder, correspondence, December 2006.

39. The final order after the Ride is dismissed by the Squadron Sergeant Major.

Index

About the Author

ROMAN JARYMOWYCZ is a lecturer at the Royal Military College of Canada and holds a doctorate in military history from McGill University. He commanded The Royal Canadian Hussars, an armored cavalry regiment, and is now retired as Dean of the Canadian Forces Militia Command and Staff College. As an author, he has published articles and books specializing on the operational art.

Recent Titles in
War, Technology, and History

Thunder over the Horizon: From V2 Rockets to Ballistic Missiles
Clayton K. S. Chun

The Development of Mine Warfare: A Most Murderous and Barbarous Conduct
Norman Youngblood

GI Ingenuity: Improvisation, Technology, and Winning World War II
James Jay Carafano

Iron Men and Tin Fish: The Race to Build a Better Torpedo during World War II
Anthony Newpower

Imagining Future War: The West's Technological Revolution and Visions of Wars to Come, 1880–1914
Antulio J. Echevarria II